ON THIS DAY IN POLITICS

Also by Iain Dale

Why Can't We All Just Get Along
Prime Minister Priti & Other Things That Never Happened
The Prime Ministers 1721–2022
The Presidents 1789–2022

ON THIS DAY IN POLITICS

IAIN DALE

ALLEN&UNWIN

Published in hardback in Great Britain in 2022 by Allen &
Unwin, an imprint of Atlantic Books Ltd.

Chapter head illustrations by Carmen R. Balit

10 9 8 7 6 5 4 3 2 1

A CIP catalogue record for this book is available from the British Library.

Hardback ISBN: 978 1 83895 475 8
E-book ISBN: 978 1 83895 476 5

Printed and bound by CPI Group (UK) Ltd, Croydon CR0 4YY

Allen & Unwin
An imprint of Atlantic Books Ltd
Ormond House
26–27 Boswell Street
London
WC1N 3JZ

www.allenandunwin.com/uk

Contents

Foreword   vii

January   1
February   33
March   63
April   95
May   127
June   159
July   191
August   223
September   255
October   287
November   319
December   351

Acknowledgements   383
Index   384

This book is dedicated to the memory of Sir David Amess MP

Foreword

When Prime Minister Harold Macmillan was asked by a journalist what his greatest challenges were, his reply was very simple. 'Events, dear boy, events'. It's an answer that any of our fifty-five prime ministers could have given, for it summed up how politicians can be blown completely off course by events. Or their names and reputations can be made or lost by a single event that they could never have anticipated. Boris Johnson expected to be the Brexit prime minister, the man who triumphantly took us out of the European Union. Instead, his legacy will probably be defined by his response to the Covid-19 pandemic, or the war in Ukraine. Events, dear boy, events.

Back in the late 1980s I bought a book in Foyles called *A Chronology of Post-War British Politics*, by political academic Geoffrey Foote. It listed all the main events in British politics day by day, month by month from 1945 until June 1987. I was flicking through it and started thinking about key dates in British politics prior to 1945. I started jotting down some examples, like the foundation of what many people view as the first English Parliament in 1265, the day in 1809 that Spencer Perceval became the first (and only) British prime minister to be assassinated, the day in 1707 when the Act of Union between England and Scotland was proclaimed. And so I went on. Within an hour I had a list of around thirty key events written down, and I realized how little I knew about most of them. I then did a quick Google search and to my absolute astonishment no one had ever written a book called 'On This Day in Politics'. Dan Snow was about to publish one called *On This Day in History*, but surprisingly no one had collated all the key political events in our political history in one handy volume.

I then started a spreadsheet and started to allocate particular events to dates. It was like putting together a jigsaw. On some days there were five or six events to choose from different years in history. For others not so much. Indeed, for some days, I really had to scratch around to find anything notable that had happened on that particular day in British political history, but even then, I always discovered something I hadn't known about before. For example, 28 December proved to be such a day. I eventually discovered that Britain's first national park, the Peak District, was declared that day in 1950. Obviously, we all know that the 1945–51 Labour government was famous for creating the NHS, nationalizations and giving India its independence. How many of us know that it also created the national parks programme? I certainly didn't, and was oblivious to the fact that the idea had been around since the 1880s. You will find little nuggets like that littered throughout this book. I've tried to cover all the main events we all know about, and to provide an introduction to some of our most interesting politicians down the centuries.

Each event is covered on a single page in around 365 words – 365 events, 365 pages, 365 words on each. Well, actually, that's a bit of a lie, as it would have been invidious to ignore events on 29 February, so it's actually 366 days.

When planning this book I was conscious that I needed to achieve a balance. That meant not just including events we are all familiar with that occurred in the last two or three decades, but also including events from the early 1900s, the 1800s and even before. When I counted up the entries, there are thirty-one entries before 1800 and forty in the nineteenth century itself. The most entries for any particular year is eight, in 1990, the year of Margaret Thatcher's defenestration and the first Gulf War. There are seven in 1963, 1967 and 1981. Since World War II there are only four years in which there are no entries in this book – 1953, 1959, 2004 and 2006.

I also thought it would be interesting to see if there was an equal share of events for the seven days of the week. There wasn't. Unsurprisingly, the fewest entries are on Saturdays (thirty-five) and Sundays (twenty-nine). Forty-two events took place on Mondays, and Tuesday proved to be the most eventful day with seventy-three events, just ahead of Thursdays with seventy-one. On Wednesdays there were fifty-six events and Friday sixty.

This book is not meant to encompass a complete political history of the last thousand, or even two hundred years. What I hope it achieves is for your interest in different subjects to be piqued, and to encourage you to read more widely about events that I can only briefly describe. My original intent was for this book to be primarily aimed at people with a mild but not obsessive interest in current affairs and our political history. However, it soon became clear that it ought to appeal to political geeks too. People like me. When I started writing, I imagined that I would be able to write about a third of the entries off the top of my head, with no research. That proved not to be the case. In the end, I probably only wrote about ten of the entries straight off the bat. I discovered things I didn't know even when writing about contemporary events with which I am very familiar.

I would like to thank the following friends and colleagues who helped in the research and drafting process for this book. Catriona Beck, Mark Fox, Corey Froggatt, Robbie Hawkins, Mathew Hulbert, Sarah Mackinlay and Jakub Szweda have gone way beyond the call of duty, but I must make particular mention also of Noah Keate and Robert Waller.

Noah is a politics student and a devout listener to my *For the Many* podcast, and has spent hours and hours helping me with both the research and drafting of many of the entries you have read. I honestly could not have delivered this book on time without him. He has a fine future ahead of him in the political and journalism world.

I first got to know Robert Waller around twenty years ago when I was running Politicos Bookstore in Westminster. He was the inventor and co-editor of the *Almanac of British Politics*. As a History and Politics teacher, his intimate knowledge of British history and politics is, I think, unsurpassed. He has corrected many errors, as well as contributed to the drafting of many of the political stories and events mentioned in the book. He has contributed to my books *The Prime Ministers* and *The Presidents*, and I could not be more grateful for his work in assisting me with *On This Day*.

Inevitably, there will be a few factual errors, which the eagle-eyed among you will spot, and I take full responsibility. Please do email me and let me know, so corrections can be made for reprints or the paperback edition. info@iaindale.com.

Iain Dale
Tunbridge Wells, June 2022

JANUARY

BRITAIN JOINS THE EUROPEAN ECONOMIC COMMUNITY

Today, Britain became a member of the European Economic Community (EEC), as it was then called, after two previous attempts to join the Common Market, in 1963 and 1967, were vetoed by the French President, Charles de Gaulle.

The Conservative Party's 1970 manifesto stated that 'it would be in the long-term interest of the British people for Britain to join the European Economic Community,' making it one of their key pledges.

Sir Edward Heath, the then prime minister and behind the accession, described the decision to join the bloc as 'very moving' and at an EEC entry celebration banquet said: 'What we are building is a community, whose scope will gradually extend until it virtually covers the whole field of collective human endeavour.'

Harold Wilson, who was the Leader of the Opposition at the time, criticized the conditions agreed by Heath as 'utterly crippling' and said that the decision to join the EEC was done without the support of the British people.

Almost a year earlier, on 22 January 1972, Sir Edward Heath signed the Treaty of Accession in Brussels which officially triggered the process of joining the community. It meant Britain was able to join the original six member states, along with Denmark and Ireland.

Both Denmark and Ireland held referendums in 1972. Norway, which was also due to join, didn't ratify the treaty after the government didn't achieve the support in a referendum for the country's accession.

From the original four countries, Britain was the only one not to put the decision to a referendum prior to January 1973. A referendum did take place a couple of years later, in 1975, under the Labour government.

The European Communities Bill was introduced to the House of Commons, debated for around three hundred hours and received the Royal Assent in October 1972. Heath's attempt to get the Bill approved relied on gaining enough support from Labour MPs to balance out the Conservative MPs against it.

Heath's decision to join the Common Market is seen by many as the most prominent achievement during his time as prime minister.

LORD GRENVILLE INTRODUCES THE SLAVE TRADE BILL INTO THE HOUSE OF LORDS

The practice of slavery was perhaps the biggest stain on the British Empire. The Slave Trade Act of 1807 prohibited the trade in slaves, but it did not outlaw slavery itself. At the time, this was considered one step too far. That came twenty-six years later. It should be noted that slavery was never legal in Britain itself, but was common in many parts of the empire.

In the twenty years prior to the Act, more than 700,000 slaves had been transported on British ships across the Atlantic. It was one of Britain's most profitable trading activities. In 1787, the Committee for the Abolition of the Slave Trade was formed, and a little-known MP called William Wilberforce led the growing opposition to the trade in Parliament. In the same year, Wilberforce wrote in his diary: 'God Almighty has set before me two great objects, the suppression of the slave trade and the reformation of manners.'

There were various attempts during the 1790s to introduce legislation aimed at outlawing the slave trade, but they foundered in the House of Lords. In addition, Henry Dundas, the leading Scottish MP and close adviser to the Prime Minister, William Pitt, persistently attempted to water down any resolutions designed to lead to outright abolition. He maintained that a gradualist approach would be better, but the suspicion remained that his amendments were designed to wreck the whole project.

The Slave Trade Bill was introduced into the House of Lords on 2 January 1807 by the Prime Minister, Lord Grenville. Hopes were high that it would pass through both Houses unimpeded, especially given that there were now a hundred new Irish MPs, who mostly supported abolition. On 23 February, it passed its second reading by 283 votes to only 16. Royal Assent followed on 25 March and the Act came into force on 1 May.

Over the next sixty years, the Royal Navy intercepted 1,600 illegal slave ships and freed 150,000 slaves from Africa.

It wasn't until 1833 that the slave trade was abolished completely in the British Empire.

'LORD HAW-HAW' HANGED FOR HIGH TREASON

William Joyce was the last person to be hanged for treason in the UK. He had achieved notoriety as the voice of Lord Haw-Haw, who made regular propaganda broadcasts to Britain from Germany during the Second World War.

Joyce was born in New York in 1894 to an Irish father and English mother, but the family moved to Galway, Ireland, when he was a small child. In his teens, Joyce was recruited by the British Army as a courier during the lead-up to the war for independence, and he was known to associate with the Black and Tans. He then moved to England, entering the Officers' Training Corps, while studying at Birkbeck College in London.

In the early 1930s, he became a key lieutenant of Oswald Mosley and was known for his powerful oratory. In 1934, he became director of propaganda for the British Union of Fascists and later became deputy leader. In 1937, he and Mosley fell out, and Mosley sacked him.

Joyce and his wife Margaret fled to Berlin just before the outbreak of war at the end of August 1939. He eventually secured a job at the 'Rundfunkhaus' scripting broadcasts for German Radio's English Language service.

The name 'Lord Haw-Haw' was coined by *Daily Express* radio critic Jonah Barrington. Joyce's broadcasts were listened to by millions in Britain and always began with the words 'Germany calling, Germany calling, Germany calling'. He constantly urged Britain to surrender and adopted a sarcastic tone whenever talking about British politicians.

The broadcasts continued throughout the war, but listenership declined. His final broadcast came on 30 April 1945, when he appeared audibly intoxicated. Twenty-eight days later he was captured by the British Army at Flensburg, near the Danish border. Due to a misunderstanding he was shot four times in the buttocks.

At the Old Bailey he faced three charges of high treason, to which he pleaded 'not guilty'. He was cleared of two charges but found guilty of the third. An appeal, on the basis he was an Irish citizen rather than a British subject, failed and he was sentenced to hang.

BURMA BECOMES AN INDEPENDENT STATE

After sixty-three years of British rule, Burma became independent in the first days of 1948. By the end of British rule, the country was in a terrible state both economically and politically, with plans to rebuild the crown colony dropped and replaced with independence talks. After the end of World War II, Burma was seen by the Clement Attlee government as less and less valuable.

The crown colony had been invaded by Japan in 1942 and was liberated by Britain with the help of the Anti-Fascist People's Freedom League (AFPFL), led by General Aung San in 1945. The General was a key Burmese political figure and seen by many as the father of the country's independence. He was also the father of Aung San Suu Kyi, the Nobel peace prize winner and later Burma's civil leader.

Aung San began to negotiate with Britain terms of the country's independence, which led to the signing of the Aung San–Attlee Agreement on 27 January 1947, almost a year before the official handover took place. Clement Attlee told Parliament the following day that 'Burma has suffered greatly in the war. Great steps have been made in rebuilding her shattered economy. It will now be for her own people, her own Government, to complete that process and build a new Burma.'

It was agreed under the terms of the treaty that the country would hold an election, which took place in April 1947, and Aung San's AFPFL party won a significant majority, effectively becoming the ruling party of the country and a government in waiting.

Only months later, General Aung San and six other members of his party were assassinated, with the former Prime Minister of British Burma, and a political rival, U Saw, held responsible for planning the killings. The assassination threw Burma's already fragile political system into chaos in the lead-up to its independence. Without clear leadership, other political groups began to challenge the AFPFL and the country was plunged into a state of unrest, with a civil war ensuing shortly after. The consequences of those events impacted the country's future for years to come and they still do today.

ROY JENKINS DIES

Roy Jenkins can lay claim to be one of the most important political figures of the second half of the twentieth century, yet he never achieved his dream of becoming prime minister.

The son of a South Wales miner, Jenkins quickly escaped his working-class roots and gained a reputation as a red wine loving, priapic bon viveur. He became an intelligence officer during World War II, and first entered parliament at the age of twenty-eight in a by-election in Southwark Central in 1948.

It was as Home Secretary in the 1960s that he set down his greatest achievements, all in the area of social reform. He stood accused of initiating the 'permissive society' by legalizing abortion, reforming the divorce laws, decriminalizing homosexuality, abolishing the death penalty, reforming the laws on theatre censorship, and liberalizing immigration laws and the laws on betting and licensing. Each reform has stood the test of time. In 1967, he replaced James Callaghan as Chancellor following the devaluation of the pound.

But it was joining the European Economic Community (EEC) which was both to dominate his political priorities and to become the issue which thwarted his leadership ambitions. In 1960, he resigned from the front bench to campaign for EEC membership, and in April 1972 he resigned from the shadow cabinet and as Deputy Leader after Labour committed itself to a referendum on the issue. Although he stood for the leadership in March 1976 when Wilson resigned, he came a poor third. Callaghan refused him the Foreign Office, and in 1977 Jenkins resigned his Birmingham Stechford seat and spent four years as the President of the European Commission in Brussels.

In March 1981, Roy Jenkins formed the Social Democratic Party (SDP) with three other former Labour cabinet ministers. He led the party for two years. They never achieved the much vaunted 'breaking of the mould' of British politics, and in 1989 merged with the Liberal Party. Jenkins remained a figure of influence and chaired a commission on electoral reform for Tony Blair.

A prolific and talented author, he wrote nineteen books, including acclaimed biographies of Gladstone, Baldwin, Attlee, Dilke, Rosebery and Churchill.

WESTLAND AFFAIR TURNS TOXIC

'I may not be Prime Minister by six o'clock if it all goes badly.' So said Margaret Thatcher to her speechwriter, Ronald Millar, hours before addressing the Commons in a censure debate on the Westland affair on 27 January 1986. Labour leader Neil Kinnock came to her rescue with a dire performance and she lived to fight another day. I was working in the Commons that day and remember saying to a colleague: 'Things will never be quite the same again.' The events of January 1986 sowed the seeds of her eventual fall from power nearly five years later.

The Westland affair became a crisis because two cabinet ministers disagreed about who should take over a West Country helicopter manufacturer. Trade and Industry Secretary Leon Brittan, a key Thatcher ally, sided with the American company Sikorsky, while Defence Secretary Michael Heseltine wanted a European consortium to prevail. The two cabinet ministers went to war.

The crisis deepened on Monday, 6 January when a letter from the Solicitor General to him, accusing him of 'material inaccuracies' in his version of events, found its way into the public domain. He accused Leon Brittan's allies of deliberately leaking it. Three days later, as Heseltine walked into the cabinet room, his dander was up. The Lady, however, was not for turning. The Prime Minister told her cabinet that in future all pronouncements by ministers on the Westland crisis must be cleared by the Cabinet Office. The Defence Secretary maintained that this should not apply to simply confirming previous utterances. He wasn't in the mood to compromise, but not a single cabinet minister supported him. As Margaret Thatcher completed her summing up, Heseltine gathered up his papers, rose and said: 'I can no longer be a member of this cabinet.' He walked out into Downing Street to declare to the waiting cameras that he had resigned.

A few months prior to these events, I had been told at a dinner party that Michael Heseltine was looking for an excuse to resign. Well, if that was true, he certainly found it.

THE DÁIL VOTES TO RATIFY THE ANGLO-IRISH TREATY

At 2 a.m. on 6 December 1921, the British Prime Minister, David Lloyd George, met Irish republican leaders Michael Collins and Arthur Griffith in the Downing Street Cabinet Room to agree the terms of a treaty to bring an end to the so-called Irish War of Independence. Negotiations had been going on since October.

Under the Treaty, Ireland would become a self-governing Dominion of the British Empire, like Canada, Australia and New Zealand. The Irish Free State would be created but Northern Ireland would be allowed to secede from it within one month. The King would be the head of state and Britain would still control several ports for the Royal Navy to operate from. The Treaty would have superior status in Irish law and the Irish Free State would take on a proportion of UK debt.

The status of the Irish negotiators was hotly contested within the nationalist movement. The Irish President, de Valera, had instructed them to refer any agreement back to the cabinet for ratification. Instead, the negotiating team decided they had a free hand to reach an agreement on terms they saw fit. This was to have tragic consequences.

Upon agreeing terms, Lord Birkenhead reportedly remarked to Michael Collins: 'In signing this treaty I am signing my political death warrant.' Collins retorted: 'I'm signing my actual death warrant.'

On 8 December, de Valera called a cabinet meeting in which he made clear his opposition to the draft treaty. However, he was outvoted by four votes to three. The two main issues were Dominion status and partition.

The House of Commons approved the Treaty on 16 December by 401 votes to 58. The debate in the Dáil started on 14 December but much of the initial debate was held behind closed doors. On 7 January, Dáil Éireann ratified the Treaty by 64 to 57 votes. Two days later de Valera resigned as president and was replaced by Arthur Griffith.

The divisions sparked the Irish Civil War in June 1922. On 22 August, Michael Collins was killed in an ambush. On 6 December 1922, the Irish Free State formally came into existence.

FIRST NON-WHITE MP ELECTED TO THE HOUSE OF COMMONS

It is the irony of ironies that Britain's first non-white MP also happened to be a slave owner, and an unrepentant one at that. John Stewart was the illegitimate son of plantation owner John Stewart Sr – who had also briefly been a Tory MP for Camelford for a few months in 1819, but had been disqualified from office over bribery and corruption – and Mary Duncan, who is believed to have been black or mixed race.

Stewart was born in the West Indies in 1789, on the Demerara Plantation in British Guiana. Little is known about his upbringing, education or pre-parliamentary life, although we do know he was the main beneficiary of his father's will when he died in 1826.

In 1832, Stewart set his sights on standing for Parliament in Lymington and skilfully won over the local newspapers and opinion formers. In the 1832 election campaign, Stewart had to defend his use of slaves and denied there was any exploitation or cruelty on his estates. The next year, he spoke on the issue in the Commons and presented a petition against the freeing of slaves in the colonies. In 1836, he maintained that despite owning the largest slave estate in Antigua it had been unprofitable until he received compensation money from the British government. When slavery was abolished, he received more than £22,400 in compensation for the loss of 433 slaves in Demerara alone. He consistently defended slavery and voted against any measures enhancing the freedom of slaves.

Stewart's ethnicity did not seem to be an issue either in Lymington or Parliament. It was only after he left Parliament that he was described as a 'man of colour' and the first 'coloured' Member of Parliament.

Despite his maverick voting record, he gradually became a supporter of Peel's Conservative leadership, especially on the issue of the Corn Laws.

In 1847, his parliamentary career came to an end, when he came third in Lymington, and he took no further part in political life. He died in 1860 at the age of seventy-one.

INCOME TAX OF 10 PER CENT INTRODUCED

Britain's war with revolutionary France in the 1790s increased significantly the amount of money spent on the Army, resulting in a desperate need to find additional funding. In the early years of his premiership, William Pitt the Younger introduced a number of financial reforms, which although they increased the annual government revenue, weren't enough to match the government's drastically rising expenditure.

Britain's first income tax, which came into force on 9 January 1799, resulted in the introduction of a levy on incomes over £60 per annum, with a fixed rate for incomes over £200 and a graduated tax on incomes between £60 and £200. The expectation was that this would increase revenues by around £10 million, but in the end only around £6 million was raised.

It was seen as a temporary measure, and its unpopularity resulted in income tax being repealed in 1802. It was then reintroduced in 1803 and repealed again in 1816, a year after the Battle of Waterloo. It became 'permanent' in 1842. Some of the opposition to income tax at the time arose because it was regarded as being too intrusive, and that the government shouldn't be looking into how much people earned.

Pitt the Younger was elected to Parliament at the age of twenty-one and became Chancellor of the Exchequer for the first time only a year later. He was the Prime Minister of Great Britain from December 1783 to March 1801, and then again from May 1804 until his death in January 1806. His ideas and policies were heavily influenced by the Scottish economic thinker Adam Smith.

Economic policies which attempted to increase revenue played a key role during his premiership. Other forms of taxation were also introduced on goods and services, affecting the more well-off citizens. The Window Tax was tripled in 1797, primarily because it was seen as much harder to evade, although it did result in people either bricking or boarding up their windows. He reduced government spending. He also reduced high duties/tariffs in an attempt to deter smuggling, which was seen by him as a key issue.

HAROLD MACMILLAN BECOMES PRIME MINISTER

It was one of the quickest transfers of power in the history of British politics. The day before, Sir Anthony Eden had submitted his resignation to the young Queen. Following the failed Suez escapade, his mental and physical health had deteriorated to such an extent that he felt unable to carry on. He immediately left the country to recuperate in the West Indies.

In those days there was no leadership election as such. Soundings were taken by party elders and a new leader 'emerged'. Lord Salisbury, known as 'Bobbety', called in the cabinet one by one to seek their views and asked: 'Is it "Rab" or Harold?', although given he couldn't pronounce his 'r's it came out as 'Is it Wab or Hawold?'. Hawold it was, as R. A. Butler's views on Suez were thought likely to split the party. Butler was also passed over for the leadership in 1963 and, along with Ken Clarke, became a nearly man of Conservative politics.

At the time, Harold Macmillan was very much a rising star, although at the age of sixty-two he was hardly inexperienced. During the war he had served as Minister for the Mediterranean, and in 1951 he joined Churchill's cabinet as Housing minister, setting an ambitious aim of building 300,000 houses a year. He was promoted to Defence Secretary in 1954, but when Eden took over as prime minister he went to the Foreign Office and six months later was reshuffled to the Treasury.

The fact that Macmillan was able to escape his strong backing for Eden over Suez, and almost make out he hadn't been in favour afterwards, says a lot about his wiliness and political nous.

Macmillan's immediate task on entering Downing Street was to repair relationships, particularly with the United States and the United Nations.

He is most remembered for his anti-apartheid 'Wind of Change' speech in South Africa in 1960 and his role in negotiating the Nuclear Test Ban Treaty following the Cuban Missile crisis. He resigned in October 1963 due to ill health. In 1984, he was created Earl of Stockton and he died two years later.

ARTHUR SCARGILL IS BORN

When discussing Arthur Scargill with millennial friends recently, not one of them knew who he was. That a man who was at one point amongst the most recognizable faces in Britain has now faded from historic memory, says a great deal about the role the union he led now plays in society.

Born on 11 January 1938 to a mining family, Arthur Scargill went on to lead the National Union of Mineworkers for more than twenty years. When he became president, in 1981, the union represented close to 200,000 members. In 2015, the membership stood at a measly 150.

Without doubt, Scargill's great impact on British life and politics came through his leadership in the 1984–85 miners' strike. The unsuccessful strike action in response to plans to close twenty-three pits, which ended on 3 March 1985, and for which many blamed Scargill, was a central moment in British political history.

For many, the strike came at the wrong time, on the wrong issue, with the wrong tactics. The failure to hold a national ballot alienated many of the Nottinghamshire miners and damaged the union's reputation and support, amongst both the trade union movement and in British public opinion more broadly.

Scargill claimed the plans to close were part of a long-term government strategy to destroy the industry. That this was confirmed to be correct in 2014 does little to change the ultimate conclusion.

It wasn't just a defeat for Scargill and the miners. It was also the moment the Thatcher government wrested back control from the unions – ten years after strike action toppled the Heath administration.

A hero to some, a maverick who hastened the closure of the mines to others, Arthur Scargill's fading from the public memory mirrors that of the outdated politics he represented. His establishment of the Socialist Labour Party in 1996, following Tony Blair's dropping of Clause 4, was a last-gasp attempt for Marxist principles, and Scargill himself, to remain relevant in British life. Its total lack of electoral success further displays Arthur Scargill's ultimate failure.

LIBERALS WIN LANDSLIDE IN GENERAL ELECTION

The election of 1906 resulted in a landslide for the Liberal Party on the scale of Clement Attlee's victory in 1945 and Margaret Thatcher's in 1983. It heralded the end of eleven years of Conservative hegemony and the beginnings of a nascent welfare state. For the next ten years the Liberals ruled under three different prime ministers – Sir Henry Campbell-Bannerman, H. H. Asquith and David Lloyd George.

On 5 December, Arthur Balfour resigned, his Conservative/ Liberal Unionist government having become very unpopular over tariff reform, the Boer War, licensing and schools. His plan was to let the Liberals take over on the assumption they would split, call an election and he would triumphantly return to power. It didn't work out like that. As soon as Liberal leader Sir Henry Campbell-Bannerman kissed hands with King Edward VII, he called an immediate general election for 12 January.

Prior to the election an electoral pact had been negotiated by Herbert Gladstone and Labour's Ramsay MacDonald. In thirty-one of the seats Labour fought, the Liberals did not put up a candidate, in order to maximize the anti-Conservative vote. Twenty-four of the twenty-nine Labour MPs who won were in these seats. It was something the Liberals lived to regret in the long term, given that within twenty years they had been totally usurped by Labour.

When the results of the election were announced, Arthur Balfour had lost his Manchester East seat after a 22.5 per cent swing to the Liberals. It is the only time a former prime minister and Leader of the Opposition has lost his seat. Only three former Conservative cabinet ministers managed to retain their seats.

In the end the Liberals won 397 seats to the Conservatives' 156, a majority of 241. Campbell-Bannerman appointed H. H. Asquith to the Treasury, Herbert Gladstone to the Home Office and Sir Edward Grey to the Foreign Office. Lloyd George became President of the Board of Trade.

It was to be one of most significant and reforming governments of the twentieth century. The shame was that within two years Campbell-Bannerman was dead. He doesn't get the credit he deserves.

13

THE FORMATION OF THE INDEPENDENT LABOUR PARTY

Until the latter part of the nineteenth century, the Liberal Party was considered the party most friendly to working-class interests. However, the Liberals, with their Whig imperialist past, flattered to deceive. With trade unions gaining in influence and popularity, the Labour Representation League was formed in 1869, designed to advance the cause of the working man within the Liberal Party and to mobilize them to vote in elections. The Fabian Society, formed in 1884, had the same aims, albeit from an intellectual viewpoint. However, as ever within the so-called intellectual Marxist left, there were some big fallings-out, as the purists thought the working-class struggle would inevitably prevail without any co-operation with 'bourgeois' political parties, like the Liberals.

In the 1892 general election, three independent candidates were elected, including Keir Hardie, with the support of the Liberal Party. It was a prelude to signing its own death warrant.

In January of the following year, at a conference called by the Trades Union Congress in Bradford, a motion was passed to form what came to be called the Independent Labour Party (ILP). It represented a coming together of the left. Those present included Karl Marx's son-in-law Edward Aveling, George Bernard Shaw and dockers' leader Ben Tillett. Keir Hardie gave the keynote speech of the conference.

The stated aim of the new party was 'to secure the collective and communal ownership of the means of production, distribution and exchange'. It called for massive social reforms, a major housebuilding programme and benefits for the unemployed, an eight-hour working day and the abolition of overtime.

The party's formative years didn't match the expectations or hopes of its founders. Only twenty-eight candidates were put up in the 1895 general election. None were elected. Even the party leader, Keir Hardie, lost his seat.

In 1900, the Labour Representation Committee was formed, with the founding of the Labour Party taking place six years later. The ILP immediately affiliated to it, and although over the years it proved to be a thorn in the Labour Party's side, many Labour MPs in the 1920s and 1930s came from its ranks. In 1975, it was renamed Independent Labour Publications.

FRANCE VETOES BRITAIN JOINING THE EEC

In January 1963, following months of intensive negotiations in both capitals and Brussels, President Charles de Gaulle of France announced his opposition to Britain's intention to join the European Economic Community (EEC). Although meetings continued for some days, soon after all member states had to halt the negotiations with Britain.

At a press conference, he raised his concerns, suggesting that Britain would want to 'impose its own conditions' on the members of the bloc and undermine its cohesion. De Gaulle was worried about Britain's 'special relationship' with the United States and who the UK would side with if another conflict was to arise. He also opposed Britain's failure to commit to leaving its Commonwealth ties behind.

On the other hand, Britain joining the EEC would potentially weaken France's influence, something de Gaulle viewed with horror. It was his aim to ensure that France would continue to lead the project and nothing would be done to undermine that. His suspicions about the United States would only worsen, if Britain was to become a member.

During the negotiations, Prime Minister Harold Macmillan and his government came up with a number of conditions as part of the application, to protect and preserve Britain's relations with Commonwealth countries. The government also attempted to preserve its role as a bridge between the US and mainland Europe. Concerns were raised across Britain's political parties around the impact of joining the bloc, and how it would affect the country's political and economic relations with other nations. However, joining the European community was an attempt by Macmillan to boost the ailing UK economy and matched his belief that Britain's future lay with continental Europe.

Macmillan was devastated by the decision to block Britain's application and considered it a huge failure. He wrote in his diary that 'all our policies at home and abroad are in ruins' and that 'the French always betray you in the end.'

Negotiations to join the EEC were resurrected under the Labour government and halted once again by a second veto from de Gaulle in 1967. Britain joined the EEC in 1973 under the premiership of Edward Heath.

BREXIT DEAL DEFEATED IN HOUSE OF COMMONS

Against all the predictions and all the odds, Theresa May had secured a Brexit deal with the European Union (EU) in December 2018. It was due to be ratified on 10 December, but it became clear that the government would be defeated if they put it to a vote. A so-called 'meaningful vote' was deferred to mid January. This was required under the terms of the European Union (Withdrawal) Act 2018, which said that any agreement with the EU had to be ratified by the House of Commons before it could be implemented.

On 9 January, the House of Commons commenced a five-day-long debate. On the final day, May declared: 'This is the most significant vote that any of us will ever be part of in our political careers. After all the debate, all the disagreement, all the division, the time has now come for all of us in this house to make a decision. A decision that will define our country for decades to come.'

She might as well have saved her breath. The motion was defeated by 432 votes to 202. This was biggest defeat for a government motion in parliamentary history. Rising to speak after the vote, Theresa May invited a vote of no confidence in her government, which opposition leader Jeremy Corbyn proceeded to table.

Theresa May now had three options left to her. Leave the EU with no deal; attempt to renegotiate the deal to make it more palatable; or hold a second referendum on leaving the EU.

Britain was supposed to leave the European Union on 29 March 2019. Two more 'meaningful votes' were held but May was defeated on each occasion. She found it impossible to renegotiate terms which would be acceptable to her party and on 24 May announced she would step down as prime minister. Her successor, Boris Johnson, after protracted parliamentary manoeuvres also failed to get a deal through. He called a general election, gained a majority of eighty and struck a deal with the EU on Christmas Eve 2019. Britain formally left the EU on 31 January 2020.

HAROLD WILSON ANNOUNCES BRITISH WITHDRAWAL
FROM EAST OF SUEZ

The Suez Canal was once described as 'the jugular vein of the empire'. When it was opened in 1869 it transformed the journey from Britain to the Far East. It became such a strategic asset that only twelve years later Britain took control over Egypt and entered a joint administration agreement over the canal with France.

It was at this time that the British Empire was at its zenith. Britannia really did still rule the waves, and Britain was adding to its territories around the world with every passing decade. Queen Victoria was not only Empress of India but head of state for around a quarter of the world's surface.

The first half of the twentieth century saw the empire's importance diminish. Independence movements started to mushroom, and a new generation of British politicians started to reconcile themselves with the fact that something would need to change in the relationship between Britain and its colonies – India, in particular. And then the Second World War happened, and it changed everything, not least Britain's financial strength and place in the world.

India gained full independence from Britain in 1947 and was quickly followed by Ceylon, Ghana, Jamaica, Kenya, Libya, Malaysia, Nigeria, Rhodesia, Sierra Leone, Singapore, Sudan, Tanzania, Uganda and Zambia. There was also a gradual drawdown of Britain's military presence East of Suez.

In 1956, the Egyptian leader, President Nasser, nationalized the Suez Canal, provoking a military response from Britain and France. The military incursion failed and signalled the 'end of empire'. Not only was it a massive embarrassment for Britain, but it gave succour to independence movements the world over.

On 16 January 1968, Prime Minister Harold Wilson made a speech announcing that all British military forces would be withdrawn within three years from British bases in South East Asia, including in Singapore, Malaysia, and in the Persian Gulf.

In 2014, the Cameron government announced the expansion of naval facilities in Bahrain. A logistics base was then established in Oman and naval deployments in the Far East are increasing to combat the military threat from China. East of Suez is back.

BARBARA CASTLE INTRODUCES 'IN PLACE OF STRIFE'

By the end of the 1960s ten million working days a year were being lost due to official and unofficial strike action. Pay rises were starting to fuel inflation. Harold Wilson's 'white heat of technology' was threatening traditional jobs, and the trade unions, far from being the mainstay of the Labour government, appeared to be threatening its very existence.

Barbara Castle, Wilson's Secretary of State for Employment and Productivity, was determined to change the relationship between the unions and the state.

She wanted unions to ballot their members before strike action and to replace the show of hands at mass meetings. She also wanted to create an Industrial Board, whose remit would be to enforce industrial agreements.

Castle had made her name as a woman of the left and she was no shrinking violet. Wilson and Castle had drafted the White Paper 'In Place of Strife' together and presented it to cabinet, but they had fatally misjudged the moment, and failed to build support within the cabinet and the Labour Party. By the standards of the Thatcher years, the reforms were fairly moderate.

The White Paper was published on 17 January, but it was never translated into legislation. Opposition in the cabinet – and there was a lot of it – was led by Home Secretary James Callaghan, who had never been a fan of Castle. When he became prime minister, in April 1976, the first thing he did was fire her from his cabinet.

'In Place of Strife' was finally killed off a few months later when an agreement was reached with the TUC. Well, more of a capitulation than an agreement, if truth be told. The unions were further emboldened and within four years had brought Edward Heath's Conservative government to its knees.

The Labour government of 1974–79 appeared to be a coalition between the Labour Party and the trade unions. They had no government ministers but had immense influence and power over the government and weren't afraid to use it, culminating in the Winter of Discontent. Had 'In Place of Strife' not been thwarted, it is entirely possible Margaret Thatcher may not have happened.

JEREMY THORPE BECOMES LIBERAL PARTY LEADER

Jeremy Thorpe had it all – charisma; a top-class education; he'd married a beautiful and intelligent woman; and he'd developed a good reputation as a parliamentary performer. In the mid 1960s, the Liberals only had twelve MPs, and when Jo Grimond announced he was standing down, three of twelve put themselves forward to lead the Liberal rump – Emlyn Hooson, the victor of the 1962 Orpington by-election Eric Lubbock, and of course, Thorpe himself. The ballot of MPs ended with Thorpe gaining six votes, with Lubbock and Hooson on three each. They both withdrew leaving Jeremy Thorpe to embark on a nine-year stint as leader of Britain's third party.

Thorpe had made his name at the bar and as a television journalist. He was telegenic and knew what the cameras wanted. Thorpe had won his North Devon seat by only 362 votes in 1959, having been selected as candidate in 1952 and fighting a losing battle in the 1955 election. He won it by a heady mixture of charisma and sheer hard work. Master of the witty and memorable one-liner, he memorably commented on Harold Macmillan's 1963 'Night of the Long Knives' reshuffle: 'Greater Love hath no man than this, that he lay down his friends for his life.' He again rose to prominence when Rhodesia declared independence from Britain and he advocated the UN bombing the main railway supply line into the country, thereby earning the nickname 'Bomber Thorpe'.

Thorpe gave the Liberal Party a profile it hadn't enjoyed since the days of Lloyd George. But the seeds of his eventual destruction were already being sowed. He enjoyed almost complete control of Liberal Party fundraising but there were justified suspicions that money was being siphoned off to pay for his own activities, not least dealing with the male model Norman Scott, who was trying to blackmail the new Liberal Leader.

In the February 1974 election, the Liberals won six million votes, but only fourteen seats. Three years later he was forced to resign the party leadership over the Norman Scott scandal. He was charged with conspiracy to murder but acquitted at the Old Bailey in 1979.

JOHN BERCOW IS BORN

John Bercow was a rarity among Speakers of the House of Commons in that he was the ultimate Marmite Speaker. People either think he was one of the greatest ever, reforming Speakers, or a self-preening, anti-Conservative, anti-Brexit narcissist.

Bercow was the hard right chairman of the Federation of Conservative Students at the University of Essex. At the same time, he was the secretary of the immigration and repatriation committee of the Monday Club.

He was elected to the House of Commons in 1997 and became a terrier-like backbench warrior, causing trouble for Tony Blair. And then he met his future wife, Sally, a committed Blairite Labour supporter. She knocked off his rougher political edges and he began a journey away from the hard right. He joined the Tory front bench but Bercow found working as a team player a bit of a challenge.

He was sacked twice from the shadow cabinet, once after rebelling against the party line on gay adoption. He then decided to succeed Michael Martin as Speaker, when the time came.

In May 2009, Martin was forced to resign in the turmoil of the MPs' expenses scandal. Bercow won the Speakership on the second ballot, thanks to the overwhelming support of Labour MPs. He started a series of internal procedural reforms and authorized the building of a creche. He controversially allowed the Youth Parliament to sit in the House of Commons chamber.

Over time he started to be accused of breaching the traditional Speaker's neutrality. He declared he was opposed to Brexit and told President Trump he was not welcome to address Parliament during a state visit. He then prevented the government from bringing its EU Withdrawal Agreement back for a third vote.

On 9 September 2019, after ten years in the Speaker's chair and amid rows over Brexit, Bercow announced he would stand down at the end of October, the date the EU Withdrawal Agreement was due to come into force.

The Boris Johnson government refused to put him forward for a peerage in the light of bullying allegations that to this day remain unresolved.

FIRST SUMMONING OF THE COMMONS

Prior to the reign of King Henry III (1216–1272) the notion of a parliament, as we understand it today, did not exist. The early Saxon kings took counsel from a network of advisers, often referred to as the Witenagemot, and they lacked any formal structure. Only in the ninth and tenth centuries did these assembles take on any kind of institutional meaning. According to historian John Maddicott, the origins of an English Parliament can be traced back to the reign of Aethelstan, when he convened his Great Assemblies. Maddicott wrote: 'These portentous gatherings were the lineal ancestors of the more brightly illuminated councils and parliaments of the post-Magna Carta world. From this time onwards the line joining the witan to the *concilia* and *colloquia* of Anglo-Norman and Angevin England, and thence to the parliaments of the thirteenth and fourteenth centuries, remained essentially unbroken.'

It wasn't until the signing of the Magna Carta in 1216 that the word 'parliament' was really used. When King John died in 1216, it was left to leading barons and churchmen to govern the kingdom until the young Henry III reached maturity. It was the first time non-royals had been able to exercise power, and there was no turning back. The first thing they did was to ensure that Henry reaffirmed Magna Carta.

However, Henry's increasingly dictatorial manner sparked a rebellion, and Simon de Montfort, Earl of Leicester, raised an army which triumphed over the King's at the Battle of Lewes in May 1264. In order to establish his authority, de Montfort summoned a parliament of the usual archbishops, bishops, abbots and barons, plus two knights from each shire and two burgesses from each borough. This later became known as the 'summoning of the Commons'.

It met on 20 January 1265 and was dissolved less than a month later. No records remain of who attended. However, the make-up of the parliament was later copied and adopted by King Edward I in his 'Model Parliaments'. Despite de Montfort's death at the Battle of Evesham later in 1265, Henry III summoned the Commons three more times in his reign.

GEORGE ORWELL DIES

There can surely be little debate about calling George Orwell one of the finest and most thought-provoking political writers of the twentieth century. Anybody with a passing interest in political literature knows the basic plots of at least two of his greatest works, *Animal Farm* and *1984*. In 2008, *The Times* ranked him second in a chart of the 50 Best British Writers Since 1945.

Born Eric Arthur Blair in 1903 in India, Orwell came from a middle-class background. His father worked in the fantastically named Opium Department of the Indian Civil Service. Even at school he dreamed of being a writer.

At the age of fourteen he gained a scholarship to Eton. After Eton he spent five years with the Indian Imperial Police in Burma, but in 1927 he returned to England and reappraised his life, deciding to become a full-time writer. For the next year or so he concentrated on essays and journalistic endeavours, writing mainly about poverty, homelessness and the plight of the poor.

It was in 1933 that his first book, *Down and Out in Paris and London*, was published by the new, radical imprint Victor Gollancz. And he now took on the pen name of George Orwell. Given the subject matter of the book, he didn't want to embarrass his family by using his real name.

But it was *The Road to Wigan Pier*, published in 1937, that set him on the road to success and fame. It also resulted in the security services monitoring him for twelve years. Orwell spent a year in Spain fighting in the Spanish Civil War, during which he was wounded, and this resulted in his next book, *Homage to Catalonia*, which turned out to be a commercial failure.

It was *Animal Farm* that really made Orwell's reputation, with its allegorical warnings about the dangers of totalitarianism. *Nineteen-Eighty-Four*, or *1984*, followed in 1949, but by then Orwell's health was failing after years of suffering from respiratory problems, first encountered in Burma. In January 1950, he died at the age of forty-six. His fame and renown now exceed anything he achieved while he was alive.

RAMSAY MACDONALD BECOMES FIRST LABOUR PRIME MINISTER

Since the fall of the Lloyd George coalition in October 1922, British politics had changed beyond all recognition. At the 1922 general election Labour had supplanted the Liberals to become the main opposition party. While respectability had been conferred at last, radicalism was on the decline. Ramsay MacDonald, the Labour leader, was the perfect exemplification of the trend. Having been anti-war and a committed socialist in earlier years, he now became the very model of a responsible opposition leader with an eye on the premiership. When Prime Minister Baldwin called an election in October 1923, few thought it would lead to a Labour government, but that's exactly what happened when Baldwin lost a vote of confidence in January 1924. King George V sent for MacDonald and Britain had its first Labour government, albeit it was only to last until October.

The new Prime Minister took on the role of Foreign Secretary too, in an effort to signal a willingness to clear up the mess created by the Treaty of Versailles and the ongoing issue of German reparations. As well as appointing Philip Snowden to the Treasury, it was notable that ten of his cabinet members had working-class origins.

It may have lasted only nine months, but the fact that a Labour government existed at all was possibly its main achievement. With the continuing widening of the electoral franchise, it sent a signal that a different future was possible. That's not to say that nothing else was achieved in its short existence. MacDonald saw to it that strikes were quickly brought to an end, unemployment and other benefits were extended, and a Housing Act meant better and more housing for working people. He convened a conference in London of the great powers to deal with the German issue and later to ratify the Dawes Plan regarding German reparations. MacDonald also formally recognized the Soviet Union.

In August the government fell over MacDonald's decision not to prosecute the communist-leaning *Workers' Weekly* over its editorial inciting servicemen to mutiny. After losing a censure motion, Labour lost the ensuing general election in October.

KIM PHILBY DEFECTS TO MOSCOW

It wasn't as if no one saw it coming. Throughout the 1940s and 1950s there were suspicions about Kim Philby's true allegiances. He had been recruited to Soviet intelligence in 1934 while at Cambridge. He became known as the most important member of the so-called 'Cambridge Five' spy ring. Guy Burgess, John Cairncross, Anthony Blunt and Donald Maclean were the other members of this traitorous group. Burgess and Maclean defected to the Soviet Union in May 1951, while Blunt and Cairncross's activities were uncovered in 1964, when they turned Queen's evidence in return for immunity from prosecution. These events did not become public until the late 1970s and 1980s.

After graduating from Cambridge Philby worked as a journalist covering the Spanish Civil War and the Battle for France. In 1940, he was recruited by MI6 and quickly rose through the ranks. In 1949, he was posted to the British Embassy in Washington, D.C., an ideal place to pass secrets to the Soviets.

While there, he tipped off Burgess and Maclean that they were about to be unmasked, resulting in them fleeing Britain to France and then on to Moscow. Although no one could prove anything, Philby became the main suspect and he resigned from MI6.

In 1955, he was publicly exonerated by Foreign Secretary Harold Macmillan in the House of Commons: 'I have no reason to conclude that Mr. Philby has at any time betrayed the interests of his country, or to identify him with the so-called "Third Man", if indeed there was one.' Philby held a press conference saying: 'I have never been a Communist.'

A year later, Philby was sent to Beirut to cover the Middle East for the *Observer*. It was there that he started an affair with a married American woman, Eleanor Brewer, who he later married in 1959. In 1961, the KGB officer Anatoliy Golitsyn defected and confirmed Philby's role as a spy. The game was up. One night he just disappeared. He had boarded a Soviet freighter and turned up in Moscow several weeks later. He died there in 1988.

WINSTON CHURCHILL DIES

On 24 January 1895, Lord Randolph Churchill died. Seventy years later, to the day, his son Winston passed away at his London residence at 28 Hyde Park Gate. The decline in his health had started in 1953 during his second term as prime minister. He suffered the first of eight strokes at a dinner in Downing Street. Somehow it was hushed up, with even the cabinet not knowing what had happened. His son-in-law Christopher Soames effectively took over the reins of power, in what would now be regarded as an unconstitutional coup. His eighth and final stroke occurred twelve years later on 15 January 1965. Nine days later he was dead. His last words were said to Christopher Soames: 'I am so bored with it all.' After the life he had lived, who could blame him.

He was without doubt the greatest Briton of the twentieth century, some would argue of all time. He was in the right place at the right time. It is one of the great 'what ifs' of history. What would have happened if Lord Halifax, rather than Winston Churchill, had become prime minister in May 1940?

The announcement of Churchill's death was made at 8.35 a.m. It led the BBC radio news bulletins at 9. Afterwards they played Beethoven's Fifth Symphony, the one which starts with three short notes and one long one, which symbolized the letter V in Morse code.

The following day, Prime Minister Harold Wilson led tributes in the House of Commons and the Queen announced that Sir Winston would lie in state for three days in Westminster Hall. More than 321,000 people queued to pay their respects.

Back in 1953, after Churchill's first stroke, the planning for his funeral had commenced on the orders of the new Queen. It was held on the morning of 30 January at St Paul's Cathedral. The twelve pallbearers included Clement Attlee, Sir Anthony Eden, Harold Macmillan and Lord Mountbatten. After the service the coffin was taken to the Tower of London, then transported up the River Thames to Waterloo Station, from where it was taken by train for a private burial in Oxfordshire.

'GANG OF FOUR' LAUNCH THE LIMEHOUSE DECLARATION

Four former senior Labour cabinet members wanted to break the mould of British politics. They had had enough of the hard left takeover of the Labour Party and its domination by the big trade unions. On a cold January morning, a few days after a calamitous Labour Party conference in Wembley, they stood together on a bridge in Narrow Street, Limehouse, in east London, and declared their intention to form the Council for Social Democracy and by implication leave the Labour Party.

Fourteen months earlier, former cabinet minister, and President of the European Commission, Roy Jenkins had delivered the annual Richard Dimbleby Lecture. He titled it 'Home Thoughts From Abroad'. He discussed the weaknesses of the British political system and what should be done about them. It led some to wonder what his agenda was. His use of the word 'realignment' led many to speculate that he might return to the UK to front a new political movement. Charles Kennedy later said: 'Every so often in life, you hear someone articulate your own thoughts – and they do so with an elegance and eloquence which make you wish you had been able to say it yourself. Roy Jenkins's Dimbleby Lecture of 1979 had that effect on me.'

The Declaration itself was a classically centrist text with a commitment to a Britain with an international outlook, a belief in both the role of the state and free markets, together with a declared ambition to reform both the political and electoral systems.

Within a week, eight thousand people had sent messages of support and a newspaper advert was signed by more than a hundred members of the social democratic left, including thirteen Labour MPs.

Two months later, Roy Jenkins, David Owen, Shirley Williams and Bill Rodgers were to launch the SDP, the Social Democratic Party. Its immediate impact was huge, and one poll showed it attracting 50 per cent of the vote. It scored some initial stunning by-election successes with Jenkins and Williams returning to the House of Commons. However, the mould of British politics proved more difficult to break in the long term.

HONG KONG CEDED TO BRITAIN

Britain occupied and took control of Hong Kong in early 1841, with the British taking formal possession on 26 January, when Britain's flag was raised, marking the beginning of colonial Hong Kong. This happened during the First Opium War, which took place from September 1839 to August 1842. The conflict was sparked between Great Britain and China's Qing dynasty by disagreements about the sale of opium by British sellers, something the Chinese opposed.

The end of the First Opium War was marked by the signing, in 1842, of the Treaty of Nanking, in which the Chinese officially ceded Hong Kong to the British. This, however, didn't solve the ongoing trade conflict about the sale of opium, subsequently sparking the Second Opium War from 1856 to 1860. The war was again lost by the Qing dynasty and concluded through the Convention of Peking, signed in 1860. As a result, the British Hong Kong was expanded by the addition of another part of the island. The Kowloon Peninsula and Stonecutters Island were officially ceded to the British Empire.

Under British rule, Hong Kong was able to flourish as a free port, becoming a crucial trade centre in the region. In 1898, it was agreed under the Convention for the Extension of Hong Kong Territory that Britain would be given an additional ninety-nine years to rule over the territory, rather than permanent ownership as initially hoped for.

During World War II, from December 1941 to August 1945, the crown colony was occupied by Imperial Japan after the Japanese invaded the territory and the British surrendered. It returned to British rule when the Japanese surrendered at the end of World War II, and Hong Kong was once again able to expand economically.

Earlier, Sir Charles Elliot had become the first Administrator of Hong Kong on 26 January 1841. The position of Governor of Hong Kong was created in 1843 and Sir Henry Pottinger was the first holder of the office. Chris Patten was the last person in that role until 1997, when Hong Kong returned to Chinese rule.

LORD SALISBURY'S FIRST GOVERNMENT FALLS

Along with Gladstone, Disraeli and Palmerston, Lord Salisbury was one of the four titans of Victorian-era politics. A scion of the Cecil dynasty, he dominated the Conservative Party for the twenty years following the death of Disraeli in 1881. He had served as Secretary of State for India and Foreign Secretary and emerged as leader of the Conservatives in succession to Disraeli, with his bitter rival Sir Stafford Northcote leading the party in the Commons. However, Gladstone was in his prime, and it was to be four years before Salisbury got the keys to Number 10 on the first of three occasions. And this didn't happen because he led the Tories to an election win, but because the Liberal government under Gladstone disintegrated over a budget revolt. In the lead-up to this, Salisbury had skilfully amended the 1884 Reform Act to ensure multi-member constituencies were abolished. At a stroke this ended Gladstone's ability to balance his MPs between Whigs and Radicals.

The Queen immediately sent for Salisbury rather than Northcote, and he formed a government on 23 June 1885. It can't be said that Salisbury's first ministry achieved much in its short seven-month tenure before it suffered a defeat by the Liberals in the Queen's Speech debate.

Gladstone formed his third administration at the beginning of 1886, but the split in the Liberals over Irish Home Rule soon forced another election in July 1886 after Gladstone was defeated on his Government of Ireland Bill.

The Liberal Unionists, led by Lord Hartington and Joseph Chamberlain, entered into an electoral pact with the Conservatives and for the first time ever the Conservatives won more than 50 per cent of the popular vote, and an overall majority. And so the Conservatives went on to rule for the next nineteen years, with a brief three-year gap from 1892 to 1895, when the Liberals regained power under Gladstone and then Rosebery.

The Irish question dominated this period of British politics. Salisbury's nephew, and eventual successor, Arthur Balfour proved to be a hard-line Chief Secretary for Ireland but neither he, nor his uncle, were able to come up with a solution. They weren't the last to fail.

LORD NORTH BECOMES PRIME MINISTER

If you enjoy drawing up lists ranking prime ministers, and let's face it, I do, most people would put Lord North fairly near the bottom, if not the bottom. After all, it was under his rule that Britain lost the American colonies, wasn't it? Well, yes it was, but the story is much more complicated than that. He governed for twelve years, from 1770 until 1782, and domestically he scored some notable successes, but we're getting ahead of ourselves.

Frederick North, 2nd Earl of Guilford, initially considered himself to be a Whig, although most of his contemporaries thought he was a Tory. And this meant he had wide appeal. He first became a minister in the Duke of Newcastle's administration and rose up the ranks throughout the 1760s. In 1767, he became Chancellor of the Exchequer and later added the leadership of the House of Commons to his titles.

In January 1770, the Duke of Grafton's government collapsed following incessant undermining from the Earl of Chatham, formerly William Pitt the Elder. Grafton had also suffered reputation damage related to his private life, after he had had an affair while his wife was pregnant with their fourth child. She divorced him, a scandal from which few politicians could recover in those days. Two cabinet resignations forced the issue and Grafton fell on his sword. King George III was determined that Lord North should take over and eventually persuaded him to do so. He retained his two other cabinet titles. North was a reluctant prime minister in some ways. He had seen how difficult it was to hold a government together and he needed convincing that he had the ability to do just that. The fact that he managed it for twelve years, while Britain was being ritually humiliated in America, is a miracle in itself.

Before the American war, North had managed to slash the national debt. It was he, as Chancellor, who established budget day in the political calendar. He also introduced important reforms to the administration of Ireland, Canada and India. So all in all, he wasn't all bad.

OXFORD UNIVERSITY REFUSES MARGARET THATCHER AN HONORARY DEGREE

Any university likes to celebrate the achievements of its graduates and often awards them honorary degrees. Oxford, which at the time was the world's leading university, decided that Britain's first woman prime minister was not worthy of the accolade and withdrew the offer of an honorary degree to Margaret Thatcher. She pretended not to care, but it hurt her deeply.

Thatcher had attended Oxford as an undergraduate between 1943 and 1947, studying for a Chemistry degree, specializing in X-ray crystallography. She later told friends that she was prouder of being the first prime minister with a science degree than of being the first female prime minister.

In late 1984, the university offered Mrs Thatcher an honorary degree and she accepted. However, a petition signed by five thousand students and protests by university lecturers over education cuts led to the university's 'Congregation' meeting in the city's Sheldonian Theatre for a two-hour debate followed by a vote. They voted by more than two to one (738–319) against awarding her the degree.

Margaret Thatcher did not comment directly but a Downing Street spokesman said at the time: 'The Prime Minister thought it was very gracious of Oxford University when the Hebdomadal Council proposed that she should be accorded an honorary degree. However, it is entirely in the hands of the university. If they do not wish to confer the honour, the Prime Minister is the last person to wish to receive it.' It was a slight she wouldn't forget, and when it came time to decide where to place her archives, she chose Churchill College, Cambridge. In 1998, her foundation also endowed an Enterprise Studies degree at Cambridge to the tune of £2 million.

In 2003, when former Thatcher cabinet minister Chris Patten was the university's Chancellor, he lifted not a finger to support Wafic Saïd, who wanted to name a wing of his Business School after her. The university refused the request, but they had no objection to naming it after a multi-billionaire arms dealer.

To this day the university has failed to honour either of its two female prime ministerial graduates – Thatcher or Theresa May.

BLOODY SUNDAY

The city of Derry/Londonderry was an unhappy place in 1972. It had a nationalist majority population, yet electoral boundaries were continually gerrymandered to ensure a loyalist majority on the city council. It had been starved of investment, and the city's housing stock was in a terrible state. The beginning of the Troubles three years earlier had turned the city into a powder keg.

Internment without trial had been introduced in Northern Ireland in August 1971. Over the ensuing four months, seven British soldiers were killed in Derry. Relations between the nationalist community and the Army were deteriorating rapidly. Although Northern Ireland Prime Minister Brian Faulkner banned all marches in the province, the Northern Ireland Civil Rights Association decided to press ahead with their protest on 30 January, following a smaller but violent march eight days earlier held at Magilligan Strand near Derry. Paratroopers were accused of using excessive force.

Fifteen thousand people set out from the Creggan Estate in Derry at 2.45 p.m. on 30 January. When the march reached the city centre, it was blocked by the British Army. At 3.55 p.m., the first shots were fired. Fourteen people were killed, with dozens more injured. It was and remains the highest number killed in any single shooting incident during the Troubles. All were Catholics. Bloody Sunday fuelled nationalist resentments and led directly to a rise in support for the IRA.

The next day in the House of Commons, the Home Secretary Reginald Maudling claimed paratroopers had been provoked. Nationalist MP Bernadette Devlin was suspended after she slapped him.

Lord Widgery was commissioned to report on what happened, and he did so ten weeks later. It proved to be a whitewash. In 1998, Tony Blair asked Lord Saville to look at the events anew in a second commission of inquiry. Hearings lasted six years and it was another six years before the report was published in June 2010. It was castigating in its conclusions. Reacting in the House of Commons, Prime Minister David Cameron said: 'There is no doubt, there is nothing equivocal, there are no ambiguities. What happened on Bloody Sunday was both unjustified and unjustifiable. It was wrong... I am deeply sorry.'

THE CORN LAWS ARE REPEALED

We all think of Brexit as the defining issue of our political age. In the 1840s, it was the Corn Laws. Their repeal in the latter part of the decade led to the Tories splitting and the emergence of a modern party-based political system.

The Corn Laws were first introduced by Lord Liverpool's government in 1815. They included duties and tariffs on imported corn-related products, like wheat, oats and barley. The purpose was to support landowners and farmers by artificially keeping the price of domestically produced agricultural products high. Cheap imports of wheat were effectively blocked. The effect was to dramatically increase food prices for the general population and reduce disposable income.

Unrest ensued, but it took thirty years and the Great Famine in Ireland, as well as a poor harvest in Britain, to prompt any kind of action. And even then, there was no political consensus on repealing the Corn Laws. However, Whig leader Lord John Russell announced on 22 November 1845 that he favoured immediate repeal, which spurred on Peel to take decisive action. Two weeks later, Peel announced he would recall Parliament in January 1846. Lord Stanley resigned from his cabinet in protest, and a week later Peel himself followed suit, after he realized he could not bring his party with him. Russell found he could not form a government and ten days later Peel was back. He pushed through the legislation with support from Whig members. Over the next three years, tariffs were reduced until complete abolition occurred at midnight on 31 January.

The repeal would not have happened without the political leadership of Sir Robert Peel, who realized from the start that it would probably spell the end of his time in front-line politics. In his resignation speech he said bread 'would be the sweeter because it would no longer be leavened by a sense of injustice.'

Looking back, this was one of the most decisive moments in British economic and political history. It set Britain on a path towards free trade. It also broke the mould of Whig/Tory politics and led to the creation of the modern-day Liberal and Conservative parties.

FEBRUARY

THE FIRST LABOUR EXCHANGE OPENS

The Liberal government led by Sir Henry Campbell-Bannerman and then Herbert Henry Asquith was one of the great reforming governments of all time. It set the framework for the welfare state, which would develop over the rest of the century.

As part of these innovative reforms, dreamed up largely by Campbell-Bannerman, but implemented and paid for by the Chancellor of the Exchequer, David Lloyd George, the Labour Exchanges Bill was introduced into the House of Commons in May 1909 by the President of the Board of Trade, Winston Churchill, following the so-called People's Budget on 29 April. It received its Royal Assent on 20 September.

Only five months later, the first state-organized labour exchanges in the UK opened their doors, and by the end of February 1910 there were eighty-three across the country. The *Manchester Guardian* declared that interest and demand was huge and there was a 'promising start everywhere'.

Labour exchanges were not a particularly new innovation in that there had been private sector or charitable exchanges for some decades. The first was opened by social reformer and employment rights advocate Alsager Hay Hill in London in 1871.

The overriding purpose of the Labour Exchanges Act was to enable the unemployed to find work more easily, as well as to improve the mobility of workers. Somewhat counter-intuitively, the creation of labour exchanges was opposed by the nascent trade union movement. The unions thought their bargaining power might be impacted, making it easier for employers to recruit cheap labour from other parts of the country. Employers weren't too keen either, at least initially, which meant that not all positions were advertised. My own grandfather moved from a farming background in Ayrshire to the Consett steelworks as a result of the local labour exchange advertising a position.

Initially, the exchanges didn't fulfil their promise and only around a quarter of the people registered with them managed to find a job through their services. However, by 1913, three thousand people each day were being placed into jobs through more than 430 labour exchanges.

BRITISH EMBASSY IN DUBLIN BURNED TO THE GROUND

On the same day that eleven of the victims of the Bloody Sunday shootings in Londonderry were being buried, protesters in Dublin burned the British Embassy to the ground. For three days more than twenty thousand people had been protesting outside the embassy in Merrion Square, not far from the Dáil.

Hundreds of petrol bombs were thrown, as well as stones and random missiles. Fire engines were prevented from getting to the scene for several hours and the crowds cut their hoses. According to the *Guardian*:

> All windows in the front of the building were smashed, and shutters torn from their hinges. Burning Union Jacks were hung on the front of the building above symbolic coffins, placed on the embassy steps by march leaders who were allowed through the police cordon around the building... watching crowds cheered as the interior of the embassy blazed fiercely. 'Burn, burn, burn,' they shouted as chunks of masonry and woodwork fell blazing on to the street. They redoubled their cheering whenever they saw the fire breaking through into new parts of the building. They stopped fire engines from getting through, and hurled petrol bombs at the building to speed the blaze.

Around twenty demonstrators and police were injured. One police officer was seriously injured when a gelignite bomb was used to blow out the front door.

All diplomats and staff had been evacuated from the building, although the Ambassador, John Peck, was in London and returned immediately.

As the embassy burned, some of the crowd moved to the nearby British Passport Office, where they were baton-charged by the police. Thirty people were injured.

Other British related organizations and buildings in and around Dublin also came under attack. Effigies of Prime Minister Edward Heath were burned. The UK government made a formal diplomatic protest over the burning down of the embassy. The Irish government responded by expressing 'regret' and said it would pay compensation.

The embassy was rebuilt in Merrion Road, a short distance away from its original site, and in 2015 it was converted into apartments.

MACMILLAN MAKES 'WIND OF CHANGE' SPEECH IN SOUTH AFRICA

Only forty years earlier, the British Empire covered a fifth of the globe. But instead of the empire making Britain more prosperous, it had started to prove a drag. Clement Attlee's Labour government had started the process of decolonization, with India in 1947 being the prime example to others. The Conservative governments of the 1950s continued the policy albeit with rather less enthusiasm.

At the beginning of 1960, Prime Minister Harold Macmillan embarked on a month-long tour of African countries, which culminated in a speech to the South African parliament on 3 February. The speech had two aims. Firstly, he wanted to make clear that Britain would not stand in the way of any British colony which wanted to gain independence. South Africa had achieved that status in 1934, but there were a whole host of African nations queuing up to unshackle themselves from British rule. The line from the speech which everyone now remembers was a direct signal that any reluctance from Britain to scupper independence movements was disappearing. 'The wind of change is blowing through this continent. Whether we like it or not, this growth of national consciousness is a political fact.'

Barbados, Botswana, Cameroon, Cyprus, Gambia, Guyana, Jamaica, Kenya, Kuwait, Lesotho, Malawi, Malta, Mauritius, Nigeria, Sierra Leone, Somaliland, Swaziland, Tanzania, Trinidad and Tobago, Uganda, Yemen and Zambia all became independent nations in the 1960s.

The second aim of the speech was to warn South Africa that its policy of apartheid was unacceptable to the international community: 'I hope you won't mind my saying frankly that there are some aspects of your policies which make it impossible for us to do this without being false to our own deep convictions about the political destinies of free men to which in our own territories we are trying to give effect.'

The speech was received in total silence.

Ironically, Macmillan had given an almost identical address in Ghana, but the press missed its significance.

CHURCHILL MEETS ROOSEVELT AND STALIN AT YALTA

By the beginning of February 1945, it wasn't a question of 'if' Germany would be defeated but when. France had been liberated, and so had Belgium. The Soviet Army was forty miles from Berlin.

With the three main Allied leaders having already met in Tehran in November 1943, it was decided that they would meet again at Yalta, in Crimea, in early February 1945. The aim of the conference was to decide the map of Europe after the defeat of Germany. Churchill and Stalin had already pre-empted this discussion by talking about 'spheres of influence' at a meeting in Moscow in November 1944, a discussion from which Stalin took much more meaning than the British Prime Minister. The French leader, General de Gaulle, was not invited to Yalta after objections from both Roosevelt and Stalin, a slight he was never to forget.

Despite the meeting being held in the Soviet Union, Roosevelt took on the role of host. America's main aim was to persuade the Soviets to join the war in the Pacific against the Japanese. Britain wanted to ensure free and fair elections and democratic government in Central and Eastern Europe, while Stalin wished to establish, as part of his war security strategy, a zone of influence in the countries on his western borders. The final agreement was given the name: The Declaration of Liberated Europe.

It was agreed that, following the unconditional surrender of Germany, the country, and its capital city, Berlin, would be divided into four occupation zones, which the USA, Soviet Union, the United Kingdom and France would administer. Germany would undergo demilitarization and 'denazification'. The borders of Poland would be redrawn and Stalin promised not to interfere in its internal affairs. Poland would lose territory in the east to the Soviet Union and gain territory in the west from Germany. The Soviet Union would join the United Nations. Stalin agreed to join the war against Japan after the defeat of Germany. Trials were to be held to hold Nazi leaders to account, and a Committee on German Dismemberment was to be set up.

Churchill and Roosevelt soon realized that the promises made by Stalin over Poland were worth nothing.

COMMONS VOTES FOR SAME-SEX MARRIAGE

Believe it or not, Michael Heseltine is in part to be credited with the introduction of equal marriage. A few days after the Coalition was formed in 2010, he gave a talk to incoming junior ministers. He told them to think of one thing they wanted to achieve while in their job. Lib Dem Home Office Minister Lynne Featherstone mulled this on the way back to her office in her ministerial car and determined to persuade her colleagues to introduce equal marriage for gay and lesbian people. It hadn't been a promise in the Conservative manifesto, but she knew the Prime Minister, David Cameron, would be sympathetic given what he said in his conference speech as Tory leader in 2006. He said marriage 'means something whether you're a man and a woman, a woman and a woman or a man and another man. That's why we were right to support civil partnerships, and I'm proud of that.' Featherstone also convinced her boss, Home Secretary Theresa May, to support her.

The Blair government had introduced the Civil Partnership Act in 2004, but the rights for same-sex couples in a civil partnership did not quite equate to those of straight couples who had married. The Bill's second reading took place in the House of Commons on 5 February 2013 and MPs were given a free vote. It passed by 400 to 175 votes. More Conservative MPs voted against than voted for (136 to 127). The Marriage (Same Sex Couples) Act received its Royal Assent on 13 July. The first same-sex marriage took place on 29 March 2014.

Civil partners were given the option of converting their civil partnership to a marriage (something I and my partner did in June 2015). However, the Act specifically prevents same-sex marriages from taking place in churches or other religious buildings, and if they do take place they are regarded as null and void. To this day, any Church of England vicar who blesses a gay marriage in a church runs the risk of being defrocked.

Lynne Featherstone proved that an individual politician really can make a difference to people's lives.

PASSING OF THE REPRESENTATION OF THE PEOPLE ACT

It is undeniably true that women played a crucial role during the First World War. With millions of men fighting on the front line, women filled key roles at home in areas such as manufacturing and agriculture. They were also part of the fight on the front line, working as nurses, doctors or translators.

With their war efforts in mind, women saw this as an opportunity to serve their country – and most importantly – gain more rights and independence.

After a struggle lasting many years, through peaceful campaigning, war endeavours and military strategy, women finally gained the right to vote for the very first time following the passing of the Representation of the People Act on 6 February 1918.

Although the significance of women gaining the right to vote was clear, there was still a long way to go in securing equal rights with men. The 1918 Act only allowed women over the age of thirty to vote, and not only that, they were required to own a property, or be married to someone that did. It took another ten years for women to gain exactly the same voting rights as men.

Although women's right to vote is arguably the most significant part of this Act, the First World War was also pivotal in extending the male franchise. For the first time, men over the age of twenty-one were now able to vote without having to own a property. This tripled the size of the electorate.

Prior to 1918, around 58 per cent of the adult population could vote. Only men who had been resident in Great Britain or Ireland for twelve months prior to a general election were eligible to vote, meaning many troops who had been serving in the war were disenfranchised. It seems clear therefore that the magnitude of the war efforts was a deciding factor in extending the vote to men further.

Although women in 1918 still faced a long road ahead in obtaining the same political rights as men, one thing cannot be disputed – the Representation of the People Act 1918 changed the face of the UK forever.

IRA LAUNCHES MORTAR ATTACK ON DOWNING STREET

In October 1984, the IRA tried to assassinate Margaret Thatcher and her cabinet in Brighton. They failed, but in 1990 decided to try again. However, before they could launch their audacious mortar attack on 10 Downing Street, she resigned. A little detail like that didn't deter them, and they continued their planning.

In June 1990, two IRA members travelled to London. They bought a Ford Transit van, rented a garage and started to manufacture the mortars. They made trips to Whitehall to work out where the van would need to be parked in order for the trajectory to be right for the mortars to hit their target – the home of the British prime minister. But it wasn't just the building they were targeting, it was the cabinet. They waited until they knew ministers would be in the Cabinet Room.

On 7 February 1991, a 'war cabinet' was taking place to discuss the Gulf War. Present were Prime Minister John Major, Douglas Hurd, Norman Lamont, Tom King, Patrick Mayhew, John Wakeham (a victim of the 1984 attack in Brighton), Peter Lilley and David Mellor, along with Cabinet Secretary Sir Robin Butler and four other senior civil servants.

As the meeting began, a van drove down Whitehall and parked on the junction of Horse Guards Avenue, only 200 yards from the Cabinet Room.

The driver was picked up and whisked away on a motorcycle. At 10.08 a.m., three mortar shells were fired from the cut-out roof of the Transit. Two overshot their target and landed on a piece of grass outside the Foreign Office. Only one exploded. But the third mortar shell landed and exploded in the Downing Street garden, 30 yards from the Cabinet Room. The cabinet ducked under the table with Prime Minister John Major declaring: 'I think we had better start again, somewhere else.'

A security officer later said: 'If the angle of fire had been moved about five or ten degrees, then those bombs would actually have impacted on Number Ten.' There is little doubt that everyone in that meeting would have been killed.

ENOCH POWELL DIES

Enoch Powell was the ultimate Marmite politician. He attracted huge loyalty and was regarded by many as the most principled and far-sighted politician of his time. Others regarded him as a pseudo-racist devil and painted him as the most dangerous man in Britain. When he died at the age of eighty-five in 1998, the country lost a politician who had himself lost his way and become a somewhat peripheral figure.

Most politicians are remembered for only one thing. Powell might be remembered for his double first in Latin and Greek at Oxford, or his ability to speak many languages including Welsh and Urdu. He might also be remembered as the Minister for Health who encouraged West Indian nurses to come to England in the 1960s. He might even be remembered for his bid to become leader of the Conservative Party in 1965, although he only won the support of fifteen MPs.

No, what Enoch Powell will always be remembered for is a single incendiary speech, made on 20 April 1968 in Birmingham, in which he warned of the dangers of immigration. It led to his immediate sacking from Edward Heath's shadow cabinet. He warned:

As I look ahead, I am filled with foreboding. Like the Roman, I seem to see 'the River Tiber foaming with much blood'. That tragic and intractable phenomenon which we watch with horror on the other side of the Atlantic but which there is interwoven with the history and existence of the States itself, is coming upon us here by our own volition and our own neglect.

The Times regarded the speech as 'evil', yet London dockers marched in his support. His words divided the country like never before. He became *persona non grata* to much of the Conservative Party and left it in 1974, standing for the Ulster Unionists. He lost his South Down seat in 1987.

In 1994, I witnessed Powell speaking to a group of Conservatives in east London. He had a way with words like few others, but he had demonic eyes. I remember thinking that he was a flawed genius.

41

NEW NUCLEAR REACTOR AT DOUNREAY ANNOUNCED

In 2020, nuclear power met 20 per cent of the UK's entire energy needs, down from 26 per cent in 1997. The country's civil nuclear programme was initiated in the 1950s, with the world's first nuclear power station opening in 1956 at Calder Hall, Windscale (now Sellafield), in Cumbria.

There are currently thirteen nuclear power plants in the UK – twelve advanced gas-cooled reactors and one pressurized water reactor.

In 1959, the Dounreay Fast Reactor went live having cost £15 million. Dounreay, on the north coast of Scotland, was a sleepy village which had hosted an RAF base in World War II. The reactor pumped electricity into the grid from 1962 until its decommissioning in 1977.

On 9 February 1966, Labour Technology Minister Frank Cousins, a former trade union leader, announced that Dounreay was to be the site of the first of the second generation of nuclear reactors, the prototype fast reactor, at a cost of £30 million. Cousins described the new reactors as 'the future'. This proved to be an illusion. Why? In the mid 1960s, stocks of uranium were thought to be dwindling, but when new reserves were discovered they became less commercially attractive, and Dounreay proved to be the first and last Plug Flow Reactor in the UK. It operated until 1994 and was the last of Dounreay's three reactors to cease operation.

In 1998, the Blair government announced that the Dounreay plant would be decommissioned following the discovery that a huge amount of uranium had gone missing, enough to build twelve nuclear weapons. It will be 2060 before the site is clear of all nuclear material and becomes a brownfield site. The famous Dounreay dome will remain in place and is classed as a listed building.

In contrast to Germany, nuclear power has never been a massively controversial political issue in Britain. In the late 1970s and 1980s, Germany experienced huge protest marches, which gave birth to the rise of Die Grünen – the Greens. In Germany all nuclear outlets are being decommissioned. In Britain successive governments delayed decisions on recommissioning or building new nuclear power stations, although the war in Ukraine has spurred the Johnson government to recommit itself to nuclear energy.

MILITARY CONSCRIPTION BEGINS

The British Army in 2022 numbers under 80,000. When war broke out in 1914 it had 710,000 members, including reservists, although only 80,000 were ready for combat in Europe, given that a third of the Army were stationed in India. By the end of the war, four years later, more than five million men were enlisted, one in four of the qualifying men in Britain's adult population. Only just over half of these were conscripts.

The Army had been shamefully neglected by 1914. Conscription was anathema and always had been in Britain. The British Army numbered six divisions, less than a tenth of the size of the French and German armies. The Secretary of State for War, Lord Kitchener, was scathing about its capabilities and regarded the Territorial Divisions as utterly useless and untrained.

When war broke out, at the beginning of August 1914, a call went out for 100,000 volunteers to join the Army. 'Your Country Needs You!' blazed the posters featuring a pointing Lord Kitchener. More than 500,000 men responded, together with 250,000 under-age boys who lied about their age. There was almost a state of euphoria. Almost 40 per cent of the volunteers were rejected for medical reasons.

Kitchener calculated he needed 92,000 recruits each and every month. By the middle of 1915, it was clear that conscription might be needed. The Prime Minister, H. H. Asquith, was firmly against, as were most of his ruling Liberal Party, but practicality started to prevail over ideology.

In the autumn of 1915, the Earl of Derby, working under Kitchener, introduced a scheme whereby canvassers would knock on doors to 'persuade' men to volunteer for war service. Nearly 320,000 men did indeed enlist, but there was substantial resistance.

As a result the government was left with no alternative but to pass the Military Service Act in January 1916. Single men and widowers who were childless and between the ages of eighteen and forty-one were required to enlist immediately. In May it was extended to married men, and in 1918 the upper age limit was raised to fifty-one. Altogether, more than 1.5 million men were conscripted.

MARGARET THATCHER ELECTED LEADER OF THE CONSERVATIVE PARTY

I was eleven years old. It was around 7 p.m. I ran upstairs to tell my ill grandmother the news. 'Margaret Thatcher has been elected leader of the Conservative Party,' I exclaimed breathlessly. And with that, she burst into tears. She told me later she couldn't believe a woman could ever be leader of a political party. Frankly, nor could most of the Conservative Party. Most MPs wondered what they had done.

Thatcher wasn't a leading light in Ted Heath's cabinet, having spent the whole of the 1970–74 period as Education Secretary. Heath couldn't stand her and often regretted giving her a cabinet job. But after the second election defeat in October 1974 it was Margaret Thatcher and Sir Keith Joseph who put their heads above the parapet to suggest that the party needed to change direction. Ted Heath, however, still popular among Tory members, refused to quit, but eventually agreed to call a leadership election in which he would stand, and dare anyone to stand against him. Sir Keith Joseph fell by the wayside after making an ill-advised speech on eugenics, and it was left to Margaret Thatcher to carry the anti-Heath banner. She astonished everyone by beating Heath by 130 votes to 119, with Hugh Fraser on 16. Heath duly resigned.

In the second round, five other cabinet ministers entered the fray, with Willie Whitelaw expected to prevail. However, a cunningly strategic campaign organized by former Colditz prisoner of war Airey Neave saw Margaret Thatcher score a clear victory with 146 votes to Willie Whitelaw's 79. Geoffrey Howe and Jim Prior trailed with 19 and John Peyton on 11. And so the first woman to lead a political party in Britain took over the reins of power in the Conservative Party.

At a press conference after the ballot, Margaret Thatcher said: 'To me it's like a dream that the next name in the line Harold Macmillan, Alec Douglas-Home and Edward Heath is Margaret Thatcher.'

She would have to wait four years to fight a general election, which she won in May 1979 and became Britain's first female prime minister.

WINSTON CHURCHILL BECOMES SECRETARY FOR THE COLONIES

Everyone knows of Winston Churchill's time as prime minister in World War II, but how many people are aware that he first became a minister in 1905 as Parliamentary Under Secretary of State for the Colonies? Sixteen years later, he was appointed to run the same ministry as Secretary of State. In 1908, he joined the cabinet as President of the Board of Trade, and was promoted to Home Secretary in 1910. A year later, he went to the Admiralty, but when the wartime coalition was formed he was demoted, only to return on 17 July to the crucial post of Minister for Munitions. After the war had ended he was reshuffled to be Secretary of State for War. He lobbied Lloyd George to hold a new title of Minister for Defence, but failed.

As Colonial Secretary, Churchill played a key part in the events leading up to the signing of the Anglo–Irish Treaty and supported the new Irish government by providing arms to combat the threat of nationalist terrorism. Churchill's other preoccupation was to protect British interests in the Middle East, especially Egypt. He was also behind the creation of Iraq and the Emirate of Transjordan, as well as implementing a pro-Zionist policy in Palestine.

Churchill left the Liberal Party in 1922 and began a journey back to the Conservatives, and in 1924 Stanley Baldwin appointed him as Chancellor of the Exchequer. He put Britain back on the gold standard, a decision he later admitted had been a huge mistake. Churchill also played a key role in defeating the 1926 General Strike.

In 1929, the Conservatives lost power again and this was to trigger more than a decade in the political wilderness for a man who had seemed destined for the top job. He fell out of sympathy with his party over protectionist tariffs and India. When the National Government was formed in 1931, Churchill was left out.

It wasn't until May 1940 that his destiny was fulfilled, and he was chosen to lead Britain through the tumult of World War II.

THE BILL OF RIGHTS IS TABLED

Britain doesn't have a written constitution, but if it did, the 1689 Bill of Rights would surely form part of it, along with Magna Carta (1215), the Petition of Right (1628), the Habeas Corpus Act (1679), the Act of Settlement (1701) and the Parliament Acts of 1911 and 1949. It formed the basis of the US Bill of Rights a century later and was the model for many other similar pieces of legislation in other countries.

During the early part of the seventeenth century, there were constant tensions and conflicts between Parliament and the Stuart monarchy. These led to the Civil Wars, also known as the Wars of the Three Kingdoms (England, Scotland and Ireland), and the Glorious Revolution of 1688. It all started with the 1628 Petition of Right, which laid out protections for individuals against the powers of the state, following the imposition by King Charles I of forced loans and the imprisonment without trial of those who refused to pay. Martial law was imposed. Parliament then asserted itself and reaffirmed Magna Carta and Habeas Corpus. To this day the Petition of Right remains in force.

Although Parliament was largely cowed during the Protectorate and the reign of Charles II, political groupings began to emerge and public engagement in debate was burgeoning with the growth of printed pamphlets. Parliament started to reassert itself and counter some of the excesses of the government.

Following the overthrow of James II, Parliament was reconvened in January 1689. Members argued that the House 'cannot answer it to the nation or Prince of Orange till we declare what are the rights invaded' and that William 'cannot take it ill if we make conditions to secure ourselves for the future' in order to 'do justice to those who sent us hither'.

The Bill set out limits on the powers of the monarch, the rights of Parliament, the rights of the individual, free elections and the royal succession. It also declared that taxes could not be imposed without the agreement of Parliament. It was truly a landmark constitutional document.

HAROLD WILSON BECOMES LEADER OF THE LABOUR PARTY

At the beginning of 1963, Labour was gaining in the opinion polls, and with an election due within eighteen months, many political commentators believed Hugh Gaitskell, who had been Labour Leader since 1955, was set to be prime minister. And then, on 18 January, he died from complications from lupus disease. His deputy, George Brown, became interim leader.

When nominations for a new leader closed, there were three candidates – Brown himself, shadow Chancellor James Callaghan and shadow Foreign Secretary Harold Wilson. George Brown was a bit of a media darling, and had the contest been fought under a different system, he might have prevailed, but in those days Labour MPs were the only ones to have a vote, and they were well aware of his heavy drinking and his tendency towards erratic and unpredictable behaviour.

James Callaghan was viewed as an outsider, and was probably putting a marker down for the future. He had been an MP for eighteen years and was seen as a safe pair of hands, but didn't have the flair or electoral appeal of Brown or Wilson.

Harold Wilson had briefly been a cabinet minister in the Attlee government, but resigned with Aneurin Bevan over the issue of prescription charges in 1951. In 1960, he had challenged Gaitskell for the leadership, and pitched himself as the most left wing of the three candidates.

The first ballot of Labour MPs took place on 7 February. Wilson topped the poll with 115 votes, way ahead of George Brown on 88. James Callaghan was eliminated after receiving the support of only 41 Labour MPs. In the second ballot a week later, Wilson triumphed with 144 votes to George Brown's 115.

At the age of forty-six, Harold Wilson's youth and vigour contrasted with an increasingly tired looking sixty-nine-year-old Harold Macmillan, and then from October 1963, the sixty-year-old Alec Douglas-Home. Wilson went on to win the 1964 general election, albeit by a very narrow majority of four seats, which increased dramatically to ninety-eight in the landslide of 1966. Wilson became the youngest prime minister since Lord Rosebery in 1894.

THE LABOUR PARTY IS FOUNDED

In 1899, a motion was passed by the Amalgamated Society of Railway Servants to suggest to the TUC that all left of centre organizations should come together with the aim of sponsoring parliamentary candidates at general elections. A special conference was held on 27 and 28 February 1900 at London's Congregational Memorial Hall.

The leader of the Independent Labour Party, Keir Hardie, proposed 'a distinct Labour group in Parliament, who shall have their own whips, and agree upon their policy, which must embrace a readiness to cooperate with any party which for the time being may be engaged in promoting legislation in the direct interests of labour'. And so the Labour Representation Committee (LRC) was formed, with Ramsay MacDonald as its Secretary. It sponsored fifty candidates in the 'Khaki' election of 1900, with Keir Hardie and Richard Bell being successfully returned.

In 1903, MacDonald came to an unofficial agreement with Liberal Chief Whip Herbert Gladstone that they wouldn't do anything to split the anti-Conservative vote. Gladstone didn't know it at the time, but he had sown the seeds of the destruction of his own party. In the 1906 election the LRC won twenty-nine seats.

At the first meeting of the parliamentary grouping, on 15 February, it was decided to use the name 'The Labour Party' for the first time. Keir Hardie was elected Chairman (i.e. leader) beating off a strong challenge from David Shackleton. Initially, the party remained based on a loose mix of left-wing organizations and trade unions. It wasn't until 1918 that individual membership was introduced. In December 1910, the party won forty-two seats and in 1918, following the expansion of the franchise, its number of MPs rose to fifty-seven. In the same year Sidney Webb drafted the famous Clause IV of the party's constitution, pledging the party to work towards 'the common ownership of the means of production, distribution and exchange'.

In 1922, the party won 142 seats and became the official opposition for the first time. In 1923, the party formed a short-lived government with Ramsay MacDonald as prime minister. Ever since, it has either been in government or the main opposition party.

CHARLES I APPROVES THE TRIENNIAL ACT

King Charles I came to the throne in 1625 and spent the first fifteen years of his reign squabbling with Parliament over the extent of his powers, and in particular the Royal Prerogative. Charles genuinely believed in the divine right of monarchs and that his views and orders should trump anything and anyone else. His dictatorial tendencies, his marriage to a Roman Catholic and his general views on religious matters all combined to make him increasingly unpopular, and eventually led to his demise.

In February 1641, Parliament passed the Triennial Act. It was determined to assert itself against the absolutist tendencies of Charles. The Act stated that Parliament must meet for at least fifty days once every three years. Charles had ignored Parliament for eleven years, and only summoned it at the end of 1640 in order to pass financial legislation to pay for the so-called Bishops' Wars in Scotland.

The Triennial Act stipulated that if the King failed to call Parliament, the Lord Chancellor would be obliged to do so, or the House of Lords could assemble and issue election writs. In addition, because Parliament had no trust in the King a clause was inserted to state that the Bill would receive Royal Assent before the end of the parliamentary session. Such was the level of distrust in the monarch.

What turned out to be the so-called Long Parliament sat until 1648 (although technically until 1660) when it was 'purged' by the New Model Army. However, it was on 4 January 1642 that the conflict between monarch and Parliament really burst into the open.

The King entered the chamber of the House of Commons, backed up by around four hundred armed soldiers, determined to arrest five MPs who he thought had behaved in a treasonous manner. He asked Speaker Lenthall where they were and received the reply: 'I have neither eyes to see nor tongue to speak in this place but as this House is pleased to direct me.' This was groundbreaking stuff, as for the first time a Speaker had effectively pledged allegiance to Parliament rather than the monarch.

PARLIAMENT VOTES TO JOIN THE EEC

Having applied to join the European Economic Community (EEC) twice, in 1963 and 1967, and been vetoed twice by the French President, Charles de Gaulle, Britain decided to see if it would be third time lucky once de Gaulle had retired. By 1970, Georges Pompidou had taken over and was much more willing to countenance Britain joining. The new Prime Minister, Edward Heath, made it his life's mission and the Treaty of Accession was signed in January 1972. By then Britain's trade with the EEC outstripped trade with the Commonwealth. Domestic political attitudes had softened too.

In October 1971, the House of Commons voted, after a six-day debate, by 356 to 244 votes to approve a white paper on EEC membership. The relatively close vote signalled that the passage of the Accession Bill was likely to be bumpy. The European Communities Bill was introduced into the Commons only four days after the Treaty of Accession was signed. Remarkably, it was only twelve clauses long.

Even more remarkably, it only just passed its second reading on 17 February 1972 by 309 to 301 votes. At the end of the debate Edward Heath threatened to call an election if the Bill fell. Had five Liberal MPs voted with Labour, things would have been very different. Some Labour MPs pushed and jostled Liberal leader Jeremy Thorpe after the vote. Fifteen Conservative MPs, including Enoch Powell, voted with Labour, five Conservatives abstained, and the sixty-eight Labour MPs, led by Roy Jenkins, who had supported membership in the vote the previous October, decided that the only way they could stay in the Labour Party and try to reverse its position on EEC entry, was to vote with the party whip on the second reading of the Bill.

The rest of its parliamentary passage ran more smoothly and Royal Assent was granted on 17 October 1972. The UK formally joined the EEC on 1 January 1973. However, on 23 June 2016, Britain voted to leave the European Union and on 31 January 2020, the European Communities Act 1972 was repealed under the terms of the European Union (Withdrawal) Act 2018.

HUNTING BAN COMES INTO FORCE

The Hunting Act banned the use of dogs to hunt and kill wild mammals in England and Wales and had faced multiple barriers before eventually being passed in 2004, and coming into force on this day.

When Tony Blair took power in 1997, his manifesto had pledged a free vote on whether hunting with hounds should be banned. Labour MP Michael Foster introduced a private member's bill, but it ran out of parliamentary time. Eventually, after a report by Lord Burns in 2000 said fox hunting 'seriously compromises the welfare of the fox' (no kidding!), the government introduced an options bill allowing each House of Parliament to choose between a ban, licensed hunting and self-regulation. The two Houses were split; the Commons voted for a ban, while the Lords voted for self-regulation. The 2001 general election was then called, which meant the Bill was abandoned due, once again, to a lack of parliamentary time.

Labour peer Lord Donoughue proposed his own bill in 2001 which would have amended the Wild Mammals (Protection) Act 1996 but it was blocked by Labour members, who had their hearts set on a more specific hunting ban.

The following year, an identical bill was introduced to the Commons. Before the final vote, the debate was interrupted by pro-hunting demonstrators storming into the Commons chamber. It was the first such invasion since King Charles I marched his troops into the building intending to arrest five MPs for disobeying his orders in 1642. The pro-hunting mob, though, were easier to handle; they were dragged outside briskly by Commons officials, where they rejoined some ten thousand protesters from groups such as the Countryside Alliance. The vote was then won by 356 votes to 166. Cheers reverberated among the crowded benches. But the Lords once again wouldn't play ball. And the Bill fell. Three years later, the Bill's aims were achieved under the 2005 Hunting Act.

ANTHONY CROSLAND DIES

When a politician dies in office, they tend to be remembered more fondly than they may deserve. In Anthony Crosland's case, he died a political hero, and among certain sections of the social democratic left he is still thought of as a spiritual guiding light today.

In 1977, he was a big beast of the Labour jungle. Although he had come bottom of the poll in the 1976 leadership election, which installed James Callaghan as Harold Wilson's successor, it was in the party where his political strength lay, not among his fellow MPs. Nevertheless, the new Prime Minister appointed him Foreign Secretary.

Crosland was the son of two parents who belonged to the Plymouth Brethren on the south coast. He had an unremarkable education but served with distinction in the war, ending up as a Captain. He then spent a year at Oxford gaining a First.

Crosland first entered Parliament in 1950 (he lost in 1955 and then won in 1959 in Grimsby, a seat he represented until his death) but it was his seminal work *The Future of Socialism*, which sought to promote a new form of social democracy, which propelled him to prominence. The book is still in print today. He was part of the Gaitskellite grouping, along with Roy Jenkins and Denis Healey.

Crosland couldn't stand Harold Wilson but served in his reforming government of the 1960s at the Treasury, the Board of Trade and Local Government. But it was as Secretary of State for Education where he really made his mark, starting the school comprehensivization process. He vowed: 'If it's the last thing I do, I'm going to destroy every fucking grammar school in England.' He didn't quite manage it, but he and his successors (including Margaret Thatcher) came very close.

Anthony Crosland was a protégé of Hugh Dalton and was married twice. He was a man of prodigious sexual appetite and had numerous adulterous affairs, including one, reportedly, with Roy Jenkins.

On 13 February, while working at home on a foreign policy speech, he suffered a brain haemorrhage and died six days later in hospital.

FOREIGN SECRETARY ANTHONY EDEN RESIGNS

With his suave and debonair good looks, Anthony Eden was very much the rising star of the Conservative Party. Appointed Foreign Secretary at the age of thirty-eight, he was seen as a future Conservative Party leader, which indeed he became, but not until much later, and we all know how that ended. He could be intensely charming, but also quite bad tempered. Rab Butler referred to him once as 'half mad baronet, half beautiful woman'. He had a point.

Eden had been elected to Parliament in 1923 for the seat of Warwick and Leamington, where his rather unlikely Labour opponent was the Countess of Warwick, who was also his sister's mother-in-law!

Eden pursued an interest in foreign affairs from the start of his career. In 1926, he became a parliamentary private secretary to Foreign Secretary Austen Chamberlain, and in 1931 he became a junior minister at the Foreign Office. He furthered his experience in 1933 when he became Minister for the League of Nations. He opposed Foreign Secretary Sir Samuel Hoare's appeasement of Mussolini over the Italian invasion of Abyssinia. When Hoare resigned over the failure of the Hoare–Laval Pact in June 1935, Eden was promoted to replace him.

Eden is often thought of as an ardent opponent of appeasement who resigned over the Munich Agreement. Neither is true. He failed to even protest about Hitler's invasion of the Rhineland and supported Chamberlain's approach to Germany. It was Italy that perturbed Eden. He tried to persuade Mussolini to agree to League of Nations arbitration but failed. Mussolini described Eden as 'the best dressed fool in Europe'. Despite this, Chamberlain was determined to maintain friendly relations with Italy, and it was this that pushed Eden over the edge. He later explained his position: 'We had an agreement with Mussolini about the Mediterranean and Spain, which he was violating by sending troops to Spain, and Chamberlain wanted to have another agreement. I thought Mussolini should honour the first one before we negotiated for the second. I was trying to fight a delaying action for Britain, and I could not go along with Chamberlain's policy.'

IDENTITY CARDS ARE ABOLISHED

In 1951, Winston Churchill's Conservative Party election slogan was 'Set the People Free'. Identity cards were introduced in the United Kingdom in 1939 under the National Registration Act, which received its Royal Assent only two days after the outbreak of war, on 5 September 1939. But why? It was simple. The government predicted there would be a widespread dislocation of the general population because of mobilization and possible evacuations from cities. The cards were successfully and speedily rolled out, and despite demands for their abolition in the aftermath of victory, Clement Attlee's government resisted such calls, arguing that they were needed because of rationing, family allowances and the need to identify people seeking payments from post offices. On the other side of the argument, it was alleged that the police habitually demanded to see identity cards, even for very trivial suspected offences. It was argued that this was fundamentally 'un-British' and the sort of practice more often used by dictators.

It was thirteen years before Winston Churchill's Minister for Health, Harry Crookshank, announced that they were to be abolished, on 21 February 1952. In actual fact, they weren't abolished, but merely transformed into NHS registration cards. In an oral answer in the House of Commons Crookshank said: 'It is no longer necessary to require the public to possess and produce an identity card, or to notify change of address for National Registration purposes, though the numbers will continue to be used in connection with the National Health Service.' The abolition would save half a million pounds and cost 1,500 jobs.

Various attempts have been made over the years by politicians to reintroduce identity cards. Margaret Thatcher came under pressure to do so to combat benefit fraud, but it was the Blair government that passed the Identity Cards Act in 2006, ostensibly as a counter-terrorism measure, to help identify illegal immigrants and counter benefit fraud. It created a national database and in February 2009 the first identity cards were issued. The Coalition government repealed the Act and destroyed the database as one of its first acts on coming to office.

NORTHERN ROCK BANK IS NATIONALIZED

To the outside world, Northern Rock was a rare symbol of private sector economic success in the north-east. It had converted from a building society to a bank in 1997 and had expanded aggressively ever since, largely funded by borrowing. The onset of the global financial crisis changed everything. It soon became apparent that it was being disproportionately affected by its exposure to the US sub-prime mortgage market (where its loans were underwritten by Lehman Brothers); its revenues were falling off a cliff and it couldn't meet its loan repayments. The news soon leaked out and for the first time in 150 years there was a run on a British bank with queues of people patiently waiting to withdraw their savings.

On 14 September 2007, the Bank of England stepped in to give short-term liquidity and provided tens of billions of pounds to prevent Northern Rock descending into insolvency. This was supposed to enable a commercial buyer to be found, but no one was willing to take on a failing bank without onerous guarantees from the taxpayer, and two possible bidders refused to make any commitment to reimburse the taxpayer. Chairman Matt Ridley and Chief Executive Adam Applegarth resigned within two months. By February 2008, the game was well and truly up.

At one minute past midnight on 22 February, Northern Rock was nationalized and shareholders lost all their money. The nil valuation of shares was later the subject of legal action by shareholders.

In March 2009, the National Audit Office slammed the government's decision to allow Northern Rock to continue offering 125 per cent mortgages, even after the taxpayer bailout. It also criticized the Treasury for realizing, in 2004, when Gordon Brown had been Chancellor, that it didn't have a plan to handle a banking emergency, but then proceeding to do nothing about it.

In early 2010, Northern Rock's assets were split from its banking operation, and eighteen months later it was put up for sale. On 1 January 2012, Virgin Money took over and renamed the business but pledged to retain its headquarters in Newcastle.

BIRTH OF SAMUEL PEPYS

Diarists write the first version of history, and so it was with Samuel Pepys, perhaps the greatest diarist of them all. Pepys lived through an important and eventful period in English history. It's easy to imagine that he kept a diary throughout his adult life, but in fact Pepys only kept a diary for ten years, but it covered some huge events in the life of England, including the restoration of the monarchy, the Great Fire of London, the second Anglo-Dutch war and the Great Plague.

The second myth about Pepys is that he was a full-time parliamentary sketchwriter and journalist. In fact he had a well-paid, full-time job as a naval administrator and served for nine years in two separate terms as a Member of Parliament in the 1670s and 1680s. He was decidedly upper middle class and lived in Axe Yard, close to what is now Downing Street, with his wife, Elisabeth. He was never a well man and suffered from bladder stones in his urinary tract. At the age of twenty-four he underwent a risky operation to remove them.

The first notable public event which Pepys witnessed was the public execution of King Charles I in 1649, which he attended at the age of seventeen.

Pepys began writing his diary on 1 January 1660 and over the next ten years would write more than one million words. It wasn't just politics, court, theatre and the military that he wrote about. He detailed his difficult relationship with his wife and his numerous affairs.

Pepys felt forced to give up his diary in 1669 due to his failing eyesight. He considered dictating it, but rejected the idea as all privacy would be lost. He was to live another thirty-four years and it is interesting to speculate how our understanding of the Glorious Revolution, the reign of William and Mary and other historical events might be different had he kept up his daily jottings.

Pepys's diaries were first transcribed in 1818, but were not published in full until 1970–83 due to concerns about some of the more obscene passages.

LABOUR NARROWLY WINS GENERAL ELECTION

If a general election is a referendum on a government's performance, the electorate blew Clement Attlee a bit of a raspberry when they went to the polls on 23 February 1950. As the results trickled in, it was clear that the result was on a knife-edge as voters began to have second thoughts about the nationalizations and performance of the economy since the end of the war in August 1945.

Labour seemed to have run out of steam and ideas. Rationing and conscription were still operating. Britain might have won the war, but austerity ruled and there was an absence of the sense of feel-good needed for any party to storm to victory.

The 1950 election was notable for a number of firsts. It was the first ever to follow a full-term Labour government, and it was the first to be fought following the abolition of plural voting and the university constituencies. It was also the first with a live televised results programme.

The main theme of the election was nationalization and whether further sectors of the economy should be controlled by the state. The Conservatives also proposed the phasing out of rationing, a measure opposed by Labour.

The Conservatives, under Winston Churchill, fought a slick campaign, while Labour leader Clement Attlee embarked on a thousand-mile-long tour of the country, chauffeured by his wife.

Prior to the election, the Labour Party had a majority of 146, but after all the results came in that had been whittled away to a mere five. Labour lost 78 seats, ending up on 315, while the Conservatives gained 90 with a total of 298. The Liberals lost three more seats to finish on six. It really was two-party politics in those days with Labour on 46.1 per cent of the vote and the Conservatives 43.4 per cent. The Liberals lost 319 deposits in the 475 seats they stood in, a record only surpassed in 2015 when they lost 335. Turnout was a record 83.4 per cent, a figure which has not been beaten since.

It was clear another election would follow soon, which it did only nineteen months later in October 1951.

CND IS LAUNCHED

The Campaign for Nuclear Disarmament (CND) is surely one of the most unsuccessful political movements in history. Aiming for the global abolition of nuclear weapons, it has achieved little since its founding in 1958. Launched by a coalition of left-wing thinkers, religious leaders and politicians in London's Westminster Hall, its inception came at the height of the nuclear arms race between the United States and the Soviet Union during the Cold War.

Initially, CND's political activism centred on marches to or from Aldermaston in Berkshire, home of the Atomic Weapons Research Establishment. The first march, Easter 1958, attracted only a few thousand individuals, but in 1961, 150,000 joined the fifty-two-mile walk from Aldermaston to London.

Attracting early high-profile supporters like the future Labour leader Michael Foot, historian A. J. P. Taylor and composer Benjamin Britten, the campaign's opposition to nuclear war inevitably felt more relevant after the 1962 Cuban Missile Crisis.

Monsignor Bruce Kent served as General Secretary between 1980 and 1985, with future Labour minister Joan Ruddock as his chair, during a revival of the nuclear arms race between the Soviet Union and America under President Reagan. A Roman Catholic priest, forced to resign due to his political allegiance, Kent served as the figurehead when hundreds of thousands attended rallies in London, Brussels and Paris. Portrayed as a communist and traitor by the media, Kent was vital in ensuring CND retained its high political profile. Indeed, in the 1983 and 1987 election campaigns, Labour committed itself to unilateral nuclear disarmament. The party was defeated by a landslide on both occasions.

CND's relevance declined in the 1990s after the end of the Cold War and the disintegration of the Soviet Union, although it still boasts a membership of 25,000.

Contemporary arguments for Trident's abolition have largely fallen on deaf ears, with Parliament voting in 2016 by 472 to 117 votes to renew Britain's nuclear deterrent. That nuclear weapons haven't been used in armed conflict since Hiroshima and Nagasaki is arguably thanks to Mutually Assured Destruction rather than CND. While a UN meeting of 122 countries in 2017 voted to abolish all nuclear weapons, action has been rather slow.

BRITAIN DECLARES IT HAS AN ATOMIC BOMB

Most people today believe that America invented nuclear weapons. It didn't. Britain did. In 1940. Eight years earlier, James Chadwick had discovered the neutron at Cambridge University, and British scientists worked out how to build a nuclear bomb. They took it to the government, and the MAUD Committee was created in order to progress the research and to ascertain if a nuclear bomb was feasible.

Fifteen months later, the committee reported its findings. It concluded that not only was a nuclear bomb technically possible, it could be built within two years. However, it was decided that the resources needed might be beyond the means of the UK and to approach the Americans, who by that time were also embarking on research but were behind the UK. In 1943, Roosevelt and Churchill signed an agreement at the Quebec Conference to merge their efforts, but only to use nuclear weapons if both governments agreed.

After the end of the war, in June 1946, President Truman ended the Quebec cooperation agreement, in part because of US fears about the extent of Soviet spying on British nuclear plans. It was a blow, which Foreign Secretary Ernest Bevin understood when he said: 'We've got to have this thing. I don't mind it for myself, but I don't want any other Foreign Secretary of this country to be talked at or to by the Secretary of State of the United States as I just have been. We've got to have this thing over here, whatever it costs... We've got to have the bloody Union Jack flying on top of it.'

Plans proceeded apace, in tandem with the development of nuclear power stations. When Churchill became prime minister in 1951, he knew nothing of the development of nuclear weapons, but on 26 February 1952 he told the House of Commons: 'I was not aware until I took office that not only had the Socialist government made an atomic bomb as a matter of research but they had created at the expense of scores of millions of pounds the important plants necessary for its regular production.' He accused Attlee of keeping the news from the Commons while accusing the Conservatives of being warmongers.

PADDY ASHDOWN IS BORN

In a list of the best prime ministers we never had, a number of names tend to come immediately to mind. Paddy Ashdown is one of them. Had he been an MP with one of the bigger parties, he almost certainly would have ended up as a senior cabinet member, and indeed he was three times offered a cabinet position.

Ashdown was a Liberal to his finger tips, and he would go on to take the third party from a paltry nineteen MPs when he took charge in 1988 to forty-six in 1997. As Ashdown himself said: 'The biggest number of Liberal/Liberal Democrat MPs since the days of Lloyd George'.

During the 1992 general election campaign, details of an affair with his secretary were released, and his openness and transparency became a template for others in how to react to political scandal.

In 1997, despite prolonged talks with Tony Blair about a possible Lab/Lib Dem coalition, Labour's landslide meant that idea proved dead on arrival. In 2009, Gordon Brown floated the possibility of him becoming Northern Ireland Secretary, but he turned it down. And a year later he decided to stay out of the Coalition government and take on the role of sage adviser to Nick Clegg.

Ashdown's political career is only one part of his exciting and diverse life. Born in Northern Ireland, as a younger man he served in the Royal Marines and as a Special Boat Service officer, as well as an intelligence officer with the UK security services.

After retiring from the House of Commons in 2001, he went on to be the High Representative for Bosnia and Herzegovina, a region he'd long had a passionate interest in, and UN Representative for Afghanistan. He was made a life peer in 2001.

Beloved by Lib Dem members, he is remembered fondly not just for leading from the front, towards the sound of gunfire, and making his party a serious political force once again but also for the same joke he told at each 'Glee Club', the annual sing-song held by Liberal members on the final night of their party conference.

Ashdown died on 22 December 2018, aged seventy-seven.

THE 'WHO GOVERNS BRITAIN' ELECTION

The Conservative prime minister Edward Heath called this winter election not because he had to, due to the five-year time limit, or because he did not have a workable majority in the Commons, but because he wanted to refresh his mandate in a national crisis. The country was mired in economic chaos and industrial disputes, and Heath was essentially asking 'Who governs Britain?' The answer provided by the electorate may overall have been inconclusive, but to his chagrin, it was certainly 'not you, mate'.

The crisis is summarized by the phrase 'three-day week', as since 1 January commercial users had been limited to that amount of electricity use, due to industrial action by the miners and transport workers – stimulated by wage caps in the face of inflation.

The campaign could hardly have gone worse for Heath, with a Pay Board report suggesting the miners deserved a rise, the worst trade balance figures ever recorded, and the unexpected call of the highly influential Enoch Powell to vote Labour over the issue of Europe.

The results produced no overall majority – although the Conservatives had a slightly higher vote share, Wilson's Labour won 301 seats to the Tories' 297. Labour did very well in the West Midlands, Powell's region. The indecision continued for four more days as Heath tried to persuade the Liberals under Jeremy Thorpe to join a coalition – they had polled six million votes but took only fourteen seats. However, Liberal demands for electoral reform were too much for Heath, and Wilson formed a minority government on 4 March.

The consequence of the photo-finish in February was that another general election was inevitable, and Wilson went to the country on 10 October – the first time there have been two in a year since 1910, and the most recent to date. That result was not very convincing either – an overall majority for Labour of just three seats. Heath had now lost four elections of five as Tory leader, and within another year he had been ousted in favour of the first female party leader in British history – Margaret Thatcher. That February gamble had conclusively failed.

DISRAELI BECOMES PRIME MINISTER

On 7 December 1837, Benjamin Disraeli made his maiden speech in the House of Commons. He was barracked by Irish MPs and declared: 'Though I will sit down now, there will be a time when you will hear me.' He wasn't wrong. After his split with Peel over the Corn Laws, Disraeli became effectively Leader of the Opposition in the Commons, while Derby led the party in the Lords, leading three separate governments.

Disraeli rose to become Chancellor of the Exchequer and Leader of the House of Commons, while at the same time playing a leading role in reforming the Conservative Party and redefining Conservatism.

After the Liberals won the 1865 general election, Lord Derby predicted that neither of them would ever hold office again. He was wrong. In June 1866, the Prime Minister, Lord John Russell, resigned over splits in the Liberal Party over parliamentary reform. Disraeli couldn't unite the Conservatives in the Commons, so Derby became prime minister for the third time on 28 June 1866.

However, Disraeli came into his own and outflanked the Liberals by persuading the cabinet to introduce a Reform Bill of their own, one which was actually more radical than the one which had floored the Liberal government. Although Lord Cranborne (later to become Lord Salisbury) resigned over the issue, Disraeli sparkled in the Commons and skilfully piloted the legislation through. Liberal MP Bernal Osborne was impressed: 'I have always thought the Chancellor of Exchequer was the greatest Radical in the House. He has achieved what no other man in the country could have done. He has lugged up that great omnibus full of stupid, heavy, country gentlemen ... and has converted these Conservatives into Radical Reformers.'

Derby's health, which had never been robust, deteriorated, and in late February 1868, an attack of gout led his doctors to advise him that he would never fully recover. He asked Disraeli if he was ready to become prime minister and advised Queen Victoria to send for him. 'I have climbed to the top of the greasy pole,' Disraeli said. But his premiership lasted less than nine months, despite some notable reforming legislative successes.

MARCH

IRA PRISONERS BEGIN HUNGER STRIKE

In 1976, there were more than 100 IRA prisoners in the Maze prison in Belfast. They were kept separate from other prisoners and were assigned a special category, which meant that they didn't wear prison clothes or do prison work. They were treated like political prisoners, or prisoners of war, rather than criminals.

This changed on 1 March 1976 when the Labour Home Secretary, Merlyn Rees, withdrew the special status of paramilitary prisoners on both sides of the divide. IRA and INLA (Irish National Liberation Army) prisoners immediately started protests, which escalated into full hunger strikes. Initially, they refused to wear prison clothes and in 1978 they started so-called 'dirty protests' in which they smeared their own excrement over cell walls. They had five demands: the right not to wear prison clothes; the right not to do prison work; the right of free association with other prisoners, and to organize educational and recreational pursuits; the right to one visit, one letter and one parcel per week; and full restoration of remission lost through the protest. All these demands were refused.

In 1980, 148 prisoners volunteered to go on hunger strike but seven were selected. In the end the British government issued a document which appeared to agree to the demands and the strike ended after fifty-three days.

In March 1981, things escalated after the British government withdrew the concessions. This time prisoners joined the strike one by one, with Bobby Sands being the first. At the same time, he contested the Fermanagh and South Tyrone by-election on 9 April and won with a small majority. Margaret Thatcher was unmoved and refused to budge: 'We are not prepared to consider special category status for certain groups of people serving sentences for crime. Crime is crime is crime, it is not political.' After sixty-six days on hunger strike, Sands died on 5 May, followed by three more prisoners over the next fortnight.

By the time the strike was called off on 3 October, ten prisoners had died. The British government made some concessions but refused to change the status of the prisoners.

THE DUKE OF PORTLAND BECOMES PRIME MINISTER

William Cavendish-Bentinck was prime minister for a mere eight and a half months in 1783. Twenty-four years later, he became prime minister for a second time, on 2 March 1807. The Duke of Portland hasn't really imprinted himself in our prime ministerial history apart from the fact that the twenty-four years between his two terms is the longest gap between terms of office of any British prime minister.

Initially, Portland was a Whig, and he served in the Marquess of Rockingham's first administration in 1765–66. In Rockingham's second ministry (March–July 1782), he was Lord Lieutenant of Ireland, a role in which he was seen as a conciliator. He resigned when Rockingham died, refusing to serve under the new Prime Minister, the Earl of Shelburne.

Portland was an implacable opponent of the French Revolution and defected from the Whigs to the Pittites over it, having previously been a strong supporter of Charles James Fox. In 1794, William Pitt the Younger rewarded him by bringing him into his government as Home Secretary. He later became Lord President of the Council and Minister without Portfolio.

When Pitt died in 1806, Portland refused to serve in Grenville's 'ministry of all the talents', but when that government fell, it was down to Portland to form a government, given he was the only figure that was capable of doing so. All the other leading contenders – Canning, Hawkesbury, Castlereagh and Perceval – were unlikely to serve under each other.

Portland's second government lasted for two and a half years, during which time the Peninsular War started, as did those between the Foreign Secretary, George Canning, and the Secretary for War and the Colonies, Viscount Castlereagh. Eventually, Canning tried to persuade Portland to sack his rival. When Castlereagh discovered Canning's plotting, he challenged him to a duel, which both men survived, although Canning was wounded in the thigh.

The resulting mockery and criticism of the duel led them both to resign. With Portland in failing health, his resignation was also not long in coming. Only a month after leaving office in October 1809, Portland was dead.

SDP AND LIBERAL PARTY MERGE

This day saw the birth of what would eventually become the Liberal Democrats, though the newly merged party would go through a number of different names before arriving at the one we know well.

From the 'Social and Liberal Democrats' (SDP) or 'Salads', to simply 'The Democrats' (a choice favoured by the party's first solo leader, Paddy Ashdown) to the Liberal Democrats.

Ashdown is often thought of as the Lib Dems' first leader, but actually the party was the first in Britain to have co-leaders, as the leaders of its predecessor parties, David Steel for the Liberals and Bob Maclennan of the SDP, were the original heads of the newly united 'third force'.

The birth of this new arrival was not an easy one, as there were opponents of a merger in both parties, but the pragmatists realized that, under the first-past-the-post electoral system, having two parties competing for the centre ground was doomed to failure and, try as they might, the voting public had never really bought into the idea of the SDP–Liberal Alliance which had been in train since pretty much the birth of the SDP in 1981.

The support of big hitters in the SDP, including former Labour Chancellor and Home Secretary Roy Jenkins, former Education Secretary Shirley Williams and future Lib Dem leader Charles Kennedy, helped to carry the vote when the proposed merger was passionately debated at the SDP's special conference called to make a decision on it.

Former Foreign Secretary David Owen, who opposed the merger, led the continuing SDP rump until its embarrassing showing in the 1990 Bootle by-election when it finished behind the Monster Raving Loony Party.

The Liberal Democrats' electoral high point would come under Charles Kennedy in 2005, when they won sixty-two seats at the general election that saw Tony Blair's Labour Party elected to a third term in government.

But it wasn't until 2010, under Nick Clegg, when, despite dropping five seats, the Lib Dems entered UK-wide government for the first time as junior partners in a Coalition with David Cameron's Conservatives.

The SDP continues to exist today, but it has drifted far from its founding principles.

THE KRAY TWINS FOUND GUILTY OF MURDER

Ronnie and Reginald Kray, commonly known as the Kray Twins, were two of the most notorious perpetrators of organized crime in east London in the 1950s and 1960s. Few British criminals are as well known as these identical twin brothers, and on this day in 1969, Ronnie was found guilty of the murder of George Cornell, and Reggie of the killing of Jack McVitie.

The jury took six hours and fifty-five minutes before returning their unanimous verdict. McVitie had been a minor member of the Kray gang, also commonly known as the Firm, who failed to fulfil a contract worth £1,000 to kill the gang's financial adviser.

At the time, the trial was the longest and most expensive ever held at the Old Bailey, lasting a total of thirty-nine days. Mr Justice Melford Stevenson, the presiding judge, recommended a life sentence for both men; these were also the longest ever sentences passed down at the court at the time. The other members of the Firm, who helped dispose of the body, also received prison sentences for being accessories to murder.

The Kray Twins earned their notoriety at the same time as mixing with prominent society and political figures of the day. As the owners of infamous nightclubs in London's East End and elsewhere during the swinging sixties, they often socialized with the likes of politicians, and entertainers such as Frank Sinatra and Judy Garland. The brothers were even photographed by legendary photographer David Bailey, and were interviewed on television. They 'befriended' the Conservative MP Bob Boothby, who had a long-standing affair with Lady Dorothy Macmillan, despite being a homosexual, and was rumoured to have been a sex partner of one, if not both, the Krays. They also had links to the promiscuous homosexual Labour MP Tom Driberg.

Following their convictions, the twins spent time in various prisons in the UK. Ronnie was committed to Broadmoor Hospital in 1979 after being diagnosed with paranoid schizophrenia – he died at Wexham Park Hospital in Slough in 1995, aged sixty-one. Reggie was freed from Wayland prison in August 2000 on compassionate grounds following a diagnosis of cancer – he died a few months later in October 2000.

CHURCHILL'S IRON CURTAIN SPEECH

It could be argued that within a year of the end of the Second World War in 1945, another global conflict was under way. It is not possible to identify exactly when the Cold War started. There is a case to be made for the declaration in 1947 of the Truman Doctrine of armed resistance against the threat of communist expansion in Europe, or the mutually suspicious Kennan (USA) and Novikov (USSR) Telegrams of 1946. But a strong early contender is Churchill's renowned and influential speech at Fulton, Missouri.

The alliance was always uneasy between Stalin's Soviet Union and the resolute heart of capitalism, the United States. They had only been brought together by a common enemy, Nazi Germany, through Hitler's double acts of aggression in 1941 – invading Russia in June, then declaring war on the USA after his ally Japan's attack on Pearl Harbor in December. Once Germany and Japan had both been defeated, the scene was set for a struggle for world domination between the two ideologically opposite superpowers that had emerged from World War II.

By March 1946, it was clear that Stalin had no intention of withdrawing from the Eastern European countries 'liberated' by the Red Army. Germany itself had been divided into zones of occupation. Communist control was being established east of a line identified by Churchill as an 'Iron Curtain' stretching 'from Stettin in the Baltic to Trieste in the Adriatic'. Further expansion, for example in Greece and even in Italy, was threatened. In the speech, Churchill called communism 'a growing challenge and peril to Christian civilisation'.

The half-American former British prime minister was claiming to speak at Fulton for peace and against tyranny, to call for the USA to rally to defend what they liked to call the 'Free World'. His words were not unheard. Unlike after 1918, the Americans did not retreat into isolation. Within three years Truman had promulgated his Doctrine and joined with Britain in the airlift that broke Stalin's blockade of West Berlin in 1949, when the military alliance NATO was formed. The Cold War was in full swing. It was to last for another forty years.

MINERS' STRIKE BEGINS

The 1984–85 miners' strike was without doubt a major turning point in modern British political history. Lasting nearly a whole year, finally ending on 3 March 1985, the strike was the result of the Thatcher government's plans to close a number of pits, something which would inevitably result in the loss of thousands of mining jobs.

The National Union of Mineworkers (NUM) was led by the divisive Arthur Scargill, whose avowed communist loyalties made him a darling of the left and a devil to the right. The 165,000 miners sought to cause a severe energy shortage and with it break the government's will. However, the government had built up coal stocks over the previous two years in the firm belief that at some stage Scargill would call a strike.

Much of the media coverage suggested that the strike just involved a catalogue of violence between miners and the police, but for those communities involved it was far more. It was a year marked by poverty, hardship and division. Though sustained through a tidal wave of support across the left, the failure of the NUM to hold a national ballot saw the strike deemed illegal by the courts, undermining its legitimacy, weakening the nation's sympathies and limiting any legal support from other unions.

At a broader level, the fight was far greater: a final pushback against Margaret Thatcher's desire to smash trade union power, which had played a major role in the collapse of Ted Heath's government in 1974. The ultimate defeat significantly weakened the trade union movement and marked the beginning of a great decline in working-class solidarity.

Had Scargill's miners not failed and the pits not closed, however, it's hard to imagine what modern Britain would look like today. In 2021, there were days when coal contributed nothing to our energy usage.

For Margaret Thatcher, the victory over the NUM was the domestic equivalent of victory in the Falklands. The Iron Lady was at the height of her powers, and she was emboldened to introduce many more industrial and trade union reforms.

IRAN BREAKS OFF DIPLOMATIC RELATIONS WITH BRITAIN

It's fair to say that Britain's relations with Iran have always been a bit rocky. Iran has rarely trusted the motives of the British government, and that remains so to this day with the recent row over the alleged £400 million debt Britain owed to Iran and the case of Nazinin Zaghari-Ratcliffe.

In 1979, Britain had broken off diplomatic relations with Iran following the overthrow of the Shah and the advent of the Islamic revolution. On 30 April, six Iranian men took over the Iranian Embassy and held hostages there for six days. Eventually, an SAS rescue team took back the building and freed the hostages, the whole thing being shown live on TV.

In September 1988, British-Indian writer Salman Rushdie published his novel *The Satanic Verses*, which contained so called 'inappropriate' depictions of the Prophet Mohammed. Thirteen predominantly Islamic countries, including Iran, promptly banned the book. Rushdie defended his work by writing that the Prophet was 'one of the great geniuses of world history'. He said it was not 'an anti-religious novel. It is, however, an attempt to write about migration, its stresses and transformations.' It cut little ice.

On 14 February, the Iranian Supreme Leader, Ayatollah Khomeini, issued a fatwa against Rushdie and offered a reward for his killing. Reacting to the news, Rushdie told the BBC: 'Frankly, I wish I had written a more critical book. I'm very sad that it should have happened. It's not true that this book is a blasphemy against Islam. I doubt very much that Khomeini or anyone else in Iran has read the book or more than selected extracts out of context.'

Margaret Thatcher gave Rushdie full police protection, which only ended when he moved to America in 2000.

On 7 March, Iran broke off diplomatic relations with the UK, days after it had demanded Britain denounce Salman Rushdie. 'By defending Salman Rushdie and his blasphemous book,' Tehran Radio quoted Prime Minister Mousavi as saying, 'Britain once again displayed its animosity toward Islam.'

Diplomatic relations weren't restored until 1998, when Iran gave an undertaking that it would 'neither support nor hinder assassination operations on Rushdie'.

HOUSE OF LORDS PASSES THE STAMP ACT

There were many things that led to the American Revolution and War of Independence, but the passing of the Stamp Act in 1765 was certainly a major factor. It may have been repealed only a year later, but its long-term effect of putting rocket fuel under the burgeoning anti-British sentiment in the American colonies cannot be underestimated. So why was it introduced?

The British victory in the Seven Years' War had come at a huge financial cost. The national debt had doubled to £130 million by 1764. The decision of the Prime Minister, the Earl of Bute, in 1763 to keep more than ten thousand British soldiers in America meant it would be difficult to reduce the debt in the short term. Bute was succeeded as prime minister by George Grenville, who was faced with a mounting financial crisis. He decided that the only way out of it was to impose taxes on the American colonies without them having any say in the matter. Bad move. The government tried to sell it as the Americans paying for their own defence against the French, but given the fact that the colonial legislatures saw no need for further defensive measures, these new taxes couldn't have been worse received.

Colonial legislators then tried a different tack in opposition to the taxes. They asserted that there was a constitutional issue involved. Precedent dictated that British subjects could not be taxed without their consent, or representation, which came in the form of elected Members of Parliament. However, the thirteen American colonies had no such representation. Their interests were assumed to be so different that they would not be able to unite in their opposition. However, this was grossly underestimated, with countless petitions being launched and seditious pamphlets published.

The Stamp Act, or Duties in American Colonies Act, passed by 205 votes to 49 in the Commons, and in the Lords it was passed unanimously on 8 March 1765. Royal Assent came on 22 March. Opposition to it didn't diminish, and only 361 days later the Act was repealed by the Marquess of Rockingham's new government, more as a matter of political expediency than anything else.

CHANCELLOR OF THE EXCHEQUER JOHN AISLABIE SENT TO TOWER

John Aislabie, Chancellor of the Exchequer between 1718 and 1721, was sent to the Tower of London in March 1721 after being found guilty of the 'most notorious, dangerous and infamous corruption' as described by an investigation launched by the Commons.

Aislabie was elected to Parliament in the late seventeenth century. He was a close ally of Charles Spencer, 3rd Earl of Sunderland, and after Spencer became the First Lord of the Treasury, effectively the prime minister, he made Aislabie the Chancellor of the Exchequer.

During his tenure, the government was dealing with the South Sea Company, which was founded in 1711 with the hope of trading predominately in slaves with Spanish America following the end of the War of the Spanish Succession. King George I of Great Britain became governor of the company in 1718, giving the company a massive boost of confidence.

The company proposed to take over the national debt, which was subsequently accepted by Parliament. Aislabie was a supporter of the proposal and negotiated the agreement between the government and the South Sea Company. Months later the market collapsed and it became apparent that due to mismanagement and overpromising, the company was simply unable to deliver what was negotiated.

In the aftermath, Aislabie failed to get a grip on the crisis in front of him and resigned in January 1721. A month later, the Commons launched an investigation into the scandal and Aislabie was accused of receiving £20,000 in company stock and negotiating in favour of the company. He was then expelled from the Commons and imprisoned in the Tower of London. Charles Spencer, 3rd Earl of Sunderland, resigned, in April 1721. As a result of the scandal, Robert Walpole became the first de facto Prime Minister of Great Britain.

After he was released, Aislabie retired to Yorkshire and spent his time creating the Studley Royal water garden. He died in June 1742. He was survived by his son, William Aislabie, who was elected to Parliament after his father's expulsion and remained a Member of Parliament for sixty years.

OSWALD MOSLEY FOUNDS THE NEW PARTY

Oswald Mosley seemed destined to reach the top of the political greasy pole. Yet his career ended in failure and disgrace.

Born in 1896 he had 'a good war' and was elected to Parliament as a Conservative MP at the age of twenty-one in the December 1918 election. Great things were expected of him and he expected great things of himself. He was a brilliant orator and spoke without notes. However, Mosley quickly fell out with his party over Ireland and he crossed the floor and sat as an Independent. In 1924, Labour formed its first government and in March Mosley joined the Independent Labour Party and switched seats to fight Neville Chamberlain. He failed to win by only seventy-seven votes. Out of Parliament he drafted a new economic plan for Labour, which was to form the basis of his views going into the 1930s.

Elected in Smethwick in 1929, he was made Chancellor of the Duchy of Lancaster, outside Ramsay MacDonald's cabinet. He was given responsibility for solving the unemployment problem but became frustrated that all his proposals were rejected. He wanted high tariffs, a major scheme of public works and the nationalization of major industry. He published a memorandum which outlined his radical policies but within the Labour Party it fell on deaf ears. When it was rejected by the Labour Party conference, he resigned from both the government and Labour, having once been seen as a future leader.

In early March 1931, Mosley announced the formation of the New Party and six other Labour MPs joined him. As with all new parties, the aim was to break the mould of British politics. However, two of the MPs resigned the next day and another after three months. The party fielded twenty-five candidates at the 1931 election but none were successful.

Mosley's dictatorial manner led many members to quit the New Party, and his increasing fascination with European fascism only made things worse. The next year he rolled the New Party into his newly created British Union of Fascists.

CHRIS HUHNE AND VICKY PRYCE JAILED

They were the golden couple of Lib Dem politics – he was Secretary of State for Energy and Climate Change in the Coalition government. She was an award-winning economist and regular pundit in the media. And then it all fell apart. Huhne had started an affair with Carina Trimingham, a Liberal Democrat activist and his PR adviser, and left his wife. Pryce decided to exact her revenge and in 2011 approached *Sunday Times* journalist Isabel Oakeshott, alleging that she had taken the speeding points for an offence on the M11, committed in March 2003. Had she not done that, Huhne, already having clocked up nine points, would have faced a driving ban. At the time he was an MEP.

When the *Sunday Times* printed the story, the police took it up and demanded the newspaper hand over tape recordings of Pryce and Huhne discussing the case. Initially, the paper refused, but in the end it was forced to comply. On 3 February 2012, both Pryce and Huhne were charged with perverting the course of justice.

Once charges were laid, Huhne had little alternative but to resign from the cabinet. At the committal hearing no pleas were entered and both were granted bail. Huhne pocketed a £17,000 ministerial severance payment. Later in the year, Pryce entered a 'guilty' plea and cited marital coercion as mitigation. On 28 January 2012, Huhne entered a 'not guilty' plea, but when the trial commenced a week later Huhne changed his plea to 'guilty'. At the sentencing on 11 March, both parties were handed eight-month jail sentences. They were released two months later, having served only two months of their terms. Pryce went on to write a book, partly about her prison experience, called *Prisonomics: Behind Bars in Britain's Failing Prisons*. Huhne's political career had ended and he resumed a business career as an environmental specialist.

It's interesting to think that in the Lib Dem leadership election in December 2007, 1,200 ballot papers were held up in the Christmas post and didn't make the deadline. Had they done so, Huhne would have become Lib Dem leader, not Nick Clegg.

SPEED LIMITS INTRODUCED FOR THE FIRST TIME

There are few Transport ministers who live long in the memory, but Leslie Hore-Belisha is one of them. He served in the post from 1934 to 1937 and introduced a new version of the Highway Code and what came to be known as Belisha beacons on zebra crossings.

Speed limits had long been a matter of controversy. First introduced in a series of Locomotive Acts in the 1860s and 1870s, the 1865 Act reduced a 10 mph speed limit for passenger vehicles to 4 mph in rural areas and 2 mph in towns. A man was also required to walk 60 yards in front with a red flag. The 1878 Act removed the need for the flag, but not the man. In 1896, the speed limit was raised to 14 mph and abolished the man. In 1903, the limit was raised to 20 mph. However, in 1931 all speed limits were abolished, both for cars and motorbikes. A reason cited was that so many people disobeyed the existing limits that their maintenance brought the law into contempt. Rather counter-intuitively, the number of road fatalities dropped each year, from 7,305 in 1930 to 6,502 in 1935.

Leslie Hore-Belisha's first act as Minister of Transport was to introduce the Road Traffic Bill. It sought to introduce a speed limit of 30 mph in urban areas with street lighting. Car ownership doubled from 1 million to 2 million between 1930 and 1940, and the number of fatalities increased from 6,502 in 1935 to 8,609 in 1940. In 2020, the number was 1,516. Speedometers were made mandatory for new cars in 1937 and a new driving test was introduced. New limits for buses, coaches and lorries were introduced too. The new legislation was bitterly opposed by those who saw the proposed speed limits as the removal of 'an Englishman's freedom of the highway'.

Night-time speed limits of 20 mph were introduced in World War II in order to counter the dangers posed by the blackout. In 1941, there were 9,146 road deaths, the highest ever.

The 1956 Road Traffic Act made the 30 mph limit permanent and in 1965 a 70 mph speed limit was introduced on motorways.

MASS SHOOTING IN DUNBLANE

Nestled in the heart of central Scotland's countryside is the small town of Dunblane. Not known as a place that would traditionally be at the centre of a media and political spotlight, the quaint Scottish town made history for one shocking event that led to a significant change in UK gun laws.

On 13 March 1996, shortly after 9 a.m., local man Thomas Hamilton entered Dunblane Primary School. He walked through the building armed with four legally obtained handguns and 743 cartridges of ammunition. While a Primary 1 class was preparing for a PE lesson in the gymnasium, Hamilton entered and shot dead sixteen pupils and one teacher. He then walked through the school, firing randomly into classrooms, before going back to the gymnasium and shooting and killing himself. To this day, it is the deadliest mass shooting in British history.

It remains unclear why Hamilton committed this atrocity – but letters he posted from 1992 onwards suggested that he became obsessed with the belief that he was being persecuted by authorities and the Scout Association, where he previously worked. It was also clear from the letters that he became hostile towards Central Regional Council's educational unit, including its teachers.

The tragedy led to wide public debate about the killings, which challenged UK gun control laws of the time. Public petitions calling for an outright ban of private ownership of handguns were launched, as well as the publication of the 1996 Cullen report after an official inquiry took place.

The Cullen report suggested that the UK should introduce tighter controls on the ownership of handguns. In response to this and the wider public debate, Sir John Major's Conservative government introduced the Firearms (Amendment) Act 1997, which banned the majority of high-calibre handguns in the UK. After Tony Blair won the 1997 election for Labour, he went further and banned all handguns from private use.

To this day, the UK has some of the strictest gun laws in the world. Since the Dunblane massacre and the introduction of the initial Firearms Act, there have only been two mass shootings in the UK (Cumbria in 2010 and Plymouth in 2021).

WILLIAM PITT RESIGNS AFTER EIGHTEEN YEARS IN POWER

There can be little doubt that William Pitt the Younger is one of our greatest prime ministers. Only twenty-four when he became prime minister in 1783, he restored Britain's reputation after the ignominy of losing the American colonies. He was a brilliant administrator and did for the Tory Party what Disraeli repeated a century later – he created a narrative which Tories could follow for the next few decades. But all premierships have to end at some point. He wasn't the first to encounter problems with Ireland, and he certainly wouldn't be the last.

The 1789 revolution in France sent shockwaves throughout the continent of Europe. It also encouraged republicans in Ireland. Pitt was alive to the rising wave of republicanism and knew that reforms would have to be introduced if these voices were to be quelled. Protestant resistance scuppered his plans to soften anti-Catholic laws.

The economic situation in Ireland was rapidly deteriorating too, which led to a breakdown in law and order and outbreaks of violence between rival Protestant and Catholic groups.

In 1797, Pitt sent General Lake to crush Protestant militias and to organize a network of spies and informers, but the situation worsened and in 1798 there was a violent rebellion, which sought to win complete independence. British forces executed 1,500 of the so-called United Irishmen. Pitt had no faith in the ability of the Dublin Parliament to govern and sought an Act of Union with Ireland with the aim of settling the Irish Question. Irish MPs were effectively bribed to support the union.

Following the Act of Union Pitt sought to placate Irish feelings with a series of conciliatory measures towards the Catholic population. However, there was one big problem. King George III was opposed to all of them, as he maintained that they would be in direct conflict with his oath of coronation, in which he vowed to protect the Church of England. Pitt lost the battle and was forced to resign, with Henry Addington taking his place.

Pitt returned to the premiership in May 1804 but it was an unhappy period, and he died in office in January 1806.

GEORGE BROWN RESIGNS

Every political generation has its larger than life characters. One of the most colourful politicians of the 1960s was George Brown. He's not much remembered now but in his day he was everywhere.

A trade union organizer, Brown was elected Labour MP for Belper in the landslide of 1945 and became a junior minister in 1951. In opposition he became a prominent figure on the right of the party and opposed the Bevanites, adherents of Aneurin Bevan. In 1955, he was elected to the shadow cabinet for the first time. He first really rose to prominence the following year when, during the visit of Soviet leaders Nikita Khruschev and Nikolai Bulganin to Britain, he engaged in a very loud contretemps with them. Later in the year he contested the Treasurership of the Labour Party but narrowly lost to Aneurin Bevan.

In 1960, following Bevan's death, Brown won the deputy leadership and three years later, when his political ally Hugh Gaitskell died, he fought Harold Wilson for the party leadership. His campaign was seen as a little amateur against the wily Wilson, and Brown's abrasive, and often rude personal conduct counted against him. His excessive drinking was widely known, and all these things added together enabled Harold Wilson to gain the support of 144 MPs to Brown's 103.

Brown vanished for a week and returned to demand the Foreign Secretaryship. Wilson instead gave him the newly created Department of Economic Affairs. He tried to resign in July 1966 after the cabinet voted against devaluing the pound but was outmanouevred by Wilson. He was then reshuffled to the Foreign Office, but his alcoholism was now affecting his work. He publicly insulted the wife of the British Ambassador to France. He also launched a bitter attack on the owner of the *Daily Mirror*, Cecil King.

His resignation came in March 1968 when the pound came under renewed pressure. He appeared at a late-night meeting with Wilson and was clearly very drunk. He stormed out and quit. Brown's main legacy may be *Private Eye*'s oft repeated description of him as 'tired and emotional'. He lost his seat in 1970.

PRIME MINISTER HAROLD WILSON RESIGNS

It was one of the best-kept secrets in politics. This and Boris Johnson's third wedding. Harold Wilson had been Leader of the Labour Party since 1963. He'd won four general elections out of five, and by the middle of March 1976 he'd served for thirteen years as party Leader and nearly eight years as prime minister. He was still only sixty. But he was tired out.

When Wilson announced to his cabinet that he was resigning, he said he'd taken the decision on timing two years earlier. Since winning the second election of 1974 in October by a majority of only three seats, his government had lurched from crisis to economic crisis. He had confided in colleagues that he no longer felt as enthusiastic for the job as he had been. He had also started drinking too much. In addition, his doctor had detected problems which were eventually diagnosed as colon cancer. The big question which no one has a definitive answer to was whether the resignation was in part down to Wilson himself realizing that his mental faculties weren't quite what they were. Whether he was conscious of the early-onset dementia which was about to afflict him, no one really knows.

And then there is the allegation that just won't go away – that the Wilson government was being destabilized by the security services, at the behest of the CIA, who thought that Wilson was a Soviet agent. There is no evidence to support this, but there is evidence, as portrayed in a 2006 ITV documentary, that a military coup was being planned by various Establishment and military figures. A 1987 inquiry held by Margaret Thatcher's government had found that the allegations were false, but they've never entirely been disproved.

Wilson's reputation has undeservedly diminished with time. He lived a rather sad retirement as Alzheimer's gradually took him prisoner. He died at the age of seventy-nine in 1995.

Wilson mainly failed in his quest to reform and modernize the British economy, but his enduring legacy will be the many social reforms enacted by his 1964–70 government.

ROBIN COOK RESIGNS

Robin Cook resigned as Leader of the House of Commons in Tony Blair's government on 17 March 2003 in opposition to the Iraq War, becoming a leading figure calling for a reassessment of the conflict. In his letter of resignation he highlighted that 'at cabinet for some weeks I have been frank about my concern over embarking on military action.'

Although his resignation was expected to trigger a bigger revolt against Blair's stance on Iraq, the government comfortably won the vote on using 'all means necessary to ensure the disarmament of Iraq's weapons of mass destruction'. Prominent figures who voted against included the future Labour Leader Jeremy Corbyn and his future shadow cabinet members Diane Abbott and John McDonnell, who currently still serve as MPs; and former Conservative Chancellor Kenneth Clarke.

Clare Short, who was the International Development Secretary, also threatened to quit the government in the lead-up to the vote but in the end remained in post for another two months before leaving her cabinet role.

Ahead of the vote and on the eve of the subsequent invasion, Cook made a statement in Parliament in which he said he couldn't 'support a war without international agreement or domestic support', and added that 'none of us can predict the death toll of civilians from the forthcoming bombardment of Iraq.' As he sat down, many MPs rose to applaud him.

Following the publication, in 2016, of the report of the Chilcot Inquiry, which assessed the UK's involvement in the Iraq War and found that – among other conclusions – peaceful options were still available, some referred back to Cook's concerns raised in Parliament at the time following his resignation.

Cook had served continuously in shadow cabinet and government from 1987, including as shadow Health Secretary under Neil Kinnock and as Foreign Secretary under Blair from 1997 to 2001.

Cook was first elected as Member of Parliament for Edinburgh Central in 1974. Following revision of the constituency boundaries, he stood and was elected as MP for Livingston in 1983, which he remained until his death on 6 August 2005 at the age of 59.

TOLPUDDLE MARTYRS SENTENCED TO BE TRANSPORTED TO AUSTRALIA

We remember the 1830s for two things – the Great Reform Act of 1832 and the ascension of Queen Victoria to the throne in 1837. But dissent was rife in this period, nowhere represented better than by the Tolpuddle Martyrs. Their name has entered British folklore, but few know their provenance of importance.

The 1825 Combinations of Workmen Act had made it legal for workers to organize in trade unions, but their activities were severely restricted.

Agricultural wages in the early 1800s were poor and falling. In Dorset in particular there was great acrimony over the issue and farm labourers had taken part in the Swing Riots which erupted across southern England in the autumn of 1830. In order to quell the riots, Dorset farmers agreed to increase wages temporarily. At the same time, there was a crackdown, with many farm workers being arrested and imprisoned. The wage rises were then reversed and in 1833 many workers were earning as little as six shillings per week. Nearly a fifth of them were in receipt of 'poor relief'.

In 1833, six farm workers from the Dorset village of Tolpuddle formed the Friendly Society of Agricultural Labourers to fight against reduced wages. Each member would be blindfolded and would swear an oath as the initiation process.

A year later, a local landowner and magistrate, James Frampton, complained to the Home Secretary, Lord Melbourne, complaining about the activities of the Friendly Society. Melbourne recommended legal action under the Unlawful Oaths Act of 1797. Six members were arrested, charged with swearing an illegal oath. All six were sentenced to transportation to Australia, where they landed in August and September 1834.

They became a cause célèbre in England with more than 800,000 signing a petition protesting at their treatment and calling for their release. A protest march was organized and in March 1836 the new Home Secretary, Lord John Russell, ordered the men's release and return to the mother country on condition of good conduct. Five of them settled in Ongar, Essex, before emigrating to Ontario. The sixth returned to Dorchester, where he died in the workhouse in 1891.

HOUSE OF COMMONS ABOLISHES THE HOUSE OF LORDS

One little-known factor of Oliver Cromwell's Protectorate was that the House of Lords was abolished in 1649, only to be recreated when the monarchy was restored eleven years later.

It was only during the reign of King Edward III (1327–77) that Parliament split into two chambers. Prior to this all power and influence had lain with the aristocracy and church. The new House of Commons consisted of borough and shire representatives while the House of Lords counted archbishops, bishops, abbots and peers as its members. As the centuries passed, both Houses of Parliament became gradually more influential and powerful. The Lords continued to reign supreme over the Commons. It wasn't until the nineteenth century, or even early twentieth, that the power was really to shift.

The civil wars of the late fifteenth century heralded a rise in the power of the Crown, given that a substantial number of noblemen were killed or executed and the Crown took over many of the bigger estates. Under King Henry VII the supremacy of the monarchy was augmented and grew during the rest of the Tudor era.

It wasn't until the reign of King Charles I (1625–49) that real conflict broke out between Parliament and the Monarchy and it led to a full Civil War. It ended with King Charles losing his head and Oliver Cromwell becoming Lord Protector.

Under the Protectorate, the House of Lords became more or less powerless, so Cromwell decided it had outlived its usefulness and he passed a law abolishing it. It stated: 'The Commons of England [find] by too long experience that the House of Lords is useless and dangerous to the people of England.' It wasn't until 1660, when the monarchy was restored, that the House of Lords was recalled. Because in 1649 the consent of both the king and the Lords hadn't been obtained, the abolition was not recognized as a proper law after the restoration of the monarchy. The House of Lords just resumed its traditional role in the governance of the country. It was as if the previous eleven years hadn't happened.

UK JOINS US-LED INVASION OF IRAQ

Tony Blair was a transformative prime minister in many ways, including seeking parliamentary approval for British military action. Previously a power of the monarchy, the prime minister had the prerogative power to commit troops to war abroad without requiring a mandate from Parliament. However, the scale and importance of the invasion led Blair to use Parliament to increase his authority and guarantee the war's legitimacy. Indeed, Blair implied his resignation would be inevitable were his motion for war to fail.

Both Labour and the Conservatives were committed to the invasion, though a quarter of MPs were opposed including all the Liberal Democrats. An amendment arguing the case for war 'had not... been established' was defeated by 396 votes to 217, while the government motion approving the invasion was carried by 412 votes to 149.

Blair had been committed to standing by President Bush and his American allies ever since the events of 9/11. In Parliament, where Labour were often seen as having a tendency to appear anti-American, he knew how important standing with the leader of the free world was. In a memo to Bush, Blair claimed he would be with him 'whatever'. Having invaded Afghanistan under Article 5 of NATO, Bush's administration had claimed Iraq was developing weapons of mass destruction, with Saddam Hussein's refusal to cooperate with UN weapons inspectors only reinforcing the assertion.

The British deployment, codenamed Operation Telic, used air and missile strikes in a 'shock and awe' operation that would neutralize Saddam's weapons infrastructure. Though Bush initially claimed 'mission accomplished' within weeks of the invasion, both America and Britain remained in Iraq until 2009 due to sectarian violence. For Tony Blair, it was the turning point that led his 'Bambi' shine to start to vanish.

The Chilcot Inquiry, which examined the UK government's handling of the Iraq War and published its findings in 2016, repeatedly argued that flawed intelligence, insufficient planning and no imminent threat made the war unjustifiable. Indeed, like the amendment from 2003, it stated the case for war had not been made.

A total of 179 British troops were killed, alongside 4,500 American personnel and 100,000 Iraqis.

DUKE OF WELLINGTON FIGHTS DUEL WITH THE EARL OF WINCHILSEA

Some men experience a lifetime of greatness and renown. Others have their fifteen minutes of fame. And so it was for the Duke of Wellington and the Earl of Winchilsea. The Duke was probably the greatest war strategist and leader this country has ever had. The Earl of Winchilsea, well, not so much. He was an easily riled man, not an ideal quality for the man appointed to be Deputy Lieutenant for Kent. In that capacity he came to preside over a meeting at Penenden Heath in Kent on 10 October 1829, when strongly worded resolutions in favour of Protestant principles were passed. He echoed these in the House of Lords a few months later when he spoke out vehemently against Catholic emancipation, a cause dear to the heart of the new Prime Minister, the Duke of Wellington.

Winchilsea was one of the very few English aristocrats to ally himself to the cause of the Orange Party in Ireland, and in very strong terms too. When the Catholic Relief Bill was put before Parliament in early 1829, Winchilsea was at his most vehement. He denounced every word of it, writing to the Secretary of King's College, London, that the Duke of Wellington 'under the cloak of some coloured show of zeal for the Protestant religion, carried on an insidious design for the infringement of our liberties and the introduction of popery into every department of the state'.

The Duke responded by challenging the Earl to a duel. Given the ridicule suffered by Canning and Castlereagh twenty years earlier, when they fought a duel, it was a surprising response to say the least.

The confrontation took place in Battersea Fields on 21 March 1829. The Earl's seconder was Viscount Falmouth, while the Duke was aided by Sir Henry Hardinge. Upon the order to 'Fire!' the Duke raised his gun, fired and missed. It is thought he missed deliberately. Winchilsea kept his arm by his side, then raised his weapon and fired into the air. He then apologized for the language in his letter, and honour was therefore served.

THE GREAT REFORM ACT IS PASSED IN THE COMMONS

In 1832, there had been no reform of who had the right to vote in Britain, or of the boundaries of the parliamentary constituencies, for centuries. There were 'rotten boroughs' with a handful of voters, and pocket boroughs dominated by aristocracy. Only about 400,000 people could vote out of a population of over sixteen million. Great cities that had emerged in the Industrial Revolution, like Birmingham, Manchester and Leeds, had no separate representation, while Cornwall had forty-four MPs. A head of steam for reform had arisen from manufacturers, middle-class radicals and workers alike.

The Whig government under Prime Minister Earl Grey had responded in 1830 with reform proposals but did not intend to introduce democracy, which was still in effect taboo among the political elite. Their mainly Tory opponents resisted any reform as leading to the catastrophe of the people's will overturning the natural dominance of rank and property. However, the Whigs thought that unless the natural leaders of the country should adapt and improve, uncontrollable waves of dangerous innovation would destroy the existing social order.

Their suggestions still shocked the opposition. Eighty-six small boroughs were to lose seats, and twenty-two new towns gain them. The electorate would be increased by about 250,000. The first Whig bill only passed its second reading by one vote in March 1831, and as it was clear it would be defeated in the Lords, Grey sought a general election. After it there was a reforming majority of over 100 in the Commons – but the Lords rejected a second bill on 8 October.

In an environment of strong popular reforming pressure, both by organized Political Unions, like that of Birmingham, and the threat of violence and riots, as in Bristol, tensions rose. The Commons voted for a third bill on 22 March 1832, but it was only the threat of the creation of many new peers that overcame Lords resistance, and it received the Royal Assent from a reluctant William IV on 7 June. With only about 7 per cent of the adult population enfranchised, this was not democracy. However, it was a start – and revolution had been averted.

FIRST LOCKDOWN BEGINS

Prime-ministerial addresses to the nation don't happen that often, and when they do, people pay attention. On the evening of Monday, 23 March 2020, Boris Johnson went on television to announce an unprecedented lockdown of the economy and society. Schools and hospitality were to shut. Socializing was to end. People were to work from home where possible. Non-essential shops would close.

Reports of a new 'viral pneumonia' in Wuhan, China, began reaching the World Health Organization at the end of December 2019, with the first reported death on 11 January 2020. China itself locked down the Hubei province after eighteen deaths had been recorded, on 23 January. The following day, Health Secretary Matt Hancock chaired the first COBRA meeting on Covid, claiming the risk to the UK public was low.

On 31 January, the first two Covid cases were confirmed in the UK. Covid-19 was officially declared a pandemic on 11 March 2020, with an eventual British lockdown seen as inevitable when other nations, including Italy, locked down quickly.

By the end of March 2020, 4,426 people in the UK had died within twenty-eight days of a positive Covid test. With the lockdown came an unprecedented level of state spending and economic intervention. The furlough scheme meant the government would be paying up to 80 per cent of people's wages.

Even though Imperial College estimated 470,000 lives would be saved by the first lockdown, more than 150,000 individuals have died with a positive Covid test. Similarly, the backlog on non-Covid healthcare, which was already huge with an ageing population, only worsened as operations were cancelled and people were told to avoid their GPs.

Though restrictions were eased with the 'Eat Out to Help Out' scheme of summer 2020, rising cases once again prompted further lockdowns in November 2020 and January 2021.

Thanks to an excellent vaccine roll-out in 2021, which was faster than in any other major country in the world bar Israel, restrictions were fully lifted on 19 July: dubbed 'Freedom Day'. In early 2022, the rapid spread of the Omicron variant first discovered in South Africa prompted a return to mask wearing and increased isolation.

STANSTED PROPOSED AS LONDON'S THIRD AIRPORT

It was back in 1942, in the middle of World War II, that the US Air Force chose to build a runway at the Stansted Mountfitchet Airfield. On D-Day, it was bombers from Stansted which led more than six hundred aircraft over the beaches of occupied France. After the war, the Americans departed, leaving the airfield in the hands of the British. By 1957, it was fully turned over to civil use.

Stansted quickly became a 'third way' in the eyes of holiday operators; it was a handy and cheaper alternative to the already-established big name airports of Heathrow and Gatwick. By 1964, Stansted was popular enough to be provisionally chosen as London's third airport, and held in reserve. But there were plenty of other options on the table; the Labour government under Harold Wilson set up the Roskill Commission to find the most viable in 1968. When it reported in 1971, it ignored Stansted altogether, suggesting four sites – Cublington, Foulness (later to be known as Maplin Sands), Nuthampstead and Thurleigh. They recommended Cublington.

However, the Heath government rejected Cublington and instead opted for Maplin Sands, which would be built on an artificial island just off the Essex coast near Southend. Then the oil crisis hit and frugal would-be Thatcherites were concerned about the rising cost. Labour MPs preferred the cheap and cheerful Stansted. Traffic gradually grew and a brand new terminal building was built. In March 2008, the airport owners, BAA, submitted a planning application for a second runway, but two years later it was withdrawn. Passenger traffic has more than doubled from 11.9 million in 2000 to 25.9 million in 2017.

A new airport in the south-east was suggested by Boris Johnson when he was Mayor of London. The site in the Thames Estuary became known as 'Boris Island'. A 2009 study by the Greater London Authority of its feasibility found 'no logical constraint' to the plan. The idea was eventually rejected.

Debates over the site of a new runway in the south-east have been going on for three decades and have still not been fully resolved.

REVEREND IAN PAISLEY JAILED

The Reverend Ian Paisley was a man of two personas – the fire and brimstone evangelical preacher and politician who demanded 'no surrender' to 'Popery' or Irish nationalism. And then there was the private man, who was kind, approachable and funny. Until old age he seemed to have an inability to compromise, yet ended up becoming one of the 'Chuckle Brothers' when he served as First Minister of Northern Ireland alongside Sinn Féin's Martin McGuinness.

That would have been unthinkable to the Paisley of the 1950s to 1970s. In 1956, Paisley helped found Ulster Protestant Action, a vigilante patrol group which became a political party, the Protestant Unionist Party, ten years later. Paisley was the public face, and he continually courted controversy. In June 1959, he was convicted of public order offences for inciting supporters to attack Catholic homes in the mainly Protestant Shankill area of Belfast.

During the 1964 election campaign, he threatened to march on the offices of a nationalist candidate who was displaying the Irish Tricolour if the RUC didn't enforce the Flags and Emblems Act, passed by the Stormont Parliament, which banned the display of any flag except the Union Jack. The RUC caved.

In the same year, a civil rights movement was formed, designed to end Catholic discrimination. Paisley saw this as an opportunity to up his public profile even further. He formed the Ulster Constitution Defence Committee along with a paramilitary wing, the Ulster Protestant Volunteers.

In June 1966, he led a march to the General Assembly of the Presbyterian Church through Catholic areas of Belfast. Violence ensued and Paisley was charged with unlawful assembly and sentenced to three months in prison. His supporters rioted outside Crumlin Road prison where he was incarcerated.

On 30 November 1968, a civil rights march was due to take place in Armagh. Paisley led a convoy of cars and took over the town centre, determined to prevent it from going ahead. The RUC halted the march leading to outrage in the nationalist community. On 25 March 1969, Paisley and his accomplice Ronald Bunting were jailed for organizing an illegal counter demonstration. Both were released six weeks later under an amnesty.

THE SDP IS LAUNCHED

A left-wing MP becomes Labour Leader, divisions grow, and after a while some moderate centre-left MPs leave and form a new party that they hope will break the two-party stranglehold on British politics. No, not Jeremy Corbyn and the formation of Change UK, but Michael Foot and the formation of the SDP.

The 'Gang of Four' – Roy Jenkins, Shirley Williams, Bill Rodgers and David Owen – launched the Council for Social Democracy in the Limehouse Declaration in January 1981, but two months later, their patience with the Labour Party ran out and they decided to go for broke and found the shiny new Social Democratic Party (SDP).

The aim was to relign British politics, or as Roy Jenkins, the party's leader, put it, 'to break the mould'. Twenty-eight Labour MPs defected to the SDP, plus a lone Conservative, Christopher Brocklebank-Fowler. An alliance with the Liberal Party was negotiated. By-election victories, strong polling numbers, and a high media profile appeared to make them strong contenders for government. But it didn't work out that way.

In the 1983 general election, the Alliance won an impressive 25.4 per cent of the vote, only 2.2 per cent behind Labour. But it only won twenty-three seats. Of these only six were from the SDP. In 1987, it won one fewer and its vote share declined to 22.4 per cent. The SDP won only five.

It's been long debated as to why, despite that early promise, the SDP/Alliance in the end fell far short of making a breakthrough. Was it the fact that in 1983 Roy Jenkins' voter appeal didn't match the slick image of the SDP? Would it have made a difference if Shirley Williams had been leader? Was it that the first-past-the-post system makes a significant breakthrough for smaller parties almost impossible? Was it the uneasy coupling of two similar but separate parties? Was it Prime Minister Margaret Thatcher's soaring popularity after the 1982 Falklands War? It was all of these reasons and more.

The SDP, of a fashion, still exists today and, prior to Brexit, had its first parliamentarian in thirty years when former *Express* journalist Patrick O'Flynn, then an MEP, defected to the party from UKIP.

THE BEECHING REPORT IS PUBLISHED

One of my first childhood memories is of watching the railway line being ripped up at the bottom of a field on my father's Essex farm. 'Why are they doing that?' I asked my father with all the innocence a five-year-old can muster. 'It's Dr Beeching's fault,' replied my dad.

Through the lens of the 2020s, the Beeching report, which recommended the closure of 2,363 stations and the ripping-up of 5,000 miles of track, is an assault on the very core of Britain's transport infrastructure. Through the eyes of the Conservative and Labour governments of the 1960s it made complete rational sense. Railway usage had been on the decline since 1945, with the proportion of journeys undertaken by rail declining from 16 per cent to 5 per cent. Car ownership and usage was increasing by 10 per cent each year. British Railways, which had been nationalized in 1948, was incurring ever-increasing financial losses. Heavy investment had not paid off. In 1956, British Railways had lost £15.6 million, rising to £42 million four years later. Something had to change. Enter Dr Richard Beeching.

Beeching became head of the British Railways Board in 1961 and was deputed by Transport Minister Ernest Marples to make the railways pay. The report made clear that revenues were unlikely to increase, so costs had to be cut. Loss-making lines would close and seventy thousand people would lose their jobs. The cuts were designed to make an improvement in British Railways' accounts of between £115 million and £147 million. At the time of the report, the Labour Party and the trade unions led the opposition to the planned cuts, yet the truth is that it was under Harold Wilson's government that many of the cuts were implemented.

In truth, not all the cuts were implemented, because of vehement local opposition. In recent years, a few of the rural lines have been reopened, with more reopenings planned over the next decade.

Beeching later described his report in these terms: 'I suppose I'll always be looked upon as the axe man, but it was surgery, not mad chopping.'

LABOUR GOVERNMENT LOSES CONFIDENCE VOTE

Governments in Britain do not often lose votes of confidence. Prior to 1979, the last time it happened was in 1924 when Ramsay MacDonald's ill-fated first Labour government was forced to call an election.

By March 1979, James Callaghan's Labour government appeared to be in terminal decline. It limped from one economic disaster to another and appeared to have no sense of direction. It was losing by-elections hand over fist and was unable to introduce any meaningful legislation as it no longer had a parliamentary majority. In 1977, Callaghan negotiated a pact with the Liberal Party, but that ended in July 1978. That September, Callaghan nearly called an election but backed out at the last minute. Callaghan won a first vote of confidence by ten votes in December 1978, having bought off the Ulster Unionists with a promise of extra parliamentary seats for Northern Ireland. A winter of industrial discontent had followed, with strike upon strike bringing the country to a standstill. The dead remained unburied and rubbish piled up on the streets.

On 1 March, a referendum on Scottish devolution took place, with a majority voting in favour. However, Callaghan decided not to implement the result as it failed to reach the 40 per cent turnout threshold legislated for in the Devolution Act. The SNP put down a motion of no confidence, quickly followed by Margaret Thatcher's Conservative opposition, for debate on 28 March. It was a bitter debate, summed up by Michael Foot's description of Liberal Leader David Steel as having 'passed from rising hope to elder statesman without any intervening period whatsoever'. Prime Minister Callaghan ridiculed the unholy alliance ranged against him. 'We can truly say that once the Leader of the Opposition discovered what the Liberals and the SNP would do, she found the courage of their convictions. ... What a massive display of unsullied principle! The minority parties have walked into a trap.'

The government lost by a single vote, with perpetually absent Irish MP Frank Maguire travelling to Westminster 'to abstain in person'.

An election was immediately called for 3 May.

THERESA MAY TRIGGERS ARTICLE 50

It was on this day in 2017 that the starting gun for Brexit was officially fired. Nine months after the referendum result, Theresa May triggered Article 50 of the Lisbon Treaty, which gave the European Council formal notice that the UK intended to withdraw from the EU. The UK's Permanent Representative in Brussels, Tim Barrow, hand-delivered a letter to Donald Tusk, President of the European Council.

The process had not been smooth, as Theresa May faced rulings from British courts on whether she, or Parliament, could trigger Article 50. While good practice for later negotiations with Brussels, it showed that extracting Britain from a relationship it had been part of for over four decades would not be easy.

Gina Miller, a relatively unknown businesswoman, shot to prominence with her legal case arguing that Article 50 should not be triggered without a vote in Parliament. Indeed, the European Parliament passed a motion on 28 June 2016, only five days after the referendum, calling for the UK to trigger Article 50 immediately. Theresa May, however, decided that Article 50 should not be triggered until 2017, in order to allow the UK time to work on its negotiating position.

What the Miller case highlighted was just how unprecedented and ambiguous such a move by the UK government was. No government had ever tried to remove itself from an international body so interwoven into its domestic governance. The government believed it could use prerogative powers to trigger Article 50 following the referendum result. However, as the referendum was not legally binding, the precedent of parliamentary sovereignty, as set out by Gina Miller, triumphed.

Some of the key principles of departure May set out in her letter included engaging 'constructively and respectfully' with the EU, alongside putting 'citizens first' and aiming to 'minimise disruption' by giving 'as much certainty as possible'. Indeed, while Theresa May called on Britons to unite, the weaker hand she inherited after the self-inflicted wound of the June 2017 election led many Remainers to believe Brexit could be stopped completely. This became the catalyst for May's ultimate failure to deliver Brexit in Parliament after agreeing a deal in November 2018.

AIREY NEAVE IS ASSASSINATED

Margaret Thatcher was to lose several close colleagues and friends to IRA bombs, but Airey Neave's loss was perhaps the biggest personal and political blow to her. And it came at the worst time.

The 1979 election campaign should have been exciting. Called after a vote of no confidence in James Callaghan's Labour government, the campaign was volatile. It was marred by tragedy following the assassination of Thatcher's shadow Northern Ireland Secretary, Airey Neave, who was killed by a car bomb as he was driving up the exit ramp of the House of Commons underground car park. The Irish National Liberation Army admitted to his murder, a lone INLA volunteer having planted the bomb under Neave's car at home.

Neave had been working in the Commons before his murder, with staff rushing to New Palace Yard following the explosion. The House of Commons was still sitting when the Chief Whip announced that someone had been injured. The MP for Abingdon since 1953, Neave had been Margaret Thatcher's campaign manager in her successful bid to become Leader of the Conservative party in 1975.

Airey Neave had never been a stranger to danger. Having visited Germany in the 1930s, he joined the Oxfordshire and Buckinghamshire Light Infantry before being wounded and captured in France. He became the first British officer to escape from Colditz Castle – a prisoner-of-war camp – during the Second World War, and was awarded the Military Cross.

Neave, as the very epitome of someone born into the Establishment, also served as a spy and lawyer during a long and distinguished career. Following his escape from Colditz, he worked for MI9 – a division of MI6 – becoming a commanding officer. Neave also served at the Nuremberg trials.

Nobody was ever convicted for Neave's death, with murder files closed and Freedom of Information requests refused.

Margaret Thatcher remained wedded to Neave's Northern Ireland manifesto commitments, written just hours before his assassination. Upon her election as prime minister, Thatcher quoted Neave as the person 'whom we hoped to bring here with us'. His influence on her ideological and political success is unarguable.

'POLL TAX' RIOTS

More than a decade after entering Number 10, Margaret Thatcher seemed unassailable, yet the storm clouds were gathering. She had had a unique ability to gauge the public mood and adapt her policies to meet it. Until the 'poll tax', that is. Introduced in Scotland in 1989, it triggered a widespread protest in central London on 31 March 1990.

The Community Charge was introduced to replace the rates system – based on property – for funding local government. Instead, a fixed charge would apply to every adult. A duke would pay the same as a dustman.

Routed from Kennington Park to Trafalgar Square, the march involved more than 200,000 people angry at a perceived clear economic inequality. Before the march, the organizers had argued to divert to Hyde Park due to the volume of people threatening to overspill Trafalgar Square's capacity. This request was denied.

A surge of protesters stuck in Whitehall meant sudden movements by riot police were seen as a provocation. The protesters clashed with police in riot uniform and on horses, leading to widespread anarchy. Banks, restaurants and cars were targeted, with rebellion regarded as pent-up fury developed during the miners' strike coming to the forefront. Cars were torched and police horses attacked.

In the course of the rioting, 113 people were injured, with 339 arrested and scuffles occurring until 3 a.m. With a 1991 police report finding 'no evidence' of left-wing groups orchestrating the riots, it suggested that the police inflated charges. Indeed, poor-quality radio and a shortage of officers further added to the pressure.

The riots generated widespread condemnation from the press and political parties, with Labour Leader Neil Kinnock dismissing the rioters as 'toy town revolutionaries' and the newspaper urging citizens to 'shop' rioters to the police.

However, public anger and discontent was widespread and growing. Some council workers refused to collect the tax, meaning, by June 1990, a third of people in England and Wales hadn't paid.

The 'poll tax' played a large part in Thatcher's defenestration in November 1990. The new Prime Minister, John Major, replaced it with the Council Tax – another imperfect system of raising money for local government, but perceived as fairer than the Community Charge.

APRIL

THE MINISTRY OF DEFENCE IS CREATED

By today's standards it seems incongruous that Britain had a War Office as recently as 1964. In addition, there were three different ministries catering for the three armed services, the Navy, Army and Air Force.

Even as far back as the 1920s there was a consensus in Whitehall that our defence and war efforts needed to be better coordinated, but there was no agreement on how. Lloyd George had rejected the creation of a single Ministry of Defence (MOD) in 1921. A chiefs of staff committee was formed in 1923, but that's about as far as it went. It wasn't until Stanley Baldwin's government created a Minister for Defence Coordination that anything changed in a material sense. But even then the minister had no say over the three services, and not being in the cabinet, Lord Chatfield had little influence. But it was a start. Things changed with the onset of war and when Winston Churchill became prime minister in 1940. He realized that the only way to coordinate defence and war policy was if he as prime minister did it. So he created a new post of Minister of Defence, and appointed himself to it.

When Clement Attlee became prime minister in July 1945, he introduced a Ministry of Defence Act, which became law in 1946. It abolished the cabinet posts of Secretary of State for War, First Lord of the Admiralty and Secretary of State for Air, and between 1946 and 1964 they all reported to the Minister for Defence.

In 1964, Harold Wilson decided that the five separate departments which served the MOD should all merge. Inter-service rivalries didn't disappear, but dissipated.

The MOD is housed in the unimaginatively named Main Building on Whitehall. Built between 1938 and 1959, it was originally meant to house the Air Ministry and the Board of Trade.

Over the years, the MOD has built up a reputation for being one of the most inefficient government departments. It has a huge land bank of some 223,000 hectares and its procurement methods have proved to be hugely wasteful and inefficient.

ARGENTINA INVADES THE FALKLAND ISLANDS

Late in the evening of 31 March 1982, Sir Henry Leach, Chief of Naval Staff and First Sea Lord, was invited to meet Prime Minister Margaret Thatcher and Defence Secretary Sir John Nott in her office in the House of Commons. She wanted an update on the rumours that Argentina was about to invade the Falkland Islands.

The discussion turned to what the British response could be. Leach proposed the sending of a task force of frigates and aircraft carriers which would take a week to put together and a further three to reach the Falklands. 'Three days, you mean?' said the Prime Minister. 'No, three weeks, Prime Minister. It's 8,000 nautical miles,' replied the First Sea Lord. 'Could we really recapture the Islands if they were invaded?' asked Thatcher. 'Yes, we could, and although it's not my place to say so, we should,' replied Leach. The Prime Minister snapped: 'Why do you say that?' Leach replied with words which were to be crucial in Thatcher's decision to despatch the Task Force only a matter of days later. 'Because if we do not, or if we pussyfoot in our actions and do not achieve complete success, in another few months we shall be living in a different country whose words count for little.' The metal in the Iron Lady's spine was tingling.

Two days later the invasion commenced, with the Falkland Islands governor, Sir Rex Hunt, forced into surrender. The next day, Parliament met for its first Saturday sitting since the Suez Crisis in 1956.

It was not a pretty debate, with Conservative MP after Conservative MP turning their fire on the Defence Secretary, who put in a hapless performance. The debate convinced Foreign Secretary Lord Carrington that he must resign, given the fact that his embassy in Buenos Aires had failed to see the invasion coming. Nott offered his resignation too, but this was refused, and he stayed in post.

The task force set sail on Monday, 5 April, only three days after the invasion, a phenomenal achievement.

ROBERT WALPOLE BECOMES BRITAIN'S FIRST PRIME MINISTER

Robert Walpole became Britain's first prime minister on 3 April 1721. He would remain so for the next twenty-one years, a record none of his successors has so far managed to exceed. Although Walpole established the office of the prime minister and also the principle that the holder was indisputably the sovereign's chief minister, he continually warned against the wisdom of any one person holding such a prominent position. He was also the first, reluctant, occupant of 10 Downing Street, a poorly built house in a dark street on marshy land near the River Thames and the Palace of Whitehall.

Walpole came to office having had a long career in government and opposition, but politics had not been his original intention. He had gone up to Cambridge University and had planned to be a clergyman, but the death of his elder brother meant he had to shoulder the burden of running the family estates and their political ambitions. He came from a political family which had built its fortune in the City and in land-owning in Norfolk. Walpole was an effective parliamentarian and knew how to provoke his opponents, but he was never totally consumed by politics. He cultivated an interest in the arts and literature, and throughout his years of influence and power did all he could to support and promote the work of musicians and artists.

Through the long years of his administration, his primary political goal remained consistent – prosperity at home and peace abroad. By the time he left office he had established the Whig Party as the dominant force in British politics, secured the Hanoverian claim to the throne and kept the country from any serious military entanglement.

The secret of Walpole's success was that he understood how to balance the exercise of the declining but still considerable powers of the monarchy with the growing power and influence of the House of Commons. As Britain's first prime minister and longest holder of the office, Robert Walpole has a good claim to being one of the country's greatest statesmen.

NATO TREATY SIGNED

NATO, or the North Atlantic Treaty Organization, was formed on 4 April 1949 after the signing of the Washington Treaty (or North Atlantic Treaty) by twelve founding member states – Canada and the United States, as well as ten European countries, Belgium, Denmark, France, Iceland, Italy, Luxembourg, Netherlands, Norway, Portugal and the United Kingdom.

The Treaty was created following the Soviet Union's expansion in Eastern Europe after the end of World War II. It was assumed that at some point the Soviets might launch an attack on Western Europe. Ernest Bevin, the Foreign Secretary in Clement Attlee's government, signed the Treaty in Washington and said at the time: 'Speaking for the British people, I can assure you that they have agreed to make their contribution to the pool of peace.'

The main premise of the Treaty – Article 5 – revolves around collective defence, essentially meaning that if a single member of NATO is attacked, it is seen as an attack on all member states, invoking a mutual response. The article has been triggered only once since its creation – by the United States following the 9/11 attacks in September 2001.

In recent years, there's been a large focus on the amount of money spent on defence, following the mutual agreement in 2014 that all NATO countries agree to committing at least 2 per cent of their GDP. According to recent data, Greece and the United States contribute the highest proportion of their GDP, while the UK meets the 2 per cent obligation.

The alliance has significantly expanded over the years and now has thirty members, including Germany, Greece, Spain, Turkey and fourteen other European countries. Former Prime Minister of Norway Jens Stoltenberg is its current Secretary General. Three Brits have led NATO, General Hastings Ismay (1952–57), Lord Carrington (1984–88) and Lord Robertson (1999–2003).

At the time of writing, Sweden and Finland have applied to join NATO as a consequence of the Russian invasion of Ukraine.

LORD CARRINGTON RESIGNS AS FOREIGN SECRETARY

As Margaret Thatcher's first Foreign Secretary, Lord Carrington is the last member of the House of Lords to serve in one of the four Great Offices of State.

Peter Carrington's political career dated back to 1938, when he succeeded his father as the 6th Baron Carrington. After a good war record, he served in the Churchill, Eden and Macmillan governments of the 1950s, with a three-year interlude as High Commissioner to Australia. His last ministerial position was First Lord of the Admiralty. Under Alec Douglas-Home he joined the cabinet as Leader of the House of Lords. Edward Heath promoted him to Defence Secretary, a position he held up until the last two months of the 1970–74 government.

Although he was eminently qualified for the job, most were surprised when Thatcher appointed him to the Foreign Office in 1979. He was never seen as a natural political soulmate of the new Prime Minister. She, however, recognized that she needed a Foreign Secretary with some experience, experience which she did not have. They became close early on, especially when he proved his uniting skills during the Lancaster House talks about the future of Zimbabwe.

On 2 April 1982, Argentina invaded the Falkland Islands. The Foreign Office had completely misread Argentinian intentions and Carrington decided that the buck stopped with him. He and his entire ministerial team offered their resignations, as did the Defence Secretary, John Nott. The Prime Minister refused to accept either Carrington's or Nott's resignation and asked them to reconsider. Nott did, but Carrington didn't. He was treated with respect by peers in the emergency debate on the Saturday following the invasion. But the mauling Nott got in the Commons made up his mind. All political disasters need a fall guy and Carrington fell on his sword rather than let it fall on the Prime Minister.

Margaret Thatcher wrote in her memoirs: 'Peter had great panache and the ability to identify immediately the main points in any argument; and he could express himself in pungent terms. We had disagreements, but there were never any hard feelings.'

NATIONAL DOCK LABOUR SCHEME IS ABOLISHED

The government of Margaret Thatcher is known for its economic reforms, trade union legislation and privatization. But few remember one reform which transformed the prospects for much of the British ports industry, and it concerned an anachronistic piece of legislation, passed in 1947, through which registered dockworkers in designated ports had enhanced employment rights and effectively a job for life – privileges other workers could only dream of. They had a guaranteed job for life, it was impossible to sack them, when they retired their jobs automatically passed to their sons and they were paid at much higher rates than other workers (and indeed dock workers in non-scheme ports). Spanish practices were rife and if a port closed down, dockers were transferred to the nearest port even if it was run by a different company and there was no need for them.

There was little to no investment in the land owned by the sixty-three Dock Labour Scheme ports (which included London, Southampton, Bristol, Cardiff, Liverpool, Clyde, Forth, Tees, Hull and Immingham – but not Dover and Felixstowe) because the port authorities were prevented by law from allowing any non-port related activity within their boundaries. If the Scheme hadn't existed they could have utilized their land however they wished.

How on earth could this scheme exist after nearly ten years of a Thatcher government? The answer was simple. Margaret Thatcher feared the economic consequences of a national docks strike.

On 6 April 1989, the Employment Secretary, Norman Fowler, announced to a stunned House of Commons that legislation would be introduced forthwith to end the Dock Labour Scheme. Tory MPs cheered, Labour MPs remained silent, but the trade unions reacted with fury and launched a strike ballot. By the time the Bill received its Royal Assent on 6 July, the strikes had petered out. It was, judges Nigel Lawson, a 'textbook example' of good government.

A new era had begun. Almost overnight, British ports became strike-free and competitive. Thousands of new jobs and businesses were created, and shipping lines became far more willing to use British ports.

ASQUITH BECOMES PRIME MINISTER

There's some dispute among historians as to the exact date that Liberal Herbert Henry Asquith became prime minister. Some think it was 5 April, others the 7th and still more the 8th.

Whichever date it was, he would go on to hold the office until 5 December 1916.

He came to the premiership with experience in two of the other Great Offices of State, having been Home Secretary (1892–95) and Chancellor of the Exchequer (1905–08), in the Gladstone/Rosebery and Campbell-Bannerman governments respectively. He was a barrister by profession before becoming the MP for East Fife in 1886, a seat he would hold until 1918. Asquith had two years out of Parliament before returning to the Commons as MP for Paisley from 1920–24.

He was a radical prime minister, from reform of the House of Lords to the introduction, via Chancellor of the Exchequer David Lloyd George, of the 1909–10 so-called People's Budget, which imposed hefty taxes on the rich to help fund a raft of social programmes seen as helping found the welfare state.

The Tory-dominated Lords spent a year opposing the proposals and, after being threatened with the introduction of hundreds of new Liberal peers, passed the Parliament Act, which ensured – in theory at least – that the government could get its legislation through.

Asquith's Liberals only squeaked through the January 1910 general election as the largest party, with only two more seats than the Conservatives, but continued to govern with the support of Irish Nationalist MPs and those of the fledgling Labour Party. A second election in November produced much the same result.

Asquith had a number of big issues to deal with, not least the increasing calls for votes for women, Irish Home Rule, which would fundamentally split the Liberal Party, and the outbreak of the First World War in 1914.

Asquith's coalition government collapsed in December 1916 and he was replaced by Lloyd George. He was the last Liberal PM to command a majority and the last of his political tradition to serve as Leader of the Opposition, which he did from 1920 to 1922. He died in February 1928, aged eighty-five.

BRITAIN SIGNS ENTENTE CORDIALE WITH FRANCE

The governments of Lord Salisbury had been pursuing a policy of 'splendid isolation' for nearly twenty years, although it could also be argued that this had dictated British foreign policy ever since the 1820s, whether deliberately or not. The world's greatest empire felt it didn't need alliances, and was confident enough to stand above the fray. However, by the turn of the century, things were beginning to change. The Anglo–Japanese Alliance was signed in 1902 and there were plenty of politicians and diplomats who were starting to think that it would be in Britain's interest to counter the so-called Triple Alliance of Germany, the Austro-Hungarian Empire and Italy. France, meanwhile, was getting increasingly nervous about the fact that Russia was its only major ally.

British–French relations had been characterized by disputes, wars and a general state of conflict for the previous thousand years. The phrase 'perfidious Albion' was invented by the French in the eighteenth century and was (and still is) rolled out whenever conflict between the two great powers was brewing.

Over a century later, at a time of seemingly constant sniping between Britain and France, it is difficult to understand the magnitude of the signing of the Entente Cordiale. It came about for many reasons but not least because of the relationship between Foreign Secretary Lord Lansdowne and the long-serving French Ambassador to London, Paul Cambon. There was no single reason that it came about, but the prospect of a Russsian–Japanese war certainly gave it some impetus, given that France was allied to Russia and Britain to Japan.

A series of colonial territorial disputes were solved with the stroke of a pen, not least in Egypt and Morocco but across Africa, the Americas, Asia and the Pacific. Zones of influence were established. But the main result of the signing of the Entente Cordiale was to send a big signal to Germany whose own diplomacy had long sought to capitalize on Anglo–French rivalry.

The Entente Coridale endured, while the Triple Alliance shattered at the start of the First World War. Yet, beyond symbolism, has it had a lasting legacy? Probably not.

JOHN MAJOR WINS GENERAL ELECTION

The 1992 election demonstrated the importance of a party leader. Marking the fourth consecutive victory for the Conservatives, voters took politicians, and perhaps themselves, by surprise in not rewarding Labour Leader Neil Kinnock with the keys to Downing Street. A personal victory for John Major, it gave the Conservatives the highest number of votes a party has ever received in an election to this day: over fourteen million.

The election came less than eighteen months after Margaret Thatcher's decline and fall. Though a less divisive figure, Major's tenure had been no less quiet with a Gulf War, replacing the 'poll tax' with the Council Tax and signing the Maastricht Treaty. Given the Conservatives had been in office for thirteen years, opinion polls repeatedly showed a Labour majority or hung Parliament were likely.

The economy was far from stable. An ongoing recession combined with 2.5 million unemployed should have worked in Labour's favour. However, Margaret Thatcher's departure meant Labour lost their momentum for change. Indeed, John Major's focus on consensus building meant he retained support from many Conservative newspapers, including *The Sun*, which published a series of ruthless anti-Neil Kinnock front pages.

Labour had further reformed themselves since their previous landslide defeat. No longer committed to radical left-wing policies, Neil Kinnock saw himself as a prime minister in waiting. Campaigning on the usual issues of taxation and healthcare, the Conservatives tried to scare voters into thinking Labour hadn't changed, using imagery of boxing gloves to suggest a 'double-whammy' of 'tax rises' and 'inflation' should they win.

Kinnock was far too jubilant and triumphalist, when the evidence did not support him. At a rally in Sheffield, an event resembling an American-style political convention, Kinnock cried out 'We're all right!' numerous times, as though victory was guaranteed before voters went to the polls. That the election had a 77 per cent turnout, the highest in eighteen years, suggests many voters deliberately turned out to ensure Kinnock did not make it into office.

While the Conservatives attracted 43 per cent of the vote, their majority declined from 102 to 21. But it was still a notable personal achievement for John Major himself.

THE GOOD FRIDAY AGREEMENT IS SIGNED

The signing of the Good Friday Agreement was certainly a huge political moment for everyone concerned, not least the new British Prime Minister, Tony Blair. It represented the culmination of a process which started under Margaret Thatcher and was given impetus by John Major, but the skills displayed by Tony Blair, his chief of staff Jonathan Powell, and the people skills of the Northern Ireland Secretary Mo Mowlam, brought about the kind of peace which few could have predicted.

By the mid 1990s, the IRA had come to realize that they could not and would never achieve their aims by a continuation of the armed conflict, and it was the backchannel discussions with the Major government that started the whole process.

The willingness of most of the Northern Ireland parties and communities to compromise and end the Troubles which had bedevilled the Province for thirty years was also a key to success, together with the input of the Irish Taioseach Bertie Ahern.

The only mainstream political party to oppose the Agreement was the Democratic Unionist Party, led by the Reverend Ian Paisley. David Trimble's Ulster Unionist Party were reluctant signatories, and although Trimble, together with the SDLP's John Hume, went on to win the Nobel Peace Prize, the UUP was finished, as many of its supporters defected to the DUP.

The Agreement covered justice, policing, demilitarization, decommissioning of weapons, release of prisoners, sovereignty, governance, civil rights and cultural rights. In fact, there were two separate but related agreements, one between the different political parties in Northern Ireland and the other between the British and Irish governments.

The two agreements were put to the populations of Northern Ireland and the Republic on 22 May 1998, with a 71 per cent yes vote in Northern Ireland and 94 per cent south of the border. The terms of the agreements came into force on 2 December 1999 and direct rule from Westminster came to an end, for the moment at least.

Tony Blair believes to this day that the Good Friday Agreement was the biggest achievement of his decade-long government. It's a claim that is difficult to argue with.

THE BRIXTON RIOTS

Urban Britain was not always a happy place in 1981. A deep recession was under way, with economic opportunities restricted for young people, and young people from ethnic minorities in particular. On top of that, the police adopted aggressive tactics towards these same groups especially in inner London, with a hostile and confrontational use of 'stop and search' powers.

In 1980, police in Brixton launched the deliberately antagonistically named plain-clothes 'Operation Swamp 81', named after Margaret Thatcher's comment in a 1978 interview where she said people were worried the UK 'might be swamped by people of a different culture'. It was clear who the police were targeting. Within five days, nearly a thousand people had been stopped and searched, leading to eighty-two arrests.

On Friday, 10 April, a young black man called Michael Bailey was being helped by a police officer after having been stabbed. A crowd gathered and when a police car arrived to take him to hospital, they assumed he was being arrested. They pulled him out of the police car. The local community wrongly believed he had been left to die by the police.

The next afternoon, more crowds gathered believing that Michael Bailey had died due to police brutality. Bricks and missiles were hurled at police cars. Shops were looted. A police van was set on fire and a fire engine was then attacked with missiles and petrol bombs. The violence escalated through the early evening with twenty-eight businesses and buildings set on fire. Police reinforcements arrived from across the capital with 2,500 officers being deployed by midnight. By 1 a.m. the sheer numbers of police had had the desired effect and calm was restored.

During the rioting, 299 police officers sustained injuries, together with 65 members of the public, while 117 cars were torched and 82 people were arrested.

The Scarman report, published in November 1981, accused the police of 'disproportionate and indiscriminate use of "stop and search" powers'. Scarman also said that 'complex political, social and economic factors [created a] disposition towards violent protest,' something completely rejected by the Thatcher government.

BRITISH TELECOM PRIVATIZATION GIVEN GREEN LIGHT

The word 'privatization' didn't feature in the 1979 Conservative manifesto, but it became one of the things Margaret Thatcher's government became best known for, and the concept was one of Britain's greatest worldwide exports of the 1980s and 1990s. The aim of privatization was to increase efficiency, competition, innovation and share ownership, and reduce waste, bureaucracy and the stifling effect of monopolies.

The privatization of British Telecommunications was not the first privatization but it was by far the biggest, and it was the first major public utility to move from the public to the private sector.

The Thatcher government had already privatized Associated British Ports, Amersham International, Britoil, British Sugar, the National Freight Corporation and assorted smaller operations. But British Telecom was the big one, and the world was watching.

On 19 July 1982, the government announced its intention to sell its stake in British Telecom. The intention was to do it in tranches, with the first tranche of 50.2 per cent being offered in November 1984. Before that, though, the enabling legislation had to pass through Parliament. The British Telecommunications Bill was hotly debated for more than 320 hours (a post-war record), with Labour implacably opposed. It received its Royal Assent on 12 April 1984. British Telecom became British Telecom plc on 6 August 1984 in preparation for the share sale.

The first share offer was a massive success and was oversubscribed by a factor of 3.2. The shares were allocated on a pro-rata basis. Institutions owned 47.4 per cent and the general public 34.3 per cent, with BT employees and pensioners getting 4.6 per cent of the shares. Ninety-six per cent of employees became shareholders. Around £4 billion was raised for the taxpayer.

The remaining government-owned shares were sold in December 1991 and December 1994 raising a further £10 billion. In April 1991, the company changed its name to BT.

The model for privatizing BT was used for British Gas two years later and was copied to one degree or another in privatizations across the world. It was a huge success. Prices were cut, waiting lists for phones disappeared, faults were repaired more quickly and new products were developed.

NEIL KINNOCK RESIGNS AS LABOUR LEADER

Neil Kinnock's nine years as Leader of the Labour Party were not without their successes, but he failed to achieve his ultimate aim of becoming prime minister. The result of the general election came as a bitter blow to him. A week out from polling day he genuinely believed he was on his way to Number 10. But on election night it wasn't to be, and the pictures of him making his concession statement, alongside his wife, Glenys, remained long in the memory.

Four days later, he formally resigned the leadership. In a statement riddled with recrimination and bitterness, he appeared to blame Conservative-supporting newspapers for his defeat. There was little self-reflection or analysis of where the campaign went wrong or the inadequate nature of Labour's policy offering. He said merely: 'There will be many opportunities to consider the causes and consequences of last Thursday's election result. I will not dwell on them here.' He went on to lambast Tory Party treasurer Lord McAlpine for paying tribute to Tory-supporting newspaper editors: 'The relationship between the Conservative Party and those newspapers which Lord McAlpine describes as being edited by "heroes" is a fact of British political life. I did think that it would be possible this time to succeed in achieving change in spite of that. Clearly it wasn't. Success will therefore have to wait. But it will come, and I will work for it.' He had only five years to wait.

The ensuing leadership election result was announced on 18 July with John Smith trouncing Bryan Gould with 91 per cent of the vote.

Neil Kinnock rescued the Labour Party from its nadir after the humiliation of the 1983 general election. He set out on a course to return the party to being a credible electoral force once again. He stood up to the far left extremism of the Militant Tendency, banishing them from the party, and adopted modern campaigning techniques. His main problem was that the electorate couldn't quite imagine him being prime minister, a fact which in later years he came to acknowledge.

THE TITANIC HITS AN ICEBERG

On 10 April 1912, a luxury steamship set sail from Southampton to New York carrying 2,240 passengers. Travelling on a five-day journey across the North Atlantic, the ship made history by being one of the largest and most modern ocean liners of its time. Not only that, it gained praise for the high level of safety measures on board – so much so, it was considered unsinkable; if four of its sixteen watertight compartments flooded, it was still technically able to remain afloat.

Four days into RMS *Titanic*'s maiden voyage, the ship collided with an iceberg off the coast of Newfoundland.

However, once the ship hit the iceberg, water started to flood into the front six compartments. The bulkheads (watertight walls which aim to prevent further flooding) were not tall enough and the water could not be contained. Only a couple of hours after the impact, the *Titanic* sank, taking the lives of 1,500 passengers and crew members.

The *Titanic* only had twenty lifeboats, not enough to save every passenger on board. The owners of the ship and the British Board of Trade believed that too many lifeboats visible on deck would make the ship seem unsafe.

The tragedy of the *Titanic* led to public inquiries in the US and the UK. Both reached similar conclusions. As a result, new international agreements were set up to prevent similar disasters, namely that there had to be enough lifeboats on board a vessel to carry every passenger on board.

An International Ice Patrol was created and it was stipulated that radios must be manned at all hours on ships carrying passengers. All of these recommendations are still in place today.

The *Titanic* disaster has captured the imagination of society ever since that fateful day in the North Atlantic. The story inspired books and films – most famously the film *Titanic* (1997) starring Leonardo DiCaprio and Kate Winslet. It is understandable why it still resonates today. With more than 1,500 people from different races, classes and backgrounds losing their lives, they all have one thing in common – they all left someone behind.

THE FIRST TELEVISED ELECTION DEBATE

It's easy to forget, in a politics so focused upon soundbites and image, that the televised debate was only very recently introduced to the UK. In the USA, political debates had long been put on telly. It was Nixon and Kennedy who first faced each other down in the autumn of 1960, in front of seventy million Americans.

Cut to April 2010, when ITV hosted the first of three election debates in the UK, hosted by Alastair Stewart at Granada Studios in Manchester. The two men vying for office had another man standing beside them – Nick Clegg. In the end, it was he who would decide the result of the election. His performance at the first debate prompted a huge, albeit transient, upswing in the polls for the Liberal Democrats. Instant polling after the debate by ITV/ ComRes put Clegg on 43 per cent, dominating David Cameron at 26 per cent and Gordon Brown 20 per cent. If audience applause hadn't been banned, Clegg might have earned a standing ovation.

Michael Gove's theory was that Clegg could 'play the role of the sparky and feisty outsider'. He presented a third way on public spending – between the supposedly lavish Labour Party and cut-heavy Conservatives. And he did it in an approachable, down-to-earth manner; looking right down the camera lens. Even Cameron and Brown acknowledged that the Lib Dems had had a good showing, having repeatedly uttered the mantra 'I agree with Nick.' But the 'yellow surge' wouldn't last. By debate number two, the Lib Dems were only level-pegging with the Tories.

The themes of this first of three televised debates related to 'domestic affairs'. The three leaders made opening statements of ninety seconds; then they entered into the argy-bargy. Smaller parties, who weren't invited to the debate, were predictably rather upset. SNP Leader Alex Salmond suggested the participants all sounded the same. Ieuan Wyn Jones of Plaid Cymru labelled the debate 'sterile', noting there hadn't been a mention of Wales in the entire thing. ITV, though, could be content. The audience peaked at 10.3 million, amounting to an audience share of 37 per cent.

BATTLE OF CULLODEN

Right in the heart of the Scottish Highlands lies Drumossie Moor. It was on this moor, three miles east of Inverness, that the Battle of Culloden took place.

In 1688, tensions between Scotland, England and Ireland were so high that civil war became a serious threat. In addition, the Roman Catholic monarch of the time – King James VII of Scotland and II of England – fled to France, having lost his nerve after William of Orange's forces landed in Devon.

When James fled, his daughter Mary and her Protestant husband, William of Orange, were invited by the English and Scottish parliaments to rule in place of him. It was then that the Jacobites were formed, aiming to confront the new king and restore the House of Stuart to the throne.

Under pressure due to the economic and political uncertainty, Scotland's parliament accepted the Act of Union in 1707, much to the disappointment of the Jacobites.

The year 1745 marked a turbulent period across Europe with war imminent. The British Army faced defeat by France in May of this year, leaving the British forces at their weakest. It was with this in mind that King James VII's grandson Prince Charles Edward Stuart (famously known as Bonnie Prince Charlie) seized the opportunity and travelled to Scotland from France to lead a Jacobite army.

His leadership of the Jacobite army was popular, until the final denouement of the Jacobite forces at the Battle of Culloden in April 1746. Facing King George II's army, the Jacobites suffered a crushing defeat. In less than one hour, nearly 1,600 men were killed. Around 1,500 of them were Jacobites.

There are a variety of reasons why they failed so drastically this time around. By April 1746, the Jacobite troops were tired and hungry – their enemies were neither. The decision to fight on a moor over higher ground also meant the Jacobites' famous Highland charge tactic could not be used to full effect. As a result, the forces at the side of the battlefield were outflanked and faced a bloody defeat, changing life in the Highlands forever.

PC YVONNE FLETCHER MURDERED

Tucked away in the sleepy and elegant St James's Square in central London, by Pall Mall, lies the site of the former Libyan People's Bureau. Libyan dictator Colonel Gaddafi didn't believe in embassies. He sent Libyan students to man the bureau with instructions to kill Libyan dissidents in the UK. Those very same dissidents decided to hold a protest outside the bureau on the morning of 17 April 1984. The students inside had telexed Tripoli for instructions. Should they do nothing, haul some of the protesters inside and beat them up, or should they fire on them? The answer came back: Fire on them. US intelligence intercepted the message and passed it on to GCHQ, who astonishingly didn't pass it on to the Metropolitan Police. That morning, a worker, who was erecting crowd barriers outside the bureau in preparation for the demonstration, was told by someone inside the building that they had guns. He passed this information on to the police, who ignored it.

Just after 10 a.m., the demonstration started, with pro-Gaddafi supporters staging a counter-demo. Suddenly, shots rang out from an upper-floor window. Eleven demonstrators were injured, but one of the seventy-five police officers present fell to the ground. PC Yvonne Fletcher had been hit. She was rushed to hospital but at midday succumbed to her injuries. The nation was profoundly shocked, but under diplomatic law, the embassy could not be stormed. Some of those suspected had escaped through an underground car park. Ten days later, on the day of WPC Fletcher's funeral, thirty people left the embassy and were returned to Libya.

The British government broke off diplomatic relations with Libya once British embassy staff in Tripoli had been evacuated. Fifteen years later, Libya accepted responsibility for the murder of WPC Fletcher and offered to pay her family £250,000 in compensation.

No one has ever been held responsible for her murder.

In 1985, a granite memorial to WPC Yvonne Fletcher, funded by public donations and organized by the film director Michael Winner, was unveiled by Prime Minister Margaret Thatcher in St James's Square.

REPUBLIC OF IRELAND COMES INTO BEING

What isn't generally known is that for one month on the cusp of 1922 and 1923, there was a completely united Ireland. The new Irish Free State, which had Dominion status, ruled over the six counties of Northern Ireland too. But under the new constitution, the Parliament of Northern Ireland could, within one month, ask to return to the jurisdiction of the United Kingdom. And this it did.

This occurred slap bang in the middle of the Irish Civil War, fought between pro-Treaty and anti-Treaty forces, who objected to swearing continued allegiance to the monarchy. The former prevailed and the political settlement remained unchanged for fifteen years.

On 29 December 1937, a new constitution came into force following a referendum, changing the name of the Irish Free State to Eire. The office of President was established. Although in theory the monarchy was still part of the constitution, the powers of the President effectively replaced those of the monarch without the country declaring itself to be a republic.

The fact that Ireland remained neutral during World War II only served to increase the growing divide over the Irish Sea. In December 1948, the Irish Parliament passed the Government of Ireland Act, which finished off what the 1937 constitutional changes had started. The Act came into effect on 18 April 1949. It terminated Dominion status, ended Ireland's membership of the Commonwealth and declared the country to be a full republic. The name Eire disappeared and instead it was henceforth to be known as the Republic of Ireland.

The only constitutional change since then came in 1998 with the referendum approving the Good Friday Agreement. Articles 2 and 3 of the Irish constitution were amended to remove any territorial claim the Republic had on the six counties of the north.

Following the 2016 Brexit vote in the United Kingdom, the Irish Taioseach, Leo Varadkar, suggested that Ireland and the UK should come to an agreement about the future of trade relations. However, the EU negotiators made clear all negotiations must be handled by them. A Northern Ireland Protocol was agreed, but it remains a constant source of trade problems which has yet to be resolved.

BENJAMIN DISRAELI DIES

Disraeli's second and final administration, which ran from 1874 to 1880, was nothing if not eventful. Disraeli has gone down in history as one of the great Conservative prime ministers, but really, does he deserve that accolade?

He used the six lonely years in opposition after his short-lived first term to remodel the Conservative Party machine, so when the 1874 election was called by William Gladstone, he was ready for it. The nation had tired of Gladstone's humourless hectoring, as had Queen Victoria. Disraeli won the first Conservative majority in three decades. The trouble was, he was flattering to deceive. His reputation had always thrived on his verve and tenacity, but by the mid 1870s Disraeli was both tired and in increasingly bad health.

He may have put all his efforts into winning back power, but rather like Gordon Brown 133 years later, once he reached the top of the greasy pole he had no idea what to do with it. The policies weren't there.

To Disraeli, just being prime minister was enough. Well, and ingratiating himself, rather successfully, with Queen Victoria. Yes, his government passed a lot of reforming legislation in the fields of health, welfare and employment, but as Edward Young puts it: '[Home Secretary Richard] Cross and his patron Lord Derby would come up with a proposal, they would bring it to cabinet, where a number of ministers would complain – but Disraeli would step in and give Cross permission to succeed... From then on the cabinet would work through the details. Disraeli, meanwhile, would fall asleep.'

In foreign policy it was so different. Disraeli loved diplomacy and in a different life would have made a great ambassador. British prestige across the world was all that mattered to him. His triumph at the 1878 Congress of Berlin was his ultimate validation and achievement. It defined his legacy. But it was all downhill from there. The domestic reform agenda faded and like Gladstone a few years before him, he had run out of steam. He lost the 1880 election and within a year was dead.

114

SAN REMO CONFERENCE AGREES A BRITISH MANDATE IN PALESTINE

The break-up of the Ottoman Empire necessitated an international agreement on how its various territories were to be governed in future. It followed the Paris Peace Conference of 1919 at Versailles, which had largely concentrated on the future of Germany. The San Remo Conference was convened primarily to determine the future governance of parts of the Middle East based on League of Nations mandates for Palestine, Syria and Mesopotamia. The four principal Allied powers were represented by David Lloyd George (United Kingdom), Alexandre Millerand (President of the French Council of Ministers), Francesco Nitti (Prime Minister of Italy) and Robert Underwood Johnson (US Ambassador to Rome). Foreign Secretary Lord Curzon and Foreign Office Permanent Secretary Robert Vansittart were members of the British delegation.

In February 1920, the Allies had met at the Conference of London to discuss initial plans for the partitioning of the Ottoman Empire. The discussions and conclusions at San Remo led to the signing of the Treaty of Sévres in August 1920.

Under the agreement reached, the main points of the Balfour Declaration of 1917 were to be implemented, including the establishment of a national home for the Jewish people. It was also made clear that nothing should be done which might prejudice the civil and religious rights of existing communities in Palestine.

The British Mandate in Palestine lasted until 1948. For the best part of thirty years, Palestine was afflicted by protests, riots and conflict between the nationalist organizations of the Jewish and Arab communities. The year 1936 saw the start of three years of insurgency by Arabs, followed in 1944 by a four-year-long Jewish revolt.

In November 1947, the United Nations announced a plan for partition, with the establishment of two new nation states. A fortnight later the British government announced an end to the British Mandate in Palestine on 15 May 1948.The UN plan failed and the Palestine war concluded with the area being divided between the new state of Israel, the Jordanian annexation of the West Bank and Egyptian control over the Gaza Strip.

JOHN MAYNARD KEYNES DIES

It is not an exaggeration to say that John Maynard Keyes was the most influential British economist of the twentieth century. The basis of his economic theories dominated three post-war decades across the world. The fact that he died aged only sixty-two, the year after the war ended, didn't diminish his influence. Keynesian economics are currently experiencing a bit of a revival after forty years of monetarist and neo-liberal domination.

After Eton and Cambridge, Keynes joined the civil service, went back into academia and became editor of the *Economic Journal*. Just before the start of the First World War, Keynes was asked by the Treasury to provide economic advice. He rapidly became very influential and played a leading part in the Versailles Peace Conference in 1919. Keynes warned Lloyd George about the dangers of exacting too high a punishment of Germany. 'If we aim deliberately at the impoverishment of Central Europe, vengeance, I dare predict, will not limp. Nothing can then delay for very long that final war between the forces of Reaction and the despairing convulsions of Revolution, before which the horrors of the late German war will fade into nothing.' His resulting book, *The Economic Consequences of The Peace*, propelled Keynes to international renown.

During the 1920s, Keynes warned against the deflationary policies being pursued and was horrified when Britain rejoined the gold standard in 1925. He advocated reflating the economy by commissioning major public works, the very kind of policies pursued by President Roosevelt in the late 1930s.

In 1930, Keynes published his *Treatise on Money*. It recommended running a deficit to combat the effects of recession. 'For Government borrowing of one kind or another is nature's remedy... for preventing business losses from being, in so severe a slump as the present one, so great as to bring production altogether to a standstill.' He built on this theme in his *General Theory of Employment, Interest and Money*.

In 1941, Keynes became a Director of the Bank of England and was made a Liberal peer a year later. His last years were spent negotiating the Bretton Woods agreement, which regulated the post-war economic settlement.

BERNADETTE DEVLIN MAKES MAIDEN SPEECH

If I were to compile a list of my Top 10 Fiery MPs of All Time, Irish republican MP Bernadette Devlin would be near the top of it. She found it almost impossible to make a speech without exploding. Perhaps her most famous incident was when she walked across the chamber to slap Home Secretary Reginald Maudling in the face after he made an incorrect assertion about the British Army over Bloody Sunday in early 1972.

Born in Cookstown, County Tyrone, in 1947, Devlin had a difficult upbringing, her father dying when she was only nine. When her mother died, she was nineteen, so she faced having to bring up her younger siblings while studying for a university degree at Queen's in Belfast.

At the age of only twenty-one she stood in the 1969 Northern Ireland general election but failed to oust the Minister for Agriculture, James Chichester-Clark. Later that year she stood in the Mid Ulster by-election as an independent 'Unity' candidate and to everybody's surprise won, thereby becoming the youngest woman ever to be elected to the House of Commons, a record held until May 2015 when the SNP's Mhairi Black won her seat at the age of twenty.

Devlin rejected the traditions of the Irish republican movement who had always refused to take their seats – something Sinn Féin MPs still refuse to do to this day.

On 22 April, only a day before her twenty-second birthday, she took the oath and within an hour rose to make her maiden speech. Devlin denounced what she called the 'Orange State' of Ulster and demanded civil rights for Northern Ireland's Catholics. One journalist hailed it as the finest maiden speech since Benjamin Disraeli in 1837.

In December 1969, Devlin was convicted of incitement to riot at the August Battle of the Bogside and was sent to jail. She was re-elected in June 1970 and sat as an Independent Socialist.

Devlin lost her seat in February 1974. She remained active in political campaigning and in 1981 was shot nine times in her home by three members of the Ulster Freedom Fighters.

Devlin, now Bernadette McAliskey, works with migrant workers in Northern Ireland.

GLADSTONE BECOMES PRIME MINISTER FOR THE SECOND TIME

The 1880 general election campaign took place following six years of Conservative government under Prime Minister Benjamin Disraeli. Disraeli's health was failing and he was leading a tired government. He had used foreign policy and in particular events in the Ottoman Empire to distract from domestic difficulties, something ruthlessly exploited by Gladstone in his series of speeches which became known as the Midlothian Campaign. He tore Disraeli apart and re-established himself as Leader of the Liberal Party, a position nominally held by the Marquess of Hartington.

His speeches lasted up to five hours, but were curated to offer maximum exposure to local electorates and the media. It was a totally innovative, new way of campaigning.

By way of contrast, Disraeli, by now the Earl of Beaconsfield, didn't campaign at all because traditionally members of the House of Lords refrained from such vulgar activities!

The Liberals attracted 55 per cent of the vote and increased their number of seats by 104 to win a handsome majority. Queen Victoria, who loathed Gladstone, invited Lord Hartington to form a government, but he declined, since he knew Gladstone would refuse to serve. And so 'The Grand Old Man' was back.

Gladstone's foreign policy in his second administration was all over the place. He resisted calls to join the scramble for colonial expansion in Africa. Egypt was conquered, much to the irritation of the French, although Gladstone himself had little to do with this achievement. There was more unrest in Ireland after the Irish Secretary Lord Cavendish was murdered in Phoenix Park. Gladstone continued to introduce parliamentary reform and widened the franchise further under the 1884 Reform Act.

Domestic policy achievements were scarce too and in June 1885 the government fell, due to the delay in sending a mission to rescue General Gordon in Khartoum, which led to seven thousand soldiers being slaughtered. Gladstone got the blame from the press, Queen Victoria and in turn, the voters. The GOM (Grand Old Man) became the MOG (Murderer of Gordon). Gladstone was down but not out. He lost the ensuing election but was back a year later.

THE EASTER RISING BEGINS IN DUBLIN

Ever since the 1800 Act of Union between Britain and Ireland, attempts had been made to introduce forms of Home Rule. Irish nationalists took the struggle to the British government in different ways, but most were peaceful and democratic. Looking back it seems almost inevitable that at some point that would change, and that violence would be used to achieve their ends.

By the time the First World War broke out, civil war seemed inevitable. The new Government of Ireland Act was suspended.

In the end, republican rebels decided to use Easter 1916 to trigger the uprising. The moderates were duped by the Military Council, by means of a forged letter, that the British were about to arrest all republican leaders and occupy their offices.

On Good Friday, a shipment of arms from Germany was intercepted and British diplomat turned republican sympathizer Sir Roger Casement was arrested. But on Easter Sunday the Military Council met and decided nevertheless to proceed with the uprising the following day.

On Easter Monday morning, 1,200 people gathered in various locations around Dublin. At midday they launched their attacks on various buildings in the city centre including the General Post Office, where Patrick Pearse read out the Proclamation of the Irish Republic. The rebels took various bridges and railway stations and cut communications links.

The attempt to take Dublin Castle, the seat of British power, ended up in failure and this marked a turn in fortunes after British reinforcements arrived. It was now that the lack of manpower among the rebels started to tell. Martial law was declared on Tuesday evening. The rebels were in retreat. By Thursday, sixteen thousand British troops had landed at the port of Dublin. But the rebels doughtily fought on. Finally, on Saturday, 29 April, Patrick Pearse bowed to the inevitable and ordered the rebels to lay down their arms and surrender.

In all, 471 people were killed over the six days of conflict – 260 civilians, 126 members of the British armed forces, 68 rebels and 17 police. Fourteen leaders of the uprising were court-martialled and executed in May. These executions turned a rising by a small minority into a turning point after which most Irish people supported Sinn Féin republicanism.

BRITISH FORCES RETAKE SOUTH GEORGIA

The Falklands conflict really started on 19 March 1982, not 2 April. It was on that day that a group of Argentinian scrap metal merchants raised their national flag on the island of South Georgia, just under one thousand miles from the Falklands. On the day after the invasion of the Falklands, Argentinian naval forces took South Georgia.

It was decided in London that retaking South Georgia would be a psychological boost and prove to the world that Britain's resolve was unwavering. A quick win was needed, and it came only nineteen days later.

The British submarine HMS *Conqueror* arrived on 18 April and carried out reconnaissance. When the SAS and their colleagues arrived, the weather was terrible with freezing temperatures and 100 mph winds. Deep crevasses hampered progress across the island. After fifteen hours, with their tents having been swept away by the strong winds, they called to be rescued. Two of the three helicopters sent to their rescue crashed, and it was thought seventeen men had perished. The news was greeted with horror in Number 10, with Margaret Thatcher bursting into tears. It turned out that all had survived.

The SBS (Special Boat Service) also had to be evacuated from their position after one of their inflatable boats turned out to be damaged, and strong headwinds and drift ice made progress impossible. However, the Argentinian submarine *Santa Fe*, which had posed a real threat, was crippled by British helicopter missile attacks and abandoned by its crew.

Late in the evening on 25 April, Margaret Thatcher appeared outside Number 10 Downing Street alongside her Defence Secretary, John Nott. He read a statement outlining how South Georgia had been taken by British Forces.

He concluded by reading a message from the Task Group Commander, Brian Young: 'Be pleased to inform Her Majesty that the White Ensign flies alongside the Union Jack in South Georgia. God save the Queen.' When journalists started to ask questions, Mrs Thatcher flashed: 'Just rejoice at that news and congratulate our forces and the Marines.' She turned to go back into Number 10 and on the doorstep turned round and repeated the word 'Rejoice!'

120

HOUSE OF LORDS VOTES AGAINST ALLOWING TONY BENN TO RENOUNCE HIS PEERAGE

One of the few figures in politics to become more left wing with age, Anthony Wedgwood Benn's desire to transform society was shaped by his own personal background. Benn's personal history was determined by his older brother Michael's death in the Second World War in 1942. Anthony then inherited his father's hereditary peerage in 1960, becoming the 2nd Viscount Stansgate.

Benn was already a Labour MP for Bristol South East, a seat he had served for a decade. One of his key campaigns had been the right for individuals to renounce their peerage, which, at the time, was against the law. Indeed, in 1955, Benn introduced a bill on this very subject, which the House of Lords rejected.

Upon becoming a Viscount, Benn lost his right to a place in the House of Commons. Standing for Labour in the resulting 1961 by-election, he won the seat with a thirteen thousand majority over his Conservative opponent Malcolm St Clair. Benn was able to galvanize widespread support from *The Times* to the *Daily Worker* in his fight to remain an MP, with 70 per cent of the public also backing him. However, his own illegitimacy meant St Clair was declared the winner and Benn was out of the lower chamber. Upon turning up to the chamber to take his seat, Benn was refused entry by the Speaker.

For three years, Benn had to fight a battle for the right to renounce his own peerage, which eventually arrived in the 1963 Peerage Act, which was introduced on 31 July 1963. Benn renounced his peerage that same day and, thanks to getting the support of Conservatives, became the MP for Bristol South East once again.

Tony Benn would remain in Parliament until 2001, representing Chesterfield from 1984 after losing his Bristol seat in 1983. He served in several cabinet positions under Harold Wilson and in 1980 failed by a whisker to become Labour Deputy Leader. Leaving the Commons in 2001 he declared he would have 'more time for politics'.

Intriguingly, in an uncontested House of Lords by-election in 2021, Tony Benn's son Stephen joined the upper chamber as a hereditary peer.

BETTY BOOTHROYD BECOMES FIRST WOMAN SPEAKER

Beyond serving as MP for West Bromwich and West Bromwich West for twenty-seven years, entering Parliament as a Labour MP in 1973, there's not a lot that Betty Boothroyd hasn't done. She's been a chorus line dancer, a volunteer on JFK's presidential campaign, an aide to politicians both sides of the Atlantic, a councillor, an MEP and a member of the House of Lords. Most significantly, however, she became the first and so far only woman Speaker of the House of Commons in 1992.

During the eight years she occupied the Speaker's chair, she became legendary, not just for her impartiality in the role but for the tongue lashings she meted out to misbehaving MPs, her shouts of 'order' reducing cabinet ministers to quivering wrecks.

Born in 1929, the daughter of Yorkshire textile workers, she was a dancer in the aftermath of the Second World War between 1946 and 1952 for the Tiller Girls. She even appeared at the London Palladium.

After Margaret Thatcher's third election victory in 1987, Boothroyd became a Deputy Speaker under Bernard Weatherill, succeeding him in 1992. For the first time in forty years, there was a contest and election for the position of Speaker, with Boothroyd facing Conservative MP Peter Brooke, though she won by a comfortable margin.

She sought to modernize the role of Speaker, declining to wear the traditional wig and challenging the Commons officials who at first insisted MPs address her as 'Mr Speaker'.

Her iconic turns of phrase, closing prime minister's questions with 'Right, time's up', and her commitment to impartiality, as demonstrated by her casting vote in the government's successful vote on the Social Chapter of the Maastricht Treaty, made her a popular and respected character across the House.

Madam Speaker Boothroyd's selection as the first woman Speaker was an important step in creating a modern parliament. Whilst the country had already elected its first female prime minister in Margaret Thatcher, Westminster had remained male dominated, with women making up only a small minority of MPs.

In 2019, Betty Boothroyd celebrated her ninetieth birthday, having become the very personification of a national treasure.

GORDON BROWN CALLS GILLIAN DUFFY A 'BIGOT'

It is every politician's worst nightmare – you get caught making an off-guard comment, and your political career hangs in the balance. Especially if you are the prime minister...

Enter Gordon Brown. Going into the 2010 election, one he was destined to lose, he called Gillian Duffy, a sixty-five-year-old pensioner from Rochdale, a 'bigoted' woman after meeting her, failing to realize his microphone was still on. Cue a PR disaster.

Brown had been conducting a TV interview in Rochdale, a marginal seat held by the Liberal Democrats, when Ms Duffy confronted him. Asking questions about immigration and her attachment to Labour, it was surely a conversation many Labour politicians were having with voters.

The Prime Minister took another view. While saying 'how nice' the conversation had been in public, in the car, he was furious. Telling his aide Sue Nye it was a 'disaster', he referred to Duffy as 'a sort of bigoted woman'. For the broadcasters, it was political dynamite. Ironically, until she heard the Prime Minister's true views, Gillian Duffy thought the conversation had gone well.

Brown's problems only went from bad to worse in a later interview on Jeremy Vine's Radio 2 show. Unaware cameras were on, he held his head in his hands as the comments were repeated, blaming a member of staff and broadcasters for his dismissive views coming to light.

Later in the day, Brown was forced to visit Gillian Duffy's home to personally apologize. He remarked that he had 'made a mistake' and had 'misunderstood' her words.

Opposition parties during the election campaign didn't pounce on his comments as much as expected. Shadow Chancellor George Osborne simply said the comments 'spoke for themselves' while Liberal Democrat Leader Nick Clegg recognized the Prime Minister's apology, and 'that's that'.

For Gordon Brown, his fate after the 2010 election is well known (though, ironically, Rochdale was one of the few Labour gains). Gillian Duffy didn't remain out of the headlines. In 2011, she confronted in a forthright manner then Deputy Prime Minister Nick Clegg on entering a coalition with the Conservatives. During the Brexit referendum, she spoke to *Newsnight* about voting Leave.

THE ACT OF UNION IS PROCLAIMED

Let's face it, England's relationship with Scotland has always been a fraught one. With the two crowns uniting under James I in 1603, there followed a series of attempts to unite the two Kingdoms.

In the latter half of the seventeenth century, the Scottish economy was failing, not least because of measures taken by England. The Navigation Acts of the 1660s had severely impaired Scotland's ability to trade. The wars between England and Holland also didn't help, as the Dutch provided Scotland with its main export market. Charles II tried to explore joining England and Scotland together in 1669 but merely as a ruse to diminish Scotland's relationship with the Dutch.

Economic pressures mounted during the 1690s, which was a decade of economic difficulty across Europe. The bigger nations were in a better position to cope with continued recession but a series of terrible harvests led to the so-called 'Seven Ill Years' and to awful famine. Depopulation followed and in some areas 25 per cent of the population died. The crisis led to the setting up of the Bank of England and the Company of Scotland Trading to Africa and the Indies. Scottish investors were encouraged to invest in the Darien scheme, a plan to build a colony in Panama for trade with East Asia. It was a disaster. The failure of the company further weakened the Scottish economy and led to further pressure for union with England.

The 1705 Alien Act designated Scots in England as 'foreign nationals' and blocked around half of all Scottish trade by boycotting exports to England or the colonies. Scottish MPs and peers were effectively offered bribes to encourage Scotland to negotiate a Union.

Thirty-one commissioners on either side were appointed to negotiate the Union. Most were Whigs, with only one Tory chosen on the English side as most opposed Union. Agreement was reached in July 1706 and the Scottish Parliament ratified it by 110 votes to 69 in January 1707.

Scotland accepted the Hanoverian succession and could now not threaten England's national security or trading ability. What it gained was economic prosperity.

IRANIAN EMBASSY SIEGE

Nowadays we are all used to following breaking news stories live on the 24-hour news channels. In 1980, they didn't exist, but even so, the nation was agog at the events in Prince's Gate in South Kensington during the five days of the Iranian Embassy siege.

Six armed men stormed the embassy, ostensibly to demand the release of ninety-one Arab prisoners in the Khuzestan Province of Iran and full independence for the region.

Twenty-six people inside the embassy were taken hostage. The captors also demanded safe passage out of the United Kingdom, something no British government could have countenanced.

Police arrived on the scene within minutes and Home Secretary William Whitelaw convened an emergency COBRA meeting. Iran then accused Britain and America of being behind the attack.

As negotiations with the terrorists proceeded, they released several hostages due to illness and then a further two in exchange for being allowed to broadcast their demands on television. Throughout the next five days, tortuous negotiations took place, with the authorities buying time for the SAS to plan a storming of the embassy if necessary.

On day six, 5 May, things came to a head. The terrorists were now frustrated at the lack of progress in meeting their demands. At 1.45 p.m., three shots were heard from within the building. Within minutes the Home Secretary was briefed on the SAS plans to storm the building. At 6.20 three further shots were heard. One hostage had been killed and the terrorist leader, Oan Ali Mohammed, threatened to kill the rest within thirty minutes. The body of the embassy's press officer, Abbas Lavasani, was thrown out into the street. The police commander requested permission from the Home Secretary to storm the embassy. He referred it to Prime Minister Margaret Thatcher, who agreed immediately.

At 7.23 p.m., the assault began with SAS men abseiling down the rear and front of the building. By 7.40, the raid was over. Around thirty men had taken part. Five of the six hostage-takers were killed. One hostage lost his life.

Margaret Thatcher's response further burnished her reputation as an 'Iron Lady' and her government's stated policy of not giving in to terrorist demands.

MAY

LABOUR WINS LANDSLIDE MAJORITY

The Labour Party had been out of power for eighteen long years. It was only with the election of Tony Blair as Leader in the wake of the death of John Smith that anyone believed that they could win an election. As the polls closed at 10 p.m. on 1 May 1997, the Leader of the Opposition was at his constituency home, Myrobella. Who was there? Alastair Campbell, his head of Communications, along with his Chief of Staff, Jonathan Powell, and his trusted adviser Anji Hunter.

As the clock struck ten, the BBC's election night show began with these words from David Dimbleby: 'According to our exit poll, Tony Blair is to be prime minister and it's likely to be a landslide.' He wasn't wrong, yet the entire Blair entourage couldn't quite believe what the exit polls were saying. Indeed, both Blair and Campbell admitted to feeling completely flat. And then the call came through from Number 10 saying that John Major would like to speak to Tony Blair. He graciously conceded, with Blair sitting in his Myrobella office in a rugby shirt and tracksuit bottoms.

By now, of course, 1 May had become 2 May and the Labour gains were piling up. While watching TV at his count, Blair remarked to Campbell: 'What on earth have we done? This is unbelievable.' After making his victory speech at the Sedgefield count, Blair and his entourage made their way to Trimdon Labour Club, where the new Prime Minister thanked all those who had made the journey with him since he was first elected in 1983. It was soon time to get a flight from Teesside airport down to London, where crowds of Labour supporters had congregated on the South Bank of the Thames at the Royal Festival Hall. The party was in full swing. I had been hosting an election night party at my bookshop, Politico's, but at around 4 a.m. I drove along the Embankment. I could hear sounds of 'Things Can Only Get Better' blaring out. Tony Blair's motorcade had arrived. The sun was already out. A new dawn had broken, had it not?

BRITISH FORCES SINK THE GENERAL BELGRANO

The sinking of the Argentinian warship the *General Belgrano* was perhaps the most significant event of the entire Falklands War, not least because it led to 323 of those aboard losing their lives, nearly half of the total Argentinian lives lost during the conflict.

The *General Belgrano* was originally commissioned as the USS *Phoenix* before World War II and survived the Japanese attack on Pearl Harbor, but was sold to the Argentinian Navy in 1951.

Following the invasion of the Falklands, Britain imposed a Maritime Exclusion Zone of 200 miles around the islands. Any ship operating inside the zone was liable to attack from British naval forces, including submarines. The British government then informed the Argentinian government via the offices of the Swiss Embassy in Buenos Aires that 'any Argentine ship or aircraft that was considered to pose a threat to British forces would be attacked.'

The next day, Argentinian ships were ordered to seek out British task force vessels and start a 'massive attack' on them. The *General Belgrano*, which was outside the Exclusion Zone, was ordered to change course. The signal giving this order was intercepted by British intelligence services. The next day, Margaret Thatcher's war cabinet agreed to a request fron the Chief of the Defence Staff to alter the rules of engagement. This would mean an attack could be launched on the *General Belgrano* outside the Exclusion Zone. Explicit authorization was given to attack the ship.

The following day, at 3.57 p.m., the British submarine HMS *Conqueror* launched three torpedoes at the *General Belgrano*. Twenty-seven minutes later, the order to abandon ship was given. A total of 772 men were rescued, with 323 losing their lives. As a consequence of the attack the entire Argentinian navy was ordered to return to port and it played no further part in the conflict.

The legality of the attack has been questioned over many years. However, in 2003, the *General Belgrano*'s captain, Hector Bonzo, said that his ship had been manoeuvring, rather than sailing away from the Exclusion Zone. He said: 'It was absolutely not a war crime. It was an act of war, lamentably legal.'

GENERAL STRIKE BEGINS

The trade union movement has certainly made an impact in the pages of this book. Organized labour arguably brought down governments such as those of Harold Wilson (18 June 1970) and his adversary Ted Heath (28 February 1974), and very likely James Callaghan after the Winter of Discontent to bring Margaret Thatcher to power (4 May 1979). Yet for all the successes, failures, and disruption, there has only been one general strike.

In left-wing mythology, the nine days of the May 1926 General Strike rank with the 'ten days that shook the world': the Russian Revolution in October 1917. However, the facts show that it was a much less pivotal, indeed a much more British, affair.

It was caused, perhaps unsurprisingly, by bitter trouble in the coal industry – which preceded it and long outlasted it. In June 1925, owners of coal mines, faced with an exports slump following the resumption of the gold standard and the end of the French occupation of the Ruhr in Germany, announced that they would be reducing their workers' wages. At first it looked like conciliation brokered by Baldwin's Tory government would work, as on 'Red Friday', 31 July 1925, an inquiry and industry subsidy were guaranteed.

However, after the Samuel report was published in March 1926, neither unions nor employers were satisfied and hostilities resumed. The miners threatened to strike, while the TUC (going through a relatively left-wing phase) promised the support of all unions, and the government again sought to arbitrate.

However, at 1.05 a.m. on 3 May, Downing Street announced that negotiations had broken down, apparently because the print union had refused to allow the *Daily Mail* to be published due to a hostile editorial. The national strike began that day, and was solidly observed.

It was hardly a revolutionary situation, though. The government took emergency powers and controlled the media, the middle classes got to drive buses, and there were no fatalities or union leaders arrested.

The General Strike ended in a predictable compromise on 12 May, as the TUC and Baldwin's government accepted the basis of the Samuel report. The miners, also predictably, fought on; but the nationwide stoppage has never been repeated.

BRITAIN GETS ITS FIRST FEMALE PRIME MINISTER

Following the Callaghan government's defeat by one vote in a confidence motion on 28 March 1979, a general election was called the following day for 3 May. The result was a Tory majority of forty-three seats, heralding eighteen years of unbroken Conservative rule. And Margaret Thatcher became Britain's (and Europe's) first female head of government.

The Conservative campaign was dominated by a safety-first approach. The party's manifesto was pretty thin gruel, with few radical policy commitments beyond controlling the trade unions and selling council houses. The campaign was dominated by attacks on Labour under the slogan 'Labour Isn't Working'. This was the theme of a famous campaign poster and party election broadcast featuring a long dole queue. Indeed, the campaign was the first in British politics where the challenger would use photos and imagery more than set-piece speeches and interviews.

The most famous picture of the campaign was when Mrs Thatcher held a calf for a full twenty minutes while the photographers got their picture. Denis Thatcher was heard to say 'Be careful, dear, or you'll have a dead calf on your hands.' It was in every single newspaper the next day. The *Daily Express* had the headline: 'Mooove over Jim'. Job done.

There were still questions about whether Britain was ready for its first woman prime minister. In an eve-of-poll election broadcast, Margaret Thatcher addressed the issue head-on, looking into the camera for ten minutes explaining to the electorate why they could trust her.

Following the overnight results, Mrs Thatcher kissed hands with the Queen on the morning of 4 May and was then driven to Downing Street, where she paused outside the famous door and quoted the words of St Francis of Assisi: 'Where there is discord, let me bring union. Where there is error, let me bring truth. Where there is doubt, let me bring faith. Where there is despair, let me bring hope.' Before she entered the building she said: 'One last thing: in the words of Airey Neave whom we had hoped to bring here with us, "There is now work to be done."'

KARL MARX IS BORN

Karl Marx may have been born and brought up in Prussia, but he spent his last three decades living and writing in London. Seen by some as the greatest political philosopher of the last two centuries, and by others as the most dangerous and divisive thinker in human history, Karl Marx is not a man with many shades of grey. Apart from in his famously very bushy beard.

Born in Trier to a lawyer, and a Mosel vineyard owner, Marx had a comfortable childhood and upbringing. His father had converted from Judaism to the Protestant Evangelical Church and if anything was a classical liberal in political outlook. Marx left Trier to study first in Bonn and then in Berlin. Marx had considered a career in academia but decided to become a journalist, but became frustrated when his articles were censored. He moved to Paris and wrote for German-language radical publications and started to write lengthy philosophical essays. It was here that his own doctrines started to form properly. When the Prussians asked the French to close down the newspaper he was writing for, and they acquiesced, he moved to Brussels. In 1848, he was arrested for allegedly funding Belgian revolutionaries, something he always denied. He briefly moved back to Germany, hoping to see a workers' revolution, but after a year he moved to London with his wife and children and it was here that he would stay.

Marx is best known for his authorship of *The Communist Manifesto*, in 1848, and the three volumes of *Das Kapital*, two of which were published posthumously.

Some hold him responsible for the fate which befell the people of Russia after the 1917 revolution, and also for the plight of the people of various Eastern European countries between 1945 and 1990, as well as people in China, North Korea, Vietnam and many other countries in the world, who were forced under the communist yoke. Marx and Engels were the declared heroes of all communist devotees. Others will say that these forms of communism would have been anathema to Karl Marx, had he lived to see what was done in his name. We will never know.

BANK OF ENGLAND BECOMES INDEPENDENT

One of the many complaints about the New Labour government was that it did not use its early years in power, with a huge majority, to be radically transformative. Far from it. Less than a week after coming into office, sweeping aside eighteen years of Conservative government, Gordon Brown announced that the Bank of England would gain independence and have control over interest rates and monetary policy.

Support for Bank of England independence, which still remains to this day, had been long-running before Labour made their move. The Liberal Democrats, in 1992, made this a key aspect of their economic policy, while Conservative MP Nicholas Budgen proposed this as a private member's bill in 1996, though neither the government nor opposition supported it. The Bank of England, located on Threadneedle Street since 1734, had been privately owned for over 250 years before its nationalization in 1946. Though still owned by the government, its independence is granted through laws allowing the Bank to follow certain policy objectives.

The Bank's committee meets eight times a year to discuss how to keep inflation at the government's target of 2 per cent. If inflation overshoots or undershoots the target by more than 1 per cent, a letter from the Governor to the Chancellor explaining the situation is required. Indeed, accountability is provided through continued public meetings with the House of Commons Treasury Select Committee, with frequent reports explaining changes in the financial system.

Interest rates were not the sole power transferred. Responsibility for government debt management was also given in 1998 to the new Debt Management Office, which has managed government cash since 2000. However, the course of the Bank since its independence has been far from smooth. Like every other financial institution, it failed to predict the 2008 financial crash, which centred on sub-prime mortgages, something which can't have been helped by the divisions in accountability between the Treasury, Bank of England and Financial Services Authority.

Under the Conservatives, the Bank was given more power to police the City of London. The Bank itself became immensely political during the Scottish and EU referendum campaigns.

FIRST SCOTTISH PARLIAMENT FOR 300 YEARS SITS

Scotland is a nation that has perhaps never truly reconciled its relationship with the rest of the United Kingdom, or England at least. Since Scotland joined with England in 1707, there were often calls for the nation to have more devolved powers recognized through a Scottish Parliament. This desire was finally achieved in May 1999, when voters north of the border went to the polls to elect their first Members of the Scottish Parliament (MSPs) since the union came together.

The idea of a proper national parliament had long been considered. Indeed, three decades previously, a Royal Commission on the Constitution examined how the UK constitution should be structured.

A referendum in March 1979 on creating a Scottish Assembly required the support of 40 per cent of the Scottish electorate to become law. Though a scheme was supported by 52 per cent of those voting, they only represented a third of the whole electorate.

The election of Tony Blair meant a key manifesto pledge of expanding devolution could be fulfilled. In a referendum on 11 September 1997, 74.3 per cent voted in favour of a Scottish Parliament on a 60 per cent turnout.

Using additional-member proportional representation, the Parliament combined seventy-three constituency MSPs with fifty-six regional MSPs. Labour won the first elections in 1999, with their Scottish Leader, Donald Dewar, leading them to fifty-six seats, nine short of a majority. He became First Minister by forming a coalition with the Liberal Democrats on seventeen seats.

The Scottish Parliament had long been part of the road to independence for the Scottish National Party. Led by Alex Salmond, they were the second-largest party at thirty-five seats.

The Scottish Conservatives, meanwhile, with no Scottish MPs in Westminster, had vehemently opposed devolution. Not winning a single constituency seat, they picked up eighteen regional seats. Indeed, the proportional nature of the electoral system allowed smaller parties like the Scottish Socialist Party and Greens to unexpectedly win seats.

The technical devolution of powers did not occur until 1 July 1999, when the Queen opened the Scottish Parliament. Originally meeting in the General Assembly Hall of the Church of Scotland, it transferred to a new Parliament Building at Holyrood in 2005.

VICTORY IN EUROPE DAY

VE Day is the day the Allies accepted the German unconditional surrender at the end of the Second World War in Europe. The German surrender document stated: 'The German High Command will at once issue orders to all German military, naval and air authorities and to all forces under German control to cease active operations at 23.01 hours Central European time on 8 May 1945...'

That evening, more than one million people hit the streets of our towns and cities and enjoyed wild celebrations. In central London the streets were thronged with men and women, boys and girls in jubilant mood. Strangers hugged and kissed each other, not quite believing their national nightmare had ended. They massed in Trafalgar Square, Whitehall and on The Mall. The royal family appeared on the balcony of Buckingham Palace, and then they beckoned Winston Churchill forward to accept the crowd's cheers.

VE Day was memorable for so many people, and for so many different reasons. It marked the end of one era and the advent of another. Although VJ Day was still more than three months away, everyone's mind turned to the post-war era. There was an air of optimism in the country, which believed that a new world dawned. Well, it did for some, but by no means all.

Britons almost took it for granted that their influence and power in the world would remain undiminished. Too many failed to understand that Britain's role as a world superpower was changing. Standing up to Hitler had more or less bankrupted the country. The colonies were thirsting for independence. The economy had to flick the switch from being a wartime command-and-control economy and revert to an economy dominated by free markets and innovation.

Later that day, Winston Churchill also addressed crowds in Whitehall saying: 'God bless you all. This is your victory. In our long history, we have never seen a greater day than this. Everyone, man or woman, has done their best.' He invited Ernest Bevin to come forward and receive the crowd's cheers. 'No Winston,' said Bevin, 'this is your day.' And indeed it was.

BORIS JOHNSON'S TENURE AS MAYOR OF LONDON ENDS

Back in the autumn of 2007, I remember interviewing Boris Johnson on the day he announced he was standing for Mayor of London. I started off with a gentle question: What would be the first thing he would do on his first day as mayor? He hesitated, he blustered, he prevaricated. In short, he hadn't got a clue. Frankly, he didn't want the job and had only been persuaded to do it against what he thought was his better judgement.

From the first day of his campaign, Labour, and the incumbent Mayor, Ken Livingstone, underestimated him, regarding the Henley MP as a joke figure with no substance. They continued to do that until the day he won an eighty-seat majority in the 2019 general election. They failed to understand his appeal to a wide cross section of the electorate. When he walked down any high street in London, he would be mobbed. And so in May 2008, he narrowly beat Ken Livingstone to become the first Conservative Mayor of London.

Boris Johnson's biggest asset as mayor was his self-awareness. He knew what he was good at and he knew what he needed help with. So he went out and recruited a team of advisers and deputy mayors who would compensate for his weaknesses. With a few bumps and resignations in the road, it worked.

Looking back, it's difficult to say he was a bad mayor, but on the other side of the coin, what were his real achievements? He was a great showman for the city, in the same way that Rudi Giuliani was for New York. Under his stewardship crime fell. Both the murder rate and knife crime went down. Road deaths fell by 43 per cent. More affordable homes (but not nearly enough) were built than under his predecessor. A cycle hire scheme was introduced. The London Olympics were a triumph. But on the debit side there were the 2011 London riots and the waste of £46 million on a never-to-be-built garden bridge.

On 9 May 2016, Johnson voluntarily left office, for greater things. He was replaced by Labour's Sadiq Khan.

CHURCHILL BECOMES PM

With the benefit of hindsight, it may seem obvious that Winston Churchill, who has more than once been voted by the public as 'the greatest Briton ever', should have been chosen as prime minister to lead the war effort in Britain's darkest hour of danger, in May 1940. Yet it nearly didn't happen.

The 'Phoney War' that had existed in Western Europe since September 1939 was broken on 9 April 1940, when German forces invaded Denmark and Norway – five days after Prime Minister Neville Chamberlain had declared that Hitler had 'missed the bus'. The British campaign to save Norway, ironically mainly planned by Churchill as First Lord of the Admiralty, was a failure. This led to a debate in the House of Commons on 7–8 May, which Labour turned into a vote of censure.

Among those decisively speaking against Chamberlain were Lloyd George (the 'winner of the Great War'), Admiral Sir Roger Keyes (in full naval uniform) and Tory backbencher Leo Amery ('in the name of God, go!'). A total of 120 Conservatives failed to support the government. Chamberlain took soundings to see if he could lead a coalition – but Labour would not serve under him.

On 10 May, Germany invaded France and the Low Countries. Who should lead a national government in this time of the greatest crisis? Chamberlain immediately summoned the two candidates, Churchill and Lord Halifax, the Foreign Secretary. Halifax was his own choice, and probably Labour's preference too – after all, Churchill as Home Secretary had sent the troops in against the Tonypandy strikers in 1910. Who, asked Chamberlain, should he advise the King to send for?

There was a long silence. Perhaps Churchill could have broken it by saying he was prepared to serve under Halifax. But it was Halifax who spoke first, saying that a member of the Lords could not be prime minister. Churchill was duly summoned to Buckingham Palace at 6 that evening. Three days later, on 13 May, he was offering his 'blood, toil, tears and sweat'. Cometh the hour, cometh the man. Churchill may have got a lot wrong at other times in his career, but surely he was the right leader for that summer of 1940.

COALITION GOVERNMENT FORMED

'England does not love Coalitions,' said Disraeli in his 1852 budget speech. Given we've had precious few of them, it is fair to say, never a truer word has been spoken.

In early May 2010, the effects of the financial crash were still rippling across the globe and there was huge market uncertainty, which was magnified by the result of the UK's general election, held on 6 May. It produced Britain's first hung Parliament since February 1974.

The Conservatives under David Cameron gained nearly 100 seats, increasing from 210 to 307. Labour, under Gordon Brown, lost nearly 100 seats, declining from 349 to 258. The swing away from the Labour government was striking.

Nick Clegg therefore became kingmaker. The Liberal Democrat Leader since December 2007, he'd enjoyed an excellent campaign, with the leaders' debates boosting his public profile. As it happened, the Liberal Democrats lost seats, declining from sixty-two to fifty-seven. But it didn't matter. Clegg, in the style of the European politicians he so admired, spent the next five days deciding whether to support the Labour government or help the Conservatives return to power.

On 7 May, Gordon Brown returned to Downing Street, having every right to do so given he was still prime minister, while that same day, Cameron made a 'big, open and comprehensive offer' to the Liberal Democrats, aware a minority Conservative government would be unsustainable. Nick Clegg began talks with the Conservatives first – the party with the most seats – as negotiating teams discussed their points of agreement and difference.

A key sticking point was electoral reform, at the core of Liberal Democrat ideology. Clegg then opened up talks with Labour, but personality clashes between the two sides led to acrimony. Brown then threw the kitchen sink and announced he would stand down as Labour Leader by September 2010. Clegg was having none of it, and eventually Gordon Brown threw in the towel. And so it was that as daylight started to fade, the Brown family left Number 10 for the final time and David Cameron walked through the front door to start the first day of his six years and two months in power, five years of which were under the Coalition.

THE DEATH OF JOHN SMITH

Had it not been for the sad death of Labour Leader John Smith at the age of fifty-five on 12 May 1994, Labour may never have won three general elections. New Labour may never have happened. We may never have gone into Iraq.

Regarded as a decent and honest man of integrity, John Smith was widely expected to lead Labour to victory at the next general election and become prime minister. However, he approached the task markedly differently to successor Tony Blair's New Labour, instead allowing economic chaos and the mistakes of John Major's government, 'the devalued Prime Minister of a devalued Government', to drag the Conservatives in the polls, with Labour coasting into power. It's hard to imagine Smith's Labour achieving the subsequent landslide victory, with the lack of the 'Blair effect' making it unlikely he would have led the party to the subsequent repeated electoral success achieved by his successor.

Entering parliament in 1970, John Smith held the Trade Secretary role under James Callaghan, subsequently becoming Labour spokesman on economic and industrial issues when the party returned to opposition. He developed a reputation as a moderate, and was appointed shadow Chancellor by Neil Kinnock in 1987. He developed a solid reputation but an ill-judged shadow budget contributed to Labour's surprise defeat in 1992. On taking over from Neil Kinnock as party Leader, he set out to unify the left and right, abolishing the trade union block vote – without which Tony Blair may never have been able to win the leadership.

During his time as Leader, Labour secured a substantial lead in the polls, with the Conservatives suffering a major defeat in the local elections just a week before John Smith's death. Two months later, Tony Blair won the leadership by a landslide, taking up where his predecessor left off, modernizing the party with the aim of winning power from a centre-left position – rewarded by the resounding victory in the 1997 general election.

A proud Scot, John Smith had been one of devolution's most ardent supporters. Five years after his death, almost to the day, a new Scottish Parliament sat for the first time. He would have liked that.

HARRY POLLITT RESIGNS AS LEADER OF THE COMMUNIST PARTY OF GREAT BRITAIN

The Communist Party of Great Britain (CPGB) was formed in 1920, ostensibly to promote communism and the interests and policies of the Soviet Union in the United Kingdom. It had five different MPs elected between 1920 and 1950, with a high point of two being elected in 1945.

Harry Pollitt was the son of a Lancashire blacksmith. At the age of twenty-five he led a strike in Southampton and was a member of Sylvia Pankhurst's Workers' Socialist Federation. He was inspired by the Russian Revolution of 1917, and when both his parents joined the CPGB when it was formed in 1920 Harry followed suit.

A year later, he travelled to Russia, where he met Lenin. In 1925, he was jailed for a year at the Old Bailey after being found guilty of seditious libel and incitement to mutiny. In 1927, he again travelled to the Soviet Union, where he met Stalin and Bukharin. Nine years later, he became the CPGB's General Secretary with the personal approval of Stalin. 'You have taken a difficult job on, but I believe you will tackle it all right,' said the Soviet leader.

Throughout the 1930s, Pollitt received his marching orders direct from the Kremlin, along with a lot of funding.

Within ten days of the outbreak of war in 1939, Pollitt was forced to resign, after refusing to take the line dictated by the Comintern. He was reinstated when Germany invaded the Soviet Union in 1941. After the war Pollitt defended Stalin's actions in Eastern Europe, including the takeover in Czechoslovakia. When Stalin died in 1953, he was bereft, describing him as 'the greatest man of our time'. Pollitt was a member of the guard of honour at Stalin's funeral.

When Khruschev attacked Stalin's legacy, the CPGB didn't know what to do. Pollitt decided that it was time to step down. He stayed loyal to Stalin until the day he died, in June 1960. A portrait of Stalin still hung above his living-room mantelpiece.

The Communist Party of Great Britain was disbanded in 1991 after the fall of communism in Russia.

ISRAEL ANNOUNCES INDEPENDENCE FROM BRITAIN

In 1917, the Balfour Declaration made clear that Britain would welcome the establishment of a Jewish homeland in Palestine, but only if it would not prejudice the civil and religious rights of existing communities there.

Once the British Mandate for Palestine was established in 1922, tensions immediately arose, not just within the British government, but also within Palestine itself. In 1937, the Peel Commission suggested splitting Palestine into two, but the proposal was rejected, leading to more violence.

In the immediate aftermath of the Second World War, violence in Palestine increased. On 22 July 1946, the British Administrative HQ in Palestine at the King David Hotel in Jerusalem was bombed by the militant Zionist group Irgun, killing ninety-one. Various peace initiatives failed as the Jewish side would not accept any solution which didn't include a Jewish state. The Palestinians, likewise, insisted on a single Palestinian state under Arab rule.

At the same time, attacks on British interests and personnel were increasing, and in September 1947, Attlee decided enough was enough and that Britain would withdraw completely. He decided to hand the issue over to the United Nations which, in November, passed a resolution suggesting giving 56 per cent of the land to the Jewish population, with Jerusalem being governed internationally and separate from a Jewish state. This plan was rejected by Arabs but it was passed by thirty-three votes to thirteen nevertheless. Strikes and violence immediately broke out in Jerusalem, and this rapidly evolved into a full-scale civil war. Britain then announced the British Mandate would end on 15 May the next year.

On 14 May, David Ben-Gurion declared the creation of the independent state of Israel. A day later, forces from Arab countries entered the territory with the express aim of preventing the establishment of a Jewish state. It provoked a full Arab–Israeli war which only ended a year later with Jordan annexing the West Bank and Egypt continuing to occupy the Gaza Strip, thereby creating the conditions for a seemingly semi-permanent conflict.

Meanwhile, Britain sat on the sidelines and did nothing.

BRITAIN EXPLODES FIRST HYDROGEN BOMB ON CHRISTMAS ISLAND

When Winston Churchill announced on 26 February 1952 that Britain had acquired an atomic bomb, what he didn't admit was that the country was years behind the US in developing the technology. But by 1957 things had moved on and Britain was ready to commence a series of nuclear tests, which became known as Operation Grapple.

Grapple was a series of nuclear weapons tests that took place on Malden Island and Christmas Island, part of the Gilbert and Ellice Islands, in the Pacific Ocean. There were nine nuclear test explosions in all. Britain thus became the third nuclear power in the world after the United States and the Soviet Union. Perhaps the most important consequence of this was the signing the following year of the US–UK Mutual Defence Agreement. After World War II America had abruptly broken off its joint arrangement with Britain, but it was now in its own interest to restore it.

Prime Minister Anthony Eden backed the tests by saying in a radio address: 'You cannot prove a bomb until it has exploded. Nobody can know whether it is effective or not until it has been tested.'

These tests, which ended in the autumn of 1958, were the first and last atmospheric nuclear tests Britain ever carried out. They were an outstanding success.

Christmas Island (now known as Kiritimati) was chosen for its remoteness and because it had no indigenous population. It was 1,450 miles from Tahiti, 1,335 miles from Honolulu and 4,000 miles from Sydney. It was claimed by both Britain and the United States, which meant Britain had to get approval for the tests from the Americans.

Opinion is divided on the medical effects on those who witnessed the explosions. In 2005, a study by Massey University, commissioned by veterans in New Zealand, found no effects but they then tested for 'chromosome translocation' and a higher rate of abnormality was discovered. Other studies have proved to be inconclusive. The Ministry of Defence continues to maintain that few people were exposed to radiation. In 1993, two veterans sued for damages but their case failed by five votes to four at the European Court of Human Rights.

JOHN GUMMER FEEDS HIS DAUGHTER A BEEFBURGER

In politics, it's generally a poor idea for politicians to get their children involved. Though it may make a politician seem more human, their offspring are unlikely to thank them later on. However, in May 1990, Agriculture minister John Gummer turned this rule completely on its head by trying to feed a beefburger to his four-year-old daughter, Cordelia, in his Suffolk constituency.

Why would this event be newsworthy? Well, in 1990, Bovine spongiform encephalopathy (BSE), commonly known as 'mad cow disease', was rife in the UK. Having repeatedly tried to reassure the public that British beef was safe, the government resorted to physically showing a minister trying to feed their child a beefburger, to convince the British public it was perfectly safe to do so and show that he didn't believe BSE could be transmitted to humans.

While his daughter refused, Gummer took a large bite and said the beef was 'absolutely delicious'. Desperate to avoid panic, Gummer had taken advice from scientific and medical experts when arguing beef could be 'eaten safely by everyone, both adults and children, including patients in hospital'. The first case of BSE in cattle had been detected four years earlier and, by the time of the infamous burger feeding, cases stood at fourteen thousand.

Government policy had always been to slaughter any animals found with the disease, to stop them entering the food chain, with 37,000 slaughtered in one year alone. However, this had not prevented fears that the disease could enter humans potentially leading to the fatal brain condition Creutzfeldt-Jakob disease (CJD). Such anxiety had led twenty education authorities to boycott beef products, taking them off the menus of hundreds of schools.

By 1992, three out of every thousand cows in Britain had BSE. Despite this, John Gummer continued to argue that his move had been the correct decision, always defining safety around whether he would be happy for his children to eat the meat.

In 1996, the government admitted a link between BSE and CJD did exist. With the EU banning the export of British beef for a decade, John Gummer's infamous photo opportunity became the one thing he is most remembered for.

ANTHONY EDEN GIVES FIRST PARTY ELECTION BROADCAST

Back in 1951, Sir Anthony Eden had made the first ever Conservative party political broadcast. Having become prime minister on 6 April 1955, Eden called a snap general election in order to get his own mandate. Eight days before polling day, Eden appeared in a remarkable election broadcast modelled on one that Dwight Eisenhower had fronted in the USA. He wrote later: 'I attached first importance to television as a medium' and was really the first UK politician to exploit it in any meaningful way. Stanley Baldwin had appeared in election films but looked incredibly stiff and uncomfortable. Eden, however, loved the camera. His appearances through the 1955 campaign had been watched by a third of the population.

According to the BBC, the Labour Party's TV appearances 'appeared shambolic and unexciting'. That was to change in 1959 when Anthony Wedgwood Benn, the Peter Mandelson of his day, took over their TV broadcasts.

This was no normal party election broadcast. Nowadays they last around five minutes. This one lasted half an hour. It took the form of Eden and four senior ministers (Harold Macmillan, Rab Butler, Iain Macleod and Sir Walter Monckton) answering questions from ten newspaper editors, including Hugh Cudlipp from the *Daily Mirror*. He asked about what he called the common impression that Eden was 'less well versed in home than in foreign affairs', Eden smiled and said it was 'a perfectly fair criticism'.

With the advent of the internet and social media, party political (or election) broadcasts have taken on a diminished significance. The parties concentrate their efforts on short, sharp Facebook adverts, which are designed to go viral. They cost less to make than a five-minute election broadcast and often reach more people.

Over the years there have been some classic political broadcasts, including Tony Benn swivelling round in his chair to face the camera in 1959, John Cleese trying to explain the virtues of proportional representation for the SDP, and John Major paying a visit to his childhood Brixton home in 1992. Happy days.

EUROPEAN CONVENTION ON HUMAN RIGHTS COMES INTO FORCE

There are many myths about the European Convention on Human Rights (ECHR). Drafted in the aftermath of World War II, its aim was to guarantee basic human rights in all the countries in Europe that signed up to it. It is most emphatically not a part of the European Union bureaucracy and is an entirely separate entity, not least since it pre-dates the then European Economic Community.

The Convention established the ECHR, which people can appeal to once they have exhausted their own domestic court procedures, in terms of potential human rights violations.

The original aims of the Convention were twofold. Firstly, to protect European citizens from the kind of human rights violations they had been subjected to in World War II, and secondly, to be a response to the human rights abuses perpetrated by Stalin's forces across Central and Eastern Europe in the immediate aftermath of the war, and to protect citizens from communist subversion. It outlines fundamental rights including the right to life, the right to a fair trial and the right to freedom of expression.

Britain played a leading part in the drafting and creation of the Convention, with Sir David Maxwell Fyfe, a Conservative MP and former prosecutor at the Nuremberg trials, one of the key figures in the process. The Convention was signed on 4 November 1950 in Rome. It took legal force on 3 September 1953 and was signed into British law on 18 May 1954.

Various ECHR judgements have proved to be controversial in the UK, most notably on prisoners' voting rights. The Conservative Party manifesto in 2019 promised to repeal the Human Rights Act and replace it. This led to speculation that Britain might withdraw from the ECHR, although this is denied by senior government ministers.

The ECHR should not be confused with the European Charter of Fundamental Rights (ECFR), which is part of EU law. This ceased to apply when Britain left the EU in January 2021. However, the human rights protections guaranteed by the ECFR continue to apply to the UK under 'retained EU law'.

SPEAKER MICHAEL MARTIN IS FORCED TO QUIT

There's an old saying in politics, that when a politician's spokesperson becomes the story, it's time for the spokesperson to leave. The same can be said for the Speaker of the House of Commons. A position of political impartiality, his or her role is not to generate attention or overshadow the proceedings of the House.

Michael Martin managed this for most of his eight and a half years as Speaker between 2000 and 2009. His departure, however, was tainted with disgrace as he became the first speaker in more than two centuries to be forced out, and it was due to the MPs' expenses scandal.

Martin was specifically accused of trying to block efforts to release details of MPs' expenses, alongside calling for a police investigation into the *Daily Telegraph* leak. His own allowance showed members of his family being flown in business class from Glasgow to London, though these figures had been publicly declared prior to the scandal.

There had been accusations of Martin's incompetence as Speaker since he first took office, with Tory backbencher Douglas Carswell leading a group of twenty-three MPs signing a motion calling for his departure. Martin's reputation had been utterly diminished when he apologized for his role in the expenses scandal, with MPs across all parties telling him to consider his position.

Michael Martin spoke when resigning about the House being 'at its best' when unity was present, using this justification to step down. His allies, including Labour MP Jim Sheridan, suggested an anti-Catholic conspiracy was taking place, calling for parliamentary sketchwriters who had tormented Martin to be censured.

His departure came as Gordon Brown sought to manage the scandal and outrage felt by the public. Brown proposed the transfer of powers over MPs' pay, expenses and pensions to an independent regulator.

Michael Martin was replaced as Speaker by the reforming John Bercow, who served until 2019. His tenure was also not without controversy, with accusations of bullying and bias during the Brexit process. It is now up to Lindsay Hoyle, the present Speaker, to prove the reputation of the Speaker can be redeemed.

THIRD READING OF THE MAASTRICHT BILL IN THE HOUSE OF COMMONS

The Maastricht Treaty heralded the transformation of the European Economic Community into the European Union, but it went far further than that. It heralded 'a new stage in the process of European integration' with a shared European citizenship, provisions for the future introduction of a single currency and also a common foreign and security policy. It contained a 'social chapter' which sought to harmonize employment conditions and regulations. No wonder it proved so controversial in the United Kingdom, and indeed elsewhere. British prime minister John Major negotiated a derogation from both the social chapter and the obligation to join a Single Currency.

Several member states found it difficult to get the ratification process through their parliaments or national referendums. Denmark had to hold a second referendum to get it through, but it was in Britain that there were real problems, despite John Major's opt-outs.

At the second reading of the European Communities Bill in May 1992, twenty-two Conservative MPs rebelled against their own government, egged on by former prime minister Margaret Thatcher, even though she had praised John Major for his skill in negotiating the opt-outs. At the time, the government's majority was only eighteen and Major had to rely on opposition support to get the Bill through to Committee stage. Eurosceptic Conservatives launched a guerrilla campaign to scupper the Bill in the Committee stage and they inflicted several important defeats.

Before the Bill could go to the House of Lords it had to pass its third reading in the Commons. Labour's official policy was to abstain, but in fact sixty-six Labour MPs voted against it and five voted in favour. But it passed easily by 292 to 112. Two months later, the government suffered a defeat at the final stage of the Bill. The next day, it resubmitted the vote under a confidence motion, which passed.

This was a fratricidal period in the Conservative Party. John Major withdrew the whip from a dozen MPs who continually rebelled. Maastricht radicalized a lot of latent Eurosceptics on the right, many of whom went on to form the Anti-Federalist League, and ultimately UKIP.

ANTONY LAMBTON RESIGNS IN CALL GIRL SCANDAL

Only ten years earlier, the Minister for War, John Profumo, had resigned over his affair with a call girl, Christine Keeler. This scandal wasn't quite on that scale, but it had everything that a tabloid newspaper would want – an aristocratic sex-mad government minister and a high-class call girl who specialized in S&M. The minister was Lord Lambton, who had renounced his title of the Earl of Durham in order to remain an MP in the House of Commons. The call girl was Norma Levy, who unlike Christine Keeler had not been sleeping with a Russian.

After being invalided out of the Army in the Second World War, Viscount Lambton, as he was then called, became an MP in 1951. His ascent up the greasy pole was slow and a huge matter of frustration for him. In 1970, Prime Minister Edward Heath appointed him Parliamentary Under Secretary of State, in charge of the Navy, at the Ministry of Defence. The job bored him and offered little challenge to what he regarded as his superior intellect.

In early 1973, the *News of the World* was tipped off by Norma Levy's husband that Lambton was enjoying hook-ups with his wife. They installed a cameraman in a wardrobe, who filmed the noble Lord in bed with Levy and a friend of hers, while enjoying a spliff. Downing Street was alerted and Lambton immediately resigned. An inquiry concluded there had been no security breaches, while Lambton claimed it was the pressure of office which drove him to have sex with Levy. He later claimed that the pressure over the renunciation of his title and the controversy over him continuing to call himself Viscount Lambton led him to engaging in 'frantic' activities like gardening and debauched sex.

The Leader of the House of Lords, the Earl Jellicoe, also got caught up in the scandal, as it turned out he was also a client of Levy's. He too fell on his sword and quit the government.

Lambton died in 2006 having lived the rest of his life in Tuscany, concentrating on gardening and more debauchery.

OPENING BATTLE OF THE WARS OF THE ROSES

Politics is about power, about 'who runs the country'. Perhaps we should be more grateful for our modern party system aiming to contest democratic elections, when we consider how differently things were done in the fifteenth century.

The first battle of what we now call the Wars of the Roses took place at St Albans, Hertfordshire. It is not quite as simple as a two-party contest, as it were, between the Houses of York and Lancaster. There were shifting coalitions and party splits as well as changes of government.

The underlying cause of the strife was the great weakness in a monarchic age of the Lancastrian King, Henry VI. He was a dramatic contrast to his father, the hero of Agincourt and Shakespeare, who died of dysentery at the age of thirty-five in 1422, leaving an heir only nine months old. Even when he reached his majority, Henry VI was far more interested in religion and architecture than effective government. What is more, from 1453 for over a year Henry fell into a catatonic trance.

The main contenders to fill the power vacuum were the King's cousin the Duke of Somerset and Richard, Duke of York. In March 1454, the Lords elected York as Protector, and Somerset went to the Tower. After Henry VI awakened on Christmas Day, Somerset was restored to power and York dismissed.

York now took up arms, and clashed at St Albans with the royal forces on 22 May 1455. The King was present but had never seen battle, and Somerset led his army. This was a rare urban battle, fought in the town centre. Nowhere near as many people were killed as at Towton, for example, in 1461, the bloodiest battle on British soil. However, St Albans was a decisive victory for York. Somerset was killed and Henry VI captured.

York did not yet claim the crown itself, but from 1460 he was to. Though Duke Richard was killed at Wakefield in 1460, his son did oust Henry VI the next year to become Edward IV – though that was far from the end of the story begun at St Albans.

MARTIN MCGUINNESS IS BORN

Terrorist or freedom fighter? Born in Londonderry on 23 May 1950, McGuinness became a key figure within both the Irish Republican Army (IRA) and its political wing, Sinn Féin.

McGuinness rose to notoriety after leaving his trainee apprenticeship as a butcher. Aged just nineteen, he joined the IRA and quickly gained influence. Second-in-command during Bloody Sunday in 1972, he oversaw the increase in membership following the shooting of thirteen unarmed civil rights demonstrators by British soldiers. That same year, McGuinness was part of a six-man delegation secretly flown to London for face-to-face negotiations with William Whitelaw, the Northern Ireland Secretary.

Imprisoned for six months in 1973 for being caught in a car with a large quantity of explosives, McGuinness contested seats for the House of Commons on numerous occasions. He won the constituency of Mid Ulster in 1997, which he held in three subsequent elections (though never took up his seat).

The chief negotiator with the British government, he was a key player in the talks which led to the Good Friday Agreement in April 1998. Sinn Féin became part of a coalition government to rule Northern Ireland, where McGuinness became Education Minister.

After a five-year suspension due to disagreements over policing, the Northern Ireland executive was restored in 2007 with Martin McGuinness as Deputy First Minister, a position he would hold for the next decade. This required him to work with the Reverend Ian Paisley, Leader of the DUP and previously his sworn enemy. The two were dubbed 'the Chuckle brothers' for their cheerful ability to put differences aside.

In June 2012, McGuinness was pictured shaking hands with the Queen during her visit to Belfast. It was quite a moment in the ongoing reconciliation between nationalists and unionists in Northern Ireland.

McGuinness resigned as Deputy First Minister when First Minister Arlene Foster refused to temporarily step down in January 2017 over the 'cash for ash' scandal. Following his resignation, McGuinness announced he was suffering from amyloidosis, a disease causing abnormal protein deposits in his organs and tissue. The disease killed him in March 2017, aged only sixty-six.

SECTION 28 COMES INTO LAW

The common perception nowadays is that Margaret Thatcher was a bigoted anti-gay prime minister. Examining the notorious Section 28 issue, it's an easy conclusion to come to. The truth, however, is somewhat more nuanced. As a relatively new MP and even newer opposition front bencher, Margaret Thatcher was one of only six Conservative MPs to support the decriminalization of homosexuality in 1967. Many of her personal staff were gay, and she always had an unusually tolerant attitude to sexual scandals.

However, one cannot ignore the fact that it was her government which incorporated Section 28 into the Local Government Bill in 1988.

Homosexuality formed no part of sex education in schools in the 1980s. In the mid 1980s, the Aids pandemic was fuelling anti-gay attitudes in society. The Greater London Council started funding LGBT groups, and right-wing newspapers highlighted a children's book called *Jenny Lives with Eric and Martin* being available in a school library in London. A Conservative MP, Dame Jill Knight, was suitably outraged and vowed to put a stop to it.

So what was Section 28? Essentially, it prohibited the 'promotion' of homosexuality by local authorities and schools. The legislation said that a local authority 'shall not intentionally promote homosexuality or publish material with the intention of promoting homosexuality' or 'promote the teaching in any maintained school of the acceptability of homosexuality as a pretended family relationship'. In today's society these would be incendiary things to say. By the standard social norms of the time, they were mainstream. However, gay campaigning groups fought a spirited campaign against Section 28, arguing it was iniquitous, an over the top reaction to a problem which didn't exist. Their pleas fell on deaf ears, with very few Conservative MPs prepared to defy the whip.

In its fifteen years of operation, there wasn't a single prosecution under Section 28. However, schools and teachers felt inhibited and many gay groups ceased or curtailed their activities in helping young people come to terms with their sexuality.

Section 28 was repealed in Scotland in June 2000 and in England and Wales in November 2003.

RICHARD DIMBLEBY IS BORN

Dimbleby is a surname synonymous with broadcasting legends. While many will know David Dimbleby for anchoring BBC general election programmes and *Question Time*, and Jonathan Dimbleby expertly hosted *Any Questions* for more than three decades, they have their father, Richard Dimbleby, to thank for offering the belief that a career in broadcasting was possible.

Born in 1913, Richard Dimbleby began his career in 1931 on the *Richmond and Twickenham Times*, which had been purchased by his grandfather in 1894. Joining the BBC as a radio news reporter in 1936, Richard Dimbleby became the corporation's first war correspondent, accompanying British forces to France, where he broadcast from the Normandy beaches.

Indeed, given television ownership did not become widespread among the public until the Queen's coronation in 1953, radio broadcasting was of extra importance. Richard Dimbleby, as an observer, was able to fly with RAF Bomber Command, even to Berlin. During the Bergen-Belsen concentration camp liberation, Dimbleby made a graphic audio recording, with the BBC deciding initially not to broadcast his dispatch. Only the threat of resignation caused a U-turn four days later.

Like his sons, Richard Dimbleby later became a well-known face on the news, commentating on public events like the funerals of George VI, John F. Kennedy and Winston Churchill. That didn't stop his appetite for lighter news, with Dimbleby also engaging in the first Eurovision television relay in 1951 and broadcasting from the Soviet Union in 1961.

Dimbleby became 'the voice of the nation'. Indeed, Richard's humorous side was never far away, with *Panorama* on 1 April 1957 featuring a family from Switzerland picking spaghetti out of a tree.

His career was brought to a tragic end aged just fifty-two in December 1965, when he died of testicular cancer. Diagnosed five years earlier, Dimbleby went public with his diagnosis in 1962 having presented a documentary on the correlation between smoking and lung cancer. Survived by his wife, Dilys, and four children – including David and Jonathan – he was commemorated by the Richard Dimbleby Cancer Fund, created to ensure investment went into cancer cures.

UKIP WINS EUROPEAN PARLIAMENT ELECTION

Having announced a referendum on the UK's membership of the European Union in his January 2013 Bloomberg Speech, David Cameron soon came to realize that he hadn't cauterized the Eurosceptic wound. If the 2014 European elections didn't teach him that, nothing would.

Voting took place on 22 May, but the results weren't announced until after polls closed in the rest of Europe at 10 p.m. on Sunday, 25 May. By the time the final Scottish results came through on the Monday lunchtime, it was clear that the governing Coalition parties had suffered a humiliating setback. The Conservatives scored 23 per cent of the vote, losing seven of their twenty-six seats. The Liberal Democrats got only 7 per cent and lost eleven of their twelve seats, as well as coming behind the Greens in the popular vote. Labour put on seven seats, but for the first time since 1984 the main opposition party didn't top the poll. That accolade went to Nigel Farage's United Kingdom Independence Party (UKIP). It got 27 per cent of the votes and finished up with twenty-four MEPs. It was the first time since 1910 that either the Conservatives or Labour hadn't come first in a national election.

European elections had never excited the British public. In fact, all polls showed that European issues never really featured among the top ten priorities of the British people. The issue excited people on the extremes of the argument, but as far as the general electorate were concerned, they were more interested in domestic political and economic issues.

The one exciting moment of the campaign came when Deputy Prime Minister Nick Clegg challenged Nigel Farage to two live debates on the whole issue of the UK's membership of the EU. It was a decision he was to regret, given that after both debates around two thirds of the people watching or listening said Farage had won.

Few commentators realized the medium-term implications of this. Revelling in the fact that the Prime Minister had taken a good kicking, they concentrated on how he might get back on track, rather than gazing into their crystal balls and analysing how this vote might work in a Brexit referendum.

OLIVER CROMWELL REFUSES THE TITLE OF KING OF ENGLAND

In 2002, Oliver Cromwell was chosen as one of the greatest Britons of all time in a BBC poll. Some historians view him as a libertarian hero, but there are even more who see him as a genocidal dictator. What is in no doubt is that he is one of the most important political figures in the entirety of British history. His brief eleven-year rule as Lord Protector did more than anything in the previous few centuries to promote the power and influence of Parliament and curtail the monarchy. Even when the monarchy was restored in 1660, there were many things the new monarch dare not do.

Oliver Cromwell's New Model Army had swept him to power in 1649 following the conclusion of the English Civil War and the execution of King Charles I. He dominated the short-lived Commonwealth of England (1649–53), conquering Ireland in the process. In 1653, he was invited to become Lord Protector after he forcibly dismissed the Rump Parliament.

Given that Cromwell had played a large part in ending the monarchy in 1649, it was somewhat ironic that Parliament invited him to become King in 1657. He seriously considered it for around six weeks. On 13 April, he made clear that his inclination was to refuse: 'I would not seek to set up that which Providence hath destroyed and laid in the dust, and I would not build Jericho again.' But it wasn't until 27 May that he formally declined. On 26 June, he was reinstalled as Lord Protector in a grand ceremony in Westminster Hall, outside of which his statue now stands. To some, it was akin to a regal coronation. It was decided that the office of Lord Protector would not be hereditary, but the incumbent would name their successor.

In his final year, Cromwell increasingly took on the trappings of a pseudo-monarch. He would be known today as a benevolent dictator, without being especially benevolent. He was to die in Whitehall on 3 September 1658 at the age of fifty-nine from malaria and kidney complications. He was succeeded by his son Richard. So much for not being a hereditary monarch.

NEVILLE CHAMBERLAIN BECOMES PRIME MINISTER

When Stanley Baldwin informed the King that he would resign shortly after his coronation, there was only one candidate to replace him – the Chancellor of the Exchequer, Neville Chamberlain. There were no leadership elections in those days; a leader 'emerged'. Baldwin recommended that George VI should summon Chamberlain, and he duly did.

Neville Chamberlain was the son of Joseph Chamberlain and brother of Austen, who sadly never saw his brother reach the ultimate office, having died two months earlier.

Neville was a late entrant to the House of Commons, joining the green benches in 1919 at the age of forty-nine. He remains the oldest man ever to be elected to the House of Commons and then go on to be prime minister.

Chamberlain had worked in the family business and in local government before becoming Director of National Service in the middle of World War I. He initially turned down a ministerial post under Lloyd George but in 1922 became Postmaster General, followed by a rapid promotion to Minister for Health in March 1923. However, when Bonar Law resigned because of ill health and Baldwin took over, he asked Chamberlain to take over as Chancellor. In eighteen months he had gone from backbencher to Chancellor. However, he only served for five months. When the Conservatives were returned to power in 1924, he asked to go back to be Minister for Health, where he remained until 1929, impressing with his radical reforms.

In 1931, Chamberlain once again became Chancellor. He continued the austerity policies of his Labour predecessor, Philip Snowden, and continued to cut expenditure, including in defence. In 1935, he reversed that policy.

Chamberlain is best known for his policy of appeasing dictators. It should not be forgotten that after the Munich Conference with Hitler, where he returned waving a piece of paper declaring it was 'peace for our time', he was hugely popular both with his MPs and the people. When war broke out in September 1939, he was the wrong man in the wrong job, and in May 1940 he was forced to resign, and Winston Churchill took over. Chamberlain died only six months later.

PAUL BOATENG BECOMES BRITAIN'S FIRST BLACK CABINET MINISTER

When four black MPs were elected for Labour in 1987, it was always odds-on that Paul Boateng would be the first of them to make it to the top. A young lawyer, he had already carved out a reputation as a leading member of the Greater London Council under Ken Livingstone.

Boateng was always a bit of a showman, ready with a pithy soundbite for the media and this was how he rapidly built a profile. On his election for Brent South he proclaimed: 'We can never be free in Brent until South Africa is free too. Today Brent South, tomorrow Soweto!'

Boateng knew, though, that in order to get to the top, he would have to temper both his views and his behaviour. Almost overnight he turned from left-wing firebrand into the very model of a moderate MP. He refused to join a Parliamentary Black Caucus set up by the other three black MPs elected in 1987, Diane Abbott, Bernie Grant and Keith Vaz. Only two years after being elected Labour Leader, Neil Kinnock appointed him to the front bench and made him a Treasury spokesman. Three years later, he switched to shadow the Lord Chancellor's Department, a post he held until 1997.

After Tony Blair's landslide in May 1997, Boateng became Britain's first ever black government minister. Over the next five years, he held a succession of posts in Health and the Home Office, where he was seen as the prime proponent of Tony Blair's mantra: tough on crime, tough on the causes of crime. After the 2001 election, he was appointed Financial Secretary to the Treasury, and a year later was promoted to the cabinet as Chief Secretary. Prior to that he had turned down the opportunity to stand for Mayor of London.

In cabinet, Boateng led two spending reviews, promoted the cause of international aid to Africa and the Millennium Development Goals. He surprised everyone by announcing he wouldn't stand in the 2005 general election. He was subsequently appointed to be Britain's High Commissioner in South Africa, a post he would hold until 2009. He was made a peer in 2010.

LABOUR WINS GENERAL ELECTION

The 1929 general election marked the second time that Labour formed a government, but as in the first they did not secure an overall majority. Therefore, the achievements of their early governments, both led by Ramsay MacDonald, were perforce limited. That of 1924 had only lasted eight months. In the May 1929 results, Labour were at least the largest party. They won 287 out of the 615 constituencies – still a substantial minority, but ahead of the 260 for the Conservatives and 59 for the Liberals.

The election had been called by Prime Minister Stanley Baldwin as the five-year term limit was approaching, but it was from a position of weakness. The Tory election slogan of 'Safety First' rang hollow. The previous five years had seen the worst industrial strife in modern British history, centred on the unique 1926 General Strike. Unemployment was rising in 1929. It was a classic 'time for a change' election, and MacDonald and Labour had already shown in their 1924 government that they would not be extreme or incompetent.

Another feature of the 1929 UK election was that it was actually the first under genuine universal and equal suffrage. Until 1928, only women aged over thirty had been allowed to vote. Now the age was twenty-one for all. Although much was made of the so called 'flapper vote' for young women, there was no detectable electoral impact.

Labour's 140 gains included many seats they had never won before, as for the first time they broke out of inner city, mining and Celtic heartlands and took 'middle England' constituencies such as Reading, Swindon and Peterborough. The Liberals were briefly reunited under Lloyd George after his long split with Asquith, and gained nineteen seats in something of an 'Indian Summer' as they campaigned on a dynamic programme, 'We Can Conquer Unemployment', based on their radical Yellow Book of 1928.

However, the political landscape was shortly to be transformed, after an event later in 1929, the Wall Street Crash. The associated economic depression was to impact profoundly, and negatively, the fortunes of both Labour and Liberal parties, as in 1931 MacDonald's government was transformed into a Tory-dominated coalition.

THE CLOCK CONTROLLING BIG BEN IS STARTED

Contrary to what most people think, Big Ben is the name of the bell which bongs on the hour. It is not the name of the clock tower, or indeed the clock mechanism which controls the bongs. Until 2012, the tower was known as the Clock Tower or St Stephen's Tower, but it was renamed the Elizabeth Tower to commemorate Her Majesty's Diamond Jubilee. The tower at the House of Lords end of the building was named the Victoria Tower after Queen Victoria's own Diamond Jubilee in 1897.

The tower was commissioned in 1845 as part of the renovation of much of the Palace of Westminster after the Great Fire of 1834. Charles Barry was the building's chief architect, but for the Tower he asked Augustus Pugin to come up with the design. Construction began in September 1845. It took fourteen years to complete.

The belfry contains four smaller bells plus the bell which became known as Big Ben. No one knows for certain but it was named after either Sir Benjamin Hall, who oversaw the installation, or Benjamin Caunt, a well-known heavyweight boxer. At the time of its installation it was the biggest bell in the world, at 13.7 tons.

The clock mechanism was started on 31 May 1859, with Big Ben bonging for the first time in July. However, in September 1859, the bell cracked at the point the hammer hit. The bell was out of action for three months before a repair was effected. It wasn't until 2007 that a new hammer was put in.

On 10 May 1941, a German plane bombed the House of Commons, destroying the Commons chamber, but also damaging two faces of the clock.

In 1965, the bells were silenced during the funeral of Sir Winston Churchill, but by and large, the only other times the clock has stopped were due to freezing weather or snow accummulations on the dials.

In 2017, a four-year programme of restoration was commenced, with the entire tower encased in scaffolding. The clock faces were restored and a lift was installed for the first time.

JUNE

COD WAR WITH ICELAND ENDS

The Cod Wars took place in the mid twentieth century over a period of twenty years. They weren't traditional wars, but a series of clashes between the British and Icelandic fishermen over fishing rights in the waters off the coast of Iceland. The term was used by a Fleet Street journalist in their reporting of the story and has stuck ever since.

The series of disputes was triggered on 1 September 1958 by Iceland's decision to extend its fishing grounds to twelve nautical miles from the country's coast, from the original four nautical miles. Ignored by the British vessels, which refused to comply with the unilateral decision, this led to confrontations with Icelandic boats and subsequently the deployment of Royal Navy warships to protect the British fishermen.

Although a deal was eventually struck in 1961 between the two sides to agree a common set of rules, in 1972 Iceland's government decided to extend its fishing grounds to fifty nautical miles. This subsequently led to more clashes between the two sides. In late 1973, a temporary deal was struck to avoid further confrontations, which set annual limits on how much fish British trawlers were allowed to catch.

The agreement expired in late 1975 and Iceland's government unilaterally extended its fishing territory once again, this time to two hundred nautical miles off the country's coast. The third, and final, Cod War began. NATO played a role in mediating negotiations between the British and Icelandic sides. In June 1976, another deal was agreed, in which the British accepted the Icelandic expansion and also a quota on the quantity of fish they were allowed to catch, effectively resulting in another Icelandic victory.

A number of other European states were involved in the clashes, including West Germany, Denmark and Belgium. Only one death has been reported as a result of the clashes; an Icelandic engineer who was accidentally killed after a collision between a Royal Navy ship and an Icelandic boat.

Decades later, in 2001, the UK government agreed to a compensation scheme for British trawlermen and the loss of their livelihoods caused by the rules agreed around fishing rights in the region.

FIRST MEETING OF THE TUC IN MANCHESTER

The birthplace of the Trades Union Congress (TUC) was the Mechanics' Institute, which also saw the origins of the University of Manchester and Manchester Metropolitan University. The first meeting, occurring on Princess Street in June 1868, brought together different representatives to see how collective action and the fight for workers' rights could be properly debated.

The creation came at a time when Manchester was becoming heavily industrialized, with factories and mills employing people without any health and safety regulation and few rights at work.

Though unions had been operating in the UK before the first meeting of the Congress, the acceleration of the Industrial Revolution, combined with the potential for employer greed, meant that regulation was difficult to achieve.

It is remarkable how many topics from the first TUC debate could still be discussed today. Though only brief handwritten notes remain, topics on hours of work and technical education were up for debate. Originally, the main purpose of the conference was to try to influence the political process through creating a 'Parliamentary Committee' that would seek to defend union interests, which in the 1920s became the General Council.

Samuel Nicholson, the President of the Manchester and Salford Trade Council, was a key figure in bringing about the Congress of Trade Unions.

It was in the 1920s that, after trying to influence government policy, the TUC really began taking an active role in industrial matters, coordinating the 1926 general strike. Moving into Congress House in central London in 1958, it became a key aspect of British political life, where governments would consult on various policy areas to ensure all voices were heard. The TUC's library is currently located at London Metropolitan University, while its archive is at the University of Warwick.

Trade union membership itself reached a high of 13.2 million in 1979. However, the role of trade unions and their power was explicitly curbed under Margaret Thatcher. Membership is now down to around 6.5 million, although there has been a marginal increase in recent years, as the effects of the gig economy become more apparent.

BOROUGH MARKET TERROR ATTACK

The final Saturday before the 2017 general election ended in tragedy due to a terrorist attack in Borough Market in London. Lasting just ten minutes, the attack started with a van being driven into pedestrians on London Bridge before it crashed on the south side of the River Thames. The three terrorists, wearing fake explosive vests, then ran to Borough Market where they stabbed people in pubs and restaurants. On a Saturday night, it was peak time for these hospitality venues. Eight people were killed and forty-eight people were injured, nineteen of them critically.

Calls to 999 were first recorded at 10.07 p.m. following the attack on London Bridge, with the attackers shot dead eight minutes after the initial emergency call was made. Forty-six rounds were fired by three City of London police and five Metropolitan police officers.

Britain was already reeling from numerous terrorist attacks that year. In March, a terrorist drove over Westminster Bridge, fatally running over four pedestrians and injuring nearly fifty more before stabbing a policeman to death. Similarly, in May, the terrorist threat level had been raised from 'severe' to 'critical' after twenty-two people were killed at an Ariana Grande concert in Manchester. That the Manchester attack had also taken place during the election campaign meant policing and terrorism dominated political debate.

The motivation for such an attack became clear when witnesses heard the attackers shout 'This is for Allah.' It was later revealed that one of the perpetrators had appeared on Channel 4's *The Jihadis Next Door* in 2016. Indeed, at least one of the perpetrators was known to the authorities through the Prevent anti-terrorism programme.

In the aftermath, a COBRA meeting was held on 4 June. Theresa May called for tighter internet regulation online, something which attracted criticism given election campaigning had been paused for a day.

Politically, the issue of police cuts, and whether this made terrorist attacks more likely, rose up the agenda to Jeremy Corbyn's advantage (he would still lose the 2017 election). Bravery awards and honours were given to those who altruistically helped others during the atrocity. Indeed, one of the recipients of the George Medal, Ignacio Echeverría, was a civilian who confronted the terrorists and lost his life doing so.

EMILY DAVISON RUNS OUT IN FRONT OF KING'S HORSE AT EPSOM

'Deeds not words' was the motto of the Women's Social and Political Union (WSPU), known popularly as the suffragettes, a nickname first bestowed in 1906 with negative intention by the *Daily Mail*. This organization had been founded by Emmeline Pankhurst in 1903 in the belief that the longer established 'suffragist' movement, which used entirely peaceful or 'constitutional' methods to gain the right to vote for women, was getting nowhere.

Led by the members of the Pankhurst family, WSPU members chained themselves to railings, broke windows and even fire-bombed houses such as that of David Lloyd George in Surrey. When imprisoned, they went on hunger strike, and were subsequently force-fed.

However, there was no starker or more tragic example of the bold deeds of the suffragettes than the actions of forty-year-old Emily Wilding Davison on Derby Day, 4 June 1913. The Royal Holloway and Oxford graduate – and also veteran of nine arrests and seven hunger strikes – made the ultimate sacrifice. It is unclear what her intentions were when she ran onto the track during the season's premier flat race (perhaps she was trying to pin the suffragette colours on a horse), and even more uncertain that she actually intended to commit suicide (she had a return rail ticket).

There is no doubt about what did happen, though. Emily Davison collided with the horse Anmer, owned by King George V, causing it to fall and leading to her own fatal fracture of the skull. She died without regaining consciousness on 8 June.

The impact of the Emily Davison incident is principally symbolic. In fact the militant actions of the WSPU did not lead directly to acquiring the vote. Women over thirty were enfranchised in 1918 after a wartime Act of Parliament, but it is most likely that the immediate cause of this advance was the valuable work women did during the war – the Pankhursts had proclaimed a truce for the duration.

Yet as Emily Davison's and the other deeds of the suffragettes show, the women who were prepared to undergo horrific suffering had kept the passion for equal political rights burning.

FIRST EEC REFERENDUM

A number of misconceptions about referendums in the United Kingdom may have arisen and need to be challenged.

One is that the first serious question of Britain leaving Europe arose in 2016. In fact, that was actually the second Brexit referendum, the first one being on 5 June 1975. We had actually joined already, under Edward Heath's leadership, in 1973 – no question of a popular plebiscite on that; parliamentary voting was deemed sufficient in line with our long-established framework of representative democracy. The vote in 1975 was about whether we should remain in or leave the European Economic Community (EEC).

Secondly, it is now often asserted that what triggers a referendum in this country is a constitutional issue. To put it simply, the people are specifically consulted when there is a proposed change to where power is located (Europe, devolution, local executive mayors) or how elections are conducted (voting system, 2011).

Yet that was not how it started. There was no referendum on the massive step of entry into 'Europe'. The reason for the 1975 referendum was internal party politics and party advantage – Harold Wilson saw it as the only way to avoid a split in his bitterly divided Labour Party and cabinet, who were free to campaign for either side.

Thirdly, some have argued that 'Brexit' is a right-wing preference, 'Remain' left-wing. However, in 1975 a subtler truth was apparent. It was the socialist left of the Labour Party, led by Tony Benn, who were for leaving (seeing it as a capitalist club), and the social democratic right (Jenkins, Owen, Shirley Williams) for remaining. The majority of Conservatives, following their party leader, were strongly in favour of the EEC. Only the fringe was against, for nationalist reasons. Therefore, it was a centrist coalition, including of course the Liberal Party, which prevailed, and both 'extremes' were defeated – by just over two to one, 67 per cent to 33 per cent.

There were important differences between 1975 and 2016. The European project had developed or mutated, from what was usually known as the Common Market free trade area to a much deeper and more invasive attempt at political union. If it had remained economic, we may never have voted to leave.

D-DAY

Hollywood made an all-star film about it called *The Longest Day*. It was the largest amphibious military invasion in the history of the world. Around 148,000 Allied troops landed on five beaches in Normandy, plus 8,000 paratroopers flew in to secure key targets. The armada of ships that crossed the Channel was nigh on 7,000 strong. Command of the skies was guaranteed by nearly 12,000 Allied aircraft. All this added up to the 'D-Day' section of an even bigger operation, codenamed Overlord.

Overlord was the invasion of German-occupied France, and a major step towards the end of the Second World War itself. Despite the immense effort of coordination that is apparent in the success of D-Day itself, there had been considerable controversy and differences of opinion between the wartime Allies.

Yes, the overall commander, the American Eisenhower, and his British immediate subordinates Tedder (his deputy, from the RAF), Ramsay (Navy) and Montgomery (Army) worked well together. However, for years previously there had been major disputes. Bearing the brunt of the land war since 1941, Stalin pressed for a 'second front' in the West. The USA was keen to take the direct route across the Channel, but Churchill had been far less enthusiastic and stalled the date of what became D-Day. He remembered the disastrous landing at Gallipoli in 1915, mainly his idea, and also the failure of the Dieppe Raid in 1942. He persuaded Roosevelt to go along in 1943 with a jump from North Africa to Sicily and Italy ('the soft underbelly of Europe') instead.

Pressure from Stalin and Franklin D. Roosevelt did eventually prise agreement out of Churchill for a 1944 date; but then the weather threatened the plan in early June. Only a brief relief from stormy conditions spotted by chief meteorologist James Stagg allowed it to go ahead.

By the end of the day, all beachheads were secure. Apart from Omaha beach, in the US sector, there was less German resistance than feared. Although progress through Normandy was slow, Paris was liberated in August and Hitler was caught in a fatal vice. The Allies never took all of Italy – it was D-Day that launched the decisive pincer movement.

Friday, 7 June 1929

MARGARET BONDFIELD BECOMES THE FIRST FEMALE CABINET MINISTER

Margaret Bondfield was a trailblazer for her sex, yet she remains a forgotten figure in the Labour movement. Not only did she become the first woman to hold cabinet office, she was also the first female privy councillor.

Bondfield was born in 1873 into a poor family in Somerset. Her father had been a radical activist in Chard. At fourteen she got an apprenticeship in a clothes shop in Hove. In 1895, she moved to London and became an active member of the Shop Assistants' Union and the Fabian Society.

In 1900, she achieved the first of her 'firsts' and became the first woman to attend a Trades Union Annual Congress. She voted for the creation of a Labour Representation Committee.

She became increasingly involved in the issue of women's suffrage through the Women's Labour League, which she helped found. She argued not just for equality with the voting rights of men, but for universal suffrage.

In November 1918, Bondfield was the first woman to be elected to the TUC General Council and in September 1923 became its first woman chair. In 1920, she stood for Parliament in a by-election in Northampton but lost, as she did in the general election in 1922. However, in November 1923 it was third time lucky. She allegedly turned down a cabinet job in the first Labour government, instead becoming a junior minister at the Ministry of Labour. At the 1924 election she lost her seat, but was only out of parliament for two years, winning a by-election in Wallsend in 1926.

Three years later, Labour was back in power and Margaret Bondfield joined the cabinet as Minister of Labour. Given the scale of the economic crash, she encountered huge problems with the costs of unemployment. She was even attacked by the TUC. Despite this she proposed a cut in unemployment benefits and to curb entitlements. The Labour Party split in 1931 and she lost her seat, never returning to the green benches.

Margaret Bondfield died at the age of eighty in 1953. She has largely been erased from Labour history, totally undeservedly.

GEORGE ORWELL'S *1984* IS PUBLISHED

George Orwell lived for less than a year after the publication of his last and most famous book, dying of a tubercular haemorrhage on the night of 21 January 1950 at the age of forty-six. But *1984* has survived the many decades since as a bestseller and a classic. Despite Orwell's decision to set his vision of a totalitarian Britain alarmingly in the near future, less than forty years after the publication date, it has lost none of its power even as we near forty years after the actual year 1984.

Indeed, into the twenty-first century one of the most popular 'reality TV' series was named after Orwell's all-seeing dictator, 'Big Brother' (and another series after his place of the worst thing in the world, Room 101).

One reason for this is that although it was written in the late 1940s during the early years of the Cold War, and although the brutal dominant system 'Ingsoc' was clearly modelled on Soviet communism, its exposure of and opposition to tyranny has a wider relevance – *1984* was not a prophecy, it was a warning.

Orwell, always an individualist radical in the English tradition, had long been hostile to the Communist Party, especially since his spell fighting on the Republican side in the Spanish Civil War. See for example his brilliant satire of the Russian Revolution, *Animal Farm* (1945). Yet he made it clear that *1984* was not an attack on socialism itself (despite its conscription by various right-wing American 'freedom' organizations), but merely its perversion.

Another reason for the book's longevity is that it is also an effective novel. It is easy to identify with the all-too-human hero, the disillusioned Ministry of Truth employee (who rewrites history) Winston Smith, his yearning for the real truth, his tragic love story, and his betrayal and terrors.

However, the main value of *1984* is that it still holds political relevance, as surveillance methods become ever more sophisticated, media manipulation more prevalent, the concept of truth more fragile even at the highest levels in world governance, and the need for democracy, respect and humanity as vital as it ever has been.

THATCHER WINS LANDSLIDE

Margaret Thatcher led the Conservative Party to three election victories, and was never defeated. Most overwhelming was 1983. The Tory overall majority jumped from 43 in 1979 to a massive 144. In her first term, Thatcher still had to gain control of her own cabinet as well as the nation, but now her power was unchallengeable.

What had led to this dominant performance? Clearly, a part was played by her resolution and leadership during the Falklands War of 1982, which may well not have happened at all but for her determination to resist the invasion by the Argentine junta. As the Russians had identified, she was now the 'Iron Lady'. It is also true that the British economy had started to recover from the severe unemployment that had replaced the inflation of the previous Labour government.

However, it has to be pointed out that the 1983 result was less an absolute Conservative triumph than the result of a perfect storm for the main opposition party, Labour. After all, the Tory share of the vote actually went down, from 43.9 per cent to 42.4 per cent, well below half of those who voted. Labour, however, fell 9.3 per cent to 27.6 per cent, their lowest since 1918. After the defeat of the Callaghan government in 1979, Labour had swung far to the left, with the leading left-winger Michael Foot as the new Leader and infiltration by the Trotskyist Militant Tendency. Linked to this was the split which saw the defection of the 'Gang of Four' and the foundation of the Social Democratic Party in 1981.

In alliance with the Liberals, this new force threatened to 'break the mould' of British politics and nearly overtook Labour in the 1983 election. However, due to the first-past-the-post system, the Alliance only won twenty-three seats despite their share of over 25 per cent (nearly eight million votes). Thatcher's landslide was therefore most of all the consequence of the evenly divided opposition.

Be that as it may, the 1983 election did give her the mandate to proceed with radical measures: privatizations such as BT and British Gas, the defeat of the miners, the abolition of the GLC. This was indeed the high summer of Thatcherism.

PATRICK MAGEE IS CONVICTED OF BRIGHTON BOMBING

Of all the IRA's terrorist attacks, surely the most remembered is their 1984 bombing of the Grand Hotel, Brighton, where they attempted to assassinate Prime Minister Margaret Thatcher and her cabinet. Five people were killed and thirty-three people injured. Patrick Magee was the man held responsible for the atrocity, convicted over eighteen months after the attack in June 1986.

The Brighton bombing occurred on 12 October 1984 during the Conservative Party conference. The bomb was time-delayed and placed in Room 629 by Magee, directly next to the room where Margaret Thatcher was working on her conference speech.

Magee pleaded not guilty, though presented no witnesses in his defence and did not testify during the trial.

Belfast-born Magee became a suspect three months after the bombing because his fingerprints were identified from a hotel registration card. Captured in June 1985 at an IRA hideout in Glasgow, Magee was accused of registering at the Grand Hotel a month before the conference under a false name – Roy Walsh – and of placing a twenty-to-thirty-pound explosive device timed to go off when guests were asleep.

Magee's lawyer, Dr Richard Ferguson, claimed the police planted Magee's print on the registration card to frame him and restore their reputation following their failure to stop the explosion.

The Old Bailey jury took five hours to reach its unanimous guilty verdict. Convicted of planting the bomb, exploding it and five counts of murder, Magee was handed eight life sentences, alongside a charge of conspiracy to bomb sixteen targets in London and around Britain. The judge recommended a minimum term of thirty-five years.

Under the terms of the Good Friday Agreement, Magee was released from the Maze prison in 1999 after serving only fourteen years. Though Home Secretary Jack Straw tried to block his release, this was overturned by the High Court. Admitting to the *Guardian* in August 2000 that he carried out the bombing, Magee continues to deny leaving the fingerprint on the registration card. Despite still defending the bombings, Magee has expressed regret at the loss of innocent lives and, in an effort to achieve reconciliation, has met with some families of his victims.

THATCHER WINS THIRD TERM

The June 1987 general election resulted in the third successive victory for Prime Minister Margaret Thatcher. The 1980s were to be an all-Conservative decade. In 1959, they had also completed a hat-trick of victories, but these were under three different leaders. For the last occasion one premier had won thrice in a row one had to go back to Lord Liverpool in 1812, 1818 and 1820 – in the days before universal suffrage.

At the time of the 1987 election, Mrs Thatcher had established her dominance. By this third election her policies of privatization and sale of council houses had matured, and since 1983 she had added the defeat of the miners in the bitter 1984–85 strike to her earlier defeat of the Argentinians. Again, she was returned with an overall majority of over 100, which is one definition of a landslide.

It could be said, though, that Labour lost the 1987 election more than the Conservatives won it. The Tory percentage of the total vote actually slipped slightly from 42.4 per cent in 1983 to 42.2 per cent. Labour still managed just 30.8 per cent, their second-lowest share since 1935, and the opposition was again split with the Alliance, which polled 22.6 per cent (though only winning twenty-two seats, a tenth as many as Labour). Although Neil Kinnock had started to rescue his party from the lowest ebb of the extremism and Militant infiltration of the early 1980s, Labour was still distrusted as divided and too left-wing, particularly on the issue of defence.

At this apparent peak of Thatcher's prestige and power it would have amazed many if they had known that she would never again lead her party into a general election, being ousted by her own party in autumn 1990. Yet in retrospect it can be argued that in the third term Thatcher's judgement lapsed, possibly in her growing resentment of the European project but certainly in her imposition of the massively unpopular Community Charge or 'poll tax'. If Margaret Thatcher had retired in 1989 after ten years in power, her political career would not have ended in such an ignominious manner.

170

DEREK HATTON EXPELLED FROM LABOUR

If one day signalled the point when Neil Kinnock began to make Labour electable again, 12 June 1986 would certainly be a contender: the day Derek Hatton was expelled from the Labour Party. It followed Kinnock's famous 1985 conference speech condemning the actions of Liverpool City Council.

Hatton had generated outrage and notoriety as the former deputy leader of Liverpool City Council by setting an illegal budget, spending £30 million more than allowed. The move was deliberately designed to protest against spending cuts by Margaret Thatcher's Conservative government. It resulted in thousands of council workers being sent redundancy notices by taxi. Though Hatton claimed it was a tactic by the council to buy more time, his move was branded 'grotesque chaos' by the Labour Leader.

Indeed, the district auditor found Liverpool City Council to have behaved in an illegal manner, committing wilful misconduct. Hatton was subsequently banned from public office. Accused in 1993 of corruption, he was found not guilty after a long trial.

His expulsion in 1986 followed revelations that he belonged to the Militant Tendency, a Trotskyite group that had begun infiltrating the Labour Party under previous Leader Michael Foot. Though Hatton argued they were a legitimate wing of the party, Labour's National Executive Committee endorsed expulsion by twelve votes to six. Neil Kinnock saw removing the hard left as vital for any electoral success.

Hatton later turned to broadcasting, hosting phone-in shows on Century FM and Talk Radio in the 1990s. He was also the subject of BBC documentaries and, in 2010, part of Channel 4's Alternative Election Night *Come Dine with Me*, with other guests including Edwina Currie and Rod Liddle.

Having applied to rejoin Labour on multiple occasions, Hatton's application was eventually approved in February 2019. Hatton spoke about his staunch support for Jeremy Corbyn, stating that his policies would benefit 'the vast majority of people' and that Corbyn had 'fresh enthusiasm and energy'.

However, he was suspended only two days later, following the emergence of an anti-semitic tweet from 2012. Hatton was later arrested in December 2020 as part of an investigation into building and development contracts in Liverpool.

PEASANTS' REVOLT COMES TO A HEAD

The working classes – or as they were much more likely to say at the time, the lower orders – figured relatively rarely on the medieval political stage, given that they comprised the vast majority of the population.

However, they did very much invade that stage, the crisis occupying the heart of the capital city too, in June 1381. Making unprecedented demands, and threatening the established fabric of a traditional society, the 'peasants' and their leaders killed some of the very top 'politicians' of the day, and engaged the dramatic personal involvement of a teenage boy king. And all this was mainly about a poll tax.

In the second half of the fourteenth century, the position of the lower orders had actually improved, due to the massive depopulation caused by the Black Death pandemic in the 1340s, which had resulted in a labour shortage. Therefore, demands could be made for wage increases and an end to the remaining practice of serfdom.

Added to this longer term cause, in Parliament in late 1380, the royal government's demand for money to finance war in Brittany took the form of a poll tax, to be levied on the entire male population. Clearly, this impacted the poor the most, and in 1381, after the government resolved to stamp out the initial 'can't pay won't pay' resistance, this sparked active rebellion, starting in the counties of Essex and Kent.

After seizing towns such as Colchester and Maidstone, the rebels of both counties headed for the capital. They protested that they were not attacking King Richard II himself, but his 'evil advisers', such as Chancellor Sudbury and Treasurer Hales, both of whom were dragged from the Tower and beheaded. A third, John of Gaunt, was in the North, but his great palace, the Savoy, was destroyed.

The situation was largely saved by the fourteen-year-old Richard, who bravely rode to both groups of rebels, listened, and convinced them to disperse. By the end of June, the rebellion was over and the hierarchy of power restored. But there were to be no more poll taxes – until 1989.

ARGENTINA SURRENDERS

On the evening of 14 June 1982, following days of advances around the capital, Stanley, a ceasefire was declared and the Argentinian commander, General Mario Menéndez, surrendered his forces to the British Major General Jeremy Moore, effectively ending the war. Both sides also agreed the terms of the surrender.

In a message to the Prime Minister, Margaret Thatcher, General Moore said 'Falkland Islands once more under the government desired by their inhabitants. God save the Queen.' On the night of the surrender, Thatcher made a speech to Parliament where she said that 'we must now bring life in the islands back to normal as quickly as possible' and added that 'the Falkland Islands should never again be a victim of unprovoked aggression.'

It was later announced that Argentina's government had agreed to withdraw its troops. The decision taken by General Menéndez to surrender was originally against the wishes of General Galtieri, head of the junta, who wanted to continue the war.

Prior to the British victory, Thatcher's popularity was at its lowest, with the expectation that she was likely to lose the next general election. This drastically changed following the success in the Falklands and in 1983 Thatcher delivered the biggest landslide majority since 1945.

As a result of Argentina's invasion and the subsequent surrender, the British government increased its military presence on the islands.

Britain and Argentina didn't restore full diplomatic relations until 1990. The islands' sovereignty status remains an ongoing dispute between the two countries. Argentina's subsequent governments have continued to claim that the islands should be returned to their control. In a referendum held in 2013, the electorate voted overwhelmingly to remain a British Overseas Territory.

The Falklands War began on 2 April and lasted seventy-four days. As a result of the conflict, 255 British and 649 Argentine military personnel, as well as 3 civilians, were killed. The day of the surrender, or Liberation Day as it's now known, is a public holiday in the Falkland Islands. The territory has a population of over three thousand, according to the latest census, more than 50 per cent more than in 1982.

MAGNA CARTA SEALED AT RUNNYMEDE

A great step in the development of our Constitution, a major guarantee of all our liberties? Well, up to a point.

The Americans certainly hold Magna Carta in high esteem. In fact, when the Kennedy Memorial monument was unveiled in 1965 at Runnymede, the meadow by the Thames in Surrey where it was sealed, the Crown actually gifted that plot of land as American soil. The document is seen as underpinning a tradition of freedom and democracy that would have been alien to its time.

However, in one sense it did have a parallel with the Declaration of Independence. Above all, it was a protest against taxation. The Plantagenet King John lost most of the dynasty's French possessions by 1204, which meant both that he spent far more time in England and that he ruthlessly raised taxation to try to recover the territory by war.

That war came to a disastrous end for John with defeat at the Battle of Bouvines in 1214. In May the next year, a baronial revolt was launched, supported by large numbers of knights and the City of London. This compelled John to negotiate the agreement sealed at Runnymede on 15 June.

This was not a universal 'Bill of Rights'. One of the clues is that it was originally called 'the Articles of the Barons'. Its restrictions on kingship centred on limited taxation, restraining his officers and preventing arbitrary 'justice'. Mostly, it applied to the powerful nobles who had forced the concessions by armed rebellion. There were clauses that referred to 'all free men', though it should be remembered that far from all were free when serfdom still existed.

Magna Carta is very important – if more for its subsequent interpretations. In the seventeenth century it was used to argue against the divine right of the Stuart monarchs, Charles I and James II, in the Civil Wars and the Glorious Revolution; then by the American colonists against George III; and even in the twenty-first century it is still cited as a precedent for the key principles of habeas corpus and the rule of law – not really understood in 1215, but still truly significant.

JO COX MP IS MURDERED

Friends remember Jo Cox MP as having an 'immeasurable' energy for life. They tell stories of Jo carrying a rucksack 'twice her size' up mountains with ease. She had a little boat on the Thames in which she shared happy evenings with her two young children and husband, Brendan. Her colleague on the Labour benches Lucy Powell said Jo was 'always putting others before herself'.

Jo Cox was murdered at the age of just forty-one in her constituency of Batley and Spen. She was shot and stabbed multiple times on her way to a surgery at Birstall Library, and died shortly after being admitted to Leeds General Infirmary. In November later that year, Jo's killer Thomas Mair, was found guilty. The judge concluded that Mair wanted to advance white supremacism and nationalism associated with modern Nazism. The extreme right-wing terrorist was sentenced to prison for the rest of his miserable life.

Such a violent attack on a sitting MP shocked the nation. It was the first such assassination for more than thirty years. In 1990, the IRA killed Conservative MP Ian Gow by placing a bomb under his car. Six years previously, Sir Anthony Berry died in the bombing of Brighton's Grand Hotel, where Margaret Thatcher was staying for the 1984 Conservative Party conference. More recently, in 2010, Labour MP Stephen Timms was stabbed twice by a student, but survived. Lib Dem Nigel Jones, similarly, survived an attack in 2000 at his surgery in Cheltenham by a man with a samurai sword. Nigel's aide Andrew Pennington was killed trying to protect him. And, of course, my friend Sir David Amess, Conservative MP for Southend West, was killed at his constituency surgery in 2021.

In Jo Cox's maiden speech in the House of Commons, she said that 'we are far more united and have far more in common with each other than that which divides us.' The Jo Cox Foundation was formed to continue her legacy, with that philosophy as one of its founding tenets. Jo brought so much positivity to politics, and her memory continues to do so. No kind of unpatriotic, depraved terrorist can extinguish that.

KEN LIVINGSTONE IS BORN

Ken Livingstone can be classed as one of the more significant left-of-centre British politicians of the late twentieth and early twenty-first centuries. He fought Margaret Thatcher in the 1980s as Leader of the Greater London Council (GLC), and so effective was he that the only way she could rid herself of this turbulent priest of left wingery was to abolish the institution that gave him his political oxygen.

Livingstone was born into a south London Conservative-voting working-class family only a month after the end of the war in Europe.

He worked as a technician as his first job, and unionized his fellow workers at a cancer research laboratory. Meanwhile, he joined the Labour Party in 1968 and was elected to Lambeth Council. In 1973, he won a seat on the GLC and it was in this era that he started to flirt with what many perceived as extreme left-wing causes. In 1981, he launched a coup against the Labour group leader Andrew McIntosh the day after Labour had won control of the council. It wasn't the last time he displayed ruthlessness. In his five years running the GLC he set himself up as the main opposition to Prime Minister Margaret Thatcher. But she had the last laugh and on 31 March 1986 the GLC was abolished.

Livingstone wasn't finished, though. He was elected to the House of Commons in 1987 and remained MP for Brent East until 2001. He hated being an MP and was never promoted to the front bench.

In March 1998, Livingstone announced his intention to run to be Labour's candidate for the newly created post of Mayor of London. However, the electoral system was rigged against him and he lost out to Frank Dobson. He then ran as an independent and won, serving two terms. However, he grossly underestimated his opponent in 2008, one Boris Johnson. Not only did he lose to him then, he repeated the experience in 2012.

In 2016, he was expelled from the Labour Party for some ill-judged remarks about Hitler, Jews and Israel. It spelled the end of his role in frontline politics.

CONSERVATIVES WIN THE GENERAL ELECTION

Few thought that Harold Wilson wasn't going to win the election. The election campaign had been going well, but then it all started to go wrong. With just four days to go before polling day, England were knocked out of the World Cup by West Germany. The next day, some unexpectedly bad balance of trade figures were published. The nation's mood began to turn, yet all the polls and pundits seemed to demonstrate that Harold Wilson would be back in Number 10, albeit with a reduced majority. Labour had been 12 per cent ahead in the polls, yet when the results came in they showed a Tory lead of 3.4 per cent. In reality, the signs had been there all along. People were tiring of the influence the unions were exerting over the government, and the constant menace of strikes. Inflation was rising, unemployment was at a forty-year high and a second devaluation was being predicted by many economists.

This was the first general election in which eighteen-year-olds could vote. In theory, Harold Wilson didn't need to call an election until March 1971, but most political observers thought he would go in the autumn of 1970, in order to avoid any difficulties over the decimalization of the currency in January 1971. Wilson always liked the element of surprise.

Some academics believe the Conservative victory was due to the Enoch Powell effect. His 'Rivers of Blood' speech in 1968 had galvanized the right and led to 2.5 million extra votes for the Conservatives according to Schoen and Johnson. Having said that, the Tory vote actually only increased by 1.7 million.

The biggest Labour casualties were George Brown and Jennie Lee. Despite an energetic campaign by new Liberal Leader Jeremy Thorpe, the party lost half of its twelve seats.

In the days following the election, Edward Heath appointed Iain MacLeod to the Treasury, Reginald Maudling to the Home Office and Sir Alec Douglas Home to the Foreign Office. Less than a month later, the new Chancellor was dead, a tragedy which had long-term consequences for the Heath government.

JULIAN ASSANGE ENTERS ECUADOR EMBASSY

Julian Assange, a previously little-known Australian editor, shot to prominence with his website WikiLeaks, which released huge amounts of classified information on American forces in military conflicts overseas and much else. Wanted by America for questioning over potential breaches of national security, he sought sanctuary and asylum in the Ecuadorian Embassy in London in June 2012, where he remained for nearly seven years.

However, it was not just America with whom Assange had a damaged relationship. The Swedish Prosecutor's Office had issued Assange with an arrest warrant in August 2010 for allegations of rape and molestation, with the UK's Supreme Court ruling in May 2012 that he should be extradited. This was the catalyst that led to his original asylum claim. The charges themselves were eventually dropped in November 2019 because of a statute of limitations.

Assange's home in the embassy consisted of a small office made into a bedroom with a bed, lamp, computer, shower and treadmill. Though able to address supporters from a small balcony where news conferences were held, and host individuals including Lady Gaga, the isolation was total.

Ecuador originally granted him asylum as they believed his human rights were under threat, a decision which baffled the UK government. The Metropolitan Police spent more than £12 million between 2012 and 2015 funding officers standing guard at the embassy.

Assange's conditions at the embassy deteriorated in 2017 when the new Ecuadorian President, Lenín Moreno, took charge. Assange hardly helped himself by appearing to 'climb up the walls' of his confinement: insulting embassy workers, riding his skateboard and playing football.

With Assange having spent a total of 2,488 days in the embassy, Ecuador eventually formally invited the Metropolitan Police in to remove him for extradition to Sweden in April 2019. Assange remains in Belmarsh prison for breaching his bail terms, with his Ecuadorian citizenship revoked in 2021. US prosecutors have charged Assange on seventeen counts of espionage and one of computer misuse because of WikiLeaks' publishing of military and diplomatic documents, with a maximum sentence of 175 years. The UK government has accepted that Assange should be extradited to America.

JONATHAN AITKEN LOSES LIBEL CASE

Jonathan Aitken appeared to have it all – dashing good looks, money, a political career, a business career, a girlfriend who was the Prime Minister's daughter. And then it all went wrong. Breaking up with Carol Thatcher and telling an Egyptian newspaper that Margaret Thatcher 'probably thinks Sinai is the plural of Sinus' scuppered his chances of ministerial preferment.

Born in Dublin during the war, Aitken went to Eton and Oxford. He was a war correspondent in the 1960s and then a television presenter. In 1970, he was acquitted at the Old Bailey of breaching the Official Secrets Act. He then started a lucrative, and sometimes controversial business career in property and arms sales.

Following the 1992 general election, John Major controversially appointed Aitken to succeed Alan Clark as Minister for Defence Procurement. He had been a director of the arms exporter BMARC. It later emerged that he suppressed documents relating to the supply of arms to Iraq by BMARC at a time when he was a director.

In 1994, he was promoted to the cabinet as Chief Secretary to the Treasury. On 10 April 1995, the *Guardian* published allegations, repeated in a *World in Action* documentary that night called 'Jonathan of Arabia', that Aitken had organized prostitutes for businessmen from the Middle East, while serving as a Defence minister.

At 5 p.m. that day, Aitken held a press conference at Conservative Central Office and denied the claims: 'If it falls to me to start a fight to cut out the cancer of bent and twisted journalism in our country with the simple sword of truth and the trusty shield of British fair play, so be it.'

In May 1997, Aitken lost his Thanet South seat and the next month his libel case against the *Guardian* and *Granada TV* commenced. It soon collapsed over his lie that his wife had paid for a hotel stay at The Ritz in Paris. It turned out that she was in Switzerland at the time.

Aitken was later sent to prison for eighteen months for perjury. He served seven. He was also declared bankrupt.

He later discovered God and in 2018 was ordained as a parish priest.

EARL OF ROSEBERY'S GOVERNMENT FALLS

Archibald Primrose, 5th Earl of Rosebery, was an undoubted political star. He was also very possibly Britain's first gay prime minister. Rosebery appeared to possess every political talent that you need to be a great prime minister, yet when he finally got the job, he seemed all at sea, and his talents deserted him. His tenure in Downing Street lasted only fifteen unhappy months.

Rosebery was born into a political and aristocratic family, his father having served in Lord Melbourne's government. In 1851, on his father's death, he inherited the courtesy title of Lord Dalmeny. On his grandfather's death in 1868, he inherited the earldom.

In 1879, Rosebery played a leading role in supporting and effectively running Gladstone's famous Midlothian Campaign, adopting campaigning tactics he had witnessed on trips to the USA. In Gladstone's brief third ministry, Rosebery was made Foreign Secretary, and he returned to the job in Gladstone's fourth and final administration in 1892. Rosebery was an old-style Liberal Imperialist, but his time at the Foreign Office was undistinguished and unmemorable.

Despite this, with his strong oratorical skills and the support of Queen Victoria, Rosebery took over as prime minister when 'The Grand Old Man' retired in March 1894. His ascension to the office was by no means guaranteed, as the Chancellor of the Exchequer, the rather aloof and very political Sir William Harcourt, had a very strong claim.

Gladstone undermined Rosebery, who wanted to stay out of the Armenian crisis, whereas Gladstone spoke out in favour of unilateral intervention. In fact, Rosebery's entire foreign policy was pretty disastrous as he continually rubbed up European leaders in the wrong way. In domestic policy he was no more successful, and the continual fights within his cabinet were a source of his increasing listlessness and depression.

In June 1895, the government lost a vote on army supply and Rosebery and his ministers resigned. Lord Salisbury called an immediate general election in which the Liberals were trounced.

Rosebery stayed as Liberal Leader for another year, but never held office again. He died in 1929 leaving an estate worth £93 million in today's money. He remains Britain's richest prime minister.

HMT *EMPIRE WINDRUSH* PASSENGERS DISEMBARK

'A misty day in June' is how the BBC news coverage described 21 June 1948, when HMT *Empire Windrush* anchored at Tilbury Docks carrying 1,027 passengers, including stowaways. The passenger list recorded 539 passengers whose last country of residence was Jamaica, while 139 gave Bermuda and 119 stated England. There were also passengers from Mexico, Scotland, Gibraltar, Burma and Wales.

The new arrivals were some of the first wave of migrants to begin a new life in Britain, helping to alleviate the post-war labour crisis. It was a long and expensive journey, costing approximately £28 – £1000 in today's money. Taking almost exactly one month to get to Tilbury Docks, the former cruise liner began its voyage in Trinidad, before calling at Jamaica, Mexico, Cuba, Bermuda and finally anchoring at Tilbury on 21 June.

Not all passengers had secured work and accommodation on arrival and these people had nowhere to go. Following some resistance, the Colonial Office reluctantly agreed to open a deep air-raid shelter beneath Clapham Common providing short-term accommodation for those who didn't have any.

At 1 p.m. on 22 June 1948, BBC news reported that the passengers had unloaded the ship themselves due to a dock workers' strike. By the time of the 6 p.m. broadcast, the report stated that eighteen stowaways had been found on board and were either fined or sentenced to several days' imprisonment.

On the same day, a group of eleven MPs wrote to Prime Minister Clement Attlee to voice their concern over the level of immigration the arrival of the ship would encourage. The Prime Minister's reply shrugged off the concern, however, noting it was unlikely their arrival would cause any 'great influx', but that if it did then his decision to keep the borders open might be reviewed: 'If our policy were to result in a great influx of undesirables, we might, however unwillingly, have to consider modifying it,' he replied to the MPs. He began the response cautioning the MPs against showing such huge concern: 'I think it would be a great mistake to take the emigration of this Jamaican party to the United Kingdom too seriously.'

BRITAIN VOTES TO LEAVE THE EU

'We're out': those words, uttered by David Dimbleby at 4.40 a.m. on 24 June, symbolized the momentous tidal wave that had just swept British politics. After weeks, months and years of argument, the British people voted on 23 June 2016 to leave the European Union after more than forty years of membership by 52 per cent to 48 per cent. This directly reversed the 1975 referendum, where two thirds had voted to remain.

The calls for a referendum stretched as far back as the 1990s, when James Goldsmith's single issue Referendum Party stood in numerous seats in the 1997 election. However, it only gained 2.6 per cent of the national vote.

Ironically, it was through the European Union that the United Kingdom Independence Party (UKIP) rose to prominence. The European elections used proportional representation, which allowed the Eurosceptic parties to win seats throughout the 2000s.

UKIP's popularity, under the leadership of Nigel Farage, increased throughout the 2010s, not least in local council elections. It was these electoral fears, alongside the prospect of backbench defections, which prompted David Cameron in 2013 to offer a referendum should the Conservatives win the 2015 election.

Cameron spent much of late 2015 and early 2016 travelling around European capitals trying to convince European leaders to help reform Britain's relationship with the EU in order to prop up support for continuing membership. The measures agreed in February 2016 were superficial and weak. The campaign then began.

Britain Stronger in Europe and Vote Leave were declared the official Remain and Leave campaigns respectively. Remain focused on the economic costs of leaving, with rising unemployment, lower household income and fewer prospects available to the British public.

Vote Leave, under the management of Dominic Cummings, organized an effective campaign around the slogan: 'Take Back Control', emphasizing the return of full British sovereignty to Parliament. Though Nigel Farage's unofficial Leave.EU campaign focused more on immigration, including a provocative 'Breaking Point' poster, the narrative of control and agency worked to excellent effect.

In the aftermath of the result, David Cameron resigned the following day.

ETON COLLEGE IS FOUNDED

When King Henry VI founded Eton College (or Slough Comp, as it came to be known in the late twentieth century), he could hardly have anticipated that twenty of our fifty-five prime ministers would have been educated there, not least because the office of prime minister was only recognized three hundred years later.

It had been thought that Eton's influence might be on the wane and Anthony Eden, Harold Macmillan and Alec Douglas-Home might have been the last three Old Etonians to enter Number 10, but not a bit of it. In the twenty-first century, two of our five prime ministers have been Old Etonians – David Cameron and Boris Johnson. Having said that, Theresa May, whose constituency is a stone's throw away from Eton, was the first Conservative prime minister not to include an Old Etonian in her cabinet, once Boris Johnson resigned as Foreign Secretary in July 2018. At the time of writing, as well as Boris Johnson, two other current cabinet ministers went to Eton.

The Duke of Wellington, himself an Old Etonian who also despatched his sons there, did not, as legend records it, say that 'The Battle of Waterloo was won on the playing-fields of Eton.' What he actually said, while passing a cricket match at Eton, was 'There grows the stuff that won Waterloo.'

While its reputation is of being the school of the upper classes, Eton has always taken boys from poorer backgrounds. The 'Eton Mission' scheme took boys from Hackney Wick in east London from as early as 1880 until 1971. Nowadays 20 per cent of the boys receive financial support. It wasn't until 1969, however, that a black boy graduated from Eton. Dillibe Onyeama later wrote a book about the racism he experienced.

Douglas Hurd, Foreign Secretary at the end of Margaret Thatcher's period in office, felt that being an Old Etonian had harmed his chances of becoming Conservative Leader in 1990, when the working-class lad John Major eventually triumphed.

Among some of Eton's old boys are George Orwell, John Maynard Keynes, Damian Lewis, Hugh Fearnley-Whittingstall and Tom Hiddleston. The school now educates actors and foodies, rather than politicians, it seems.

COMMONS VOTES FOR THIRD RUNWAY AT HEATHROW

Theresa May's government comfortably won the vote on plans to build a third runway at Heathrow Airport, which took place on 25 June 2018, by 415 votes to 119, a majority of 296. Labour MPs were given a free vote and the majority of other MPs either voted against or abstained; eight Conservative MPs rebelled and voted against.

The vote was highly controversial because of the opposition from some MPs, as well as environmental organizations and campaign groups. Supporters of the expansion believed it was a necessary step to support aims to grow as a global power, compete with other major airports and create new jobs.

Boris Johnson, who was the Foreign Secretary in Theresa May's government at the time, was criticized for missing the vote. In 2015, as the then London Mayor and newly elected MP for the constituency of Uxbridge and South Ruislip, which neighbours Heathrow airport, he said he would lie 'in front of those bulldozers and stop the building, stop the construction of that third runway'.

Since Tory MPs were whipped to vote in support of the expansion, if Johnson was to vote against he would have to either resign or be sacked by Theresa May. He instead travelled to Afghanistan in his role as Foreign Secretary, widely seen as an excuse to miss the vote, avoid embarrassment and keep his job in the cabinet. He said at the time that resigning would 'achieve absolutely nothing'. Greg Hands, Conservative MP and Trade Minister at the time, resigned a few days prior to the vote in the Commons.

The third runway was first approved in 2009 by the Labour government under Gordon Brown and later scrapped by the Conservative–Lib Dem Coalition in 2010, before the plans were brought back a few years later. In early 2020, the Court of Appeal ruled that it had been unlawful to approve the expansion since current climate change targets weren't properly considered. Later that year, the Supreme Court reversed the decision, allowing Heathrow to continue working on its plans to build a third runway and expand the airport.

BRITAIN SIGNS THE UNITED NATIONS CHARTER

After the utter failure of the League of Nations, there was considerable scepticism about the likely success of a similar body, were it to be created after the Second World War. The fact that such an organization was being planned for as early as June 1941 is something of a surprise, given America hadn't even entered the war at that stage. The Allied nations of Europe and the Dominions came together to publish the Declaration of St James's Palace. It set out the goals and principles of a post-war international order.

Churchill then persuaded the United States to issue a joint statement expanding on the declaration, which became known as the Atlantic Charter. It called for self-determination for everyone, the restoration of self-government to occupied countries, free trade, global cooperation and the abandonment of the use of force and disarmament. There were also worthy statements about freedom from fear and want and freedom of the seas. These came to be the founding principles of the UN Charter.

On New Year's Day 1942, less than a month after the US entered the war, four countries came together to sign the Declaration by United Nations – the UK, US, China and the Soviet Union. The next day, a further twenty-two nations added their signatures.

The Declaration of the Four Nations was signed in 1943 by the leading four countries calling for a 'general international organization, based on the principle of the sovereign equality of all peace-loving states'.

In the autumn of 1944, the United States hosted the Dumbarton Oaks Conference to work out in detail how the United Nations organization would work. It came up with the idea of a limited membership Security Council, operating alongside a General Assembly. The Yalta Conference in February 1945 rubber-stamped the proposals and proposed a Conference of United Nations for 25 April 1945, which turned out to be just a fortnight before Germany surrendered.

The conference took place in San Francisco, with Britain and forty-nine other nations signed up to the Charter. It came into force on 25 October 1945 with the first General Assembly being held in London the following January.

GORDON BROWN BECOMES PRIME MINISTER

Gordon Brown's premiership can easily be described as a tragedy. A classic example of a politician who yearned for the keys to Downing Street, he never really got to grips with the burdens of the office of prime minister. When he took over from Tony Blair on 27 June 2007, everyone assumed he had a long-worked-out plan. That assumption proved to be wrong.

Brown's obsession with getting the top job came to a head in September 2006, when numerous MPs, including Brown's key ally, junior Defence minister Tom Watson, signed a letter urging Blair to resign. Subsequent resignations by Parliamentary Private Secretaries forced Blair to state that the 2006 Labour conference would be his last as Leader.

Brown's election resembled more of a coronation. A challenge from future shadow Chancellor John McDonnell fizzled out, with the ardent left-winger unable to gain enough nominations to stand.

Even Brown's political opponents can't argue that his first few months as prime minister weren't successful. He enjoyed a honeymoon period of dealing with near-miss terrorist attacks, handling a new outbreak of foot-and-mouth disease and responding to flooding. Brown appeared to offer competent leadership.

Riding sky-high in the opinion polls, Brown let speculation grow that a snap election was in the offing. He was desperate for his own mandate. When internal polling showed Labour would lose seats, he announced to Andrew Marr that no such election would be happening, and indeed he had never thought of holding one.

Hubris never goes down well with the British electorate. His position never really recovered. With his credibility shot, his remaining two and a half years as prime minister were defined by instability and indecision.

Brown's greatest legacy was his handling of the global financial crash, where he provided worldwide leadership, with his characteristic indecision nowhere to be seen. His hosting of the London conference attended by more than one hundred world leaders in April 2009 was masterly.

The 2010 election can almost be looked back upon as a victory for Brown, in that Brown didn't lose as badly as everyone expected him to. Eleven years on he remains a towering figure in British politics.

TREATY OF VERSAILLES SIGNED

The Treaty of Versailles, as part of the Paris Peace Treaties, dealt with the future of Germany. It intended to make sure that the 'war to end wars' was never repeated. In this it proved a signal failure, and it could be argued that it led to another and even greater world war just twenty years later.

This was a winners' settlement. The terms of Versailles were essentially hammered out between President Woodrow Wilson of the USA and prime ministers David Lloyd George of the UK and Georges Clemenceau of France – as losers, the German leaders of the democratic republic recently founded at Weimar were given no say and forced to sign.

Wilson had espoused liberal internationalism and Lloyd George was also disinclined to destroy Germany, as he pursued the traditional British foreign policy, a balance of power on the Continent – he did not want overwhelming French dominance. However, Clemenceau, nicknamed the Tiger, whose country had actually been invaded, was implacable.

The consequences were that after Versailles, Germany lost its empire, and territory was stripped from its edges. The Rhineland was demilitarized and Germany's armed forces were severely restricted. What is more, they were to accept the guilt of causing the war, and pay massive reparations for decades to make up the damage caused.

As Germany had sought an armistice before it was itself invaded, nationalists (like Hitler and his followers) could claim that the signing of Versailles was another 'stab in the back' and they vowed to take over and reverse it. As John Maynard Keynes pointed out, the economic effects added to the national humiliation, enhancing support for the Nazis, especially when stimulated in the international depression of the early 1930s.

It could be concluded that Versailles was either too harsh or too mild. Harsh, because its terms generated a sense of victimhood in Germany and stoked the fires of Nazism. Mild, because it did not actually take away Germany's massive basic strength as the largest nation in Europe – it did not split and occupy, as happened after World War II. The worst of both worlds, it was like wounding a bear – and the Second World War followed.

SIR ROBERT PEEL FALLS FROM HIS HORSE

It was an ignominious end to a stellar political career. Peel was riding on Constitution Hill when he was thrown from his horse, which then fell on him. He died three days later.

Peel was born into a wealthy textile manufacturing family in Bury in 1788. At the age of twelve he was sent to Harrow, and then was the first ever student to achieve a double first-class degree in classics and mathematics at Oxford.

At only twenty-one he became a Member of Parliament in 1809, for the rotten borough of Cashel in County Tipperary. His sponsor? None other than the future Duke of Wellington, then Sir Arthur Wellesley, the Chief Secretary for Ireland.

After only a year he was appointed as a War Office minister, and two years later became Chief Secretary for Ireland. He resigned in 1818 over the issue of Catholic emancipation, which he then opposed.

In 1822, Peel joined Lord Liverpool's cabinet as Home Secretary. He was to be one of the great reforming Home Secretaries of all time, reducing the number of crimes punishable by death and reforming prisons. While Peel refused to serve under Canning and Goderich, he returned to the Home Office when Wellington became prime minister in 1828.

Peel came to realize that if something wasn't done about Catholics in Ireland, a serious political situation might develop. Peel then took the controversial Catholic Relief Bill through the Commons. Peel was sent to Coventry by many a Tory Protestant.

In 1829, Peel created the Metropolitan Police force, a model which was then copied throughout the country.

In 1830, the Tories lost office, but they were returned in 1834, and it was Peel (who wrote the famous Tamworth Manifesto that was to be the bible for modern Conservatism) who became prime minister, albeit only for four months.

Peel returned to power in 1841. He brought in a Factory Act, protecting the working conditions of women and children in particular. However, his five years as prime minister were dominated by the issue of the Corn Laws. Peel knew that repealing them would mean the end of his ministry, but repeal them he did, nonetheless.

THERESA MAY STANDS FOR THE CONSERVATIVE PARTY LEADERSHIP

Theresa May became Britain's fifty-fourth prime minister because she was the last woman standing. She was seen by her parliamentary colleagues as the adult in the room, yet they turned a blind eye to her obvious political and personal flaws.

When David Cameron resigned only hours after Britain voted to leave the European Union, Boris Johnson looked odds-on to succeed him. He was the effective leader of the Leave campaign, a born campaigner and his two terms as Mayor of London appeared to make him a shoo-in. But the favourites rarely win Conservative leadership contests and so it proved here. Johnson's shambolic personal administration and lack of organization led Andrea Leadsom to desert him and announce her own candidacy, quickly followed by his ally and campaign manager Michael Gove, who deserted Johnson on the morning of 30 June only minutes before he was due to formally launch his campaign. Gove was immediately seen as a backstabber and only attracted 48 votes to Leadsom's 66 and May's 165 in the first round of voting. In the second round Gove was eliminated with 46 votes to Leadsom's 83 and May's 199. There was supposed to be a two-month-long campaign among the Tory Party membership, with May and Leadsom facing each other, but after an embarrassing interview with *The Times*, in which she appeared to suggest that she would make a better prime minister because she was a mother, Leadsom came under fire from all sides. She was also concerned that she was so far behind May in terms of MP support that if she won among party members, her position as leader and prime minister would be unsustainable. On 11 July, Leadsom phoned May to tell her she was withdrawing.

Theresa May thus became prime minister without being tested, either by party members in hustings or by the media. Although she had mainly kept her counsel in the Brexit referendum, she had voted Remain, yet she was about to lead Britain out of the European Union. That was the plan, anyway. And it also proved to be her undoing. Perhaps her ultimate failure was inevitable.

JULY

HONG KONG GOES BACK TO CHINA

Hong Kong was returned to China on 1 July 1997 after 156 years under British rule. The handover was marked by a ceremony on the same day, which was attended by a number of high officials, including Prime Minister Tony Blair, Hong Kong's last governor Chris Patten, President and General Secretary of the Chinese Communist Party Jiang Zemin, as well as Prince Charles.

The process of Hong Kong returning to China began in the early 1980s. At that point the Chinese government began to officially raise their intention of regaining the city's sovereignty, and in 1982, China and Britain, under Prime Minister Margaret Thatcher, agreed to start negotiating the future of the territory. The process concluded in 1984 with Chinese and British leaders signing the Sino–British Joint Declaration, under which Hong Kong would revert to Chinese rule in 1997. In a speech at the signing of the formal pact, Mrs Thatcher called the agreement 'historic' and 'a landmark', but she also highlighted that 'the negotiations were not always easy.'

The Joint Declaration, which resulted in the end of the colonial rule, came with a set of agreements around what life in Hong Kong would look like following the handover, under the 'one country, two systems' policy. It was agreed that the territory would preserve many of its capitalist principles by 'enjoy[ing] a high degree of autonomy, except in foreign and defence affairs' and would also be 'vested with executive, legislative and independent judicial power' for fifty years from the day of the handover. This allowed the city to continue its expansion as a major economic hub in Asia without the restrictions on freedoms experienced in mainland China.

The 'one country, two systems' principle is set to expire in 2047 and what exactly happens at that point remains unclear. In recent years, Britain has accused China of being in breach of the 1984 declaration on a number of occasions. Most recently, after China's top legislature passed the Hong Kong National Security Law in 2020, which reduced the city's judicial autonomy and made it much easier to prosecute activists who dare to speak against the government.

WOMEN GET FULL VOTING RIGHTS

On 2 July 1928, five million women were added to the electoral register, as the Representation of the People (Equal Franchise) Act received Royal Assent. At the general election the following year, women comprised 52 per cent of the entire electorate. It was a hugely significant moment in the movement for women's rights, and for the suffragettes and suffragists who had fought through both democratic and violent means for a woman's right to vote for the previous half a century.

The aim of the legislation was to bring voting rights for women fully into line with those for men. Up until then, only women over the age of thirty who owned property or were wives of property-owning men, or were graduates were allowed to vote. The Bill gave all women over the age of twenty-one the right to vote, irrespective of property ownership.

The passage of the Bill was surprisingly uncontroversial and it passed through both Houses of Parliament with relative ease. Millicent Fawcett, who started arguing for a woman's right to vote in 1868 when she was only twenty-two, wrote in her diary on 2 July: 'It is almost exactly 61 years ago since I heard John Stuart Mill introduce his suffrage amendment to the Reform Bill on 20 May 1867. So I have had extraordinary good luck in having seen the struggle from the beginning.'

The 1928 Act was not the end of the reform of the voting system. In 1948, a further Representation of the People Act abolished plural voting in general elections and eradicated the twelve university constituencies. Prior to this, university graduates were able to vote in two places. Constituencies with two MPs were also abolished. For the first time, candidates would forfeit their deposit if they failed to receive more than an eighth of the votes cast.

In 1969, a new Representation of the People Act extended voting rights to those aged eighteen to twenty-one, although it wasn't until 2006 that eighteen-year-olds were allowed to be candidates.

FOOD RATIONING ENDS

It seems ridiculous to think that it took more than nine years following victory in the Second World War for food rationing to end in Britain. It is possible to attribute Labour's defeat in the 1951 general election in large part to the growing anger among British housewives that they were still having to endure food rationing and shortages. Indeed, in the 1955 election the Tory majority increased from seventeen to sixty seats, largely based on the fact that food rationing had ended, the white goods revolution was in its infancy and the feel-good factor had returned to Britain for the first time in decades.

Nowadays we tend to think that Britain used to be self-sufficient in growing its own food. Not a bit of it. At the outbreak of war the country was importing twenty million tons of food per annum, including 80 per cent of fruit, 70 per cent of cheese and sugar and 50 per cent of meat products. Right from the start of the conflict, the Germans made it their business to try to starve Britain into submission by intercepting and sinking ships in the Atlantic which were heading for the ports of Liverpool, Glasgow and Bristol to unload their provisions.

A new Ministry of Food was created in September 1939, and in April 1940 Lord Woolton was brought in to run it and create a proper system of food rationing. The Ministry and its fifty thousand employees controlled virtually all sales of food in the country by implementing a ration book system. It worked, and although there was a black market in most goods, it ensured that the population maintained basic nutrition needs.

By the middle of 1941, food imports were only 50 per cent of what they had been two years earlier. However, Woolton's strategic planning and motivational skills proved successful, and complaints were few.

As the war went on, it wasn't just food that was rationed. Petrol, clothing, soap and newspaper print were also rationed. In 1946, bread rationing was introduced and lasted two years.

With rationing continuing, the Conservatives exploited public weariness, which developed into anger to good political effect. Ignoring this anger proved to be Labour's undoing.

AMERICA DECLARES INDEPENDENCE FROM BRITAIN

As national humiliations go, this was about as big as it gets. For the supreme power in the world to lose thirteen of its biggest colonies in one go wasn't just embarrassing, it was almost unthinkable. It could have been very different but a series of missteps in British government policy towards the North American colonies needlessly enraged American political leaders. What was astonishing was that the Prime Minister, Lord North, held on to his job for a further five and a half years.

Relations between the Colonies and Great Britain had been getting worse since 1763. A series of measures taken by the British Parliament outraged public opinion in the colonies, especially the issue of taxation without representation. The King and Lord North were determined to enforce British law and British will. In 1775, a full-scale revolutionary war broke out. There were still many colonists who hoped for conciliation with Britain, but King George III was having none of it.

The Declaration of Independence is without doubt one of the most beautifully written and important political documents ever published. Its aim was to elucidate why the American Colonies now regarded themselves as thirteen independent states. It was to create the United States of America.

It was on 4 July 1776 that the Second Congressional Congress met in Philadelphia and the Declaration was published. It was signed by fifty-six of America's Founding Fathers. Drafted by Thomas Jefferson, John Adams wrote that its passing by Congress 'will be the most memorable Epocha in the History of America'. He was right. The original copy of Jefferson's draft is retained in the Library of Congress.

The Declaration justified independence on the basis of twenty-seven complaints against the behaviour of King George III and Great Britain and it asserts various basic rights. The key sentence, often quoted from the Declaration is this: 'We hold these truths to be self-evident, that all men are created equal, that they are endowed by their Creator with certain unalienable Rights, that among these are Life, Liberty and the Pursuit of Happiness.'

The Declaration provided a model for other similar declarations in other countries down the ages.

THE NHS IS FOUNDED

The National Health Service has had many midwives. Founded in July 1948 by the then Labour government, the Health minister, Aneurin Bevan, trumpeted it as Labour's crowning glory, something all Labour politicians have repeated down the years.

The founding principle of the NHS is that healthcare should be available to all, free at the point of use. Discussions about the state provision of healthcare dated back many decades before 1948. The Conservative government at the beginning of the twentieth century commissioned a Royal Commission on the Poor Law, which looked at how the health of the poor was (or wasn't) catered for. The 1934 Labour Party conference committed the party to the creation of a state-run health service.

In 1942, the Liberal politician William Beveridge recommended the creation of a 'comprehensive health and rehabilitation services for prevention and cure of disease'. There was cross-party agreement on the Beveridge report's recommendations, with Conservative Health minister Henry Willink issuing a consultative white paper on the creation of a national health service two years later.

When Bevan became Health minister in 1945, his immediate aim was to work out how best to introduce a truly national health service. He went out on the stump and argued for it in typically fiery speeches.

The war had, ironically enough, helped in this endeavour given that all the nation's hospitals had already been merged under one umbrella organization. Some Conservative MPs were fearful that a national organization would mean that the personal relationship between doctor and patient might be diminished, and they argued for local control over hospitals and services. Their amendments to the Bill were defeated.

Bevan's tenure in charge of the NHS lasted only three years and ended with his resignation when the Treasury insisted on the introduction of charges for dental treatment. The following year, Churchill's second administration introduced prescription charges. Harold Wilson later abolished them, but when they were reintroduced, the low-paid were exempted from charges.

Since 1948, the NHS has expanded its remit into mental health and health education, yet the argument about how best to pay for it continues to this day.

FIRST INDIAN MP ELECTED TO THE HOUSE OF COMMONS

Although Dadabhair Naoroji is considered the first Asian or man of Indian extraction to be elected to the House of Commons, fifty years earlier, in July 1841, the constituency of Sudbury had elected an Anglo-Indian, David Ochterlony Dyce Sombre. He wasn't to last long, and only nine months later was disqualified from the Commons after having been found guilty of bribing electors.

Even today Naoroji, one of the founders of the Indian National Congress in India, is still considered a hero of Indian nationalism. So how did he come to be elected as Liberal MP for Finsbury Central in the 1892 general election, which returned Gladstone to power for the final time?

Naoroji was a true polymath and seemed to be able to turn his hand to anything. He was an ordained priest, a publisher, a missionary for the Zoroastrian religion and a professor of mathematics and natural philosophy. In 1855, he travelled to England and became a partner in Cama & Co, the first Indian company to open in Britain. He resigned three years later having had some ethical concerns about the company's activities and established his own eponymous cotton trading company. At the same time he became Professor of Gujarati at University College London. In 1865, he launched the London Indian Society.

When he took his seat in 1892, he refused to swear the oath on the Bible because he was a Zoroastrian and took it on the Khordeh Avesta instead. He spoke often in the Commons about India, but also took on subjects such as Irish Home Rule. He also employed a young researcher in the Commons called Muhammad Ali Jinnah, the future founder of Pakistan.

In 1895, he lost his seat, having only attained a majority of five votes in 1892. His seat fell to the Conservative William Massey-Mainwaring, who beat him by 805 votes. He returned to India and in 1906 was elected President of the Indian National Congress.

Naoroji is today regarded as the 'Grand Old Man of Indian Nationalism', and deservedly so.

In June 2022, there were fifteen MPs of Indian extraction in the House of Commons.

TERROR ATTACK ON LONDON

London – Thursday, 7 July 2005. It began like any normal day in the capital. Londoners began their commute in the same way they always did – they headed to the tube and made their way to work.

At approximately 8.49 a.m., three bombs were set off on the London Underground within fifty seconds of each other. The first was on the Circle Line near Aldgate, the second, also on the Circle Line, at Edgware Road, and the third, on the Piccadilly Line between King's Cross and Russell Square. Around one hour later, a fourth bomb was detonated on a number 30 bus near Tavistock Square.

In this coordinated attack by four Islamist terrorists, fifty-two people were killed and more than seven hundred were injured. It was the deadliest terrorist attack in the UK since the bombing of Pan Am Flight 103 in 1988 over Lockerbie.

In the investigation that followed the deadly attacks, the four suicide bombers were revealed to be 'ordinary British citizens', who carried out the bombings using easily accessible materials. As a result, authorities were not able to detect the plan, a shortcoming which initiated a huge change in British counter-terrorism policies, which had previously been focused on foreign threats.

A day after the attacks, the Prime Minister, Tony Blair, declared: 'There is no hope in terrorism nor any future in it worth living. And it is hope that is the alternative to this hatred.'

However, his response to the bombings, and the investigation thereafter, came under scrutiny. In 2006, the government decided against a public inquiry, describing it as a 'ludicrous diversion', with a full independent inquiry 'undermin[ing] support' for MI5. The Leader of the Opposition, David Cameron, disagreed, saying a full inquiry would 'get to the truth'. When David Cameron became prime minister in 2010, an independent coroner's inquest of the bombings began.

Lady Justice Hallett reported on 9 May 2011. She found that the fifty-two people who died were killed unlawfully but their deaths could not have been avoided or prevented. If the emergency service response had come earlier, they probably still would have lost their lives.

DAVID DAVIS RESIGNS AS BREXIT SECRETARY

David Davis is a politician who is no stranger to resignation. In 2008, he resigned as shadow Home Secretary and MP for Haltemprice and Howden to fight a by-election on the issue of civil liberties. Yet it was his resignation as Secretary of State for Exiting the European Union on the evening of Sunday, 8 July 2018 that caused the most publicity and, perhaps, can be seen as the beginning of the end for Prime Minister Theresa May.

To his own surprise, Davis had been appointed by May as the first Brexit Secretary when she formed her government in July 2016. May had voted Remain and needed a Leave supporter to run Brexit. Davis would be responsible on the British side for negotiating the Withdrawal Agreement that would see Britain leave.

Or so he thought. Davis was sidelined as May came to entrust more power to her chief adviser on Europe, Olly Robbins. A Europhile, he aimed to negotiate a closer relationship with the European Union than Davis could stomach. Both the sequencing of negotiations and concessions on Northern Ireland were anathema to him. Following the ill-fated election of 2017, May's position in Parliament, and Davis's ability to extract a credible Brexit deal, were further weakened.

On 6 July 2018, May invited her entire cabinet to Chequers, where she sought to present the UK's negotiating strategy. Throughout the day, May's central vision was a Common Rulebook between the UK and EU, which essentially involved remaining in the single market for goods.

Davis took the weekend to contemplate his options, eventually resigning late on the Sunday evening. He argued that it was simply not a version of Brexit he could credibly support or negotiate. Followed the next day by the Foreign Secretary, Boris Johnson, it demonstrated just how difficult it would be to formulate a shared Brexit strategy among the cabinet, let alone Parliament.

Despite trying three times (Davis voted for it twice) to pass the deal which was eventually agreed with the EU, May could not find a majority in Parliament and was forced to resign as prime minister in July 2019, just over a year after Davis's fateful resignation.

EDWARD HEATH IS BORN

The Prime Minister between 1970 and 1974 was born during the Great War, and was very much shaped by being a young adult during the approach of, as well as the course of, World War II. It was Edward Heath's experiences then that so strongly created the chief theme of his whole life – a theme that can be crystallized in one word: Europe.

As an undergraduate (Organ Scholar) at Balliol College, Oxford, between 1935 and 1939, Heath supported the anti-appeasement candidate, Sandy Lindsay, in the renowned 1938 Oxford by-election against the official Conservative Quintin Hogg. Heath's hatred of Fascism had matured during visits to Nazi Germany in 1937 and Spain during the civil war in 1938, experiences he never forgot. Together with his service in the 1939–45 war, which he ended as a major, this generated his determination to bring unity and peace to the continent that had been so brutally torn apart.

Having become an MP in 1950, Heath was therefore the ideal choice to lead the first negotiations when Harold Macmillan decided in 1960 that Britain's future lay in a link across the Channel rather than in the embers of empire. That application was vetoed by the French President, de Gaulle. However, having become Conservative Party Leader in 1965, Heath made entry to the (then) EEC his first priority after winning the 1970 general election; his passionate advance was accepted this time and consummated in UK entry on 1 January 1973. There was no question of an approving referendum, a concept Heath always loathed.

Edward Heath will be remembered for other things: being the first grammar-school-educated and arguably working-class Tory Party Leader; and for losing three general elections to Harold Wilson and perhaps one to the miners ('Who Governs Britain?', February 1974); being a racing yachtsman, musician and bachelor; and his marathon feud with his Eurosceptic successor, Margaret Thatcher. Nevertheless, he himself in his last years had no doubt about his key achievement. He had got his country into the EU. It is perhaps fortunate that Heath died in 2005, when Brexit was not even seen as a serious possibility.

BATTLE OF BRITAIN STARTS

It was actually on 18 June 1940 that Prime Minister Winston Churchill declared in the House of Commons that 'the Battle of France is over. I expect the Battle of Britain is about to begin. Upon this battle depends the survival of Christian civilisation. Upon it depends our own British life...' In fact there is no agreed date for the start of the battle, but the head of the RAF's Fighter Command, Air Chief Marshal Sir Hugh 'Stuffy' Dowding, later suggested 10 July as the best date – and who is to argue with the single most important individual in Britain's vital and historic victory?

As Churchill's speech reminds us, in that summer of 1940, Britain was fighting Hitler's Germany almost alone, but for its empire. The Continent had fallen, the USA was still neutral and the USSR was in the cynical pact with the Nazis. Hitler's plan was to establish air superiority before launching the cross-Channel invasion of England, Operation Sealion. He had been assured this was achievable, by the Luftwaffe's ambitious chief, Hermann Goering.

However, it was the RAF, who defeated a German air force three times more numerous, who were triumphant, led by flexible and imaginative chiefs like Dowding and the New Zealander Keith Park, and including charismatic air aces such as the legless Douglas Bader and the South African 'Sailor' Malan, flying the two great warplanes, the iconic Spitfire and the workhorse Hurricane. The RAF were assisted by the first use in warfare of radar, following the work of the British pioneer Robert Watson-Watt, by the German mistake in mid August of switching their attacks from airfields to bomb London, and vitally by the masses of Britons who contributed from observing the skies to making and repairing fighters.

On the climactic 15 September 1940, the largest Luftwaffe attack was repulsed with the loss of sixty aircraft. Five days later, air superiority signally remaining British, Hitler postponed the invasion indefinitely. We may end by considering another Churchill speech, his tribute to the 'Few' – just over two thousand Allied pilots. Yet it was also a victory for the whole of Britain, and the first reverse for Hitler.

LORD SALISBURY RESIGNS

Lord Salisbury is Britain's fourth-longest-serving prime minister. He served in three separate stints: 1885–86, 1886–92 and finally from 1895 until 1902. He was the last prime minister to govern from the House of Lords.

Born in 1830, he entered the Commons in 1854. He served as Secretary of State for India in Derby's and Disraeli's administrations, before becoming Disraeli's Foreign Secretary in 1878.

You can sum up Salisbury's political philosophy in two words – unionist and imperialist. He believed in the power and greatness of the United Kingdom and went to great lengths both to preserve and extend its power and influence.

In 1885, he defeated Gladstone's Home Rule for Ireland Bill and became prime minister for seven months. After five months out of office he then won, with the help of Liberal Unionists, an election in July 1886, and was back for six years. His goal was to preserve existing European alliances and he led the so-called 'Scramble for Africa' and presided over relative peace and prosperity at home.

In 1892, Gladstone returned to power for a final hurrah, but was then succeeded by the hapless Earl of Rosebery. Salisbury's Conservatives were swept back to power in the 1895 election with a large majority.

In foreign affairs, his preferred area of operation, Salisbury faced many challenges, as alliances in Europe ebbed and flowed. Salisbury's preferred policy of 'splendid isolation' continued but was coming under strain. Britain saw off French aggression in East Africa after the 1898 Fashoda Incident, and Salisbury resolved border disputes with the USA in Venezuela and Alaska, but it was South Africa where Salisbury encountered his main challenges. Tensions with Germany – already mounting over German naval expansion – over the Transvaal led to the ill-fated Jameson Raid in 1895, and then four years later full-scale war broke out with the Boers. Victory was somewhat inevitable given the resources Britain put into the war effort, but it came at a huge cost in terms of lives and international reputation.

Salisbury won the so-called Khaki election in 1900 but resigned two years later due to ill health.

ARTHUR BALFOUR BECOMES PRIME MINISTER

Arthur Balfour was a remarkable man who was a rather unremarkable prime minister. The nephew of the outgoing Prime Minister, Lord Salisbury, he is perhaps best known for the 1917 declaration that bears his name, which acknowledged the Zionist cause in Palestine. He remains one of the few former prime ministers to have had an important career after leaving Number 10.

Born in the year of European revolution, 1848, Balfour was always destined for a political career, entering the House of Commons in 1874 at the age of twenty-six. He joined his uncle's first ministry in 1885 and two years later became Chief Secretary for Ireland, a position he held until 1891. He was a vehement opponent of Home Rule for Ireland. From 1892 he led the Conservatives in the House of Commons.

When the Tories returned to power in 1895, Balfour became Leader of the House of Commons. He was not a lover of the ways and traditions of the House of Commons and always preferred influencing matters of foreign policy.

When Lord Salisbury resigned due to ill health on 11 July 1902, there was no real debate about who should take over.

Balfour's three and a half years in office were dominated by the never-the-twain-shall-meet arguments between advocates of free trade and those who wanted a more protectionist trade policy. Cabinet resignations included the arch supporter of tariff reform, Joseph Chamberlain.

However, a major achievement was the 1902 Education Act, which set the course of primary education policy for decades to come.

Balfour's foreign policy was dominated by a desire to effect a rapprochement with the French. In 1904, he signed the Entente Cordiale.

In December 1905, he resigned in the hope that the Liberals would be unable to form a government. It was a massive misjudgement and the Liberals stormed to a landslide in the January 1906 election. He remained party Leader until 1911, but returned to the cabinet, eventually, as Foreign Secretary in December 1916, and served in the coalition government until 1922.

The quotation which perhaps sums up Balfour's laconic attitude to life reads: 'Nothing matters very much and few things matter at all.'

HOUSE OF COMMONS VOTES AGAINST RESTORING DEATH PENALTY

The United Kingdom regularly used the death penalty as a punishment from ancient times until 1964. That was the year the final hanging took place, before the death penalty was suspended for murder under Home Secretary Roy Jenkins (and later abolished in 1969).

However, the House of Commons continually held debates on reintroducing capital punishment, the most influential of which was perhaps in July 1983, when the House of Commons voted overwhelmingly against restoring the death penalty. Why? Because Margaret Thatcher and her government supported the motion making terrorism a hanging offence.

By 361 votes to 245, MPs rejected the proposal. The vote was a free one despite Thatcher's recent 144-seat landslide majority, as the Prime Minister wanted to ensure MPs could vote with their individual conscience. Labour, the Social Democrats and Liberals were naturally opposed, which, combined with sceptical Conservatives, helped to guarantee the death penalty remained a punishment of the past.

The 1983 debate took place less than twenty-four hours after a horrifying terrorist attack on British security forces in Northern Ireland, where four Ulster Defence Regiment members were killed by a land mine. Though amendments in the debate included advocating capital punishment for killing police officers and prison guards, the Home Secretary, Leon Brittan, argued he could only defend hanging applying to terrorists.

In a previous vote, in 1982, 111 of the Conservative Party's 332 MPs opposed restoration while 36 Tory MPs abstained. Given that France, West Germany and the Netherlands had abolished capital punishment with no chance of a subsequent debate, it was clear that the IRA and the threat of violence from terrorism were key in keeping British support high.

Public opinion since the abolition of capital punishment had long supported its return, with 75 per cent endorsing its reintroduction in 1983. It was only public institutions, using the example of America where crime remained rife, that stopped its usage. Indeed, it took until 2015 for public support for the death penalty to drop below 50 per cent, compared to 75 per cent in 1983.

ABORTION BILL RECEIVES ITS THIRD READING

On 14 July 1967, the Abortion Act passed its third reading in the House of Commons with a majority of 262 to 181. Introduced by David Steel MP, the future Liberal Leader and subsequently Lord Steel, the legislation changed women's reproductive rights in the UK forever and is considered a progressive move for the time.

Although Steel brought the Bill in as a private member's bill, the government at the time supported its aims and as a result appointed Sir John Peel – the then President of the Royal College of Obstetricians and Gynaecologists – to oversee a medical advisory committee, which approved its passing.

The Act came into full effect in April 1968, ultimately legalizing abortions under certain conditions in England, Scotland and Wales. It allowed an abortion approved by two medical practitioners if a woman was up to twenty-eight weeks pregnant, with the added safeguarding of this being provided free via the NHS.

The key to this Act was allowing abortion on a much wider scale, emphasizing that 'the continuance of the pregnancy would involve risk, greater than if the pregnancy were terminated, of injury to the physical or mental health of the pregnant woman.'

However, the Act did not pass without passionate debate and has since been challenged in parliament by pro-life campaigners, but all attempts at reform, or even abolition, have been unsuccessful. With this in mind, it is also important to note that only recently has Northern Ireland legalized abortion, on 21 October 2019, with the issue still one that divides the nation.

Since the 1967 Abortion Act was passed, there have been a number of amendments, such as the Human Fertilisation and Embryology Act of 1990, which most notably changed the gestation period from twenty-eight weeks to twenty-four weeks, with some exceptions relating to risk of life.

Without doubt, this Act holds a huge amount of significance for women across the UK – by allowing safe and legal abortion, it truly helped to lay the groundwork for an advancement in women's rights, helping bring about real social change.

NATIONAL INSURANCE ACT IN EFFECT

Which government first created the distinctive welfare state in Britain, with its network of benefits in support of citizens 'from cradle to grave'? The most common answer would surely be: the Labour government led by Attlee from 1945, following the wartime publication of the Beveridge report. However, this view may be challenged.

If we consider the first introduction of key benefits such as old age pensions, instead we must turn to the Liberal government of Asquith after 1908, with Lloyd George as Chancellor also playing a key role. Pensions were first paid in 1909. Then in 1911, the National Insurance Act, coming into effect in July 1912.

For the first time the state took responsibility for benefit payments to assist those suffering from sickness or unemployment. This was in line with the 'New Liberal' principles of positive freedom. That means the belief that people cannot be truly free and in a position to fulfil their potential as individuals if they are held back by poverty or ill health – unlike the philosophy of classical Liberals like Gladstone, it is not just a matter of freedom from external constraints such as that of excessive government. Government can, just sometimes, in fact be part of the solution, not part of the problem.

Interestingly, many like George Lansbury in the early Labour Party were very dubious about the National Insurance Bill. They objected to the workers having to make contributions and argued it should be a universal benefit paid for by progressive taxation, which is a more radical policy. As it was, the principle was established that national insurance benefits should be paid for jointly by worker, employer and government.

The 1911 Act was, it has to be said, not as comprehensive as it later became. Only some occupations were covered, with many, such as domestic service, omitted. Benefits were not generous and were strictly time limited.

Nevertheless, the introduction of National Insurance marked a key and enduring turning point in the role of government in Britain – as did that Asquith government as a whole. Over a hundred years later, after much extension and modification, National Insurance is still going strong.

STATE OF EMERGENCY DECLARED

States of emergency are not declared very often, especially not by prime ministers who are only a month into their term of office. The last State of Emergency had been declared during the General Strike in May 1926. But in 1970, the country's dockworkers had the power to bring the country to a standstill, and they weren't afraid to exercise it.

Forty-eight thousand Registered Dock Workers in the Dock Labour Scheme ports had demanded a pay rise of more than 100 per cent. Unsurprisingly, the government said no. As a consequence the Transport and General Workers' Union called its members out on strike on 15 July. Half of them had already commenced unofficial strike action anyway. The employers' side showed weakness right from the start and made what looked like an attractive counter-offer, which would have meant dockworkers could have earned £55 per week, when the average wage in the country was only £35.

So united were the dockers that the new Home Secretary, Reginald Maudling, asked the Queen to declare a state of emergency because of fears of food shortages. The decision was supported by opposition leader Harold Wilson. Initially, imports came to a standstill. The Army was put on standby, but in the end dockers agreed to handle perishable foodstuffs. The strike affected 90 per cent of UK imports and exports.

A court of inquiry was convened under Lord Pearson and reported on 27 July. It recommended a 7 per cent pay increase. Initially, the dockers rejected the offer, but a revised offer, which included enhanced overtime and holiday rights, was accepted on 30 July. The strikers had lost more than £4 million in pay and the strike had cost the economy up to £100 million.

A year later, another national dock strike ensued over job security, and this became a pattern over the next eighteen years, until the Dock Labour Scheme was abolished in April 1989. Containerization led to the rise of ports which didn't fall under the remit of the Scheme and so had a competitive advantage. The newly created Felixstowe started to eclipse the Port of London.

THE HUMBER BRIDGE OPENS

Why, you may ask, is the opening of a bridge included in a book of 365 significant British political events? Simple. It's the most blatant example in our history of US-style 'pork barrel' politics entering British elections.

On 7 November 1965, the obscure Labour MP for Kingston upon Hull North, Harry Solomons, died. His was a key marginal seat, with majorities of under a thousand in three of the previous five general elections. Solomons had wrested it off the Conservatives at the 1964 election, but with a Commons majority of only four, Harold Wilson's government could not afford to lose the by-election called for 27 January 1966.

Labour's worries only increased when the left-wing radical (and future *Guardian* features editor and KGB contact) Richard Gott announced his candidacy for the Radical Alliance. Opposing the Vietnam War, Gott threatened to split the left-of-centre vote. In the end he attracted a paltry 253 votes.

Harold Wilson was desperate to think of a ploy which could solidify the increasingly weak Labour vote. He asked his cabinet ministers for ideas. It was his trusted ally Barbara Castle who came to the rescue.

Proposals for a bridge or a tunnel across the Humber had been around since 1883 and firm proposals were drawn up in the 1930s, but it was only in early January 1966 that the Secretary of State for Transport, Barbara Castle, dramatically announced that construction would begin.

Well, it did, but not until six years later. By that time, the Conservatives were back in power. However, it wasn't until nine years later that the bridge was actually completed.

The bridge was officially opened by HM The Queen on 17 July 1981, although traffic had been crossing it since 24 June. This was more than fifteen years since Barbara Castle first announced the project.

Given the cost of the scheme, and the low traffic levels, the Humber Bridge has gone down in history as one of the biggest ever white elephants ever constructed. But at least Labour won the by-election with a 4.4 per cent swing...

THE BALLOT ACT RECEIVES ROYAL ASSENT

Believe it or not, ballots have not always been secret in this country. We take it for granted nowadays, but up until 1872 your landlord or employer had a perfect right to stand with you and watch you as you filled in your ballot paper. When the franchise was widened in the 1867 Second Reform Act, this become much more of an issue. The skilled working classes were enfranchised and would have a real influence on the outcome of constituency elections. The power of the landowners and business owners was on the wane. The Chartists had long campaigned for a secret ballot, but the political classes had always resisted for reasons of self-interest. Interestingly, support or opposition to the legislation did not split down party lines. There were plenty of Conservative MPs who spoke out in favour and plenty of Liberals who didn't. Given he had been a firm advocate of parliamentary reform, it was somewhat surprising to see the former Liberal prime minister Lord John Russell (now Earl Russell) speaking out against. He criticized what he called the 'culture of secrecy in elections'. He believed there was nothing wrong with knowing how others had voted and saw the measure as an 'obvious prelude from household to universal suffrage'. From his point of view, this would have been a very bad thing, and this view exemplified the split between the older and younger generations of politician.

The other issue of the time was the fact that election candidates could spend whatever they liked, on whatever they liked. Many voters would be bribed by both sides and thought nothing of it. It wasn't until 1883 that the Corrupt and Illegal Practices Prevention Act was passed, which banned such activities.

In addition, two other pieces of legislation were key to modernizing electoral law and heralding the kind of system elections are administered under today. Following the passing of the Ballot Act, the Municipal Elections Act and the Parliamentary Elections Act both followed two years later.

William Ewart Gladstone was one of our greatest prime ministers, and all these reforms came in under his stewardship and oversight.

MPS VOTE TO TELEVISE THE HOUSE OF COMMONS

It is surprising to think such televised broadcasts are only a little over thirty years old. BBC Parliament (formerly known as The Parliamentary Channel), which broadcasts live and recorded coverage of legislatures around the UK, was established in 1992 before the BBC purchased it in 1998. With the service attracting, on average, 1.2 per cent of the UK's population a week, the public have not, so far, shown great interest in televised parliamentary proceedings.

As early as 1964, a select committee under the Labour government argued a trial period should take place. However, MPs believed the character of the Commons would be changed by the introduction of cameras and voted against televising. Subsequent proposals were defeated in 1972 and 1975.

A compromise of broadcasting via radio was reached in 1975, with extracts from the Commons used for programmes on Radio 4 like *Today* and *Yesterday in Parliament* from 1978. Tony Benn was one of the first voices to be heard.

Surprisingly, it was the House of Lords which led the way with a three-day TV experiment in 1968 and then experimentally broadcasting from 23 January 1985, making the change permanent soon afterwards. A vote in the House of Commons that year meanwhile narrowly rejected televising by 275 votes to 263. In 1988, MPs debated televising the Commons for the eleventh time in twenty-two years.

Eventually, a free vote led to a majority of fifty-four in favour of experimenting for six months with broadcasting, with the first televised speech ever from the Commons broadcast on 19 November 1989. Conservative Ian Gow was the first MP to be shown speaking. The decision to televise was made permanent on 19 July 1990. Rules originally only allowed a close-up or wide shot, but these were eventually relaxed.

BBC Parliament has recently significantly cut back its coverage. Currently, only live and recorded coverage from Westminster and the devolved chambers is broadcast. Previously, party conferences were shown alongside specialist shows. That the BBC has cut these back suggests a long-term commitment to the scrutiny of Parliament is on the wane.

IAIN MACLEOD DIES

Iain Macleod was Chancellor of the Exchequer in the government led by Edward Heath for barely a month before he died. It is one of the great 'what ifs' of political history as to what might have been had he lived. He was by common consent one of the most talented, if maverick, politicians of his generation.

With deep Scottish ancestral roots, Iain Macleod was born a Yorkshireman in 1913. From the age of ten he was educated in Scotland, latterly at Fettes College, the Scottish Eton. He spent an unremarkable four years at Cambridge, apart from the fact that he became an international bridge champion. He was earning around £150,000 a year at today's prices playing bridge and gambling, which lessened the need to find a proper job. He signed up for Army service in 1939 and soon became a commissioned officer. He was injured in 1940 in the Battle of France and was part of the D-Day landings in 1944. He ended his war service as a Major.

Elected to the House of Commons in 1950 for Enfield West, Macleod was promoted quickly into government. A gifted orator, he made his name in a speech in the House of Commons in March 1952 attacking Aneurin Bevan. Six weeks later, Churchill made him Minister of Health. In 1955, he was promoted to the cabinet as Minister for Labour and then in 1959 he went to the Colonial Office and oversaw the ramping up of the decolonization programme.

In 1963, Macleod was horrified by Sir Alec Douglas-Home becoming prime minister and refused to serve under him, instead becoming the editor of the *Spectator*. After the Tories lost power in 1964, he rejoined the front bench as shadow Chancellor. Over the next six years, he fashioned the tax and spend policies he hoped to implement in office. It was not to be.

Having been appointed Chancellor of the Exchequer after the Tories' surprise election win on 18 June 1970, he only got to make one major speech in the Commons, on 7 July. Later that day, he was hospitalized and on 20 July died after a massive heart attack. The Heath government never really recovered.

UK AMBASSADOR TO IRELAND MURDERED BY IRA

Christopher Ewart-Biggs had been the UK's man in Dublin for less than a fortnight when he was assassinated by the IRA on 21 July 1976. Despite varying his route to work many times, a vulnerable spot connected his residence to the main road. It required the ambassador to choose between going left or right. He chose right. Due to attend his first meeting with the Irish Minister for Foreign Affairs, Dr Garret Fitzgerald, he instead hit a landmine full of hundreds of pounds of explosives. It was 9.40 a.m. and he was killed instantly. He was fifty-four and survived by his wife and three children.

Ewart-Briggs was born in Kent and educated at Wellington College and University College, Oxford. During the Second World War, he served in the Royal West Kent Regiment of the Army, where he lost his right eye. Joining the Foreign Office in 1949, Ewart-Biggs had served in Lebanon, Qatar and Algiers, as well as Brussels and Paris.

Judith Cooke, a civil servant and passenger in the car, was also killed, while driver Brian O'Driscoll and passenger Brian Cubbon (the highest-ranking civil servant in Northern Ireland) were severely injured. The Irish government launched a manhunt involving more than two thousand soldiers, with the Taoiseach Liam Cosgrove condemning the 'atrocity'.

Jim Callaghan, the Labour Prime Minister, was among those who resolutely said they would aim to 'bring to justice those responsible for this atrocity'. The government cancelled all ministerial engagements and offered a reward of £20,000 for information leading to the arrest and conviction of those responsible. Though thirteen suspected members of the IRA were arrested, nobody was ever convicted of the killings.

Ewart-Biggs's widow, Jane, had travelled to England by ferry to purchase curtain materials for the embassy when she learned of her husband's murder. She later became a life peer in the House of Lords, where she sought to improve Anglo–Irish relations and promote peace, and also established the Christopher Ewart-Biggs Memorial Prize for literature.

In 2016, a tree was planted at the British ambassador's residence by Kate Ewart-Biggs, forty years after the assassination of her father.

NICK GRIFFIN BANNED FROM BUCKINGHAM PALACE

The fact that Nick Griffin, the leader of the British National Party (BNP), was invited to attend a garden party at Buckingham Palace came as something of a surprise. The fact that he was 'disinvited', less so. Why was his invitation withdrawn? Well, the idiot posted a message on social media asking members of the BNP what they would like him to ask the Queen. He had been invited as an elected member of the European Parliament, and told his supporters: 'I'm attending to represent the patriots who made this possible; I'll be there for you,' and asked for their suggestions on what he should say 'if – presumably due to some ghastly blunder by a courtier – I actually meet her?'

The Palace, putting on its best po-face, issued a statement: 'Nick Griffin MEP will be denied entry to today's garden party at Buckingham Palace due to the fact he has overtly used his personal invitation for party political purposes through the media. This in turn has increased the security threat and the potential discomfort to the many other guests also attending. Mr Griffin's personal invitation was issued to him as an elected member of the European Parliament. The decision to deny him entry is not intended to show any disrespect to the democratic process by which the invitation was issued. However, we would apply the same rules to anyone who would try to blatantly politicise their attendance in this way.'

Griffin served as leader of the BNP from 1999 until 2014, and in 2009 was elected to the European Parliament as MEP for North West England. He notoriously was invited to appear on BBC's *Question Time* programme following that election, and was eviscerated by the other panel members, who included black playwright Bonnie Greer.

He had had a long career in the National Front after graduating from Cambridge in 1980 and in 1998 was convicted of publishing or distributing racist material. He faced further incitement to racial hatred charges in 2004 but was eventually cleared.

In 2014, he was expelled from the BNP and was declared bankrupt. He has barely been heard of since.

CHANNEL TUNNEL BILL RECEIVES ROYAL ASSENT

Though we take the Channel Tunnel for granted nowadays, it has only been open for just over a quarter of a century. The Channel Tunnel Bill received Royal Assent in July 1987 and opened eight years later.

Britain had tried to dig to Europe for over a century. In 1880, work started on experimental tunnels near Folkestone using hand tools. However, these initial plans were abandoned because of the political volatility in the relationship between the UK and France over centuries. Planning for a tunnel in the 1970s was scrapped by Labour in 1975 due to continuing economic crises.

Initially, Margaret Thatcher had favoured a road tunnel because it is believed she thought cars represented 'freedom and individualism'. However, this proposal was rejected as unsafe.

Following Royal Assent, hundreds of thousands of small shareholders bought shares in Eurotunnel, believing they were safe. However, due to debt and disagreement between shareholders, a deal was nearly sunk, with shareholders not receiving dividends until 2009. Three tunnels were built – one in each direction and a middle tunnel for service work, with Margaret Thatcher's support based on an absence of public funding.

The infrastructure process was initially delayed due to difficult terrain and water infiltration, though a British and French worker were eventually able to shake hands in 1990. Starting in Folkestone in Kent and ending in Calais, the journeys of the future would take only thirty-five minutes.

The tunnel was eventually opened in May 1994, a year later than planned, by Queen Elizabeth II and French president François Mitterrand, who cut the inaugural ribbon to link the two nations. Utilizing twelve thousand engineers, the project cost £4.65 billion (£8.5 billion today). The tunnels are thirty-one miles long, and hold the record for the longest undersea tunnels in the world, currently carrying more than 10 million passengers and 1.6 million lorries annually.

It is less well known that proposals for a second tunnel were originally made when Eurotunnel won the contract for the Channel Tunnel. Thatcher had wanted this second tunnel as the road tunnel, but safety and environmental concerns scuppered it.

BORIS JOHNSON BECOMES PM

The political ambitions of Boris Johnson have been apparent ever since he admitted, as a child, he wanted to become 'World King'. Throughout his time at Eton and Oxford, Johnson climbed the greasy pole, becoming President of the Union.

After university, Johnson joined *The Times*, where he was sacked for inventing a quote. Best known for working at the *Daily Telegraph*, he became its Brussels correspondent from 1989 to 1994, when his Euroscepticism became apparent. He edited the *Spectator* between 1999 and 2005, when his notoriety for sending in copy late continued to irritate colleagues.

Elected as Conservative MP for Henley in 2001, Johnson was sacked from the front bench by Michael Howard for lying about an affair. He was persuaded to stand as candidate for Mayor of London. His ability to twice win a Labour city in 2008 and 2012 demonstrated an electoral appeal which most Conservative politicians lack.

Johnson became the public face of the Vote Leave campaign in the Brexit referendum and, with Michael Gove, was the co-leader. Following the narrow Leave win, he was going to run to replace David Cameron, but a stab in the back from his erstwhile ally, Gove, ensured his withdrawal.

Appointed Foreign Secretary by Theresa May, Johnson lacked direction. The highpoint was his handling of the diplomatic response to the poisoning of the Skripals by Russia in Salisbury.

Launching his candidacy for Leader following his, and then May's inevitable resignation, he won a stonking 66 per cent of votes against Jeremy Hunt.

As prime minister, he presided over renegotiating a Brexit deal, which again failed to receive a full mandate in the House of Commons. In the ensuing December 2019 election, he won an eighty-seat majority, which allowed Johnson to agree a Brexit deal on 31 January 2020.

The next stage of his premiership was dominated by the Covid-19 crisis, a virus from which he nearly died. He presided over more than 150,000 deaths, and this, combined with accusations that he lied to Parliament over lockdown parties in Downing Street, nearly ended his political career in early 2022.

LOUISE BROWN IS BORN

The name Louise Brown might seem a fairly ordinary one but it represents someone born in truly extraordinary circumstances. On 25 July 1978, shortly after midnight, Louise Joy Brown became the first ever human to be born after conception by in vitro fertilization (IVF). Born in Oldham General Hospital in Lancashire, by planned Caesarean section, she was delivered by registrar John Webster.

Her parents, Lesley and John Brown, had attempted to conceive naturally for nearly a decade, but Lesley's blocked fallopian tubes prevented this from happening. On 10 November 1977, Lesley Brown underwent IVF, developed by Patrick Steptoe, Robert Edwards and Jean Purdy, which they had been working on for more than a decade. A mature egg was removed from one of Lesley's ovaries and combined with her husband's sperm to create an embryo, which was then planted into Lesley's uterus. Edwards, as the surviving partner, won the Nobel Prize for Medicine in 2010 for this achievement.

Louise Brown weighed 5 pounds, 12 ounces, and was informally dubbed the 'test tube baby', despite her conception taking place in a Petri dish. Hordes of reporters from across the globe descended on Oldham to report on what was called 'the most awaited birth in perhaps 2000 years' by *TIME* magazine. Brown's sister Natalie was also born via IVF four years later and, in May 1999, became the first human born after IVF conception to give birth herself (without IVF).

Brown's birth has often been called one of the most 'remarkable medical breakthroughs of the 20th century'. While her parents were aware the procedure was experimental, they had not been told that no case had yet resulted in a baby. Having attempted impregnation in 282 women, only five had previously become pregnant with none giving birth to a live baby. This raised questions about whether informed consent had been achieved.

Faith groups have often been critical of IVF, worrying about science trying to 'play God'. In 1978, the man who became Pope John Paul II worried about women being used as 'baby factories'.

Politicians and legislators the world over have since struggled to keep up with the science.

LABOUR WINS MASSIVE ELECTION LANDSLIDE

The reason this day marks the 1945 result, rather than election day itself, is that the polls remained open for two weeks from 5 July to 19 July, and the counting of the votes was delayed by another week to allow for the collection of the ballots cast by Britain's servicemen still overseas – the war in the Far East would continue till August, for example. Around 1.7 million 'service' votes were cast, and they contributed to a set of results that shocked many, not least the Prime Minister, Winston Churchill.

Churchill, as the charismatic leader who had piloted the victory over Germany, expected that his Conservative Party would be returned in this election that followed the end of the wartime coalition. However, any respect was not extended to his party. When all the results had been declared, the Conservatives had 189 losses – nearly half of all their seats. Labour by contrast gained no fewer than 239, to win 393 in all. This constituted their first ever overall majority, a massive 156 seats.

Churchill had not had a good campaign personally, being jeered by the crowd at Walthamstow Stadium on 4 July, having made a very ill-received remark in a radio broadcast about Labour (his partners in government for the past five years) being likely to attack free speech like 'some form of Gestapo'.

However, the main reason why Labour won was because they were far more in tune with the mood of the country in 1945. Much had changed in the ten years since the 1935 election, though the memory of the unemployment and depression of that decade, presided over by a predominantly Conservative government, had not faded. After the first ever 'total war', involving massive efforts on the 'Home Front', the British people felt they deserved a different future as a reward.

In 1942, the Beveridge report had been published, recommending in essence a Welfare State to slay foes such as poverty and ill health. It had become an instant bestseller. Labour promised to bring in the major reforms, but Churchill and the Conservatives were unenthusiastic. The scene was thus set for Attlee's government, perhaps one of the most radical ever in Britain.

SEXUAL OFFENCES ACT RECEIVES ROYAL ASSENT

It hardly seems possible that, only fifty-odd years ago, homosexuality was still illegal in England and Wales. Indeed, in Scotland and Northern Ireland it remained illegal until the early 1980s. Gay men were routinely prosecuted for 'importuning' another man. In the 1950s and 1960s, there were more and more court cases, ruining the lives of the men concerned. The police would even tempt men to commit acts of gross indecency in public toilets in an effort to get more convictions. However, public attitudes to homosexuality were becoming more tolerant. In 1957, the Wolfenden report was published, and it examined whether laws on homosexuality should be altered. Incidentally, the law only applied to gay men. There were no restrictions on lesbian acvitity. Wolfenden recommended decriminalization for men over the age of twenty-one. However, the Conservative government kicked it into the long grass, believing (wrongly) that the public wouldn't stand for it.

It took another eight years before a real attempt was made to change the law. Labour MP Leo Abse tabled a private member's bill, with the support of the maverick Conservative MP Humphry Berkeley and Lord Arran. The Bill's passage through Parliament was interrupted by the 1966 election. Labour achieved a massive majority, which encouraged Home Secretary Roy Jenkins to adopt the cause in a government sponsored bill. However, although homosexuality was legalized, there were still restrictions. The homosexual age of consent was to be twenty-one, higher than that for heterosexuals, and only private sexual acts would be within the law. Homosexuality would remain illegal in the armed forces.

The Bill was not whipped at second reading, but virtually all Conservative MPs voted against, with only seven voting in favour, including both Margaret Thatcher and Enoch Powell.

In 1979, a Home Office Committee recommended equalizing the age of consent at eighteen, but that didn't happen until 1994. In 2002, gay people were allowed to adopt, and in 2005 the Civil Partnerships Act was passed, leading to the Equal Marriage Act in 2013. In January 2022, the government announced that all homosexual-related criminal convictions were be scrubbed from the records, with formal pardons issued.

IRA DECLARES AN END TO THE 'ARMED STRUGGLE'

July 2005 proved to be quite a momentous month in Britain. There were two terror attacks in London, it was announced London would host the 2012 Olympics and the IRA declared an end to what it called 'the armed struggle'.

Most people think back to the 1998 Good Friday Agreement as the moment when peace came to Northern Ireland, but it was merely a step on the road to peace. In some ways, 28 July 2005 was a more significant day in the whole process, as it signalled that the IRA recognized it could never achieve its aims through violence.

Although the IRA had declared a ceasefire in 1997, it still retained a vast cache of weapons and explosives. This had always rankled with unionist politicians, who understandably said they could never trust that the IRA meant peace while it retained the ability to conduct violent terror attacks.

The unexpected and sudden declaration on 28 July read:

> All IRA units have been ordered to dump arms. All Volunteers have been instructed to assist the development of purely polit-ical and democratic programmes through exclusively peaceful means. Volunteers must not engage in any other activities what-soever. The IRA leadership has also authorised our representative to engage with the IICD to complete the process to verifiably put its arms beyond use in a way which will further enhance public confidence and to conclude this as quickly as possible.

Sinn Féin president and alleged IRA leader Gerry Adams called it a 'courageous and confident initiative'. Well, he would, wouldn't he...

This led to the decommissioning of IRA weapons under the supervision of the Independent International Commission on Decommissioning. On 26 September 2005, it was announced that all IRA weapons had been decommissioned. The IRA's military structures were also dismantled. However, not all IRA leaders had backed these events and small splinter groups remained active, including Continuity IRA and the Real IRA.

In 2015, the UK government concluded that the IRA continued to exist, albeit in a diminished form.

During its reign of terror the IRA killed more than 1,700 people, including around a thousand members of the British security forces.

219

WILLIAM WILBERFORCE DIES

If you drew up a list of nineteenth-century politicians who made an impact on the world, William Wilberforce would surely feature near the top. It was he who was the driving force behind the campaign to end the slave trade.

Born in Hull in 1759, Wilberforce was the son of a wealthy sugar merchant.

In the mid 1780s, Wilberforce became an evangelical Christian and, having been elected to Parliament at the age of twenty-one, toyed with leaving politics, but instead decided to devote himself to reform. In 1786, he was approached to take up the issue of the slave trade in Parliament.

Between 1789 and 1791, he made several parliamentary speeches and presented evidence to committees and hearings. In April 1791, he presented his first Abolition of Slavery Bill, and embarked on a four-hour-long oration. The Bill was defeated by 163 votes to 88.

A year later, Wilberforce introduced another bill. In response, with the support of Prime Minister William Pitt, the Home Secretary, Henry Dundas, proposed that the slave trade should be phased out over a number of years. The Bill was passed by 230 to 85. However, the onset of the war with France scuppered things.

Throughout the 1790s, Wilberforce plugged away, but public support for abolition was ebbing away. It wasn't until 1804 that things started to change. A new bill passed through the House of Commons but there was no time for it to complete its passage through the Lords. In 1806, the government itself introduced the Foreign Slave Trade Bill and it became law on 23 May. On 23 February 1807, a further Abolition Bill passed both Houses and received Royal Assent on 25 March. Wilberforce sat in his place with tears streaming down his face.

However, it wasn't until 1833 that slavery itself was abolished. By this time, Wilberforce had suffered from ill health for a number of years. He died just days after hearing that the Slavery Abolition Act was about to receive Royal Assent and become law.

He is buried in Westminster Abbey, near the grave of William Pitt.

IAN GOW IS MURDERED

Margaret Thatcher's premiership was bookended with the murder of two of her colleagues by the IRA. In March 1979, Airey Neave was assassinated by a car bomb, while in July 1990, fellow Conservative MP Ian Gow suffered the same fate. The MP for Eastbourne since February 1974, Gow was killed when a bomb exploded under his car at his East Sussex home.

Gow was born in 1937 and educated at Winchester College. He qualified as a solicitor in 1962, working for the London practice Joynson-Hicks and Co.

A long-time Conservative activist, Gow achieved a 10 per cent Liberal to Conservative swing in the October 1974 election in Eastbourne, doubling the majority. Though Gow voted for Margaret Thatcher in the first round of the 1975 Conservative leadership election, he switched his support to Geoffrey Howe in the second.

Gow worked with Airey Neave on Northern Ireland policy in the run-up to the 1979 election. Appointed as Parliamentary Private Secretary to Margaret Thatcher in her first term, his loyalty to the Prime Minister was absolute, and he was promoted to a ministerial role after the 1983 election.

Despite being seen as on the right of the Conservative Party, Gow consistently opposed reintroducing the death penalty.

Gow resigned from the government in November 1985 over the Anglo–Irish Agreement, which would later lead to devolved government. Staunchly opposed to any compromise with Irish nationalists, Gow continued to support the Prime Minister, not least in the challenge she faced from Sir Anthony Meyer in 1989.

Unlike many MPs, Gow left his home address and telephone number in Who's Who. On 30 July 1990, a 4.5 lb bomb was planted under his Austin Montego car, which detonated at 8.39 a.m. as Gow reversed out of his driveway. He died ten minutes later. The IRA claimed responsibility, accusing him of being a 'close personal associate' of Thatcher and advising her on Northern Ireland issues.

Nobody was ever charged with Gow's murder. The Liberal Democrat candidate David Bellotti triumphed in the subsequent Eastbourne by-election, with Conservative MP Ann Widdecombe charging him with being the 'innocent beneficiary of murder'.

VIOLENCE BREAKS OUT AT MOSLEY RALLY

Once seen as one of the brightest prospects in British politics, former fascist leader Sir Oswald Mosley might have disappeared into obscurity following his wartime detention. Not a bit of it.

After the war, he started the Union Movement whose aim was to create a United States of Europe. It didn't take off and its meetings were often disrupted by violent protesters. In 1950, he suggested Africa should be divided up between white and black areas. He was one of the first deniers of the Holocaust, maintaining that the only deaths that occurred in the camps were due to Allied bombing and disease, and that Hitler knew nothing about them. In 1951, he moved to Ireland but returned to stand for Parliament in the 1959 general election in North Kensington, an area of high immigration from the West Indies. He scored 8.1 per cent of the vote. He then moved to Orsay, France.

On one of his trips back to England, in July 1962, he sought to address a rally in Dalston, in east London. Accompanied by men dressed in black shirts, he and they were set upon and punched to the ground. Police made fifty-four arrests, including Mosley's son Max, the future Formula One entrepreneur. Seven thousand people had gathered to hear Mosley speak from the back of a lorry. When he recovered from being knocked to the ground, he got on to the lorry but faced a barrage of rotten fruit, coins and stones. The crowd broke into chants of 'Down with the fascists'. Eventually, he was forced to give up and was driven away in a car that was attacked by protesters as it drove through them.

Mosley's last intervention in British politics came in the 1966 election, where he gained a paltry 4.6 per cent of the vote in Shoreditch and Finsbury. He then announced his retirement and moved back to France. He published his memoirs *My Life* in 1968, writing in the same year: 'I am not, and never have been, a man of the right. My position was on the left and is now in the centre of politics.'

He died in 1980.

AUGUST

ACTS OF UNION BETWEEN BRITAIN AND IRELAND

Ninety-three years after the union between England and Scotland, the Acts of Union between Britain and Ireland were passed separately in the British and Irish Parliaments on 1 August 1800 and implemented on 1 January 1801.

Until 1542, Ireland was a more or less independent nation, with few governmental ties to Britain, albeit since 1171 the English monarch had been titled Lord of Ireland by the Holy See. In that year, the Irish Parliament passed the Crown of Ireland Act, making Henry VIII King of Ireland too, which, in light of Henry VIII's split with Rome in 1534, seems a little incongruous given Ireland's current religious affiliations. It is easily forgotten that most of the ruling classes in Ireland were Protestant until well into the nineteenth century.

In 1707, when congratulating Queen Anne on the union of Scotland and England, the Parliament of Ireland wrote to her: 'May God put it in your royal heart to add greater strength and lustre to your crown, by a still more comprehensive Union.'

In 1782, Ireland gained effective total legislative independence from Britain through the Constitution of 1782. Most of the power in Ireland was concentrated in Protestant hands, something the Catholic majority became increasingly irritated by. This eventually led to a rebellion in 1798, which involved a French incursion. The rebellion was easily (but brutally) crushed.

Although Catholic emancipation had not yet happened, it was becoming more frequently discussed in Britain. There were genuine fears that if the issue wasn't dealt with, a newly enfranchised Catholic majority would lead to major changes in the governance of Ireland. It wasn't long before the issue of full Union with Ireland became a serious prospect for the British government.

However, the Irish Parliament voted against Union in 1799, but a year later it passed by 158 to 115 votes. Under the terms of the Act, 100 Irish MPs would join the existing English, Scottish and Welsh MPs in the House of Commons. However, it would be another twenty-nine years before Catholic emancipation, thanks mainly to the fact that King George III refused to countenance it, on the basis that it would have broken his Coronation Oath.

IRAQ INVADES KUWAIT

The fact that Iraqi tanks had rolled into Kuwait seemed to catch the whole world by surprise. Few had seen it coming, and even now, historians and commentators are divided on the reason for the invasion. Was it because Iraq couldn't pay back $14 billion of loans? Was it because, according to Iraq, Kuwait had been stealing its oil on the border through slant drilling?

The US had already signalled to Iraqi leader Saddam Hussein that it would have 'no opinion' on an Arab–Arab dispute, and Assistant Secretary of State John Kelly, one week before the invasion, had told Congress that America had no treaty obligations towards Kuwait.

Whatever the cause, on the morning of 2 August, Iraqi tanks rolled over the border. Iraqi forces met little resistance and by the end of the next day the whole of Kuwait had been conquered.

Margaret Thatcher and President George H. W. Bush were attending a conference in Aspen, Colorado, and together they held a press conference reacting to the invasion. Thatcher stated: 'Iraq has violated and taken over the territory of a country which is a full member of the United Nations. That is totally unacceptable and if it were allowed to endure then there would be many other small countries that could never feel safe.' She froze Kuwaiti assets in the UK to avoid them being expropriated by Iraq.

Britain and America led the opposition to the Iraqi invasion at the United Nations, which, for once, was surprisingly united, with both the Soviet Union and China expressing concern. Resolution 660 was passed by fourteen votes to zero at the Security Council, ordering Iraq to withdraw its forces.

Later a deadline of 15 January was set for withdrawal. Over the next few months, Allied forces were deployed to the region as part of Operation Desert Shield. Meanwhile, Margaret Thatcher had resigned as British prime minister and was replaced by the inexperienced John Major. On 17 January 1991, Desert Storm was launched and within five weeks Kuwait was retaken.

By then, more than 400,000 people, half the Kuwaiti population, had left the country.

ROYAL ASSENT TO BUTLER'S EDUCATION ACT

The years 1939 to 1945 evoke nothing but memories of the Second World War. However, post-war social reforms were being planned for and few were more important than R. A. Butler's 1944 Education Act. It was instrumental in helping to reduce inequalities that existed within the education system.

The proportion of 'free places' within grammar schools had already increased from a third in 1913 to almost half in 1937. However, for cost reasons parents often had to turn down places.

The key component of Butler's new legislation was requiring Local Education Authorities to create three streams of education schooling – grammar schools, secondary moderns and technical schools. Children would sit an exam aged eleven, known as the 'eleven-plus'. The school-leaving age was also raised to fifteen, and then sixteen in 1972. Previously, in 1938, 80 per cent of children left school aged fourteen, having just attended an all-age elementary school, as fewer than 1 per cent of children went to university.

The role of religious groups like churches in delivering education was also adapted, through religious education being absorbed into the state sector, with Butler encouraging non-sectarian religious teaching in secular schools. As a result, a third of Anglican schools become voluntary aided and could access more state subsides.

The British historian Paul Addison argued that the Act received nearly universal acclaim: Conservatives liked the social hierarchy, Labour enjoyed the new opportunities for poorer children, and the public enjoyed free secondary education. Butler himself saw the Act as being the bedrock of one-nation conservatism that mirrored Disraeli's paternalism towards the working class.

The eleven-plus has subsequently received widespread criticism for dividing children on the basis of intelligence and leading those who attended secondary moderns to feel like failures.

The Act clearly demonstrated that children were staying in the education system for longer. For example, in 1947 there were just 5.5 million children in maintained schools, which rapidly increased to 9.1 million by 1967. However, the small number of technical schools meant 80 per cent of children attended secondary modern schools of variable quality.

OUTBREAK OF WORLD WAR I

The total number of casualties in what was once known as the Great War was over forty million, with around twenty million deaths, half of them civilians, and at least the same number seriously wounded.

Although it was described as the war to end wars, it did no such thing. But did Britain have to become a participant? Its roots were very much on the continent of Europe, and for a time it seemed quite possible to avoid being drawn in.

Tuesday, 4 August strictly speaking marks not the start of the Great War, but the entry of the United Kingdom. Germany had been at war with Russia since the first day of the month, and on the 3rd it had declared war on France. The short-term causes of this massive crisis lay in the Balkans, with the assassination of the heir to the throne of the Austro-Hungarian Empire by a Bosnian Serb at Sarajevo on 28 June.

In addition, the structural problem was the existing system of alliances. When Austria–Hungary responded by giving an ultimatum to Serbia, this brought in Serbia's ally Russia, and Austria's – Germany. France was in turn committed to Russia. Britain too had signed an Entente Cordiale with France in 1904 and completed the Triple Entente by including Russia in 1907.

However, were Britain's 'ententes' strong enough to inveigle us in the escalation? Not all the cabinet thought so in the tense days of late July and early August 1914. In the last week of July, there was strong opposition within the cabinet from John Morley, John Burns and others, even including Lloyd George. However, by the end of Sunday, 2 August, the cabinet had taken the crucial steps towards intervention, the mobilization of the fleet and the guarantee of Belgium's borders.

The decisive influences were the strong commitment of the Foreign Secretary, Sir Edward Grey, to the entente philosophy and the defence of France, supported by Prime Minister Asquith – and the gung ho attitude of most of the press and, indeed, public opinion. On 3 August, Grey famously remarked that 'the lamps are going out all over Europe.' How right he was – in that, at least.

PIRATE RADIO STATIONS FORCED TO CLOSE DOWN

Pirate radio stations have been a part of radio since the 1960s, with changes to digital and internet radio failing to bring about their complete demise. However, their peak was during the 1960s, with a revival in the 1980s and 1990s. Nonetheless, the government tried to ensure their end in August 1968 by forcing pirate radio stations to close down.

Pirate radio stations began broadcasting on medium wave from offshore ships in the mid 1960s. At the time, this was not illegal, as, if a ship was moored three or more miles off the British coastline, it was regarded as being in international waters. This meant the government, police, Navy and Coastguard had no say or jurisdiction over what was broadcast.

Set up to meet the growing demand for pop music not provided by the BBC, the first pirate radio station was Radio Caroline.

By 1967, ten pirate radio stations were broadcasting to a daily audience of ten to fifteen million, with notable DJs like Kenny Everett and Johnnie Walker attracting big audiences. Using a Top 40 format, Radio Caroline and its ilk started to challenge the BBC's monopoly.

The BBC eventually caught on and realized it was losing listeners. It responded by launching BBC Radio 1, Radio 2, Radio 3 and Radio 4, with some Radio 1 DJs, including Tony Blackburn, being directly poached from pirate radio. The UK government then followed suit by introducing the Marine Broadcasting Offences Act 1967, which outlawed offshore stations (except for Radio Caroline).

This was seen as deeply ironic given the Labour government had been liberalizers in many social policies, including decriminalizing homosexuality, legalizing abortion and abolishing capital punishment. Yet they, unlike the Conservative opposition, were willing to be censors. Transmitters were silenced and, temporarily, the radicalism of pirate radio was bought to an end.

Originally broadcasting from ships, pirate radio stations can more commonly be found today in tower blocks across the UK, with Ofcom estimating more than 150 pirate radio stations were still in operation in 2009. Yet it was Radio Caroline and the ingenuity to broadcast internationally that meant it became the ship which rocked the world.

JOHN STONEHOUSE CONVICTED

John Stonehouse was a Labour politician like no other. Best remembered for unsuccessfully faking his own death in 1974, it was later discovered he had been a Czechoslovak spy. Though already in prison, insufficient evidence was found to bring him to trial.

Born in 1925 in Southampton, Stonehouse joined the Labour Party aged sixteen and was elected to represent Wednesbury in 1957. Serving as junior minister for aviation, he began spying for Czechoslovakia, though defended himself against accusations in 1969 during questioning from MI5.

Stonehouse had many business interests after 1970 and these became highly precarious, leading him to adopt deceptive, creative accounting. Realizing the Department of Trade and Industry was about to investigate him, he created a new identity: Joseph Markham – the husband of a deceased constituent.

On 20 November 1974, Stonehouse left a pile of clothes on a beach in Miami, leading to speculation he had drowned. Though obituaries were published, he was actually travelling to Australia to begin a new life with his mistress and secretary Sheila Buckley, twenty-one years his junior. Eventually, he was spotted depositing money in Australia under the name Joseph Markham, which led to local police investigations.

Initially thought to be Lord Lucan, who had disappeared two weeks earlier, Stonehouse was arrested in Melbourne on Christmas Eve 1974 and held in Brixton prison until August 1975. Staggeringly, throughout this whole period, he remained a Labour MP and was not expelled by the party.

Defending himself in court, Stonehouse was charged on twenty-one counts of fraud, theft, forgery, conspiracy to defraud, causing a false police investigation and wasting police time, with his trial lasting sixty-eight days. Convicted on 6 August 1976, he was sentenced to seven years in prison, resigning his parliamentary seat and Privy Council membership in the same month. Imprisoned in Wormwood Scrubs, he was released in August 1979 for good behaviour after suffering three heart attacks.

IDI AMIN EXPELS UGANDAN ASIANS

There is a lot of competition for the title of Africa's most brutal dictator, but Uganda's Idi Amin must surely be near the top of the list of contenders. Seizing power in 1971 from Ugandan president Milton Obote, Amin presided over Uganda for eight notorious years in which up to 500,000 Ugandans were brutally murdered and tens of thousands were forced to leave the country.

Within a year of taking power, Amin decided to rid the country of its Indian population. Ugandan Asians had played a key role in any successes the Ugandan economy had experienced over previous decades. They had originally been brought to the country by the British colonial rulers in the 1890s to help build the Ugandan railway. Of the 32,000 who came, around 7,000 decided to make their homes in the country permanently. By the early 1970s, the Ugandan Asian population amounted to around 80,000 people, a quarter of whom were officially Ugandan citizens. Many were employed in banking and business, and were the personification of high-achieving immigrants.

On 7 August, Amin announced that Ugandan Asians had ninety days to leave the country. They were, he said, 'sabotaging Uganda's economy and encouraging corruption'.

The government of Edward Heath was presented with a problem. In theory, 50,000 Ugandan Asians had the right to enter Britain. Heath tried in vain to negotiate a compromise with Amin, but the Ugandan leader remained intransigent. Up until then, Britain had hugged Amin close and seen him as a pro-British ally.

In the end, nearly 30,000 Ugandan Asians came to Britain, initially housed in reception centres on former RAF airfields. Many arrived with no means of supporting themselves, having been expelled without compensation for business, property and assets.

Edward Heath said: 'It is our duty. There can be no equivocation. These are British subjects with British passports. They are being expelled from their country which in many cases is the land of their birth. They are entitled to come here and they will be welcome here.'

Fifty years on, many of the homes of Ugandan Asians who settled here still have pictures of Edward Heath on their walls.

GEORGE CANNING DIES

George Canning became famous for two reasons. He was the last prime minister to fight a duel, and he became Britain's shortest-serving prime minister, dying after only 118 days in office.

Unusually in those times, Canning was not born to rule. He was the son of a failed Irish businessman and an actress. However, his uncle was persuaded to be his guardian and funded his education at Eton and Oxford. He entered politics at the age of twenty-three and soon climbed the ranks of ministerial office, eventually becoming Foreign Secretary in the Duke of Portland's government, having also been an ally of William Pitt the Younger. He was a success, not least in masterminding the British victory in the Battle of Copenhagen in 1807, a key strategic victory in the Napoleonic Wars.

Two years later, Canning became embroiled in a series of disputes with his cabinet colleague Viscount Castlereagh, Secretary of State for War and the Colonies. It all revolved around troop deployment to Portugal. Canning threatened to resign unless Castlereagh was sacked. The Duke of Portland, who by this time was in failing health, agreed, but Castlereagh found out about the deal and challenged Canning to a duel, which took place on 21 September 1809 on Putney Heath. Unlike his opponent, Canning had never fired a gun in his life. He missed, but was wounded in the thigh. The country was appalled.

When the Duke of Portland resigned, Canning should have succeeded him, but the King decided to plump for Spencer Perceval instead.

He refused to serve under Perceval but returned to public office under Lord Liverpool, eventually returning to the Foreign Office for a successful five-year stint in 1822.

When Liverpool stood down due to ill health in April 1827, it was Canning who the King chose over Peel and the Duke of Wellington. They refused to serve under Canning, who was forced to bring Whigs into a supposedly Tory administration. Canning's health was already on the decline and he died a few months later. He became known as 'the lost leader'.

INTERNMENT INTRODUCED IN NORTHERN IRELAND

Internment began in Northern Ireland for the first time during the Troubles as Operation Demetrius. Involving the mass arrest and imprisonment without any trial of those suspected of being involved with the Irish Republican Army (IRA), the policy had been proposed by the unionist Northern Ireland government led by Brian Faulkner and approved by the British government under Conservative prime minister Edward Heath.

Starting on 9 August 1971, 342 individuals – all of whom were Irish republicans – were arrested by officers launching dawn raids at 4 a.m. This sparked four days of violence in which twenty civilians, two IRA members and two soldiers were killed. Naturally, the use of internment meant seven thousand fled or were forced out of their homes and violence dramatically increased. The British Army faced sustained attack from the IRA with many civilians affected.

From February 1973, loyalist unionists also began being detained. Detainees were generally held at Crumlin Road prison or HMS *Maidstone*, a prison ship in Belfast Harbour. Many of those arrested complained of mistreatment and abuse.

However, faulty intelligence meant that many of those arrested were no longer involved with republican militant activities and had no links to the IRA at all. Though violence eventually began to wane, protests took place in Derry/Londonderry through strike action by over eight thousand workers on 16 August, with sixteen thousand households withholding rent payments for council houses. The crisis had become so disruptive that, by March 1972, direct rule from Westminster had returned.

The interrogation techniques – being beaten, subjected to loud noise, deprived of food and being kicked in the genitals – used to obtain information were ruled as 'inhuman and degrading' by the European Court of Human Rights (ECHR), but weren't seen as torture. It later emerged that the British government had withheld information from the ECHR, and that torture had been authorized.

Internment eventually ended in December 1975, with nearly two thousand having been interned over the four years. This did not mark an end to the Troubles by any means. It also did not deter any kind of nationalist terror threat, with terror attacks on Great Britain only increasing.

232

MPs ARE PAID FOR THE FIRST TIME

MPs' pay has long been a contentious issue. However, parliamentarians even receiving a salary had only been introduced less than a century before. In August 1911, Parliament decided that members of the House of Commons should receive an official salary of £400.

MPs had received pay in medieval and Tudor times – two shillings a day for city MPs and four shillings for county MPs in 1327. As the prestige of being an MP increased, payment was seen as unnecessary as so many MPs came from the aristocracy. Radical campaigns by the Levellers and Chartists called for MPs to be compensated as part of a wider set of parliamentary reforms.

Victorian radicals like John Stuart Mill – a staunch supporter of female suffrage – strangely opposed paying MPs, fearing it would create the tyranny of the majority and reduce the independence of MPs. William Gladstone meanwhile argued that the working-class electorate preferred wealthier candidates. Aspects of snobbery emerged with some arguing that paying MPs would lead to a decline in the number of well-educated MPs.

Eventually, the widening of the electoral franchise led to the issue of paying MPs becoming partisan. Liberals supported the policy officially from 1893 while the Conservatives remained opposed. Trade unions funded the salaries of the first Labour MPs.

The Osborne Judgment, which banned political contributions by trade unions, so angered Labour MPs that Herbert Asquith's Liberal governments, which did not enjoy a parliamentary majority after 1910, introduced a salary at the level of a junior clerk in the civil service. By comparison, the average annual earnings in 1908 were £70.

MPs' pay was regularly reviewed by the Senior Salaries Review Board, having been linked to the pay of civil servants since 1983. The damning nature of the expenses scandal meant that MPs were no longer allowed to set their own pay, and in 2009, the Independent Parliamentary Standards Authority was created to set pay.

Pay for ministers, whips, the Speaker and shadow ministers has always been higher due to the additional responsibilities their employment involves. Currently, the basic salary of an MP is £81,932.

BRITISH LEYLAND IS NATIONALIZED

After the Second World War, the UK's economy was falling out of shape. Its industries, once the envy of the world, were being run down and neglected. Over decades, the situation worsened. Britain's motor manufacturing fell behind France, Germany and the United States. When Labour won the election in 1964, Harold Wilson saw it as his personal mission to get stuck in, and mobilize government intervention, to fix the problem.

Alongside his technology minister, Tony Benn, he developed grand ideas, envisioning enormous conglomerates in manufacturing which would go out and compete with the global big hitters. The theory was that competition between British manufacturers held them back, and by amalgamating, they could present a unified force, prioritizing global exports.

In 1968, after months of negotiation and political pressure from Benn in particular, Leyland Motors, which had a lot of experience in marketing and was responsible for the Triumph and Rover cars, merged with British Motor Holdings, which had enormous manufacturing capability. British Leyland was born.

It didn't take long, though, for things to start going wrong. Sir Donald Stokes of Leyland Motors, encouraged by Tony Benn to take up the role as chief executive of the new British Leyland, was said by the *Financial Times* to have 'the toughest job held by any boss in Britain'. He was tasked with keeping on top of an enormous beast of a company, riven by union disagreements, plagued with bad management and shoddy workmanship. The outcome, as James May puts it, was that 'the cars weren't terribly well built and quite a few bits fell off.' Customers were unhappy. In April 1975, the company collapsed, having run up £200 million in debt. Stokes ran for the hills. Wilson and Benn had to step in to maintain stability, nationalizing the company.

But by 1977, Britain had become a net importer of cars. Wilson and Callaghan, and then Thatcher, kept British Leyland going with bailouts. In 1986, the Leyland brand was so tainted, so synonymous with bad quality, that the name was changed to Rover Group. In 1988, it was fully privatized, as Margaret Thatcher's Conservative government sold their shareholding to British Aerospace.

VISCOUNT CASTLEREAGH COMMITS SUICIDE

I met Murder on the way –
He had a mask like Castlereagh –
Very smooth he looked, yet grim;
Seven bloodhounds followed him.

That was Shelley, in *The Masque of Anarchy*. Lord Castlereagh could be one of the most unpopular politicians ever in Britain. The bicentenary of the Peterloo Massacre of 1819 gave a renewed boost to his portrayal as the brutal, repressive villain of the piece. Yet the manner of his death was by any standard a tragedy in itself.

Castlereagh was born Robert Stewart in Dublin in 1769, went to school in Armagh, and died as the Marquess of Londonderry, having succeeded to his father's title the year before, in 1821. Many of his fellow countrymen regarded him as a traitor for his role in suppressing the 1798 Irish rebellion and then pushing the 1801 Act of Union through the Irish Parliament, thus abolishing that body.

He was Foreign Secretary in the Tory governments of Perceval and Liverpool between 1812 and 1822, and was criticized for supporting the return of the reactionary monarchies in Europe at the Congress of Vienna in 1815 after Napoleon's final defeat. Castlereagh was also Leader of the House of Commons during these years, which associated him with repressive legislation such as the notorious Six Acts, passed in 1819 after Peterloo.

Despite the controversies, as a friend of George IV, who succeeded in 1820, Castlereagh was a strong candidate to replace Liverpool as prime minister in 1821. However, after his father died, his mental health rapidly deteriorated. In 1822, he claimed he was being blackmailed about a homosexual affair. On 12 August, he cut his throat with a small knife and died almost instantly.

Many of the criticisms of Castlereagh's policies are unfair. He had wanted Catholics to be emancipated as part of the Irish settlement. Some said he was a great enemy to civil liberty, but the oppressive measures were those of Lord Sidmouth, the Home Secretary. Castlereagh was an early and strong opponent of slavery. If indeed he was pushed over the edge by the revelation of sexual orientation, that is a condemnation of the attitudes of the age, not of him.

EAST INDIA COMPANY BROUGHT UNDER GOVERNMENT REGULATION

Imagine if a new continent was discovered by a British explorer working for Amazon. And that Amazon then controlled all trade with that continent and its governance. Well that's kind of what happened with the East India Company in South Asia. It became so powerful that it became a law unto itself, before it was brought under government regulation in 1784.

Formed in 1600 to trade in the Indian subcontinent, it rapidly expanded its trading activities into South East Asia, China and Hong Kong, as well as Persia. It was instrumental in colonizing many parts of the regions and by the mid 1700s accounted for half of the world's trade.

India remained a core area of the company's operations and it took on all the functions of government of the country, exercising both military and administrative powers. Following the Battle of Plassey in 1757, it governed for the next century until the 1858 Government of India Act heralded the commencement of the British Raj.

The company had been involved in various financial and political scandals over the years and many leading politicians were caught up in them, which explains why successive administrations proved so reluctant to bring it to heel.

Having seen off the Spanish and Portuguese, the East India Company's main rivals were from France and the Netherlands. Indeed, so stark was the competition that it spiralled into four Anglo–Dutch wars, the last beginning in 1780 and ending in 1784.

The Regulating Act of May 1773 sought to overhaul the management of the East India Company but it had little effect. The company was in a terrible financial position. In return for its monopoly trading position it was supposed to pay an annual premium to the government of £40,000 (around £50 million in today's money), but for several years it had failed to meet its obligations.

William Pitt introduced the India Act in 1784 to address the shortcomings of the Regulating Act. It introduced a Board of Control and joint control of India between the company and the government.

CHURCHILL AND ROOSEVELT SIGN THE ATLANTIC CHARTER

Ever since he had become prime minister in May 1940, Churchill had been trying to persuade the American President, Franklin Delano Roosevelt, to enter the war. But America was still in the grip of isolationism and there was no appetite for a repeat of 1917. Roosevelt was happy to subtly supply materials, armaments and hardware to Britain, but that was as far as he would, or could, go. Pearl Harbor would change that, but that was still some months away.

In the middle of 1941, things still looked bleak for Britain, so it was quite something for Churchill to be looking towards what a post-war international environment might look like. The Atlantic Charter effectively became the document which the future United Nations was modelled on.

Churchill and Roosevelt met first on 9 August on board the British battleship HMS *Prince of Wales* and the following day on the American cruiser USS *Augusta* at Placentia Bay, Newfoundland. They drew up goals and aims for the world after the war, including the universal right to self determination, lower trade barriers, global economic co-operation, the advancement of social welfare, a world free of want and fear, disarmament of aggressor nations and a guarantee of no territorial gains by the USA and the UK.

Part of the aim was to learn from the mistakes made in the Treaty of Versailles. There was no formal document for signing. Churchill quoted Roosevelt as saying that the Atlantic Charter was 'like the British Constitution – the document did not exist, yet all the world knew about it. Among his [Roosevelt's] papers he had found one copy signed by himself and me, but strange to say both signatures were in his own handwriting.'

The Charter was endorsed six weeks later by the governments in exile (France, Belgium, Poland, Norway, Netherlands, Yugoslavia) and the Soviet Union.

INDIA GAINS ITS INDEPENDENCE

Since the creation of the British Raj in 1858, independence was something that always seemed far away, but on the other hand, was always inevitable. As the decades passed, a nationalist movement gained traction, but uniquely, under the inspirational leadership of Mahatma Gandhi, it advocated non-violent means of persuasion through civil disobedience. The pressure built, even during World War II. In addition, Churchill had had to promise that Britain would divest itself of its colonies after the war in order to get full support from the USA. India had also provided huge support to the Allied war effort, both in terms of manpower and resources. The promise of independence was unavoidable even for a devout supporter of the empire like Churchill.

When independence came, it came quickly. Attlee had replaced Churchill as prime minister in July 1945 and immediately set about planning how best to give India its independence.

On 20 February 1947, Attlee announced that Britain would grant full self-government to India by the end of June 1948. Initially, Britain had wanted to preserve India's unity as a single state, but Attlee delegated the decision on India's future structures to the Viceroy, Lord Louis Mountbatten. It proved to be a fateful decision.

On 3 June 1947, Mountbatten declared that India would be partitioned into two separate states – India and Pakistan. Things then moved very quickly, perhaps too quickly. The India Independence Bill proceeded apace through Parliament and gained Royal Assent on 18 July.

At 11.57 p.m. on 14 August, Pakistan was declared a separate nation. Then at 12.02 a.m. on 15 August, India at last became an independent nation. Both were declared Dominions and remained within the Commonwealth.

Massive outbreaks of violence ensued between Hindus and Muslims. Partition had displaced between ten and twenty million people. Millions of refugees were on the move and it is estimated that up to two million people lost their lives. The enmity between India and Pakistan has lasted to this day.

Could things have been done differently, to avoid the violence and deaths? Probably, but no one has yet been able to explain how.

THE PETERLOO MASSACRE

The significance of the Peterloo Massacre in the fight for universal suffrage and meaningful parliamentary reform has never had quite the acknowledgement it deserves. Only historians can answer as to why that is.

The glacial process of political reform had juddered to a halt in 1793, but following the victory at Waterloo in 1815 there were genuine hopes that a new day was dawning and it would resume. Lord Liverpool, who had become prime minister in 1812, was a Conservative to his core. Giving the masses the vote was not on his political agenda. As the war came to an end, hundreds of thousands of troops were demobilized. There weren't enough jobs for them. It was not a good time to be a member of the working classes, especially when the new Corn Laws, designed to protect the interests of landowners, led to a dramatic increase in the cost of bread. The country was not quite in a state of revolutionary foment, but the conditions had been laid for huge disquiet. More than seven hundred petitions, with a million signatures, were delivered to Parliament, encouraged by the populist writer William Cobbett. That's the equivalent today of six million people signing a petition.

Things came to a head in Manchester in August 1819 when thousands of protesters gathered in St Peter's Field, in the culmination of a summer of protests across the land. Many were dressed in their Sunday best. There was a festival atmosphere, which was soon shattered by the arrival of three hundred truncheon-bearing special constables, accompanied by close to a hundred members of the Manchester and Salford Yeomanry, alongside the regular cavalry of the 15th Hussars. They galloped into the crowd, initially killing a small child and a special constable. The hustings were smashed to pieces. Exits were blocked by bayonet-toting infantry, leading to a stampede. Women were twice as likely as male protesters to be injured, and they were deliberately targeted. Eighteen people ended up being killed.

The Peterloo Massacre sparked a countrywide series of protests that autumn. Revolution never came, but the Great Reform Act did, albeit thirteen years later.

ANIMAL FARM IS PUBLISHED

Animal Farm is widely regarded as one of the greatest political novels ever written. Penned by George Orwell, it told the story of animals rebelling against their human farmer in a bid to create a freer and more equal society. Naturally, such a utopia failed to materialize, as the animals themselves became as corrupted as their human leaders.

The book is undoubtedly a satirical take on the Soviet Union, which was founded on the same premise.

What remains fascinating about the book was that Orwell was a democratic socialist and undoubtedly a figure of the left. Fighting in the Spanish Civil War against fascism, his admiration for liberal democracy was unarguable. Indeed, it was seeing the purging by communists that inspired him to recognize where the threats to liberty can emerge from. His greatest quality was the ability to criticize his own side, and condemn anything that claimed to be on the left while not respecting individual freedom.

Orwell crafted the book between November 1943 and February 1944, during the period when the UK was in an alliance with the Soviet Union to defeat Nazi Germany. Initially, publishers were immensely resistant to publishing the book – such was the obviousness of the metaphor – for fear of worsening relations. Four publishers rejected the book, with one disapproving of it after checking with the Ministry of Information. It was eventually published by Secker & Warburg in the immediate aftermath of the war.

The relatively simple plot of *Animal Farm*, which can be examined on a surface and deeper level, was demonstrative of Orwell's desire to speak in a clear and concise manner in his writing. Orwell described the book as fusing 'political purpose and artistic purpose' for the first time. Writing a preface, Orwell criticized the suppressing of criticism of the Soviet Union, though this was removed from later editions. Initial reviews weren't positive, with schools over following decades sometimes, in an ironic twist, seeking to censor the book. Not in my school, however, where the book was on my O Level English syllabus.

PARLIAMENT ACT RECEIVES ROYAL ASSENT

The twentieth century was one of immense constitutional change in Britain, especially with regard to the House of Lords. The 1911 Parliament Act dramatically changed the upper House's powers by removing its ability to reject financial bills of the House of Commons. It heralded the start of a gradual weakening of the Lords' ability to be a barrier to the elected government of the day.

The need for the Parliament Act was sparked by the constitutional crisis of November 1909, when a Conservative-dominated House of Lords full of hereditary peers rejected the Liberal government's 'People's Budget', which included pensions for people over seventy and increased taxation to redistribute wealth. Led by Prime Minister Herbert Asquith, Chancellor David Lloyd George's budget was passed following the first 1910 general election. A second election that year had reforming the House of Lords at the core of the campaign.

The Parliament Act, which the House of Lords agreed to by 131 to 114 in August 1911, removed the Lords' ability to wholly veto Commons bills. Peers only agreed to this after King George V threatened to create 250 Liberal peers to remove the Conservative majority. Instead, they could only delay legislation by up to two years. Along with reducing the maximum length of a Parliament from seven to five years, the Act clearly sought to make Parliament more accountable. Before this, the only way to resolve disputes between the two Houses had been the creation of more peers by the monarch.

The Parliament Act has only been used seven times to force bills through. Most recently, the New Labour government forced through the hunting ban, equalizing the age of consent and introducing proportional representation for elections to the European Parliament without the consent of the Lords.

It proved to be another move on the road to democratizing the British parliamentary system. Less than a decade later, universal suffrage was introduced in 1918, which was wholly extended in 1928. In 1949, a subsequent Parliament Act reduced the Lords' delaying powers to just one year, and in 1958, life peers were introduced for the first time.

MO MOWLAM DIES

Mo Mowlam died on 19 August 2005, aged just fifty-five, from a brain tumour. One of the main female architects of New Labour, she was undoubtedly an individual with a long and enduring legacy. Best known as Northern Ireland Secretary during the signing of the Good Friday Agreement, which bought peace to Northern Ireland after three decades of the Troubles, she was always keen to highlight the good that politics can do.

Then Irish Taoiseach Bertie Ahern labelled her someone with 'courage and sincerity', while Tony Blair said she had one of the 'most remarkable and colourful personalities' in British politics.

Born in Hertfordshire in 1949, Mo grew up in Coventry and attended one of the nation's first comprehensives – Coundon Court School. She studied sociology and anthropology at Durham.

Before entering Parliament, Mowlam worked as an academic at the University of Wisconsin–Milwaukee, before relocating to the UK to teach at the University of Newcastle. She was elected for the seat of Redcar, which she won in 1987. That same year, she became Labour's spokesperson on Northern Ireland.

Immediately following John Smith's death in 1994, Mowlam became one of the earliest supporters of Tony Blair's bid for the leadership, which he rewarded with the post of shadow Northern Ireland Secretary.

Diagnosed with a brain tumour just weeks before the 1997 election, Mowlam gained weight and lost her hair, but was not deterred. Mowlam was still recovering from treatment when Blair appointed her Northern Ireland Secretary. Influential in ensuring peace talks worked, she entered the infamous Maze prison in 1998, where she spoke to convicted paramilitaries. She was successful in persuading them to enter peace talks.

In 1999, she was moved to become Minister for the Cabinet Office before standing down from Parliament in 2001.

Mowlam's last few months in 2005 were characterized by her strong spirit, but her health was evidently deteriorating. Struggling with her balance because of radiotherapy treatment, she suffered a fall in August 2005 after which she never regained consciousness. She passed away in the Pilgrims Hospice – an apt name – in Canterbury less than two weeks after former Foreign Secretary Robin Cook died.

CHURCHILL'S 'NEVER IN THE FIELD' SPEECH

On 10 July, the Battle of Britain commenced. Day after day, night after night, the planes of the German Luftwaffe had attacked Britain's coastal defences, airfields and infrastructure. The onslaught lasted until 10 October. Initially, heavy damage was inflicted by the Luftwaffe, but slowly the British airmen in their Hurricanes and Spitfires gained the upper hand. It was the first military campaign fought entirely in the air.

The objective of the onslaught was to force Britain to sue for peace. The methods were twofold – to attack ports and shipping, with Portsmouth coming under particularly heavy attack initially, and then to achieve air superiority by attacking airfields. As the Germans became ever more desperate they also bombed civilian targets.

By mid August 1940, Churchill had only been prime minister for three months. But he knew he was the one person the public looked to, to keep their spirits up. His 'blood, sweat and tears' speech had galvanized the nation. After six weeks of German bombing, he knew he had to do something similar.

On 20 August, he spoke in the House of Commons, paying tribute to the bravery of those he called 'The Few', the RAF pilots who were trying to keep the Luftwaffe at bay.

It is said that Churchill first used what became one of his most famous sentences on a visit to the Operations Room (now the Battle of Britain Bunker) at RAF Uxbridge on 16 May. Emerging into the daylight he told Major General Pug Ismay: 'Don't speak to me. I have never been so moved.' After a period of silence, he then said: 'Never in the history of mankind has so much been owed by so many to so few.'

He decided to use this in his speech four days later, but travelling to the Commons, when he repeated it to Ismay, Ismay warned: 'What about Jesus and his disciples?' Churchill acknowledged the point and changed it to 'Never in the field of human conflict'.

Churchill was effectively telling his people: 'Don't despair. We've turned the corner.' And it was true. Victory in the Battle of Britain proved to be the first setback for the Nazi war machine.

BBC STARTS TV BROADCASTS FROM ALEXANDRA PALACE

The BBC was an established radio broadcaster – and had already come up against opposition from politicians on numerous occasions.

The first such significant battle was fought back in 1926 when, for nine days in May, the UK's industry ground to a halt in a General Strike. The TUC had triggered the action to prevent wage reduction for coal miners, and it meant that many newspapers were unable to print. The Conservative government, led by Stanley Baldwin, needed an effective way of getting messages out to the population. Chancellor Winston Churchill believed that radio was the best way to cut through the chaos, and he lobbied Baldwin to seize the British Broadcasting Company, which had already caused the government a fair amount of grief in its reporting of the strike. Stanley Baldwin eventually ruled that the broadcaster should remain independent.

Ten years later, in a converted wing of Alexandra Palace, the BBC (now British Broadcasting Corporation) began test television transmissions under government licence. The special programmes included short musical performances and speeches. The image was so low-definition that viewers had to take breaks from looking at the screen after a limited duration. In November, with the official launch of BBC television, the resolution was much better – at 240 lines rather than 30. Programmes were broadcast Monday to Saturday, from 3 to 4 p.m. and 9 to 10 p.m.

The BBC's TV service has been no stranger to hostility from government, either. A notable example was the reporting and programming around the Falklands War in 1982. Margaret Thatcher's government became furious with the BBC for casting doubt on British military sources when Peter Snow said 'If we believe the British...' when presenting *Newsnight*. After a few other such cases, Home Secretary William Whitelaw invited both the BBC's Chairman and Managing Director of Television to attend a meeting with Tory backbenchers. When they arrived, they found more than a hundred MPs, ready to showcase their fury. It turned into a ritual defenestration.

Somehow, perhaps by public demand, the BBC has survived and kept its independence, despite pressure brought on it by governments of both colours. There are plenty of challenges to come.

ENGLISH CIVIL WAR BEGINS

On this day Charles I raised his standard at Nottingham, the traditional act of a King going to war – however, not against a foreign power such as France or Spain (or even Scotland, before the unification in the persons of the Stuart kings themselves). It was Charles's own Parliament, or those within it who so strongly opposed him. This was civil war, internal strife, and it was to culminate in Charles's beheading and our only experiment in living without a monarchy.

There has been much controversy about the reasons for the civil war (or wars – the role of conflicts in Scotland and Ireland have been stressed by recent historians). It is now unfashionable to agree with the great Marxist historian Christopher Hill that this was the 'English Revolution', the transition from aristocratic feudalism to bourgeois capitalism. Arguments that the civil war was caused by either the rise or fall of the gentry are similarly unsupported by agreed evidence.

If the social and economic causes are now downplayed, there can be less doubt about the importance of religion and politics. Charles's religious policy had been seen as flirting dangerously with Catholicism, with his wife aggressively following the Roman faith, and his Archbishop of Canterbury William Laud's Arminianism at the opposite end of the Protestant spectrum from the Puritanism that would play such a large role in the next twenty years.

Above all, as so often, this period of history was shaped by the struggle for power. For eleven years, from 1629 to 1640, Charles had attempted a 'Personal Rule' without calling Parliament. This looked like royal autocracy on the continental model. When he felt forced to recall Parliament he was met by a battery of reproachful protest, indeed remonstrance.

Charles dissolved the first recalled 'Short' Parliament after three weeks. Its successor, later in 1640, lasted for twenty years – to outlive him, indeed. Skilfully led by MPs such as John Pym, Parliament so harassed Charles that he decided to fight; but having faced superior military forces and leadership such as that of Oliver Cromwell, the King was led to the scaffold and the block in 1649.

WESTERN HOSTAGES APPEAR ON TV WITH SADDAM HUSSEIN

Following the Iraqi invasion of Kuwait in early August 1990, the Iraqis held many Westerners hostage, viewing them as human shields. Some had been on a British Airways flight to Kuwait which actually took off from London after the invasion had begun.

On 23 August, Saddam Hussein appeared on state television with a group of predominantly British hostages including five-year-old Stuart Lockwood. Saddam told them they had been detained to 'prevent war', but were guests, not 'human shields', and Iraq's only motive was to ensure their safety. He chatted to the dozen captives, ruffling the blonde hair of Stuart while doing so. He asked him if he was getting his milk.

The pictures provoked widespread revulsion. British Foreign Secretary Douglas Hurd said: 'The use of children in that sort of way is contemptible.' A spokesman for the Gulf Support Group, set up to support the families of stranded British people, said the scene 'made all of us feel sick'.

The women and child hostages were allowed to fly home in September, but the men were detained until December.

It was subsequently rumoured that the reason why BA flight 149 was allowed to proceed, and then land in Kuwait, was that it had SAS operatives on board. It also later transpired, following the release of official papers under the thirty-year rule, that the situation could have been avoided if the contents of a call by the British Ambassador to Kuwait had been passed on to British Airways. By that time the flight was in the air, but it could have been diverted.

The Gulf Support Group has been fighting for compensation for the ordeal of the passengers for thirty years. In November 2021, the Foreign Secretary, Liz Truss, denied any UK government culpability and said: 'responsibility for the passengers being taken hostage lies solely with the Iraqi government at the time.'

The fact remains that had the BA flight captain been aware of what was happening before he landed, he wouldn't have.

One day, the whole truth will out.

BRITAIN BURNS DOWN THE WHITE HOUSE

Those who don't know their transatlantic history probably imagine that the 'special relationship' between Britain and the United States has always existed. Far from it. From the loss of the colonies under Lord North in the 1770s, right up until the turn of the twentieth century, the two countries were, if not at war, certainly at loggerheads. It was only during World War II that the 'special relationship' was struck.

In 1812, war broke out between the United States and Britain over long-standing differences about territorial expansion and British support for Native Americans who opposed it. Britain had been interfering with American trade with France, in particular impressing American merchant seamen. Britain had tried to avert war, given it was already at war with France, but by the time concessions were transmitted to America, Congress had already voted for war. Despite making initial gains, the American forces gradually lost ground to the British, whose army was reinforced following the abdication of Napoleon in early 1814. In August, British troops burned down most of the capital, Washington, D.C., including the White House. The war ended in a draw with the signing of the Treaty of Ghent, later in the year.

On 24 August, British forces routed the Americans at the Battle of Bladensburg, ten miles north-east of Washington. They continued on to the capital under the leadership of Major General Robert Ross. They razed most of Washington to the ground. The whole city was ablaze, including the White House, which was at that time called The Presidential Mansion, and the US Capitol Building. So confident was President James Madison of American victory that he had prepared a celebratory banquet that evening. When news of the defeat came, the President's wife, Dolly, packed up as many of her possessions as she could and together they fled to Maryland. When Ross's men burst through the doors of the White House, they found pigs roasting on spits. They ate the food themselves and drank a toast to His Majesty. Chairs were then piled up on the banqueting table and the room was set ablaze. A 'special relationship' indeed.

RAMSAY MACDONALD FORMS NATIONAL GOVERNMENT

Coalitions have been rare in British politics in the past century. It has been thought appropriate to suspend party competition in the interests of national unity during major wars, hence the coalitions of Asquith in 1915, Lloyd George in 1916 and Churchill in 1940. On one occasion, in 2010, the parliamentary arithmetic after an indecisive general election led to the Cameron–Clegg agreement to form a peacetime coalition, but that was unusual – previously hung parliaments had tended to lead to minority governments, shortly followed by another election, as in 1974. The circumstances of the coalition formed in August 1931 are unique.

It is true that at the time, Ramsay MacDonald's Labour government did not have an overall majority, but that had been the case since the 1929 election. The cause of his highly controversial decision to form a 'National Government' was an unprecedented international economic crisis, the depression provoked by the Wall Street Crash.

On 24 August 1931, MacDonald announced that he would be forming a coalition. The leaders of the Conservative and Liberal parties, Stanley Baldwin and Herbert Samuel, agreed to serve under him. In a reduced cabinet of ten members there were just three others from the Labour Party (Snowden, Thomas and Lord Sankey), outnumbered by four Conservatives and two Liberals. This was the first act of the 'great betrayal' identified by Labour supporters thereafter.

Why did MacDonald take this dramatic step, instead of resigning himself and going into opposition or retirement? Some, like Sidney Webb, later accused him of pursuing a deliberate plot – claiming that he had long intended to drop the Labour Party and carry on himself. But the evidence does not support this theory. MacDonald's diary suggests that on 23 August he expected to leave office the next day. However, the intervention of King George V may well have been critical. On the morning of 24 August, he implored MacDonald to stay on for the benefit of the country in the grave economic emergency. MacDonald was always strongly influenced by the conception of 'duty'. Ironically, it was this that led him to a step that culminated with his vilification by his own party.

POLITICAL DOCUMENTARY MAKER MICHAEL COCKERELL BORN

If Sir Robin Day was the best political interviewer we have ever had in Britain – and he was – then Michael Cockerell is our most renowned political documentary maker. His profile films and documentaries about leading politicians and documentaries about the political process still stand the test of time and most of them can now be watched on Youtube, reaching a whole new generation.

As a political broadcaster, one thing I learned from Michael Cockerell is to let people speak and they might just say something interesting, and that often leads to a news headline.

The BBC, to its credit, would give Cockerell both the time and resources he needed to make a top-class hour of television, in a way it just doesn't nowadays.

He started off on the BBC Africa Service before spending twelve years as a go-getting reporter on *Panorama*. In 1979, he conducted an interview with Margaret Thatcher on the eve of the election, where his interviewing style led the future Prime Minister into some self-reflection. 'How many Mrs Thatchers are there?' he asked. She smiled and replied confidingly: 'Oh, there are three at least. There is the intellectual one, the intuitive one and there's the one at home.' Her voice was so low and breathy, her manner so intimate – even coquettish – that the late Sir Robin Day, watching in the studio when the filmed interview went out, joked: 'the untold story of the election campaign: Margaret Thatcher is having an affair with Michael Cockerell'.

Politicians almost fell over themselves to be a subject of one of his films, all of them memorable. Edward Heath opened up to him. Alan Clark was revelatory. Roy Jenkins was a sex maniac (I exaggerate), Michael Howard came across as human. And Boris Johnson? Well...

How to Be a Chancellor, *Foreign Secretary* and *Home Secretary* were a trilogy of documentaries which let us into the secrets of what those three government departments actually do. And then came another trilogy explaining the relationship between Britain and America, France and Germany.

Michael Cockerell. A political broadcasting legend.

LORD MOUNTBATTEN IS MURDERED BY THE IRA

Lord Louis Mountbatten was the very personification of the British Establishment. He was a minor, but influential member of the royal family, had had a good war record, and had been the last Viceroy of India. He was the man the royal family turned to in times of trouble, especially Prince Charles, for whom he had become something of a father figure.

The Mountbatten family had a holiday home on the Irish border in County Sligo. Mountbatten had long been on an IRA target list. In 1978, they had tried to shoot him while he was on his boat, but bad weather intervened. On 27 August 1979, not quite four months after her election as prime minister, the IRA decided to send Margaret Thatcher a message. The method would be to assassinate Lord Mountbatten. He was out lobster-potting with his daughter, son-in-law, their twin sons and their paternal grandmother, along with a young local crew hand, Paul Maxwell. The boat, *Shadow V*, had been moored in the harbour at nearby Mullaghmore and the previous night IRA member Thomas McMahon had affixed a 50 lb remote-controlled bomb to its underside. Mountbatten had only piloted the boat a few hundred yards out of the harbour when it blew up. Mountbatten was cruelly injured, with both his legs being almost blown off. He was pulled alive from the water by local fishermen, but died before he could be brought ashore.

Mountbatten's grandson Nicholas and Paul Maxwell were killed instantly, while Doreen, the Dowager Lady Brabourne, died the next day in hospital.

Margaret Thatcher said: 'His death leaves a gap that can never be filled. The British people give thanks for his life and grieve at his passing.'

Some time later, Sinn Féin leader Gerry Adams said: 'He knew the danger involved in coming to this country. In my opinion, the IRA achieved its objective: people started paying attention to what was happening in Ireland.'

On the same day, the IRA also ambushed and killed eighteen British soldiers at Warrenpoint, sixteen of them from the Parachute Regiment. It was the deadliest attack on the British Army during the Troubles.

THE LAST BRITISH PLANE LEAVES AFGHANISTAN

In February 2020, Donald Trump signed the Doha Accords with the Taliban, which committed the United States to withdraw its forces from Afghanistan by 1 May 2021. The Taliban failed to meet most of the commitments they made, but nevertheless the incoming President, Joe Biden, stood by the agreement but extended the deadline to 11 September, the twentieth anniversary of the 9/11 attacks.

Then, with no warning to the US's allies, he unilaterally announced on 8 July that the date would be brought forward to 31 August. Governments in Europe were horrified. The Taliban was encouraged to speed up its conquering of Afghan territory. By mid August, they were almost at the gates of Kabul. It was at that point that the UK Foreign Secretary, Dominic Raab, and his permanent secretary at the Foreign Office decided it was appropriate to go on holiday.

An emergency airlift began with the aim of rescuing all British citizens still in Afghanistan. It began on 14 August and rescue efforts became increasingly frantic as the Taliban encircled the Afghan capital, then took it over. Planes were landing and taking off from Kabul airport every few minutes rescuing Western citizens and Afghan nationals who had helped Western countries during the occupation.

Members of Parliament complained bitterly that their representations on behalf of constituents with relatives in Afghanistan were going unanswered, even when a bespoke email address had been set up by the Foreign Office. Dominic Raab eventually returned from his holiday after enduring days of humiliating newspaper coverage, but by then the damage to his reputation was irreparable.

At the same time, a former soldier, Pen Farthing, who ran an animal rescue centre in Kabul, demanded that he, his staff and animals should be given priority in the airlift. The country then divided between those who thought rescued Afghan animals should be given priority over humans, and those who didn't. Eventually, more than fifteen thousand people were rescued by the British airlift, but several thousand Afghans, who were eligible for rescue, were left behind.

This was the most abject failure of American intelligence and foreign policy since, well, the last one.

BRITAIN SENDS TROOPS TO KOREA

Korea had been occupied by Japan since 1910, but at the end of the Second World War it was liberated. The United States came to an agreement with the Soviet Union to split Korea into two occupation zones. The Soviet-supported North became the Democratic People's Republic of Korea, whilst the American-backed South was the Republic of Korea. In 1949, Soviet and US forces were withdrawn, but they left behind a tense pair of nations, each claiming legitimacy over the whole peninsula. In June 1950, North invaded South.

Two days after hostilities began, Clement Attlee's Labour government held a cabinet meeting. Korea was listed as the fourth item on the agenda, and ignorance in cabinet was obvious. Some ministers didn't even know where it was. Cabinet Secretary Sir Norman Brook said to Attlee that 'Korea is rather a distant obligation,' to which the PM replied: 'Distant, yes, but nonetheless an obligation'. Cabinet was reluctant for British troops to get involved; they didn't consider the invasion as any real threat to the UK's interests.

In the end, the UK agreed to join seventeen other UN countries and support the Americans, whose troops had been pushed back down through the country to the southern coastal port of Busan, as the North Koreans captured the Southern capital of Seoul. On 29 August 1950, British soldiers arrived in Busan.

As UN forces pushed north through Korea and neared the border, China became involved to push them back. Battles were bloody and casualties mounted. In 1951, the fighting paused and armistice negotiations began. So began two years of stalemate, in which soldiers faced extreme conditions of hot and cold weather, sat in trenches on either side of the Korean border. An agreement was signed in July 1953. Nearly sixty thousand British troops had seen action during the Korean War, over a thousand of whom lost their lives. To this day, the war hasn't officially ended – no peace treaty has been signed.

The war had been unpopular with the British public, having occurred so soon after World War II. Clement Attlee had paid a heavy price politically by agreeing to join in the conflict.

MPS REJECT MILITARY ACTION AGAINST SYRIA

A special summer recall of Parliament saw MPs rejecting the Coalition government's proposals for military action against Syrian president Bashar al-Assad's regime. Nine days earlier, a suspected chemical weapons attack had taken place on the outskirts of the capital Damascus, where hundreds of people were killed. While the Assad government blamed Syrian rebels, the UK and US governments put responsibility firmly at Assad's feet. Assad had crossed President Obama's red line and used chemical weapons.

David Cameron sought a mandate from Parliament endorsing military action if UN weapons inspectors produced evidence demonstrating government responsibility. This precedent – seeking a mandate from Parliament before partaking in warfare – had been set by Tony Blair's Iraq War vote of 2003 and David Cameron receiving an overwhelming mandate for his Libyan intervention in 2011. However, that same mandate was not repeated this time, with a Joint Intelligence Committee document unable to ascribe a motive for the attack, meaning intelligence agencies failed to deliver a definitive verdict on whether military action would be lawful.

MPs voted 285 to 272 against the government, ruling out the prospect of joining US strikes. Thirty Conservatives and nine Liberal Democrat MPs rebelled against their own government, alongside the opposition parties, to ensure British military action was thwarted.

Ed Miliband was the main architect of the defeat. As Leader of the Opposition he argued that the public opposed a 'rush to war' and 'reckless and impulsive leadership', despite initially having assured David Cameron of his support. That David Cameron failed to ensure such a motion passed Parliament undoubtedly made him a diminished figure on the world stage, with the already questionable 'special relationship' put under further strain.

Following the Paris terrorist attacks in November 2015, the UK sponsored a UN Security Council Resolution by France urging UN members to take 'all necessary action' in the fight against ISIS. MPs in December 2015 thus voted by 397 to 223 for the UK to participate in airstrikes against ISIS in Syria, though there would be no ground troops. The UK may have U-turned on its international involvement, but the internal crisis in Syria remains as far from resolved as ever.

SIR DAVID FROST DIES

'Hello, good morning and welcome.' Five very simple words, yet everyone knew that when they were uttered by Sir David Frost at the beginning of his Sunday morning programme, they were in for an hour of brilliant political TV entertainment.

His interviewing style was deceptive. He wanted a conversation, and his softly, softly approach, which other interviewers often derided, invariably reaped dividends. And he could turn his hand to any type of interview, from heads of state to ordinary people in the street. He was a man of rich and many talents. He could pick up the phone to any world leader and they would take his call. That's power. That's influence.

David Frost first rose to fame in the early 1960s, hosting the weekly satirical show *That Was the Week That Was*. He remarked that 'Talking to the camera seemed the most natural thing in the world.' America soon came calling and for the rest of his life he commuted between the UK and the US working on various broadcast projects. Perhaps his most famous moment came in 1977 when he persuaded former president Richard Nixon to take part in three extended interviews, which became known as Frost v Nixon. They were eventually turned into an award-winning film and stage play.

Frost enjoyed huge success throughout his broadcasting career, but there were failures too. He led the successful bid for Britain's first commercial breakfast television franchise in 1983, TV-am. It flopped, despite a stellar line-up of presenters including Frost himself. However, he stayed with TV-am, hosting a weekly *Frost on Sunday* show, and then when TV-am lost its franchise, he presented *Breakfast with Frost* each Sunday for twelve years from 1992, attracting all the leading politicians.

Over his career he interviewed each of the eight British prime ministers from 1964 to 2016 and the seven US presidents from 1969 to 2009.

I appeared on his show several times as a newspaper reviewer. He had such a clever way of putting me at my ease. With seconds to go to air, he'd tap my knee and wink at me.

David Frost died on a Mediterranean cruise on 31 August 2013 at the age of seventy-four.

SEPTEMBER

GLADSTONE'S SECOND HOME RULE BILL FALLS

In 1885, Gladstone's son Herbert decided to fly what was known as the Hawarden Kite. Hawarden was William Gladstone's home, and the kite was a well-placed story in the press that the Grand Old Man of British politics had converted to the cause of Home Rule for Ireland. Whether Gladstone himself knew of his son's 'kite flying' is unknown, but it had a dramatic effect. The eighty-six Irish Nationalist MPs in the House of Commons immediately withdrew their support from Lord Salisbury's administration and transferred their allegiance to the Liberals. This only served to entrench Salisbury's anti-Home Rule views, which had up until that point been softening. While Gladstone became prime minister for a third time, it was a short-lived triumph. When he introduced his First Home Rule Bill in 1886, ninety-three of his own MPs voted against it. Salisbury was back in power for another six years.

Returned to office in 1892, Gladstone decided to have another go and introduced a new Home Rule Bill. However, by this time, the Irish Nationalists had split into two factions. Gladstone decided to draft the Bill himself in order to keep its contents secret. None of his colleagues or indeed the Irish MPs had any idea of what was in it. This proved to be a calamitous mistake when, at Committee stage, it was discovered that there had been a major error in calculating how much Ireland should contribute to the Treasury each year.

The Chancellor, Sir William Harcourt, already an enemy and rival of Gladstone's, was already enraged at having not been consulted on the Bill, but this made matters ten times worse. Although it eventually passed the Commons by a narrow majority, it was never going to get past the Conservative-dominated House of Lords. Sure enough, it fell by 419 votes to 41.

Gladstone retired not long afterwards, having essentially been the architect of his own defeat. It was a sad way to end such a long and illustrious political career.

Home Rule simmered away, but it was to be another twenty years before it was seriously considered again.

THE GREGORIAN CALENDAR IS INTRODUCED

Brits are always suspicious of change. We like what we're used to. So when Henry Pelham, who was Britain's third prime minister, agreed to proposals to change the calendar from the Julian calendar to the Gregorian calendar, it proved somewhat controversial in the population at large.

Most Catholic European countries had already adopted the Gregorian calendar, but it was still greeted with suspicion in most of the Protestant parts of the continent. They viewed it as a papist plot, designed to persuade them all to return to the followings of Rome. However, they all gradually followed suit, but it wasn't until 1923 that Greece relented, to become the last European country to fall into line.

The Gregorian calendar was introduced in 1582 by Pope Gregory. Its purpose was to space leap years differently, in order to make the average calendar year 365.2425 days, rather than 365.25. The Gregorian calendar shortened the average year by 0.0075 days which stopped the drift in the calendar with regard to the equinoxes. By the time the Pelham government introduced the change, the difference between the two calendars was eleven days. In order to rectify this, it wasn't Thursday, 3 September that followed Wednesday, 2 September in 1752, it was Thursday, 14 September. New Year's Day would also change from March to 1 January.

The main instigator of the change in Britain was the Earl of Macclesfield, a fellow of the Royal Society. He was supported by the Earl of Chesterfield, who managed to persuade Prime Minister Henry Pelham that the reform should be introduced. In 1751, Chesterfield introduced a 'Bill for Regulating the Commencement of the Year and for Correcting the Calendar Now in Use'. It proved to be remarkably uncontroversial and passed through both Houses with little opposition. It received Royal Assent in May 1752.

It is commonly thought that there were rioting mobs in the streets, chanting 'give us back our eleven days'. However, modern-day historians dispute this, saying there is little evidence to support it. Some people, however, continued to observe Christmas Day on 5 January for many years to come.

BRITAIN DECLARES WAR ON GERMANY

At 11.15 in the morning on Sunday, 3 September 1939, the sepulchral tones of Prime Minister Neville Chamberlain were broadcast on BBC radio to the nation: 'Unless we heard by 11 o'clock that they were prepared at once to withdraw their troops from Poland, a state of war would exist between us. I have to tell you now that no such undertaking has been received, and that consequently this country is at war with Germany.' Yet just a year earlier, Chamberlain had been feted like a hero on his return from Munich for avoiding just such an eventuality. On the other hand, he has subsequently been condemned as an arch-appeaser, a 'Guilty Man' for not standing up to the Nazi menace earlier.

Chamberlain has been accused of being fooled by Hitler. He did say that he thought Hitler was a man whose word could be trusted when he said that he had no more territorial demands in Europe, and on 30 September 1938 that he believed he had secured 'peace with honour... peace for our time'. What this actually meant was that he had refrained from going to war with Germany in 1938 to save Czechoslovakia, a country in Central Europe that Britain could not directly help.

So why did the same man declare war in 1939 because Germany had invaded Poland, another country to the east of Germany? It could be argued that Chamberlain had been quite rational to give Hitler another chance and delay for a year. This is not mainly because it gave Britain another twelve months to rearm, and develop vital weapons such as the Spitfire – after all it also gave Hitler another year to prepare.

However, it certainly should be remembered that it was widely expected that when the next war came it would bring the scale of death and destruction from the skies that we now associate with a nuclear attack – 'the bomber will always get through.' That is why Chamberlain's speech on 3 September was immediately followed by mass evacuation. It did not – yet – bring devastating bombing. But it *was* followed by six years of world conflict.

GREENHAM COMMON PROTEST COMMENCES

Throughout history, peaceful protests have been powerful political statements. The Greenham Common protest, opposing US nuclear cruise missiles on British soil, was a prime example. Started by four women in west Wales – Ann Pettitt, Karmen Cutler, Lynne Whittemore and Liney Seward – the presence of women by the RAF base lasted nineteen years and is imprinted on the public conscience.

The women walked 120 miles to Greenham Common in Berkshire, with their march leaving Cardiff on 27 August attracting thirty-six women, four men and some children, who were part of Women for Life on Earth. Ten days later, they arrived at the base, with some marchers chaining themselves to the base fence like the suffragettes.

The presence of US nuclear missiles had been sparked by the Soviet Union deploying an intermediate-range missile (SS-20) which could destroy Europe's NATO bases. The United States therefore responded by placing its own medium-range missiles in Europe, with ninety-six based in Greenham from 1983.

The peace camp, which contained feminist, religious and New Age strands, quickly gained international fame, with thirty thousand women arriving in December 1982 for an 'Embrace the Base' human chain along all nine miles of the perimeter. By the time the missiles arrived in November 1983, authorities struggled to balance defending the right to protest with ensuring the work of the base could continue.

Portrayed as lesbian separatists by the media, the women faced attack from some right-wing groups including RAGE (Ratepayers Against the Greenham Encampments). One protester, Helen Thomas, was tragically killed by a police van aged only twenty-two in 1989, though her death was ruled an accident.

The protest began to end after the Reykjavik Summit between Ronald Reagan and Mikhail Gorbachev in 1986, which agreed to eliminate intermediate-range missiles on both sides. Gorbachev himself admitted the Greenham women influenced his decision to attend the summit, while a Reagan adviser argued the 'zero option' was copied from the women's banners.

Missiles started being removed in 1989 and the final missile left in 1991. The base was returned to full RAF ownership in 1992 before closing, becoming common land in 1997.

CHRISTINE KEELER ARRESTED AND CHARGED WITH PERJURY

Politics has always been full of scandal and rarely more so than in the Profumo Affair. It involved married cabinet minister John Profumo having an affair with Christine Keeler, a model and showgirl. However, Keeler was also sexually involved with Yevgeny Ivanov, a Soviet naval officer.

Born in Uxbridge – now Boris Johnson's constituency – Keeler became a topless showgirl at Murray's Cabaret Club in Soho, where she met Stephen Ward. In her autobiography *Secrets and Lies*, Keeler argued that Ward was working as a double agent for both MI5 and the KGB, passing secrets between the two.

Ward introduced Keeler to John Profumo, the Secretary of State for War, in July 1961 at Cliveden in Buckinghamshire. The affair ended after Profumo became aware of the security risk of continuing the relationship. Keeler's subsequent relationships with individuals included jazz promoter Johnny Edgecombe. When their relationship ended, Edgecombe turned up at Stephen Ward's house – where Christine Keeler had sought refuge – and fired several shots.

It was this incident that sparked the publicity for the Profumo Affair. As ever, it is the cover-up which catches the politician out. Initially denying any kind of relationship with Keeler in the Commons, Profumo later admitted he had lied in the chamber, which forced his resignation.

However, neither Christine Keeler nor Stephen Ward were out of the woods. Keeler accused jazz singer Lucky Gordon (another of her partners) of attacking her. Protesting his innocence, Gordon said two witnesses could prove he was not guilty.

These witnesses were eventually named at the closing stages of the trial of Stephen Ward, who claimed Keeler had given false evidence about Gordon. Accused of being bent on political revenge, Ward was on trial for the earnings he obtained from Keeler through her work as a prostitute. Overdosing on barbiturates before being sentenced, he went into a coma and died. Keeler herself pleaded guilty to perjury and served six months in Holloway prison.

Keeler lived a mostly solitary life after her release from prison. Following two brief marriages, both of which failed, the money she had earned from selling her story to newspapers ended up being spent on legal fees.

DIANA, PRINCESS OF WALES IS LAID TO REST

For a week most of the country had been in a state of shock. The level of grief exhibited by people who had never known the Princess of Wales bordered on hysteria. In the early hours of 31 August, Princess Diana had been killed, along with her friend Dodi Fayed and driver Henri Paul, when the car they had been travelling in had hit a concrete barrier in a Paris underpass. It later transpired that Henri Paul, the deputy head of security at the Ritz hotel in Paris, was drunk.

I remember watching the horror as it unfolded on the TV news channels. It wasn't clear at the outset that the Princess had died, but the sad news was broken at around 4.30 a.m. I had never met the Princess, although I did own her Audi Cabriolet. It felt like a member of my own family had been killed.

As the nation woke up to the news of her death, Prime Minister Tony Blair spoke outside his local church: 'I feel like everyone else in this country today. I am utterly devastated. We are today a nation in a state of shock, in mourning, in grief that is so deeply painful for us... She was the People's Princess and that is how she will stay, how she will remain in our hearts and our memories for ever.'

On the morning of 6 September, princes Philip, Charles, William and Harry walked behind the coffin, carried on a gun carriage, down the Mall to Westminster Abbey. During the funeral service, Diana's brother, Charles Spencer, gave the eulogy, directly criticizing the press and, indirectly, the royal family for their treatment of his sister. Applause rang out in the Abbey and rippled through the crowds outside. Elton John sang a new version of 'Candle in the Wind', dedicated to Diana's memory.

More than three million people lined the streets of London and 2.5 billion people watched the funeral ceremony worldwide.

After the service, Diana's coffin was driven up the M1 to the family's ancestral home at Althorp, where it was buried on an island in the middle of a lake.

JAMES CALLAGHAN RULES OUT AUTUMN ELECTION

Gordon Brown wasn't the only Labour prime minister to regret bottling calling an election. Despite his honeymoon popularity, and letting election speculation run rife, at the last minute he decided not to call an election in September 2007, only three months after taking office. He failed to learn the lesson of his predecessor but one, James Callaghan.

On 7 September 1978, Callaghan ruled out an autumn election, which most analysts think he would have won, against insurgent Conservative Leader of the Opposition Margaret Thatcher. Callaghan believed his 'Sunny Jim' persona would ensure he could survive any Winter of Discontent. How wrong he was.

At the time, elections were usually held four years apart. However, Callaghan wanted to retain power for as long as possible, going into a fifth year, even as his parliamentary majority rapidly diminished. The Lib–Lab pact had already fallen apart, forcing Callaghan to rely on the Scottish National Party and Ulster Unionist MPs. Yet Labour were ahead in the polls, as Thatcher's net positive rating fell to -13 per cent.

While holidaying on his Sussex farm, Callaghan had spoken to trade union leaders, with the majority advising him to call an early election. Speaking at the TUC conference on 5 September, he said: 'I have promised nobody that I shall be at the altar in October.' He then sang a line from the the chorus of the music hall song which begins, 'There was I, waiting at the church.' Two days later, in a TV broadcast, he announced to an expectant nation that there would be no election that autumn.

Callaghan's over-optimism caused him to believe an understanding on pay restraint on wages could be reached. It was a fatal miscalculation on his part.

Pay restraint by the unions was largely abandoned and most industries experienced strikes. The Winter of Discontent gave the Conservatives a 19 per cent lead by January 1979, with the government losing a vote of confidence by one vote in March.

After the election in May 1979, Callaghan remarked that there are times when you can't hold back the tides of change, and this was one of them. He was right.

PENGUIN CHARGED WITH OBSCENITY OVER LADY CHATTERLEY'S LOVER

We British can be a prudish lot. Or could. Today anything goes, and the thought of censoring a book for 'taste and decency' would be anathema in 2022. But as the drab 1950s turned into the swinging sixties things were different. Labour MP Roy Jenkins, who was later to be dubbed the architect of the 'permissive society', persuaded Harold Macmillan's Conservative government to support a reform to the Obscene Publications Act, and a new, liberalized version became law in 1959.

However, when Penguin Books published the full version of D. H. Lawrence's final novel, *Lady Chatterley's Lover*, in 1960, they were sued over breaching public decency. The book's plot revolved around an aristocratic woman who was at it with her gardener and in every conceivable position. And it contained regular uses of the words 'fuck' and 'cunt'.

The prosecuting counsel demonstrated how in touch with the times he was by asking if this was the kind of book 'you would wish your wife or servants to read'. Collapse of stout case. The prosecution clearly hadn't studied the new Act in enough detail. It had made it possible for publishers to escape the long arm of the law if they could demonstrate the work in question was of 'literary merit'. E. M. Forster and others testified that it was.

The trial opened on 20 October, and on 2 November 1960 the trial ended. The verdict was 'not guilty'. The floodgates were opened and there have been very few obscenity trials since.

Penguin published a second edition in 1961 which contained the dedication: 'For having published this book, Penguin Books was prosecuted under the Obscene Publications Act, 1959 at the Old Bailey in London from 20 October to 2 November 1960. This edition is therefore dedicated to the twelve jurors, three women and nine men, who returned a verdict of 'not guilty' and thus made D. H. Lawrence's last novel available for the first time to the public in the United Kingdom.'

Lady Chatterley's Lover is now on the school curriculum. Proof, if ever there needed to be, that times have changed.

QUEEN ELIZABETH II BECOMES LONGEST-SERVING MONARCH

When Queen Victoria died in 1901, she had reigned for sixty-three years, seven months and two days. It was assumed that this record would never be broken. However, on 9 September, Queen Elizabeth II overtook her great great great grandmother. And in February 2022, she celebrated her Platinum Jubilee, marking seventy years on the throne.

Her first prime minister was Winston Churchill, and since then she has had weekly audiences with fourteen more prime ministers. When Boris Johnson became prime minister, she overtook King George III, who had fourteen different prime ministers in his sixty-year reign. Queen Victoria had ten.

The relationship between monarch and prime minister has fascinated many historians over the years. Early prime ministers served at the pleasure of the monarch rather than the voters, but in the three hundred years since Robert Walpole came to power in 1721, the power of the monarchy has been on the decline. There was a time when if the monarch didn't like the cut of your jib, you were highly unlikely to ever become *primus inter pares*. Queen Victoria was the last monarch to exert any real influence and power over who would enter Number 10. Since then, the electorate has decided.

HM The Queen has clearly enjoyed the company of some prime ministers more than others, but has been very discreet about which ones she liked and disliked. Rumour is that Harold Wilson was her favourite prime minister. She herself was once asked and she replied: 'Winston, of course, because it was always such fun.'

A servant once commented 'I could not hear what they talked about, but it was more often than not punctuated with peals of laughter – and Winston generally came out wiping his eyes!'

Whole books have been written about the Queen's relationship with Mrs Thatcher and there has even been a stage play, *Handbagged*. In *The Crown*, it was portrayed as very prickly. While it is true that Mrs Thatcher was a bit of a revolutionary figure, and the Queen is anything but, they got on far better than is widely supposed.

GIBRALTAR REFERENDUM

After Spain made a formal proposal to Britain in 1966, about the future of Gibraltar, a referendum was organized in which Gibraltar citizens were asked whether they wished to pass to Spanish sovereignty or retain their current status under British rule.

The result of this referendum, held on 10 September 1967, was overwhelming, with 99.19 per cent in favour of remaining under the sovereignty of the British crown.

By 1969, the Labour government had introduced a new constitution for Gibraltar. Meanwhile, the fascist regime in Spain closed the border between Gibraltar and Spain, and it did not open again until the new democratic government in Spain sought admission to the European Union.

The 1969 constitution contained an important preamble, which stated: 'Her Majesty's Government will never enter into arrangements under which the people of Gibraltar would pass under the sovereignty of another state against their freely and democratically expressed wishes.'

Despite being enshrined within the constitution, it was this principle that foreign ministers Jack Straw and Peter Hain unilaterally and arbitrarily ignored in 2002, when they embarked upon talks about joint sovereignty with Spain. They completely ignored the words cited in the 1969 constitution – despite having no mandate to embark on such conversations.

This act by Peter Hain and Jack Straw resulted in a further referendum in 2002. The result was comparable to the referendum of 1967.

In the light of the result of the referendum, and United Kingdom public opinion which was supportive of Gibraltar's resolve to remain British, the then Prime Minister, Tony Blair, instructed that there should be no further pursuit of talks with Spain regarding joint sovereignty.

A further result of the 2002 referendum was that both the United Kingdom and Gibraltar governments drafted a fresh constitution. It effectively granted the Gibraltarian Parliament full internal self-government. The Gibraltarian government has powers in excess of those exercised by the Scottish government. In essence Gibraltar has devo max.

9/11

Tony Blair was in Brighton for a speech to the TUC conference. He was staying in the hotel where, seventeen years earlier, the IRA attempted to kill Margaret Thatcher with a bomb. For his security detail it was an ordinary day; but that was about to change.

At 12.46 p.m. UK time, the first hijacked plane was flown into the North Tower of the World Trade Center. When the second plane hit the South Tower at 1.03 p.m., Blair and his team knew it couldn't have been accidental. The PM's security staff immediately assessed the potential danger around him. It was decided he would shorten his TUC speech, then get back to London as quickly as possible.

An air of confusion and, perhaps, panic descended. Where in London might be vulnerable to such attacks? Canary Wharf, certainly, had a building tall enough; the Transport Secretary, Stephen Byers, quickly closed the adjacent City Airport. But what of Buckingham Palace, the Houses of Parliament and Downing Street itself? Police were deployed to reinforce the streets, but all nervous eyes were looking to the skies. It fell to Geoff Hoon, Defence Secretary, to scramble fighter jets to enforce a no-fly zone above the entire capital.

Richard Wilson, then Cabinet Secretary, called Tony Blair shortly after the attacks. He recalls that the PM focused very keenly on how George Bush would react, and what he would do next. Blair felt that it should be his role to intervene to stop the President going too far. This meant the UK standing closely with the US on foreign policy, to strengthen relations and, Blair thought, increase his government's influence around the world.

In the days following the attack, as the Bush administration focused its blame for the attack on al-Qaeda founder Osama Bin Laden, Blair fell into line. He issued an ultimatum to the Taliban government in Afghanistan that if it didn't give up Bin Laden, there would be war. Sure enough, twenty-six days after the Twin Towers fell, a US-led coalition began military operations in Afghanistan. Two months after that, the Taliban was overthrown, to be kept out of power until it seized it back in August 2021.

JEREMY CORBYN BECOMES LABOUR LEADER

'Sharon in Brent wants you to run for leader.' Those were the words I said to Jeremy Corbyn on LBC the day after Labour had badly lost the 2015 general election, and on the day Ed Miliband resigned as leader. He roared with laughter and retorted: 'I don't think there would be many of my colleagues supporting that view!' Yet, only three weeks later, on 3 June, he announced he would run.

Thanks to a dozen MPs like Margaret Beckett and David Lammy 'lending' their nominations, he crept over the line with minutes to spare and was officially nominated on 15 June, along with Liz Kendall, Andy Burnham and Yvette Cooper. No one expected him to come anywhere but last, but no one had considered the effects of the leadership election rule changes introduced by Ed Miliband, which took power out of the hands of Labour MPs and trade unions and empowered ordinary members and supporters. As Corbyn built momentum, the other three candidates struggled to define themselves and floundered against a man whose quiet resilience impressed Labour members, who had grown tired of what they saw as three right-wing candidates. They began to let their hearts rule their heads.

When the result was announced on 12 September, everyone knew who the winner was going to be, and sure enough, Corbyn won with 59.5 per cent of the vote. Corbyn struggled to make headway in his first few months, having picked a shadow cabinet in his own image. Many of them fell by the wayside and a year later he faced a leadership challenge from Owen Smith, which he saw off with ease, gaining an increased majority.

When Theresa May called an election for 8 June 2017, she was expected to win a landslide. Instead, Labour gained thirty seats and attained 40 per cent of the vote. It was still a loss, however Corbyn's supporters tried to portray it. Even they couldn't portray the 2019 result as a win. Corbyn had endured a miserable two years, plagued by accusations of anti-semitism and incompetent leadership. Labour lost fifty-eight seats and dropped 8 per cent of the vote. Corbyn finally resigned.

IAIN DUNCAN SMITH BECOMES CONSERVATIVE LEADER

Leadership elections usually dominate the political landscape, especially if they involve one of the two main parties.

The same cannot be said for the 2001 Conservative leadership election. Called after the party's second landslide defeat, with a net gain of just one seat, it failed to capture the political imagination. The Conservatives simply looked so far from power, a far cry from their repeated victories under Margaret Thatcher. That the result itself was announced on 13 September 2001, not as had been intended, forty-eight hours earlier, further highlighted its limited significance.

The winner? Iain Duncan Smith, beating rival Kenneth Clarke – by more than 55,000 votes. Overall, he received 61 per cent of the vote to Clarke's 39 per cent.

Within the campaign itself, key divisions were, unsurprisingly, mainly over Europe. In the first ballot of MPs, both David Davis and Michael Ancram tied for bottom place. With both refusing to withdraw, a second ballot was held in which Ancram lost, but both withdrew. Michael Portillo, who had re-entered Parliament under William Hague and served as his shadow Chancellor, lost the final MPs' ballot to Iain Duncan Smith by a single vote following a faltering campaign.

That only eight hustings were held among local constituency parties, with one televised debate on *Newsnight*, just showed how little momentum the campaign enjoyed.

As Leader, Duncan Smith was unable to command any authority. At the 2002 Conservative Party conference, Duncan Smith called himself the 'quiet man' and said his confidence for leadership should not be underestimated, acknowledging his quietness and timid persona was not a strength. Instead, it only reinforced his public image: unable to communicate effectively, disorganized with no central vision, a vote of confidence in his leadership was a matter of when, not if. In November 2003, after numerous rumours of plotting, Duncan Smith lost an MPs' vote of confidence by ninety votes to seventy-five.

After resigning, Duncan Smith sought to improve the conditions of the poor by creating the Centre for Social Justice think tank, the policies of which he implemented as Work and Pensions Secretary in David Cameron's Coalition government.

DUKE OF WELLINGTON DIES

Draw up a list of the top ten most important Britons of the nineteenth century and there's a fair chance most people would include one of the greatest military commanders ever to lead UK armed forces – Arthur Wellesley, the first Duke of Wellington. He is of course most remembered for his trouncing of Napoleonic forces at the Battle of Waterloo, but in all he fought sixty battles. His political career is relegated to second place in people's memories, despite him twice being prime minister.

Born in Dublin in 1769, he was elected to the Irish House of Commons in his twenties, but his military career came first. He had been made a duke during his period as Ambassador to France in 1814, but it was only on Boxing Day 1818 that he entered government as Master-General of the Ordnance in the administration of Lord Liverpool. In 1827, he became Commander-in-Chief of the British Army. When Lord Liverpool's government fell in 1827 and George Canning took over, Wellington, along with many other ministers, quit too. Three months later, Canning died, and six months later, his successor Viscount Goderich was forced out. Wellington's time had come, even though he was a reluctant prime minister. Along with the progressive Robert Peel, he had become increasingly influential in the Tory Party, and his more conservative approach provided a balance to Peel.

Wellington's period as prime minister was certainly not as memorable as his time as a military leader, but he does have one big achievement to his name, the long overdue issue of Catholic emancipation. It had been assumed that Wellington would stand firm with the Anglican Settlement, but he knew the time had come to push reform through. The Tories were split and he had to persuade Peel not to resign. He even became the last prime minister to fight a duel with the Earl of Winchilsea after the latter accused him of introducing 'popery'.

The rest of Wellington's premiership was characterized by splits, economic problems and riots and in November 1830 he resigned. He returned for a three-week swansong in 1834, and remained active in the House of Lords until his death in 1852.

FUEL PROTESTS END

During the fuel protests in September 2000 it was almost impossible to fill up your car with petrol. People would drive from petrol station to petrol station and face queues of hours or miles. Fights would break out on forecourts. I remember saying to my partner: 'This is not the country I know.'

Rising petrol and diesel fuel prices caused independent lorry owner operators to form a protest group called 'TransAction'. They blockaded oil refineries and fuel depots in Essex, leading to widespread disruption of supplies of petroleum products.

The main aim of such protesters was to force a reduction in fuel duty, which the government had ruled out. The rise in fuel costs had led to the UK going from being one of the cheapest fuel-providers in Europe to one of the most expensive. The UK haulage sector was becoming increasingly uncompetitive.

The Conservative opposition were determined to exploit the government's problems. After the price of crude oil hit $35 per barrel, the main blockading began on 8 September 2000, when a Cheshire refinery was blocked by Farmers for Action, with other protests occurring across the country. By 10 September, the Manchester Fuels Terminal, the largest inland oil terminal, had also been blockaded, meaning fuel became rationed and petrol stations closed.

On 11 September, the government took emergency powers under the Energy Act 1976 to ensure fuel arrived at essential services, with three thousand petrol stations closed due to a lack of fuel. The government's COBRA committee also sought to utilize the military to guarantee more fuel deliveries. The level of daily deliveries plummeted from 131 million litres to five million.

Supermarkets warned they would run out of food because of panic buying, while seventy schools had to close. From 14 September 2000, the protests began ending as protesters gave the government sixty days to act.

Following the end of the protests, the government froze fuel duties and announced changes would be made to road vehicle taxation. Similar protests occurred in 2005 and 2007, causing panic buying, though these were not on the same scale.

September 2000 was the only time in the Blair years that the Conservatives were ahead in the opinion polls.

BRITAIN LEAVES THE ERM

'Black Wednesday' in September 1992 marked the effective end of John Major's government. He would remain prime minister for another five years, but his economic credibility was shot. The day marked Britain's withdrawal from the Exchange Rate Mechanism (ERM) and, along with the Maastricht Treaty, signalled the first step on the long road to Brexit.

Throughout the 1980s, Margaret Thatcher's government had repeatedly struggled to control the pound and inflation. A stable currency was needed to help businesses plan. It was also linked to the process of further European integration, where the government agreed to ensure the pound would not exceed three deutschmarks (DM).

The ERM itself was introduced in 1979 as a means of stabilizing monetary policy. It was always intended to be the first step on the road towards a single currency. Though Margaret Thatcher had always resisted joining the ERM, political weakness forced her hand and in October 1990 the new Chancellor, John Major, announced Britain was joining. The timing was a huge mistake, as was the high entry level of £1 – DM 2.95. Inflation and interest rates in the UK were far higher than the major European economies, and productivity much lower. The seeds of withdrawal had already been sown.

By the summer of 1992, the pound was under constant pressure, as were the weak Italian lira and Spanish peseta. Each was in constant danger of breaching the 6 per cent fluctuation limit. The Chancellor, Norman Lamont, stepped in to support the pound but traders continued to sell the currency. It was a fruitless task. Things came to a head on 15 and 16 September. No matter how much was pumped in, and no matter how many increases in interest there were, the pound continued to flounder. Appeals to the Bundesbank to step in fell on deaf ears. At 7 p.m. on 16 September, the Chancellor announced in sombre tones that Britain was quitting the ERM. It was a day of national humiliation, from which the Major government never recovered.

However, in retrospect, leaving the ERM proved something of a boon. It may have cost the taxpayer £3.3 billion, but inflation started to fall and growth started to rise.

271

BNP WIN FIRST COUNCIL SEAT ON THE ISLE OF DOGS

September 1993 will always be a tainted month for British politics, for it marked the far right, racist British National Party (BNP) winning their first ever local council seat, in the London Borough of Tower Hamlets. Unemployed lorry driver Derek Beackon beat Labour by seven votes to win the Millwall by-election on the Isle of Dogs in east London. Their vote increased from 20 per cent in 1992 to 33.9 per cent at the by-election, which prompted many fears within the local Asian community.

Labour even accused the Liberal Democrats of helping the BNP to win by using racism in their own election literature within the ward, suggesting resources were being diverted to Asian communities. Raja Miah from the Tower Hamlets Race Equality Council argued the result had pushed the area back several years in race relations and left the Asian community 'very sad and frightened' as a consequence.

The result was blamed on unemployment and widespread deprivation, with previous versions of the far right including the British Union of Fascists and British Movement generating an appeal. The BNP's campaign emphasized 'Rights for Whites' through canvassing and leafleting.

Beackon himself was regarded as a poor representative with little knowledge of bureaucracy and council debates. He lost his seat in May 1994 following a Labour landslide in the East End, with the Liberal Democrats also being removed from power in Tower Hamlets.

The BNP did not win any future council elections until May 2002, when they won three seats in Burnley, where 11 per cent of the population were of ethnic minority heritage. They later won seats in Barking and Dagenham, winning a by-election in September 2004 with a 470 majority, with London Mayor Ken Livingstone arguing this was a threat that needed to be taken seriously.

In 2009, they won two seats in the European Parliament, including one for their leader, Nick Griffin. After a notorious appearance on *Question Time*, where Griffin was roundly humiliated, the BNP gradually declined into obscurity. Griffin himself was later expelled from the BNP, highlighting the party's full transformation into irrelevance.

SCOTLAND HOLDS INDEPENDENCE REFERENDUM

This date could have marked the end of the 307-year-old union between Scotland and England. Even though, on an 84 per cent turnout, the Scottish electorate voted by 55 per cent to 45 per cent to reject independence, the momentum of the Scottish National Party (SNP) and broader Yes coalition only increased in the months and years after their defeat, especially after the 2016 Brexit referendum.

Calls for Scottish independence had become ever more vocal since the creation of the SNP in 1934, but even the launch of a Scottish Parliament under Tony Blair in 1999 did not extinguish the fires of independence. In 2007, the SNP took over the government of Scotland, and their power has only grown ever since.

The charismatic Alex Salmond became First Minister, and in 2011 gained an absolute majority, which encouraged him to apply for a Section 30 order at Westminster, which would allow a referendum to take place.

Prime Minister David Cameron, as Leader of the Conservative and Unionist Party, was personally strongly opposed to independence, but he recognized the damaging implication of being seen to deny the mandate of Scottish voters. As such, the Edinburgh Agreement, signed in October 2012, set out the timetable for a referendum.

In November 2013, the Scottish Independence Referendum Act was passed, which allowed all EU and Commonwealth citizens over sixteen to vote. Nonetheless, campaigning had begun long before then, as both sides formed campaigns – Yes Scotland and Better Together.

The complacency and arrogance of the No campaign in assuming victory was certain in the final weeks of the campaign was striking. This allowed Yes to creep ahead in the polls, leading to David Cameron, Ed Miliband and Nick Clegg to make a dramatic statement cancelling prime minister's questions to travel to Scotland and save the union. Following a fiery, engaging, determined speech from Gordon Brown, the Yes side was defeated, though Glasgow voted for independence and the 45 per cent in favour was higher than expected.

David Cameron's comments in the aftermath of his victory were ill-judged. He said it was now important to prioritize 'English Votes for English Laws'. Timing is everything in politics.

ALEX SALMOND RESIGNS AS SCOTTISH FIRST MINISTER

Alex Salmond is one of the most significant figures to have emerged in the last century of Scottish politics. He took Scotland to within a whisker of leaving the Union, and eight years on from the independence referendum, which was supposed to settle the issue for a generation, Scotland looks more likely than ever to vote to leave, should there ever be a second referendum.

Born in 1954 to civil servant parents, Salmond grew up and was educated in Linlithgow. He graduated from the University of St Andrews and followed his parents in going into the civil service, where he spent two years in the Scottish Office as an economist. He was then recruited by the Royal Bank of Scotland, spending seven years as an oil economist.

He entered the House of Commons in 1987 as MP for Banff and Buchan and three years later defeated Margaret Ewing to begin the first of two stints as SNP Leader. In 1999, he was elected to the Scottish Parliament, but left in 2001, only to stand again in 2007. It was after this election that he first became First Minister, entering a coalition with the Greens. In 2011, he led the SNP to a majority win, which gave him the mandate to call an independence referendum.

A charismatic campaigner, Salmond led the Yes campaign from a position where it only had 29 per cent support in the polls, to coming within five points of winning. On the afternoon of 19 September 2014, Salmond announced he would stand down and a new First Minister would take over from 14 November. He said on that day: 'My time as leader is nearly over, but for Scotland, the campaign continues and the dream shall never die.'

He returned to Westminster in 2015, but was defeated two years later. He then faced fourteen charges including two counts of attempted rape, nine of sexual assault, two of indecent assault and one of breach of the peace. He was cleared by a jury of all charges.

In 2021, he left the SNP and formed the Alba Party, which failed to win a single seat in the ensuing Scottish Parliament elections.

Salmond's deputy, Nicola Sturgeon, became First Minister in November 2014, a position she holds to this day. A formidable politician, she has used every opportunity to push forward the cause of independence and is committed to holding another referendum at the earliest opportunity.

BRITAIN LEAVES THE GOLD STANDARD

In 1924, Winston Churchill achieved a Lazarus-like political come-back. He had been out of Parliament and without a political party. But he was returned in the 1924 election as a 'Constitutionalist' and his comeback was complete when Prime Minister Stanley Baldwin astonished the entire political world by making him Chancellor of the Exchequer.

His first action in his April 1925 budget – and it was the equivalent of Gordon Brown making the Bank of England independent in 1997 – was to return Britain to the gold standard at its pre-war rate of $4.86 to the pound. The decision was greeted by Conservative MPs waving their order papers. The Bank of England was euphoric. Top economist John Maynard Keynes was a lone voice warning that British exports would be severely damaged.

A gold standard is a monetary system in which the standard currency is based on a fixed quantity of gold. It formed the core of the international monetary system from the 1870s for the next fifty years. However, with the advent of the Great Depression in 1929, many countries abandoned the gold standard because it hampered their ability to expand the money supply and inflate the economy. This meant higher interest rates, lower investment and this all led to higher unemployment – a perfect economic storm. Many economists attribute the whole depression of the 1930s to the fact that the US and the UK were on the gold standard. However, by way of contrast, the ex-head of the Federal Reserve Alan Greenspan attributes the bank failures of the early 1930s to the fact that Britain came off the gold standard.

By mid 1931, unemployment had risen to close to three million. Labour's austerity Chancellor, Philip Snowden, had presented a budget with dire forecasts. He refused to countenance budget deficits. Labour became hopelessly split on cuts to unemployment benefit. On 24 August, the government fell and a general election was called for October. Runs on the pound and London as a financial centre forced the decision to come off the gold standard on 21 September. Almost immediately, the economic conditions became more favourable for a recovery.

NORTH SEA OIL IS DISCOVERED

It was thought that the discovery of oil in the North Sea could rescue Britain's ailing economy. It didn't. All it did was mask the structural weaknesses endemic in the UK economy in the 1970s and 1980s. Compare how Norway has grown a sovereign wealth fund on the proceeds of its own oilfields with the parlous state of the UK's finances, and it's clear to see that Britain has wasted the huge boon that North Sea oil should have given it.

It was in September 1965 that the *Sea Gem* barge-cum-oil-rig struck gas sixty-five miles off the Lincolnshire coast. Tragedy ensued, however, as the *Sea Gem* then sank, taking thirteen oil rig workers with it. Other gas and oil finds soon followed, but further exploration was put on hold when the price of gas fell dramatically.

In December 1969, Phillips Petroleum discovered what came to be known as the Ekofisk oilfield in Norwegian waters and Amoco located the Montrose oilfield 135 miles east of Aberdeen. They were drilling for gas but found oil. A year later, the massive Forties field was discovered, followed by the Brent field in 1971. Further discoveries came over the next few years.

After the 1973 and 1979 oil crises and a huge spike in the price of oil, government devoted huge resources to encouraging oil and gas companies to speed up production. By 1985, Britain had become a net exporter of oil and in the mid 1990s a net exporter of gas.

Gas production peaked in 2001 and oil in 1999. Aberdeen soon became the oil capital of Europe, with huge operations also in Great Yarmouth.

Safety has been a constant concern, especially after the Piper Alpha disaster in July 1988, when the oil rig exploded and sank, killing 167 men. The ensuing report by Lord Cullen was a crucial landmark in North Sea safety.

In the mid 1980s, oil and gas production were worth around £10 billion per year, although this has now dropped to around £1 billion a year.

New fields continue to be discovered but it's highly unlikely they will be exploited given the debate surrounding climate change.

SIR ROBERT WALPOLE MOVES INTO NUMBER 10 DOWNING STREET

Number 10 Downing Street is an address that is renowned the world over. Next to the White House and the Kremlin it is one of the most famous seats of government in the world. It is here that the cabinet meets, where the prime minister lives, and where many historic decisions have been made over the centuries.

Sir George Downing, who had been a spy for Oliver Cromwell, bought the site in 1654, but due to legal wrangles wasn't able to commence building on it until 1682. He built a row of terraced properties, designed by Sir Christopher Wren. Downing's portrait still hangs in the entrance hall.

In 1735, King George II offered 10 Downing Street, by then property of the Crown, to Prime Minister Sir Robert Walpole in recognition of his achievements over fourteen years in office. Walpole said he would live there but it should remain government property. However, of the thirty-one prime ministers between then and 1902, only sixteen actually lived there, given most of them possessed much more grand properties.

Two little-known facts are that, until 1787, Number 10 was actually Number 5, and that the famous black door wasn't added until the 1780s.

Twice the building has experienced bomb damage. In 1941, a German bomb landed in neighbouring Horseguards Parade, while in 1991 the IRA launched a mortar attack from Whitehall when a cabinet meeting was being held. On both occasions windows were blasted inwards.

As an eleven-year-old, I was able to pose for a picture in front of the famous door, but in 1990 the whole street was blocked off by gates due to the continuing IRA threat.

On the 250th anniversary of the building, Margaret Thatcher wrote: 'How much I wish that the public... could share with me the feeling of Britain's historic greatness which pervades every nook and cranny of this complicated and meandering old building... All Prime Ministers are intensely aware that, as tenants and stewards of No. 10 Downing Street, they have in their charge one of the most precious jewels in the nation's heritage.'

AUSTRALIAN COURT LIFTS BAN ON PUBLICATION OF SPYCATCHER

The publication of books by former spies has always been controversial and this was never more true than with *SpyCatcher: The Candid Autobiography of a Senior Intelligence Officer*, written by Tasmania-based former MI5 officer Peter Wright. The British government attempted to stop the book's publication in the late 1980s in Australia, following its ban in England.

Core allegations in the book included Wright unmasking a Soviet mole in MI5 and MI5–CIA plotting against Labour prime minister Harold Wilson. Though the book had been banned in England, it was due to be published by Heinemann in Australia, with a New South Wales Supreme Court case brought by the British government.

British newspaper reportage on the case was extremely limited, with contempt of court applications applying. During the ban, bookshops would give the book away with another book of equivalent value to get around the ban on selling.

As it happened, Peter Wright's book was eventually published after the Australian courts lifted the ban in September 1987. The case had been defended by republican movement leader Malcolm Turnbull, who would become Australian prime minister in 2015. Facing the British Cabinet Secretary, Sir Robert Armstrong, it soon became clear nothing in the publication would threaten national security. The court argued that much of the information contained within *Spycatcher* was no longer confidential and that the technological methods mentioned were no longer used.

The British government tried to appeal the decision, which was dismissed by the NSW Court of Appeal and Australia's High Court in 1988. With controversy about the role of Australia in investigating the potential national security risks to the UK, publication now went ahead. Politicians including Tony Benn and Alistair Darling read extracts of the book out loud and condemned the continuing restrictions in England.

Seeking to ban the book was key to its success. *Spycatcher* became a bestseller, selling two million copies, allowing Wright to die a millionaire in 1995 from the proceeds.

In 2021, the Cabinet Office was still blocking Freedom of Information requests on the *Spycatcher* affair.

SUPREME COURT RULES ON PROROGUING OF PARLIAMENT

Exactly two months after taking office as prime minister, Boris Johnson sparked a constitutional crisis. The Supreme Court, under President Lady Hale, declared Johnson's advice to the Queen, that Parliament should be prorogued for five weeks between 9 September and 14 October during the Brexit crisis, was unlawful. All eleven justices unanimously agreed after a three-day hearing that the proroguing was 'unlawful, void and of no effect'.

Prorogations in themselves are nothing unusual, taking place for a short period between the end of one Parliament and beginning of another, which is marked by a Queen's Speech. Indeed, Johnson wanted to present his new prime ministerial agenda on 14 October. He was desperately trying to ensure the UK left the EU by 31 October.

Tempers were already flaring after a group of rebellious MPs ensured the passing of the Benn Act, which mandated the government to seek an extension to Article 50 if no deal had been agreed by 31 October.

Businesswoman Gina Miller, who had taken both the Article 50 case and prorogation to the Supreme Court, argued it was a 'win for parliamentary sovereignty' and that the Prime Minister 'must open the doors of parliament'. Though it had been predicted the court would rule against the Prime Minister, the unanimous nature of the rejection came as a shock.

The Prime Minister, unsurprisingly, argued that he 'profoundly disagreed' with the ruling, but would 'respect' it and accepted Parliament would return. Brexiteers like Steve Baker regarded the ruling as an 'earthquake moment', with calls for a general election to end the paralysis only intensifying.

Eventually, Johnson was able to negotiate a new Withdrawal Agreement that he presented to MPs. In a 'Super Saturday' sitting, MPs supported his agreement but disagreed with the short amount of time given to scrutinizing it. An inevitable general election delivered an eighty-seat majority for Johnson's Conservatives and allowed his deal to pass and Brexit to happen on 31 January 2020.

The ruling raised continued questions about the powers of the Supreme Court and judiciary in challenging the actions of government, adding further to claims that the legal profession was biased against Brexit.

BBC BROADCASTS FIRST EDITION OF QUESTION TIME

On 12 October 1948, the BBC broadcast *Any Questions?* for the first time on the BBC West of England Home Service. It took more than thirty years for a television producer to work out that the format would work on screen too. And so it was that in late September 1979, veteran political interviewer Robin Day hosted the first show with a panel consisting of Labour MP Michael Foot, former Conservative MP Teddy Taylor, the Archbishop of Liverpool, Derek Worlock, and the author Edna O'Brien. The first run of shows were all broadcast from the Greenwood Theatre in south London. The show only started going 'on the road' around the country in the early 1990s. Initially, there were always four panellists, but nowadays there are more usually five, and on occasion even six. The show was an immediate ratings hit and has now been going for forty years.

Recorded in front of a live audience on a Thursday night, it is then broadcast later in the evening. Occasionally, it is broadcast live.

In its forty years, *Question Time* has only had four regular hosts: Sir Robin Day (1979–89, 303 episodes), Peter Sissons (1989–93, 149 episodes), David Dimbleby (1993–2018, 914 episodes) and the current host, Fiona Bruce (2018–).

The guest who has appeared most often is Kenneth Clarke (fifty-nine appearances). Shirley Williams is second with fifty-eight, with Menzies Campbell third on forty-seven.

I've appeared on the show three times, firstly in 1986 when I summoned up the courage to comment on a question on the American bombing of Libya, and then in 2018 and 2019 when I appeared on the panel. On both occasions I was terrified, and was worried that I might dry up. As if. Like most guests, I ended up thoroughly enjoying the experience, although on the second occasion there were six panellists. I only managed to speak for three minutes and I was constantly interrupted by the SNP MP Ian Blackford. I nearly ended up walking off the set. Strangely, I haven't appeared since...

THEATRE CENSORSHIP ENDS

It seems incredible, but until 1968 theatres were regulated for taste and decency. The Licensing Act 1737 and the 1843 Theatres Act gave the Lord Chamberlain powers to close down any theatre which was putting on a play which was deemed too controversial. The 1737 Act was designed to protect Sir Robert Walpole's government from being lampooned. By the late 1960s, this anachronism had been dealt with as part of the Labour government's liberal progressive reforms. For those opposed to the so-called permissive society, like anti-porn campaigner Mary Whitehouse, the Theatres Act of 1968 represented all that was bad about freeing up society.

Until 1968, the Lord Chamberlain could ban any new play from being performed for any reason, and remarkably he did not have to give a justification for doing so. Initially, the two so-called Patent Theatres (the Theatre Royal, Drury Lane, and the Theatre Royal, Covent Garden) were licensed to host spoken word plays. In 1843, the powers of the Lord Chamberlain were reined in and he was only allowed to ban a theatrical work if 'it is fitting for the preservation of good manners, decorum or of the public peace to do so.' Local authorities were also allowed to license theatres. And that's the way the law remained for the next 126 years.

By the 1960s, theatre managers, critics, actors and producers were united in their opposition to censorship. Many of the political satirists of the early 1960s, such as David Frost, Richard Ingrams and Willie Rushton, pushed the barriers of acceptability on television and in print, but there was also growing pressure for works like D. H. Lawrence's *Lady Chatterley's Lover* to be performed on stage.

The trigger for legislation came in 1966 when the producers of Edward Bond's play *Saved* were successfully prosecuted. There were others too and the public response led the Labour Home Secretary, Roy Jenkins, to introduce the latest piece of his legislation designed to bring Britain into the modern age.

It wasn't until 2008 that the common law offences of blasphemy and blasphemous libel were outlawed in England and Wales. Scotland had to wait until 2021.

MAUREEN COLQUHOUN DESELECTED

Maureen Colquhoun was a trailblazer, a woman ahead of her times. She wasn't just Britain's first openly lesbian Member of Parliament, she spoke out in favour of all sorts of social reforms, which nowadays we take for granted.

First elected to parliament for Northampton North in February 1974, Colquhoun was quick to display her left-wing credentials by becoming treasurer of the Tribune Group, always a thorn in the side of the Labour leadership. In 1974, she castigated her own Labour Party for paying lip service to International Women's Day and failing to provide creche facilities at its annual conference.

She introduced a Balance of the Sexes Bill to ensure that equal numbers of men and women should be appointed to public bodies, and in 1976 signed a letter to *The Times* advocating the withdrawal of British troops from Northern Ireland. Ever the controversialist, as her parliamentary swansong in 1979, she introduced a Protection of Prostitutes Bill, and invited fifty prostitutes to the House of Commons to put their case for decriminalization.

But it was her sexuality for which she became infamous. When selected as a candidate she was a married mother of three children. However, in 1973, she left her husband to start a relationship with the publisher of *Sappho* magazine, Barbara Todd.

She was then outed by the *Daily Mail* gossip columnist Nigel Dempster, who had managed to gain an invitation to a housewarming party held by Colquhoun and her partner. She complained to the Press Complaints Commission and won.

On 27 September 1977, Colquhoun's constituency Labour Party management committee voted by twenty-three to eighteen to deselect her, citing her 'obsession with trivialities such as women's rights'. Colquhoun maintained that her ability to do her job as an MP had nothing to do with her sexuality.

The deselection vote was overturned in January 1978 by Labour's National Executive Committee. However, her local constituency party refused to work with her, and at the May 1979 general election she experienced an 8 per cent swing against her, higher than the national average, and lost to the right-wing Conservative Antony Marlow.

She died in February 2021, an undeservedly forgotten figure in Labour Party and gay history.

UK PASSES LAW OUTLAWING CANNABIS

There are plenty of politicians who have admitted to smoking a spliff during their university days. However, the drug has been outlawed for nearly a century. Use of the drug was common in British Empire territories throughout the nineteenth century, and prohibition was gradually introduced in British India.

The 1925 International Opium Convention led the UK to prohibit cannabis as a drug in 1928, which was added to the 1920 Dangerous Drugs Act. However, this did not deter cannabis use in the long term, with arrests and convictions increasing dramatically in the 1960s. At the start of the decade, there were 235 arrests, rising to 4,683 by 1969.

A tough Misuse of Drugs Act, passed in 1971 under Conservative prime minister Edward Heath, declared cannabis a Class B drug. This removed the ability of doctors to prescribe cannabis for medical use. Nonetheless, just two years later, cannabis possession convictions in the UK had reached 11,111 annually. The drug remains at Class B classification, apart from between 2004 and 2009 under New Labour, where it was briefly reclassified as a Class C drug.

Despite cannabis charges potentially bringing sentences of up to fourteen years, an unlimited fine or both, 7.2 per cent of those aged sixteen to fifty-nine in 2017 reported using the drug, a figure that is, in reality, likely to be far higher. With a 2014 police survey finding cannabis offences accounting for 67 per cent of all police recorded drug offences, various forces including County Durham Police have argued they will not prioritize criminalizing those taking the drug for personal consumption.

Calls for legalization have largely fallen on deaf ears. In 1997, the *Independent on Sunday* launched a 'decriminalize cannabis' campaign. The Liberal Democrats and the Green Party have long supported legalization but were unable to reach an agreement in coalition with the Conservatives.

In November 2018, medical cannabis was legalized after the plight of two epileptic children was raised, both of whom had benefited from using cannabis.

Given that proponents of cannabis legalization have stated it could raise £1 billion for the Exchequer, liberalizing drug laws is not an issue which will disappear from political debate soon.

THE METROPOLITAN POLICE SERVICE IS FORMED

'The police are the public and the public are the police,' wrote Home Secretary Sir Robert Peel, considered the founding father of modern policing. The Metropolitan Police Act of 1829 was introduced as a result of the significant body of work Peel had undertaken in order to establish a centrally organized, formal system of law enforcement. The Peelian Principles, as they became known, laid the foundations for a modern, ethical system of policing by consent. The Peelian Principles continue to be recognized and embraced by the forty-three police forces in existence today.

As the Home Secretary, Sir Robert Peel recognized that an organized, structured system of policing was necessary and that officers should be paid a wage – which attracted men of good character. Implicit in Sir Robert Peel's model was the notion of policing by consent – police officers were regarded as citizens in uniform and as such were unarmed.

Nicknamed Peelers or Bobbies, after Peel, 895 police constables, 88 sergeants and 20 inspectors were recruited to the Metropolitan Police when it began its operations on 29 September. They had responsibility for the Metropolitan Police District, covering a seven-mile radius from Charing Cross. To avoid accusations that the force would be a military organization, officers were issued with blue uniforms – a tail coat and top hat – to distinguish them from the military who wore red. To further avoid any military connotations, officers had little in the way of protection; each officer was given just a ratcheted rattle, to raise the alarm, and a wooden truncheon.

The first PC killed in the line of duty was Joseph Grantham, who had intervened in a fight and was beaten to death in June 1830, less than a year after the Metropolitan Police was formed.

Grantham's murder, and the subsequent inquest, illustrated the strength of feeling among some members of the public who feared the new system of law enforcement was a threat to civil liberties. At Grantham's inquest the jury returned a verdict of 'justifiable homicide' and argued he had contributed to his death by 'over exertion in the discharge of his duty'.

MUNICH AGREEMENT

An aggressive regional power led by a ruthless dictator demands rights for a population who speak its language, within a much weaker independent and democratic state on its borders. It threatens military action if its long-standing grievances are not remedied. This causes a crisis across Europe, as Western powers such as Britain decry the claims of the dictatorship, but believe they cannot act militarily to save the threatened, and fear escalation of extreme danger into possible world war.

No, this is not Ukraine in 2022. The state under threat was Czechoslovakia. The minority were the German speakers in the Sudetenland, on its western edges. The aggressive tyrant was Adolf Hitler – and the year was 1938.

The Nazis claimed Czechoslovakia, a state created in the Paris Peace Treaties of 1919 (imposed on Germany to such bitter resentment), was a threat – it was shaped like a dagger thrusting into Germany's vitals, at least after Hitler seized Austria in the Anschluss earlier in 1938.

What were the Western powers to do about Hitler's aggression? Above all, the aim of the Prime Minister, Neville Chamberlain, was to avoid war. Three times in September 1938 he flew to meet Hitler, at Berchtesgaden, Bad Godesberg and finally at Munich. As the crisis (and Hitler's demands) escalated, some such as the Labour Party and Churchill bridled at the threats to a democratic state (whose leader, President Beneš, was not included in Chamberlain's negotiations). However, driven by the overwhelming fear of weapons of mass destruction falling from the sky, preparations were made, such as trenches in Hyde Park and 38 million gas masks being distributed.

Therefore, when on 30 September Chamberlain flew back to Heston airport, waved the paper containing the agreement, and announced 'peace for our time' from Number 10, there was a massive wave of relief. This was temporary.

Chamberlain has been accused of selling out a democratic nation by the appeasement of a dictator at Munich. The policy brought at best delay. Six months later, in March 1939, Hitler seized the rest of Czechoslovakia, without resistance. Six months after that, he invaded Poland, and this time Chamberlain declared what was to become World War II.

OCTOBER

MOSLEY FORMS THE BRITISH UNION OF FASCISTS

Oswald Mosley is perhaps the only British politician to always have the word 'fascist' associated with his name. The founder of the British Union of Fascists (BUF), Mosley created the group in October 1932 following the defeat of the New Party in the 1931 general election. Initially claiming fifty thousand members, it had a strong initial level of support, including Lord Rothermere, whose family owned the *Daily Mail*.

Mosley himself went on a long political journey, initially being the youngest ever Conservative MP in 1918 before defecting to Labour in 1922. He was a minister under Ramsay MacDonald but left Labour in 1931 after it rejected his protectionist Keynesian economic paper. Mosley then formed the New Party, which failed to achieve electoral success.

The conversion to fascism came after Mosley visited Mussolini in Italy in January 1932. By this point, Mosley had lost his seat in Parliament and spent the summer of 1932 writing his manifesto before forming the BUF. Though none of its candidates were ever elected, the party was able to gain a following in the East End of London. Polling almost eight thousand votes in the London Council elections in 1937, its threat appeared real.

In 1934, a rally took place at Olympia, attended by twelve thousand people. There was trouble when anti-fascist protesters were attacked by the BUF's paramilitary wing, the Fascist Defence Force. This prompted support to decline, with the overt embrace of anti-semitism in 1936 leading to violent anti-fascist protests. Famously, the 1936 Battle of Cable Street in London's East End had 'blackshirt' fascists fighting a coalition of anti-fascist groups.

The group metamorphosized into the British Union of Fascists and National Socialists in 1936, before becoming the British Union in 1937. Proscribed by the British government at the onset of war in 1939, when membership had fallen to twenty thousand, it was disbanded in 1940. Mosley had married his mistress Diana Mitford in 1936, with Hitler as a guest of honour, and the couple were detained for three years in Holloway prison during World War II.

Mosley's fascism did not waver, however. In 1948, he founded the Union Movement, which called for a single nation state across Europe.

KEIR HARDIE BECOMES LABOUR'S FIRST MP

Some Jeremy Corbyn supporters, angry at Keir Starmer's leadership of the party, call him 'Keith'. Why? For one reason among many, they dislike the fact Starmer shares his name with the founder of the Labour Party, and its first MP, Keir Hardie.

Hardie had worked as a mineworker and union organizer, where he began to recognize the importance of socialism in delivering fairness. Thinking the Liberal Party, at the time the main opposition to the Conservatives, were unwilling to embrace the required radicalism, he became the first Secretary of the Scottish Labour Party in 1888. Hardy was then elected for the seat of West Ham South in an 1892 by-election, refusing to wear a suit in the chamber.

The ideas that Hardie espoused would not seem unusual today, but were profoundly radical in the late nineteenth century. Advocating free schooling, pensions and female suffrage, these were not within the political Overton Window.

After losing West Ham South in 1895, Hardie spent five years building up the Labour movement before a Labour Representation Committee – the Labour Party – made up of trade unions and socialists was created in 1900.

Hardie was then elected for Merthyr Tydfil in South Wales in 1900, with only one other Labour MP (Richard Bell in Derby) also successful. By 1906, this had increased to twenty-six. Hardie served as Leader of the Labour Party, but, like many of his successors, was unable to cope with internal divisions and so resigned just two years later in 1908.

Despite his prominence, Hardie was not always popular in the Labour Party. An ideological pacifist, he opposed the First World War and sought to organize a general strike. Other battles after his involvement with the Labour Party included campaigning with Sylvia Pankhurst for votes for women. What remained a continued part of his ideology was a belief in defending the underdog and campaigning for justice. This was rooted in his Christianity, with Hardie saying the teaching of 'Jesus of Nazareth' drove him into the Labour movement.

ANEURIN BEVAN SPEECH TO LABOUR CONFERENCE

Aneurin Bevan will long be remembered as both one of the great orators of the twentieth century, and the man who ushered in the National Health Service in 1948 as Minister for Health. He is a towering figure in Labour history and mythology, albeit, like most brilliant men, deeply flawed.

As shadow Foreign Secretary, Aneurin Bevan had part responsibility for developing Labour's policy on nuclear disarmament. Of course, he had been a member of Attlee's government, which had put in place Britain's own independent nuclear programme after the war. Bevan himself had been a firm opponent of nuclear weapons, having been horrified by the devastation wrought by the bombs dropped on Hiroshima and Nagasaki. As Minister for Health he had no direct involvement in the decisions taken by Attlee and Bevin in the immediate post-war period. However, as shadow Foreign Secretary he couldn't avoid the issue and gave it deep thought. The Labour Party itself was split down the middle, with the left decrying nuclear weapons, but the right realizing that if Britain didn't have them, its worldwide role and commitments would be affected adversely.

In 1955, Bevan had led a backbench revolt against the testing of a hydrogen bomb. As a result, the Parliamentary Labour Party voted by 141 to 113 to withdraw the whip from him, although it was restored a month later. When Attlee finally stood down as Leader, Bevan contested the ensuing leadership context against Herbert Morrison and the eventual winner, Hugh Gaitskell. He then became shadow Colonial Secretary, and in 1956 Gaitskell promoted him to shadow the Foreign Office.

At the 1957 Labour Party conference, the issue came to a head, with the party debating the issue of nuclear disarmament. Bevan astonished both his allies and foes in the party by reversing his position. He said unilateral nuclear disarmament 'would send a British Foreign Secretary naked into the conference chamber'. The obvious interpretation of this remark was that he had changed his mind on the issue of nuclear weapons. However, his allies denied this, alleging that he meant his negotiating position would be damaged by a loss of allies, rather than the lack of nuclear weapons. Hmmm.

SPENCER PERCEVAL BECOMES PRIME MINISTER

Spencer Perceval had the potential to become a really memorable prime minister. Sadly, the only thing we remember about him is that he remains the only one of our fifty-five prime ministers to have been assassinated.

Born at the end of 1762 to an Anglo-Irish earl, Spencer Perceval had a classic education for the time – Harrow and Trinity College, Cambridge. He then trained as a lawyer, entering Parliament as MP for Northampton in 1795. An admirer of William Pitt, he first became a minister in the Addington government after being made Solicitor General. He then rose to be Attorney General, the only one ever to rise to be prime minister. Under the Duke of Portland he became first Leader of the House of Commons and then Chancellor of the Exchequer. He remained opposed to Catholic emancipation and the wider reform of Parliament. He was a firm supporter of the war against Napoleon and argued in favour of abolishing the slave trade.

Following the resignation of the Duke of Portland, due to ill health, in October 1809, Perceval became prime minister, mainly because his name wasn't Canning or Castlereagh. Their mutual hatred and antipathy (as well as fighting a duel) effectively ruled them out. Grenville and Grey refused to serve, and so it was that the cabinet recommended Perceval to the King.

Spencer Perceval was in office for less than three years, and he took some time to establish himself in the job, given his position was inevitably quite shaky. However, he dealt deftly with a number of crises including the madness of the King, Luddite riots and economic problems. He trenchantly promoted the Peninsular War against stiff opposition at home too. By May 1812, people were speaking positively of their Prime Minister.

At teatime on 11 May 1812, Perceval made his way from Downing Street to the Commons. As he entered Members' Lobby, just outside the chamber, he was shot in the chest at point-blank range. A few minutes later he was dead.

His killer was John Bellingham who believed he had been cheated by the government. Five days later he was hanged.

CHEQUERS DONATED TO THE NATION

Chequers is a beautiful, Grade I listed, sixteenth-century manor house, situated near Princes Risborough in Buckinghamshire. It is the official weekend residence of the British prime minister, and has been since early 1921. The house was given to the nation by its then owner, Sir Arthur Lee.

The house is most likely named after the chequer trees that grow in its grounds, although it could also be named after the first owner of the land on which the house is built, Elias Ostarius. His surname signified he was an usher at the Court of the Exchequer.

The house was built by William Hawtrey in 1565. In 1715, the then owner married Oliver Cromwell's grandson John Russell. And to this day the house contains items of Cromwell memorabilia.

In 1909, Arthur Lee took Chequers on a long lease and undertook a restoration of the inside of the house, before taking on outright freehold ownership. During World War I it became a field hospital and a convalescent home. With no children to leave Chequers to, as the war approached its end, Lees decided to donate the house to the nation, for the exclusive use of prime ministers. In previous times, most prime ministers came from the aristocracy and usually had big houses to live in and relax or entertain. Since the turn of the twentieth century that had not been the case.

Prime Minister David Lloyd George approved and the Chequers Estate Act of 1917 was born. Lee was awarded a peerage and the house was handed over on 8 January 1921. A stained-glass window in the Long Gallery reads: 'This house of peace and ancient memories was given to England as a thank-offering for her deliverance in the great war of 1914–1918 as a place of rest and recreation for her Prime Ministers for ever.'

Prime ministers often use Chequers to meet foreign leaders. Macmillan met Nikita Khruschev there and it was at Chequers that Margaret Thatcher first met Soviet leader Mikhail Gorbachev, after which she proclaimed he was 'a man I can do business with'.

BARBARA CASTLE IS BORN

Barbara Castle was the most prominent female Labour politician of her generation. Serving as MP for Blackburn between 1945 and 1979, she had a close political relationship with Harold Wilson and served in his cabinet for twelve years.

Castle was born in Chesterfield into a politically active home. Her father became editor of the *Bradford Pioneer*, the city's socialist newspaper, in 1935, with her sister Annie also being elected as a Labour councillor.

Winning numerous academic awards at Bradford Girls' Grammar School, Castle read PPE at St Hugh's College, Oxford, serving as Treasurer for the Oxford University Labour Club, though she disliked the social elitism within the university. Before entering Parliament, Castle worked for *Tribune* magazine and the *Daily Mirror*.

Castle only became a parliamentary candidate for Blackburn (as it then had two members) by women threatening to quit unless she was added to the shortlist. Though she had no connections to Blackburn, she studied weaving and spinning in a bid to demonstrate her commitment.

A vehement supporter of decolonization and the anti-apartheid movement, Castle became the first Minister for Overseas Development under Harold Wilson in 1964. She was moved a year later to the Ministry of Transport, where she introduced motorway speed limits, the mandatory fitting of seat belts in new cars, and the breathalyser, despite widespread opposition. Road deaths dropped by 16 per cent. Despite pre-election commitments, she also ripped up two thousand miles of railway.

As Employment Secretary between 1968 and 1970, Castle was unafraid to cause controversy, penning the ill-fated white paper 'In Place of Strife', which sought to reduce union power. She also introduced the Equal Pay Act in 1970.

After Labour returned to power in 1974, Castle became Health and Social Services Secretary, but her fierce rivalry with James Callaghan led to her immediate removal from the cabinet after he became prime minister in 1976.

Opting to leave Parliament in 1979, she served for ten years as a Member of the European Parliament, before joining the House of Lords in 1990. She died in May 2002.

ABOLITION OF GLC ANNOUNCED

Ken Livingstone has arguably been the most effective left-wing politician of the last fifty years. Unlike many of his contemporaries, Livingstone was able to repeatedly win elections. Most notably, he ran the Greater London Council (GLC) in the 1980s and then spent eight years as Mayor of London at the start of the twenty-first century.

The GLC had been created by the London Government Act of 1963, which initiated a new body to better manage the administration of London. Responsible for running strategic services like the fire service, emergency planning and waste disposal, it also had joint responsibility with London boroughs for managing roads, housing and city planning.

In all of the six elections to the GLC, the main opposition party triumphed, while the party in government came second. With Labour winning the 1981 election, the moderate leader Andrew McIntosh was deposed immediately after the election by Ken Livingstone, who was supported by thirty of the fifty members of the GLC.

It was Livingstone's belief in ultra-socialist policies that put him in opposition to Margaret Thatcher. He indulged in publicity stunts like putting London's unemployment figures on the side of County Hall and meeting Gerry Adams during the Troubles. Livingstone also cut public transport fares by 25 per cent, funded by higher rates.

This provoked Margaret Thatcher in October 1983 to announce that the GLC should be abolished due to its perceived ineffectiveness, with powers transferred over to the boroughs.

The Local Government Act 1985 passed narrowly in Parliament, leading to the abolition of the GLC on 31 March 1986, with at least seven thousand jobs cut. At a rally on the South Bank, 250,000 people gathered to witness the council's demise. County Hall, which housed the GLC, is now home to the London Aquarium and Dungeon and a Marriott Hotel.

Tony Blair's New Labour government was committed to reintroducing London-wide government, with a 1998 referendum establishing a London Assembly and Mayor endorsed by over 60 per cent of voters. Ken Livingstone, though not selected as the Labour candidate, won the first London Mayoral election in 2000, a position he held until 2008.

CLEMENT ATTLEE DIES

Clement Attlee was not the first Labour prime minister – that was Ramsay MacDonald – but he was the first to win an overall majority that gave him effective power, in 1945. He led the party to another majority in 1950 and even in defeat in 1951 Labour received the highest share of votes, a remarkable 48.8 per cent.

Many observers think this success was deserved. He is one of the two post-war prime ministers who could truly be regarded as transformational, Margaret Thatcher being the other one. The main reason for this extraordinary rating is that his 1945–51 government was one of those that truly marked a turning point in British history. It introduced a thorough Welfare State, typified by the foundation of the NHS in 1948, and the biggest ever series of nationalizations, from the mines to the Bank of England. It may well have been the only UK government that could genuinely be classed as socialist.

Attlee was an unlikely 'president' of this 'red revolution'. The son of a wealthy solicitor, he attended Haileybury, the public school established to train East India Company staff, and Oxford. He himself became a barrister. In the Great War he was a major. However, his life changed direction from its privileged course when, exposed to poverty as a volunteer in the East End, he became Mayor of Stepney and in 1922 MP for Limehouse.

This solidly working-class base enabled Attlee to survive the massive losses Labour suffered in the 1931 election, and therefore to be in a position to replace the idealist Lansbury as party leader in 1935 – a position he held for twenty years. During the Churchill coalition between 1940 and 1945, Attlee played a quiet but significant role as the great man's deputy, in particular on the home front; yet Churchill was shocked when Labour won a landslide victory in the July 1945 election.

It is said that Churchill called Attlee a modest little man with a lot to be modest about. Modest, definitely – his idea of election campaigning was to be driven around the country by his wife, Violet, in a humble Hillman saloon; yet Attlee actually had a lot to be proud, not modest, about.

HAROLD MACMILLAN RESIGNS

Harold Macmillan was a prime minister not removed by a general election, or his colleagues, but by his own prostate.

Macmillan followed a fairly conventional route into British politics. The son of an American mother and grandson of the Macmillan publishing house founder, he was educated, unsurprisingly, at Eton and Balliol College, Oxford. His undoubted patriotism and sense of duty was evident by serving in both World Wars, being sent to north-west Africa in 1942 as British Minister Resident at Allied Forces Headquarters.

Rejoining the House of Commons as MP for Bromley after a 1945 by-election, he became Minister for Housing following Churchill's return to Downing Street in 1951. He achieved the Conservative pledge of building 300,000 homes in a single year. Macmillan would serve in a range of positions, including two of the Great Offices of State: Foreign Secretary and Chancellor of the Exchequer. His chance to serve in a third came following Sir Anthony Eden's resignation in January 1957 after the Suez Crisis.

Macmillan was regarded as a stable figure who could restore Britain's reputation. On taking office he told the Queen he thought the government would not last longer than six weeks.

Macmillan presided over increased living standards and prosperity, famously telling the British people they had 'never had it so good'. By October 1959, Macmillan was called 'Supermac' and steered the Conservatives towards an increased majority when he called a general election.

Macmillan was an Atlanticist and forged close relations with both presidents Eisenhower and Kennedy. He accelerated the process of decolonization and applied for membership of the EEC, although that was scuppered by a veto from President de Gaulle of France.

Economic difficulties and various scandals, including the resignation of the War Secretary, John Profumo, saw Macmillan's political authority on the wane. His 'night of the long knives' reshuffle, where six cabinet ministers were sacked, failed to change his fortunes.

In October 1963, he was diagnosed with a prostate problem – which he was told he would make a complete recovery from – but he nevertheless resigned on 9 October 1963.

Macmillan became an earl in 1984. He died two years later.

THATCHER TELLS HER PARTY 'U TURN IF YOU WANT TO'

When Margaret Thatcher came to power in May 1979 her initial aim was to apply drastic surgery to the UK economy. Out went the economic theories of John Maynard Keynes, and in came the monetarist ideas of Milton Friedman. The pain was almost immediate. Unemployment rose by 500,000 within a year. Following the Winter of Discontent, widespread strikes continued to afflict the economy. The spectre of inflation still haunted the government and by the autumn of 1980 it was still a stubborn 15 per cent, although the decline had started.

Politically, Margaret Thatcher was vulnerable. She did not enjoy support for her austere economic policies and reforms from the majority of her cabinet. Many, including Peter Walker, James Prior, Ian Gilmour and Francis Pym, argued for her to halt the cuts in public spending, and to reflate the economy to stop unemployment still further. Thatcher was unrepentant and took the fight to the Conservative Party conference in Brighton:

> If our people feel that they are part of a great nation and they are prepared to will the means to keep it great, then a great nation we shall be, and shall remain. So, what can stop us from achieving this? What then stands in our way? The prospect of another winter of discontent? I suppose it might.
>
> But I prefer to believe that certain lessons have been learned from experience, that we are coming, slowly, painfully, to an autumn of understanding. And I hope that it will be followed by a winter of common sense. If it is not, we shall not be diverted from our course.
>
> To those waiting with bated breath for that favourite media catchphrase, the 'U-turn', I have only one thing to say: 'You turn if you want to. The lady's not for turning!' I say that not only to you but to our friends overseas and also to those who are not our friends.

Party members rose as one and cheered her to the rafters. Meanwhile, on the platform, her predecessor, Edward Heath, sat stony-faced. At that moment, he realized there was no way back for him.

LABOUR NARROWLY WIN GENERAL ELECTION

For only the second time in the twentieth century, two general elections were held in the same year, in 1974. It was an indication of the seriousness of the economic and political crisis facing Britain. Earlier in the year, the Conservative government under Edward Heath had lost power, even though it had won more votes than Labour in the 28 February general election. Having won three fewer seats, Heath found it impossible to form a government and resigned in favour of Labour's Harold Wilson.

As head of a minority government – the first in Britain since 1929 – Wilson knew it couldn't last long, and after only seven months he called another election, hoping to win a meaningful majority. He won a majority, but meaningful it was not.

The election campaign itself did not have the buzz or excitement of its February counterpart. Turnout fell by 6 per cent. Labour were able to ask the electorate to give them a mandate on the basis of having ended the miners' strike, albeit having given in to the National Union of Mineworkers' demands.

Both the Conservatives and Liberals saw their vote share decline. The SNP won nearly a third of the votes, winning eleven seats, their highest total ever. Labour won 319 seats, with the Conservatives dropping to 277. The Liberals dropped one seat to thirteen. This gave Labour a majority of three seats.

No one thought the new government would last very long, but in 1977 James Callaghan, who had taken over as prime minister in March 1976, negotiated a pact with the Liberals. In the event the Parliament ran for nearly a full term, only ending when the government lost a vote of confidence in March 1979.

Edward Heath's luck had run out, and having only won one election out of the four he had fought as Conservative Leader, he was turfed out in February 1975, to be replaced by Margaret Thatcher.

Wilson, and then Callaghan, were beset by strikes and industrial unrest, along with deteriorating public finances, and Labour lost by-election after by-election. It was almost a relief when the electorate put the government out of its misery in May 1979.

THE BRIGHTON BOMB

Ray Walsh was no ordinary guest at the Grand Hotel on Brighton's seafront. He knew the layout of the hotel like the back of his hand. He knew how it was built. He knew its vulnerabilities. He also knew which suite Prime Minister Margaret Thatcher would be staying in during the Conservative Party conference a few weeks later. His name wasn't really Ray Walsh. It was Patrick Magee, the thirty-five-year-old IRA terrorist. He constructed a makeshift bomb with a long-term detonator, wrapped it in clingfilm to avoid sniffer dogs being able to detect it, and placed it carefully under the bath of room 629, five floors above the prime ministerial suite.

At 2.53 a.m. on the morning of Friday, 12 October, Margaret Thatcher was in her bedroom putting the final touches to her conference speech. Her husband, Denis, had just got into bed, having emerged from the bathroom. A minute later, there was a flash, a bang, then everything went dark. The bathroom had disappeared. Having located Denis, Margaret Thatcher opened the bedroom door and went into the corridor. The scene was one of total chaos.

The blast killed five senior Conservatives including the Deputy Chief Whip, Sir Anthony Berry. Trade and Industry Secretary Norman Tebbit and his wife, Margaret, lay trapped in the rubble for hours before being rescued, with the pictures broadcast live on TV. Margaret would be paralysed for life.

Margaret Thatcher was whisked away to Lewes Police Station but not before she told the BBC Political Editor John Cole that the conference would go on as usual. And it did. She opened proceedings by declaring the bombing was 'an attempt to cripple Her Majesty's democratically elected Government. That is the scale of the outrage in which we have all shared, and the fact that we are gathered here now – shocked, but composed and determined – is a sign not only that this attack has failed, but that all attempts to destroy democracy by terrorism will fail.' While attending church the following Sunday, she thought to herself 'This is the day I wasn't meant to see.' The tears started to flow.

UKIP GETS ITS FIRST MP

Douglas Carswell had been a Conservative MP since 2005. A maverick right-winger, he was always an original thinker and argued vehemently against Britain's membership of the European Union (EU). He argued passionately for an In/Out referendum (and introduced a private member's bill in 2009 to bring it about), and although he took the same position as UKIP leader Nigel Farage, he became convinced Farage was actually a barrier to Britain leaving the EU. He regularly met his old friend and Conservative MEP Daniel Hannan for conspiratorial dinners at Tate Britain on Millbank and together they came up with a plan. They decided the only way to achieve their aim was for Carswell to sacrifice his political career in the Conservative Party and to challenge Farage's strategy from within UKIP.

Prime Minister David Cameron had already announced there would be an EU referendum in his January 2013 Bloomberg speech. On 28 August 2014, Carswell announced he was resigning his parliamentary seat and would fight the ensuing by-election as a UKIP candidate. Few expected him to win and retain his seat, but he did, and with some style. He later said he had 'jumped ship with the express goal of changing the image of UKIP and ensuring that it was an asset rather than a liability in the referendum campaign... to decontaminate the brand'.

The by-election was held on 9 October. The Conservatives poured in huge resources but Carswell triumphed and won with an increased majority. By this time, his former colleague Mark Reckless had also defected to UKIP, announcing his decision in the middle of the Conservative Party conference.

Four days later, Douglas Carswell was introduced into the House of Commons as UKIP's first MP. He was joined by Reckless, who also won his by-election two months later.

Carswell and Farage soon fell out, with the latter accusing the former of being disloyal. In the 2015 election, Carswell was re-elected, but with a much smaller majority. In the 2016 referendum, Carswell supported Vote Leave rather than Farage's Leave.eu.

Douglas Carswell lost his seat in 2017. He now runs the Mississippi Center for Public Policy in Jackson, Mississippi.

CECIL PARKINSON RESIGNS

Cecil Parkinson was Margaret Thatcher's choice to succeed her as prime minister. It was not to be. His political career was damaged, like so many, over a sex scandal. Fathering a child with his secretary Sara Keays, it made his resignation in October 1983 an inevitability.

Parkinson was born and raised in Lancashire, reading English and Law at Emmanuel College, Cambridge, before training as an accountant. Elected to represent Enfield West in a 1970 by-election, replacing the late Chancellor, Iain Macleod, his political rise mirrored Margaret Thatcher's ascendancy. Appointed Minister of State for Trade following her first election victory in 1979, he was promoted to Chairman of the Conservative Party in 1981.

A member of Thatcher's Falklands War cabinet, he was rightly seen as a total Thatcher loyalist. He was a good media performer and made the government's case effectively on TV and radio.

However, his fortunes were not to last. After overseeing a brilliant election campaign in June 1983, in which Thatcher was returned with a 144-seat majority, he was pencilled in as Thatcher's new Foreign Secretary. However, in the midst of election night celebrations, Parkinson confessed his long-term affair with Sara Keays to Margaret Thatcher, admitting she was about to have his baby. She abandoned plans to appoint him to the Foreign Office and instead he was allocated the less high-profile Department of Trade and Industry. In just four months he managed to privatize British Telecom and reform the Stock Exchange.

His resignation came during the Conservative Party conference, following the publication in *The Times* of a myriad of allegations from Keays. She stated Parkinson had promised to marry her before reversing his stance. It appeared he was finished.

However, after the 1987 election, Thatcher reinstated him in the cabinet, where he served as Energy Secretary and Transport Secretary, jobs which never quite satisfied him.

Leaving the cabinet after Margaret Thatcher's removal from office, he was appointed to the Lords in 1992, and founded Conservative Way Forward. Returning as party Chairman for a year under William Hague between 1997 and 1998, it was not a happy period.

Parkinson died aged eighty-four in January 2016, leaving nothing in his will for his daughter Flora Keays.

SIR DAVID AMESS MP IS MURDERED

Most MPs hold constituency surgeries on a Friday or Saturday. It's an essential part of our democracy that the public are able to meet their Members of Parliament and lobby them on an issue of concern to them.

David Amess was first elected to Parliament in the Thatcher landslide of 1983. He was the youngest member of his intake. He represented Basildon for nine years before becoming MP for Southend West in 1992. A popular MP on all sides of the House, he never attained ministerial office, but this didn't seem to matter to him. He wasn't consumed by ambition, he was consumed by helping his constituents and his many campaigns, of which making Southend a city became the most important.

David had been a friend since I met him when I was working as a parliamentary researcher in 1985. In May 2021, I recorded an hour-long interview with him (available on Youtube) about his book *Ayes & Ears*, a guide to how Parliament works. I then agreed to be the guest speaker at his annual Conservative dinner on 15 October. A few days before that fateful day, we ran into each other at the Conservative conference. He told me he was very much looking forward to turning the tables on me, and interviewing me after the dinner in front of his members. 'I'm going to do a Paxman on you,' he chortled as he walked away. Those were the last words he ever said to me.

At 12.31 p.m. on 15 October, I received an email telling me David had been stabbed multiple times at his constituency surgery. I was in a state of shock for some moments. Thoughts of the murder of Jo Cox five years earlier came back to me. Three hours later, the terrible news came that he was dead. The whole of politics, and indeed the country, was appalled.

In March 2022, Ali Harbi Ali was convicted of David's murder.

On 1 March 2022, Southend finally became a city. I can see David's smile as I type that sentence. Rest in peace, my friend.

PARLIAMENT BURNED DOWN

The Palace of Westminster might represent the mother of all parliaments, but that hasn't stopped the building facing widespread damage. While its bombing during the Second World War is well remembered, less attention is given to the Great Fire of 1834, which resulted in the destruction of the Palace.

There had been warnings that a fire was inevitable since the 1790s. Medieval timbers lay under the stone exterior, a material which easily caught fire during the Great Fire of London. The precise cause of the fire however was a Tally Stick, a stick of hazel or ash wood used by the Exchequer.

On 16 October 1834, a clerk, Richard Whibley, instructed two labourers – Joshua Cross and Patrick Furlong – to burn two cartloads of tally sticks in the Palace's furnaces, which provided under-floor heating for the House of Lords. However, this meant that for nearly eleven hours they threw tallies into the furnaces without consideration. The senile Housekeeper ignored the warning signs of disaster facing the building.

By late afternoon, smoke was circulating throughout the Palace, as a fire rapidly spread. The combination of strong winds and poor fire equipment led to much of the rest of the Palace catching fire. Eventually, a huge fireball exploded, attracting hundreds of thousands of people to observe what was happening. Legend has it that it could be seen at Windsor Castle, twenty miles away. Indeed, only a change of wind direction stopped the historic Westminster Hall from also facing destruction.

Hundreds of fire fighters and the London Fire Engine Establishment battled the blaze, with volunteers manning the pumps. Fire crews remained for five days until the last of the fires were extinguished. Amazingly, there were no deaths.

By February 1835, temporary chambers and committee rooms were available for occupation, with a government competition announced to design the new Palace. Charles Barry won the commission, designing the building in a nineteenth-century Gothic style, which had come back into fashion.

Only Westminster Hall, the Chapel of St Mary Undercroft and part of the Cloister survived 1834, and the damage cost £2 million.

SIR DAVID BUTLER IS BORN

Watch any BBC election programme over the last sixty years and almost three things are certain: the appearance of a Dimbleby (Richard or David), Peter Snow or Jeremy Vine demonstrating the excellent swingometer – and analysis from one Sir David Butler. Someone with both a deep knowledge of psephology and the enthusiasm to explain things to others, he remains a titan of broadcasting election analysis.

Butler was born into a political family during the 1924 election campaign, where his mother ran the campaign for his grandfather Albert Pollard, who was standing as a Liberal. Educated at St Paul's School and New College, Oxford, where he read Philosophy, Politics and Economics, Butler was tutored by the philosopher Isaiah Berlin. He interrupted his studies to serve in the Second World War, where he became a Lieutenant and crossed the Rhine as a tank commander.

Butler attended Princeton University as a Visiting Fellow between 1947 and 1948, when, during the 1948 presidential election, he hitch-hiked around America. His obvious intelligence took him to high places, including serving as personal assistant to Britain's Ambassador in Washington.

Throughout his academic career, he taught at Nuffield College, Oxford, where he served as a Fellow until 1992 (and remains an Emeritus Fellow). Having written a doctoral thesis in just two years on the British electoral system, a career in academia seemed inevitable. At the college, he compiled the Nuffield Election Studies of each UK election since 1945. Other co-authors included Richard Rose and Anthony King. Between 1974 and 2005, Butler wrote the series with Dennis Kavanagh.

Butler's prime on-screen appearances, as an expert on UK election night programmes, occured between 1950 and 1979. He was part of ITV's election night show in 1997 and Sky's in 2001. Crucial was his invention of the idea of swing between the parties. An author of numerous books, his *Political Change in Britain: Forces Shaping Electoral Choice* was seen as a pioneering analysis that used American political science in the UK.

Elected a fellow of the British Academy in 1994, Butler was appointed CBE in 1991 and knighted in 2011 for services to political science.

BBC FOUNDED

The British Broadcasting Corporation (BBC) is an organization like no other. Giving the UK major soft power, its global transmission of news, entertainment and sport has played a key role in cementing Britain's clout during an era of Britain coming to terms with a new role in the world.

The BBC was originally called the British Broadcasting Company upon its founding on 18 October 1922 by wireless manufacturers. Daily broadcasting began from the 2LO transmitter in The Strand, being the first daily radio service in London. News was supplied by an agency, while music, drama and talks filled the airwaves for a few hours each day. The news of its launch made almost no impact, with barely any newspaper coverage.

John Reith, aged thirty-three, became the BBC's first Director-General (then General Manager) on 14 December 1922. And by February 1924, the electronically generated pips had begun, which marked the Greenwich Time Signa on BBC radio.

It took until January 1927 for the British Broadcasting Corporation to be properly established by Royal Charter, which outlined the BBC's objectives and obligations.

The BBC's coverage of politics has always been contentious, with the corporation censoring Oswald Mosley, the leader of the British Union of Fascists, and Harry Pollitt, the leader of the Communist Party of Great Britain. During the war, television broadcasting was suspended, with radio broadcasts used to maintain the nation's spirits.

Since then, the Corporation has inevitably become involved in many a controversy, usually involving politicians accusing it of a lack of balance or impartiality. Conservative politicians think it's stuffed with left-wingers determined to portray a certain view of the world, while Labour politicians believe it swings to the right. Under virtually every government these sorts of rows break out, and then eventually everyone calms down. Until the next time.

The biggest 'spat' between government and the BBC occurred in 2003 when *Today* correspondent Andrew Gilligan accused the Blair government of 'sexing up' a dossier about weapons of mass destruction in Iraq. The resulting inquiry led to the resignations of both the BBC Chairman, Gavyn Davies, and Director-General, Greg Dyke.

CARLTON CLUB MEETING DITCHES LLOYD GEORGE

The Carlton Club may sound like a location only for the elite, but a decision there in October 1922 dramatically impacted the course of history. On 19 October, Conservative MPs gathered to decide whether the party should remain in government as part of the coalition government led by Liberal prime minister David Lloyd George.

The parties had come together in a coalition during the First World War under Herbert Asquith, though Lloyd George replaced him in December 1916. The coalition continued after the 1918 election, even though the vast majority of coalition MPs were Conservatives. The Liberal Party split between those who continued to support Asquith and those who supported Lloyd George.

The main Conservative opposition was fuelled by discontent over the government's policy towards Turkey. Lloyd George had been willing to launch a war over Turkey's threat towards British and French troops in Canakkale. But Lord Curzon, the Conservative Foreign Secretary, eventually persuaded French troops to agree an armistice rather than withdraw, and stabilized the situation.

Public attacks on the coalition led to the cabinet announcing an election on 10 October 1922, with Lloyd George and Austen Chamberlain, leader of the Conservatives, both defending the coalition. Andrew Bonar Law had led the Conservatives for a decade before Chamberlain took over, and still retained strong public support within the Conservative Party. He was one of the main opponents of the coalition's continuation.

Austen Chamberlain tried to defend the government and coalition at the Carlton Club meeting of Conservative backbenchers, arguing this was an ideological battle, between those who favoured freedom, and socialism. Stanley Baldwin and Bonar Law were the key speakers against the coalition, suggesting Lloyd George had been able to destroy the Liberal Party and could do the same to the Conservatives.

The rebel voices were able to win the day, with Conservative MPs voting 187 to 88 against continuing the coalition. Austen Chamberlain resigned and Bonar Law was invited to form a government following the November 1922 election.

The Carlton Club meeting also marked the foundation of what would become known as the 1922 Committee of Conservative backbenchers.

ALEC DOUGLAS-HOME FORMS A GOVERNMENT

Alec Douglas-Home was a unique prime minister. The first and only born during the Edwardian era, he was the last to enter Downing Street as a member of the House of Lords. Renouncing his peerage thanks to Tony Benn, he rejoined the House of Commons. Prime Minister for less than a year, he entered office in October 1963.

Born in July 1903 to aristocracy, he was educated at Eton. Where else? After Oxford, he rose through the ranks of the Territorial Army – lieutenant, captain, major – during the 1920s and 1930s.

His title did not prevent election to the House of Commons, though Douglas-Home, or Lord Dunglass as he was then, demonstrated little interest in politics. Elected in 1931 for the National Government representing Lanark, he became Parliamentary Private Secretary to Chancellor Neville Chamberlain, retaining that post when Chamberlain became prime minister.

Dunglass was a supporter of Chamberlain's policy of appeasement, accompanying him to Munich in 1938. He suffered his own health crisis when a hole in his spine surrounded by tuberculosis was discovered. In July 1943, he attended the House of Commons for the first time since 1940, gaining a reputation for foreign affairs expertise.

Losing his seat in the 1945 landslide, he regained it in 1950 before inheriting the title of the Earl of Home in July 1951. Serving in the Commonwealth Relations Office from 1957, he became Foreign Secretary in 1960.

Following Macmillan's resignation during the 1963 party conference, Douglas-Home was not initially a top contender. Rab Butler, the front runner, gave an uninspiring speech and this helped Douglas-Home to decide to run. Gaining Macmillan's support, he was invited by the Queen to form a government on 18 October.

Though Enoch Powell and Iain Macleod refused to serve, the cabinet eventually united around Douglas-Home. Becoming MP for Kinross and West Perthshire, his main interest remained foreign affairs. His main legislative act was abolishing resale price maintenance, which allowed price reductions. Despite economic prosperity, Douglas-Home was defeated by Harold Wilson in October 1964.

Retiring as Leader of the Conservatives in July 1965, Douglas-Home returned as Foreign Secretary during Edward Heath's premiership. He died in October 1995 aged ninety-two.

THE ABERFAN DISASTER

In Aberfan, a small Welsh village near Merthyr Tydfil, it had been raining for weeks. There was a build-up of water in a colliery spoil tip, atop a hill, which eventually led to disaster. At 9.15 a.m., the tip's contents slid down into Aberfan, where the slurry enveloped a primary school and a row of houses. One hundred and sixteen children and twenty-eight adults perished.

That morning, the National Coal Board (NCB) met to discuss the disaster. NCB Chairman Lord Robens sent two men to Aberfan to investigate. Labour's Welsh Secretary, Cledwyn Hughes, arrived on the scene at 4 p.m. He asked after Lord Robens; the NCB said he couldn't be there, but that he was personally directing relief work. He was, in fact, being invested as the Chancellor of the University of Surrey, clearly far too busy to respond to a catastrophe caused by the negligence of his own organization.

Prime Minister Harold Wilson made it to Aberfan by 9.40 p.m. He visited rescue workers and was briefed by local police. He quickly ordered an inquiry to be headed by a judge and assisted by an engineer and a planning lawyer. HM The Queen also visited eight days later.

A year later, in August 1967, the inquiry's report was scathing in its criticism of the National Coal Board and its 'bungling ineptitude'. A major contributing factor in the disaster was that the tip in question sat on top of water springs. The springs were not 'unknown', as Lord Robens had initially said. They were in fact on the Ordnance Survey map. Locals knew about the springs.

In a Commons debate on the disaster a few months later, Labour MPs from Welsh mining towns found themselves unable to come to terms with the NCB's failure – after all, it was their hero Clement Attlee's creation. But Margaret Thatcher, then Power spokesman for the Conservatives, was on hand to help them. She asked why a key member of the NCB had remained at a conference in Japan when the disaster occurred. She asked why the NCB had promoted their Director of Production after he was criticized for ignoring the tip's instability. Answers came there none.

SAME-SEX MARRIAGE AND ABORTION BECOME LEGAL IN NORTHERN IRELAND

One of the downsides of devolution is that some issues, which most people assume are UK-wide, are, in fact, decided within the three devolved administrations. Although gay people have been allowed to marry in England since 2014, the Northern Ireland government refused to legislate to mirror the English legislation. Even the deeply Catholic and religious Republic of Ireland legalized it in 2015 following an emphatic referendum result. It was the same with abortion, which was legalized in England in 1967. Any woman in Northern Ireland wanting an abortion had to travel to England or Wales.

Opinion polling in Northern Ireland shows a consistent majority for the legalization of both same-sex marriage and abortion, yet the DUP blocked it at every point, refusing to even allow debates on the subject in the Stormont Assembly. The impasse was broken in 2017 when the Assembly collapsed. This led to a power vacuum, so MPs in Westminster decided to step in and fill the void. In July 2019, they voted by 333 votes to 73 to extend equal marriage legislation to the Province after an amendment to a government bill was proposed by Labour MP Conor McGinn, who was born and raised in Northern Ireland. Minutes later, MPs voted on an amendment tabled by McGinn's colleague Stella Creasy on abortion rights, and this passed by 332 to 99. The government promised to abide by the results of the votes, despite coming under huge pressure from the DUP and religious communities in Northern Ireland not to do so. The first gay marriage took place in February 2020.

The situation with abortion was more complex. In March 2020, Stormont was restored and the UK government published details of a new legal framework for abortion services. Fatally, though, it was up to Stormont's Department of Health to actually commission the services. In June, the Assembly backed a non-binding motion rejecting the law change. In March 2021, Parliament voted to give Northern Ireland Secretary Brandon Lewis the powers to compel the Northern Ireland Executive to implement abortion laws.

Legal challenges ensued but in February 2022, the courts ruled in favour of Brandon Lewis.

THE WAR OF JENKINS'S EAR BEGINS

Wars between Britain and various European powers during the eighteenth century were not, it has to be said, unusual. For one to be named after a merchant ship's captain was, however, not a common occurrence.

This war was a nine-year-long conflict between Britain and Spain that started in 1739. It was the nineteenth-century British historian Thomas Carlyle who called it the War of Jenkins's Ear, albeit 120 years later. Robert Jenkins was captain of a British merchant ship, who had his ear cut off by representatives of the Spanish Coastguard when they climbed aboard his ship in search of illicit goods. Jenkins later said in testimony that the Spanish captain, 'took hold of his left Ear and with his Cutlass slit it down, and then another of the Spaniards took hold of it and tore it off, but gave him the Piece of his Ear again.' This happened in 1731, eight years before the actual war began. In 1739, Jenkins appeared before Parliament so parliamentarians could see the damage inflicted on him by the dastardly Spanish. The public and politicians were outraged, and the frenzy that ensued bolstered support for war with Spain. The South Sea Company was also pushing for confrontation with Spain, which it felt would help boost its trading position in the West Indies. In addition, Britain was keen for Spain to adhere to the valuable 'asiento' deal which allowed British slave traders to ply their evil trade in Latin America. In Spain, the War of Jenkins's Ear is called the 'Asiento war'.

On 28 March, the House of Commons voted by 257 to 209 to seek redress from Spain. On 10 July, King George II ordered British warships to take action against Spanish ships, although the actual declaration of war didn't come until 23 October.

The war didn't go well initially and there were a lot of casualties. However, in 1742, the war against Spain became a side battle in the War of the Austrian Succession, which in effect was a wider European conflict. It wasn't until 1748 that the war ended with the signing of the Treaty of Aix la Chapelle.

ROBIN DAY IS BORN

Sir Robin Day styled himself as the 'Grand Inquisitor', a pioneer of interrogating politicians to elicit answers of importance. One of the titanic figures of British political journalism throughout the twentieth century, he was born in October 1923 in Hampstead. Educated in London, Gloucester and on the Isle of Wight, he served in the British Army's Royal Artillery from 1943 to 1947.

Day's passion for debating and reaching the truth can be seen in his choice of degree at St Edmund Hall, Oxford: Law. Alongside becoming President of the Oxford Union, Day took part in a US debating tour. Practising law only briefly, he worked at ITN from 1955, becoming the first British journalist to interview Egypt's President Nasser after the Suez Crisis.

His journalistic strategy aimed to break the deference traditionally shown by interviewers towards politicians. Interviewing the Prime Minister, Harold Macmillan, in 1958, Day's combative approach was labelled a 'most vigorous cross-examination' by the *Daily Express*.

Day's own political views leaned Liberal, standing as a candidate for the party in Hereford at the 1959 election. Following his defeat, Day defected from ITN to the BBC.

Working on all the BBC's election programmes from the 1960s to 1987, he also presented *Panorama* and launched *Question Time* in 1979, where he served as the Chair for a decade. His recognizability came not only from his interrogative questioning but also his heavy-rimmed spectacles and a trademark bow tie.

Television was not the exclusive format for Sir Robin, with radio also allowing him a chance to reveal his broadcasting capabilities. Presenting *It's Your Line* from 1970 to 1976, it allowed the public to phone in and question politicians themselves, something widely seen as groundbreaking. He also presented *The World at One* from 1979 until 1987. In 1981, he was awarded a knighthood.

Having campaigned for over two decades to see Parliament televised, first presenting arguments in favour to the Hansard Society in 1963, Day saw his argument eventually win out in 1989.

Day died of heart complications, aged seventy-six, on 6 August 2000. Baroness Thatcher argued Day was 'tough and relentless' but she 'always enjoyed the joust'.

CHURCHILL WINS 1951 GENERAL ELECTION

Clement Attlee's government had run out of steam and was looking tired. Bevin was dead. Bevan had resigned. Cripps had retired. In 1950, Attlee had only been elected with a majority of five, and another general election seemed inevitable. Bizarrely, it was provoked by King George VI, who was due to go on a foreign tour (in the end he was too ill to go) and was worried the government might fall while he was away. The party was still riven by the Bevanite splits over the NHS and other issues, which hadn't exactly helped the party win the previous year. On top of that, Attlee had been embarrassed by the defections of Guy Burgess and Kim Philby, and sterling was under strain following a set of disastrous trade figures. As the historian John Charmley put it, the government was 'exhausted in mind, body and manifesto commitments'.

These were not propitious circumstances for an election, but nevertheless Attlee dissolved Parliament in September. Polling day was set for 25 October.

Labour fought the campaign without ever really getting out of second gear. Mrs Attlee drove her husband round the country to promote a message of 'stick with nurse for fear of worse'. Labour's manifesto concentrated on peace, full employment, cost of living and fairness. All the usual fare, but the Conservatives, with Churchill as leader, had successfully renewed themselves in opposition and put forward some eye-catching policies, promising to build 300,000 houses a year and reverse Labour's nationalizations. The party Chairman, Lord Woolton, had also reinvigorated the party organization. Labour also suffered for its support for America's war in Korea, which also played into Churchill's hands as the great war leader.

Labour won more votes than any party had ever done before (this record stood until John Major's victory in 1992), and their tally outnumbered the Conservatives and National Liberals combined. But the Conservatives won 321 seats to Labour's 295. As in 1874, a political party had won an overall majority, while losing the popular vote. It was the last election in which the Conservatives did better in Scotland than England.

Winston was back in Number 10.

312

HOUSE OF LORDS VOTES TO ABOLISH HEREDITARY PEERS

In its 1997 election manifesto, New Labour promised meaningful constitutional reform. This included reform of the House of Lords.

Nonetheless, the House of Lords was initially resistant to change, as it always has been. In 1649, the House of Lords was abolished for more than a decade after voting against the execution of Charles I. Previous Lords reform Acts in 1911 and 1949 had diminished the ability of the Lords to block or veto Commons legislation and in 1958 life peers were introduced.

Within the first year of Tony Blair's government, the Lords had returned government bills thirty-eight times, opposing the European Elections Bill five times alone. The huge disparity between a Labour-dominated House of Commons and a Conservative House of Lords gave Blair the chance to demonstrate how the Lords undermined democratic legitimacy.

As part of its reforms Labour wanted to ensure that 751 hereditary peers lost their 800-year right to sit at Westminster. Indeed, the Conservatives intended to vote against the Bill because of the intended removal of the hereditary peers before a royal commission had reported on the future of the Lords.

Lords Tory leader Lord Strathclyde compared the 'bows and arrows' of the opposition to the 'machine guns' from New Labour. They eventually abstained. In the end, the Lords voted by 221 to 81 to abolish hereditary peers, with the Act receiving Royal Assent on 11 November.

Eventually, the New Labour government compromised with the hereditary peers by allowing ninety-two hereditary peers to remain. When a hereditary peer died, there would be a by-election among hereditary peers to allocate their replacement, a system widely seen as farcical given the narrow electorate. And it's that system which is still, scandalously, in operation twenty-three years later.

If the Bill had been defeated, a constitutional crisis would have been provoked due to the Salisbury Convention, which committed peers to allowing legislation through which had been included in a party's election manifesto.

Nick Clegg, in the early period of the Coalition after 2010, tried to institute further Lords reform, but it was thwarted by an implacable Conservative opposition.

THE STOCK MARKET EXPERIENCES THE 'BIG BANG'

Vested interests always fight any form of deregulation. 'It will be the ruin of us.' 'It will cost the economy millions.' 'We've always done it this way.' Siren voices in the City of London were horrified when, in 1983, Cecil Parkinson – all too briefly Trade and Industry Secretary – announced that he intended to deregulate the financial markets and the London Stock Exchange. He didn't exactly order the slaughter of the First Born, but judging by the reaction of some, he might as well have done.

What provoked this radical move was an important anti-trust case launched by the Office of Fair Trading against the London Stock Exchange under the Restrictive Practices Act of 1956. Restrictive practices in many sectors were rife, but especially in the hallowed halls of the London Stock Exchange. There were fixed commission charges, and the so-called 'Single Capacity' rule laid down a separation between brokers acting as agents for their clients on commission, and jobbers who created the markets and provided liquidity by holding stashes of stocks and shares on their books. Brokers and jobbers were not allowed to be part of larger financial groups and no foreigners were allowed to be members of the Stock Exchange.

After three years of preparation, the big day came on 27 October 1986. All the old practices were swept away and the Stock Exchange became screen rather than paper based. What could possibly go wrong? Well, not a lot, actually. Many of the old traditional stockbroking firms were gobbled up by bigger financial institutions, and some of the most famous names in the City disappeared, but apart from that, the 'Big Bang' spurred London as a financial centre on to even greater things. London is now the indisputable number two most important financial hub in the world, behind New York. Some even posit that it has overtaken the 'Big Apple'. Without 'Big Bang' that simply would not have been possible.

Cecil Parkinson may have other legacies, but he could certainly be proud of this one, even if in 2008 Gordon Brown blamed too much deregulation for the world financial crash.

HOUSE OF COMMONS VOTES TO JOIN EEC

Though many politicos will remember the late-night Brexit votes as Theresa May sought to pass her Withdrawal Agreement in Parliament, few now recall Edward Heath conducting the reverse in 1971 to guarantee British entry into the European Economic Community (EEC).

British entry had been vetoed by French president Charles de Gaulle twice, in 1963 and 1967, due to concerns about Britain's economic performance and the influence of the USA. Following his departure as president, British membership was put firmly on the agenda.

Conservative prime minister Edward Heath was a staunch Europhile, possessing a guiding, almost biblical ambition to take Britain into the EEC, having experienced the horrors of the Second World War. Triumphing over Harold Wilson in the 1970 election, he managed to persuade the French government of the merits of British entry. Negotiating a deal with Brussels, his slim Commons majority meant there was no guarantee of Parliament approving a deal.

Indeed, numerous Conservative MPs were opposed to EEC entry. Despite Harold Wilson applying for membership in 1967 as prime minister, as Leader of the Opposition he opposed Heath's deal, arguing it was not good enough for the UK and that the government did not have a mandate for such a big decision.

Six days of debate about Britain's entry took place in October 1971, titled 'The Great Debate' by historians, as 176 MPs contributed. Initially wanting to whip his MPs, Heath was persuaded by his Chief Whip, Francis Pym, to allow a free vote of Conservative MPs to vote as their consciences demanded.

Strategically, this was brilliant. Many Labour MPs, including the party's Deputy Leader, Roy Jenkins, were staunchly pro-European and wanted to back Heath's membership deal. By not whipping Conservative MPs, Labour MPs could therefore justify defying a Labour three-line whip.

In the end, MPs voted to join Europe by 356 votes to 244, with 39 Conservative MPs voting against EEC membership. However, sixty-nine Labour MPs voted to support membership, with twenty MPs abstaining. This allowed Heath's government to attain a majority of 112, far beyond their expectations.

Heath's lasting goal had been achieved. On 1 January 1973, Britain officially joined.

1924 GENERAL ELECTION

This was the election that ended the 'experiment' of the first ever Labour government in Britain after just ten months. In the previous general election in December 1923, the sitting Prime Minister, Stanley Baldwin, had failed to achieve endorsement for his adoption of a protectionist economic policy and therefore resigned. With the Liberals unwilling to form a government, the opportunity arose for Ramsay MacDonald to do so, even though Labour won only 191 out of the 615 seats.

Not surprisingly, his administration did not record any major achievements in legislation or domestic policy, but it did succeed in showing that Labour could be a competent 'party of government'. There were no disasters either, at least until in the autumn of 1924, when MacDonald was accused of misleading the Commons in the Campbell case, which related to the prosecution of the editor of the communist-leaning newspaper *Workers' Weekly*.

Therefore early in October, both the Liberals and Conservatives supported a motion of censure against the Prime Minister. MacDonald decided that this was to be treated as a matter of 'no confidence'. In effect, the opposition parties had decided to combine and end his government – as they could have done at any time.

The most notable feature of the campaign was the Zinoviev letter, published by the *Daily Mail* four days before the poll, which implied that MacDonald's recognition of the USSR had encouraged communist subversion within Britain. Now regarded as a fake, it impacted the result, but probably not significantly to Labour's disadvantage – a large Conservative overall majority such as the 209 they achieved was always likely in October 1924.

In fact, the main losers in the election results were the Liberals, who were very short of money and squeezed to the Tories' benefit by the anti-socialist sentiments generated by the Zinoviev letter. They were reduced from 158 seats to 40. Labour, with 151 MPs, was now clearly in second place, and actually increased its votes compared with 1923 – up from 4.3 million to 5.3 million. The Liberal decision to censure MacDonald had backfired, and another nail had been hammered into the coffin of its long career as a governing party.

HOUSE OF LORDS PLANS REVEALED

Reforming the House of Lords has been a consistent theme of governments ever since the universal franchise arrived in 1928. Parliament Acts had limited the amount of time the upper chamber could limit legislation. This was further exacerbated by reforms announced in October 1957 under Prime Minister Harold Macmillan.

Previously, the upper chamber had contained only individuals with hereditary peerages who came from the aristocracy. Undoubtedly with a Conservative leaning, this social divide was widely condemned in the post-war consensus. As such, while the upper House would remain unelected, life peerages were created, something Queen Victoria herself had been an early supporter of. While Macmillan referred to them as 'day boys', the proposal was seen as radical at the time.

The advent of life peerages allowed apparently experienced and distinguished individuals who might not be able to receive hereditary titles to join the House. Previously existing in medieval England, they were given to mistresses of monarchs. At the discretion of the prime minister, new peers would also be chosen by party leaders, with expenses paid. The reforms also allowed women to enter the upper chamber for the first time.

Lord Home, the Conservative leader in the House of Lords (and later prime minister), argued that admitting women would recognize their rights to be part of a modern society, also adding, in a note of the different times, that 'taking women into parliamentary embrace is, after all, only an extension of the normal privileges of a peer.'

Though the reforms seemed extensive, the government was unwilling to countenance reducing the rights of hereditary peers.

The 1958 Peerages Act thus allowed the Queen to create life peers, whose peerages would expire upon their death. Further reforms in 1963 also allowed hereditary peeresses to sit in the House of Lords, while peers could also give up their title if they wished to sit in the Commons. Both Tony Benn and Alec Douglas-Home would take advantage of this reform. By 2018, 1,419 life peers had been appointed in the sixty years since the scheme was first introduced.

317

BRITAIN AND FRANCE TAKE SUEZ CANAL

In July 1956, after months of increasing tension, Egyptian president Gamal Abdel Nasser announced the nationalization of the Suez Canal Company, which had been in operation since 1869 and was run jointly by the British and the French.

The Egyptians had seized control of a vital conduit between Asia and Europe upon which the UK depended for its oil. Prime Minister Anthony Eden was furious, and convened a series of secret meetings with French and Israeli military leaders. He wanted a prompt return to the status quo and feared that anything else would further cement the UK's image as a declining world power. So, in spite of pressure from President Eisenhower of the United States to find a peaceful solution with the UN, he sent British troops into Egypt alongside the French.

The Conservative government faced loud and continued opposition from Labour under Hugh Gaitskell even, and perhaps unusually, after war had begun. In an impassioned speech, he referred to the idea that the UK had 'colluded' with Israel and France and accused Eden of turning his back on the Commonwealth, the Americans and the UN.

The military action had initially seemed successful, but the UN quickly threatened Britain with sanctions if there were any civilian casualties, and Nasser shut the canal. The British economy was in a state of panic. There was a run on the pound, and the Treasury faced having to devalue its currency. A scorned Eisenhower pressured the International Monetary Fund to deny the UK any help. Public pressure was mounting too, as anti-war protests and civil service resignations were triggered by the international embarrassment. Eden had to accept a ceasefire.

The only thing achieved in the long-term by intervention was a cementing of Egypt's control of the Suez Canal, backed by the UN and US. The standing of the UK in the Middle East was severely damaged. Britain could no longer take such military action without the backing of the Americans. Anthony Eden's own reputation was in tatters, and he resigned as prime minister in January 1957 after less than two years in the job.

NOVEMBER

SIR GEOFFREY HOWE RESIGNS

The fate of Margaret Thatcher's premiership was perhaps sealed the night after Halloween in 1990. Marking the resignation of her Deputy Prime Minister, Sir Geoffrey Howe, it precipitated the events which led to Thatcher, within a month, being toppled from power after more than a decade as prime minister.

Having briefly served as MP for Bebington between 1964 and 1966, Howe re-entered the Commons in 1970 as the MP for Reigate. Serving as Solicitor General under Edward Heath, he stood against Margaret Thatcher in the second round of the Tory leadership contest of 1975. Though Thatcher triumphed, she saw Howe as a political soulmate and made him shadow Chancellor.

As Chancellor from 1979 to 1983, he was a steady reformer. He abolished exchange controls and created tax-free enterprise zones. His 1981 budget made balancing the books a priority and it instituted swingeing public expenditure cuts. Howe reduced inflation from 11.9 per cent in early 1981 to 3.8 per cent in February 1983, as interest rates also fell from 14 per cent to 10 per cent.

After 1983, Howe served as Foreign Secretary for six years. However, the Foreign Office also marked the start of souring tensions with Number 10, not least over Europe. As a pro-European, Howe increasingly felt at odds with Thatcher's more strident tone, threatening to resign over her opposition to joining the Exchange Rate Mechanism.

In 1989, Howe became Deputy Prime Minister, refusing the office of Home Secretary. He felt incensed at having been replaced by the little-known John Major and having to give up Chevening, the grace and favour residence of the Foreign Secretary. Demoted to Leader of the House of Commons, tensions increased in October 1990 as Margaret Thatcher made her famous 'No, No, No' statement opposing further European integration.

Two weeks after his departure, Howe made an incendiary resignation statement from the backbenches. He said serving in Margaret Thatcher's cabinet was akin to going into bat with the team captain having already broken it. It was one of the most dramatic parliamentary moments of the last forty years. The speech was widely seen as a catalyst for Michael Heseltine to challenge Thatcher for the leadership.

BIRTH OF EDWARD COLSTON

Would Edward Colston have merited a mention in this book, had his statue not been ripped down and dragged into Bristol Harbour in 2020? Probably not, but his story is one which resonates through the centuries as a Member of Parliament, philanthropist but, above all, a slave trader.

His story is certainly not unique, as there were plenty of MPs of his generation intimately involved in the slave trade.

Colston was born in Bristol to a merchant, who later became High Sherriff of the city. The family had lived in Bristol since the thirteenth century. After the Civil War, the Colstons moved to London, where at the age of eighteen he became an apprentice in the Mercers' Company. He became involved in the textile sector as well as importing fine wines from Portugal and Spain. In 1680, he became a member of the Royal African Company, which traded on the west coast of Africa in gold, silver, ivory and also slaves. Nine years later, he became deputy governor of the company but his association with it ended in 1692. During his twelve years with the Royal African Company, it transported around 85,000 Africans to the Caribbean and North America. It is estimated that around nineteen thousand may have died on the journey.

During this time, he started to donate large sums of money to good causes and charities in Bristol. He founded alms houses, endowed schools and a hospital, and streets were subsequently named after him.

Colston entered Parliament in 1710 but was an MP for only three years. He died in 1721.

In 1895, 174 years after his death, a statue was erected in his honour in the centre of Bristol. When a biography uncovered his connection to the slave trade, there were immediate demands for it to be removed, demands which were ignored for the next hundred years. In response to the Black Lives Matter movement protests, on 7 June 2020 the statue was torn down and pushed into Bristol Harbour. It was later retrieved and is now on display at the M Shed museum. The protesters who tore it down were found not guilty of causing criminal damage eighteen months later.

ACT OF SUPREMACY

The English Reformation, the transformation of the country from overwhelmingly Roman Catholic to Protestant, started in the reign of one of our best known and most formidable monarchs, Henry VIII. This was of immense importance in a religious age. Yet Henry himself always remained a strong Catholic, and it was not at all his intention to follow the groundbreaking ideas of such reformers as Martin Luther on the Continent. The Reformation was the unintended consequence of Henry's power politics.

Henry's marital policy is among the best-known issues in the whole of English history. Essentially, he wanted – and felt he needed – a male heir to prolong and safeguard the Tudor dynasty. As he could not obtain permission from the Pope for a divorce from Catherine of Aragon, he founded a Church of England with himself as its Supreme Head. The man who played a major role in realizing this plan – his chief minister in the 1530s, Thomas Cromwell – has also now become very familiar through the multiple Booker Prize-winning novels of Hilary Mantel.

A key element in Cromwell's strategy was the Act of Supremacy of November 1534. The King would now have the right to decide how the English Church should be organized, its central beliefs, and who would be appointed to its key positions. The Act of Supremacy had immediate serious consequences, not least for those who opposed it. Among those executed for refusing the Oath of Supremacy was Henry's former Chancellor, Sir Thomas More, who was to be canonized as a Catholic saint in 1935. Ironically, Thomas Cromwell himself also lost his head, after losing the favour of the King in 1540.

Among the rapid developments in religion in England in the rest of the century, Henry's Act of Supremacy was repealed in the reign of his Catholic daughter, Mary Tudor, in 1555, but re-established under her Protestant sister, Elizabeth I, in 1559. We may have moved on from Tudor politics, in which monarchs are autocrats and chief ministers struggle to keep their heads on their shoulders, but the Church of England is still our official religion, and the Queen is still its Supreme Governor.

PAUL EDDINGTON DIES

Paul Eddington was an actor best known for playing Jim Hacker, a fictional Minister for Administrative Affairs, and later Prime Minister, whose departmental management bore more than a hint of resemblance to reality. Eddington starred as Hacker between 1980 and 1984 in *Yes Minister*, before resuming the role in its sequel, *Yes, Prime Minister*, from 1986 to 1988.

Eddington was born in Paddington in June 1927. His family were Quakers, and he was brought up with strict family values and registered as a conscientious objector to warfare. He began acting with the Entertainments National Service Association during the Second World War, and later he worked for a Sheffield theatre company.

Making inroads into TV didn't appear too tricky for Eddington, where he starred in programmes including *The Adventures of Robin Hood*, *The Avengers* and *The Prisoner*. Nonetheless, he remained low-profile for many years, with his wife Patricia threatening to leave him if he quit acting. Yet it was the sitcom *The Good Life*, first broadcast by the BBC in 1975, which first brought Eddington to national fame. Eddington starred opposite Penelope Keith as Jerry Leadbetter, Margot's henpecked businessman husband.

But it was *Yes Minister* and *Yes, Prime Minister* which really raised Eddington's profile. The shows were broadcast throughout Margaret Thatcher's premiership, and she was said to have enjoyed them immensely. The show was shortlisted four times for BAFTA Best Light Entertainment Programme, but Eddington lost out for Best Actor to Nigel Hawthorne, playing civil servant Sir Humphrey Appleby, whose catchphrase gave the show its title. The programmes cemented in the public psyche the idea that civil servants, rather than politicians, are the individuals in charge of decision-making.

Hawthorne and Eddington appeared in a sketch of *Yes, Prime Minister* supposedly written by Margaret Thatcher, in which she herself played the Prime Minister. In fact, it was penned by her press secretary, Bernard Ingham.

Made a CBE in the 1987 New Year Honours, Eddington published his autobiography, *So Far, So Good*, in 1995. Just five days before his death, an interview with the BBC was broadcast where Eddington said he would like to be remembered as having done 'very little harm'.

GUNPOWDER PLOT

'Gunpowder, treason and plot'. The fifth of November is certainly one of the best remembered days in British history. There may have been others who have thought that the fiery destruction of both houses of Parliament (and, indeed, the monarch) may be a good idea, but Robert Catesby and his co-conspirators, such as the Yorkshireman Guy (or Guido) Fawkes, came nearest to achieving such an impact.

Those still celebrating annually with bonfires, 'guys' and fireworks may have some understanding that thirty-six barrels of explosive, along with Fawkes, were discovered at the eleventh hour in the cellars under the Lords before the royal opening of Parliament. But it is less likely that the wider intentions of the plotters are still known, or the political significance of the celebration.

As with most of the politics of the sixteenth and seventeenth centuries, religion was at the core of the issue. Two years earlier, in 1603, Queen Elizabeth I had died. She had re-established the Protestant Church of England after the turmoil of the middle of the previous century, and as a result had faced Catholic plots and threats such as those involving the Spanish Armada and Mary Queen of Scots. Under her successor, James Stuart (the latter's son), Roman Catholics in England had high hopes that their persecution might end. They were to be disappointed.

In February 1604, James ordered all Jesuits and other Catholic priests to leave the country, and reinstituted fines for open Catholic worship ('recusancy'). It was this that motivated Catesby, a landed gentleman from the Midlands, and the other conspirators. They aimed too to kidnap James's daughter Elizabeth, and install her as queen, to be married to a Catholic. Thus would the Roman faith be restored.

The plot completely failed. Fawkes and the gunpowder were discovered, and Catesby died in a shoot-out at Holbeche House in Staffordshire. In January 1606, Parliament designated 5 November as a day of thanksgiving. Due to the anti-Catholic sentiment of the time, an effigy of the Pope was burned as well as the 'guy'. Few, if any, now celebrate for that reason – but the symbolism does refer to the troubled history of religion in Britain.

MICHAEL HOWARD IS ELECTED CONSERVATIVE LEADER

The Conservative Party in 2003 was in a parlous state. Having spent six years in opposition, it was led by Iain Duncan Smith, who had found it difficult to make any inroads into the popularity of Tony Blair and New Labour. In the end, Conservative MPs lost patience with the 'quiet man' who had in his own words failed to 'turn up the volume'.

Michael Howard was born in Swansea in 1941. His father was a Jewish Romanian immigrant who settled in the UK in 1939. Howard joined the Young Conservatives at the University of Cambridge, before becoming a lawyer in 1964.

Unsuccessfully contesting Liverpool Edge Hill in 1966 and 1970, he was elected to represent Folkestone and Hythe in 1983. The first of his intake to be made a minister, as Minister for Local Government, he introduced Section 28, which banned local governments from 'promoting' homosexuality, and just as notoriously, the 'poll tax'.

Joining Margaret Thatcher's cabinet as Employment Secretary in January 1990, he was appointed Environment Secretary and then Home Secretary by John Major. He adopted a tough approach to crime, arguing that 'prison worked'. During his tenure the prison population increased from 42,000 to 85,000. Despite voting for the reintroduction of the death penalty in 1983 and 1990, he opposed it in 1994.

Famously asked fourteen times by Jeremy Paxman about prison escapes, he stood for the Conservative leadership in 1997. Ann Widdecombe's label that there was 'something of the night' about him was without doubt a contributing factor in his failure to win.

Becoming shadow Foreign Secretary under William Hague, he was appointed shadow Chancellor under Iain Duncan Smith in 2001. Winning praise, he took the leadership unopposed in November 2003 after Duncan Smith quit.

Despite radiating competence, Howard's public image did not improve. Focusing on immigration during the 2005 election, he was criticized for dog whistle politics. Gaining only 33 seats nationally, the Conservatives still only held 198 seats to Labour's 356.

Following the May 2005 election defeat, Howard announced he would stand down that October, giving time for leadership candidates to tout their wares. The Cameron era was about to begin.

LORD LUCAN DISAPPEARS

The 7th Earl of Lucan appeared to have it all – matinee idol good looks, a beautiful wife, three children and inherited wealth. In reality, by the time of his disappearance in November 1974, he had become a tortured soul.

John Bingham was born in 1934 into a left-wing aristocratic family. He was evacuated to Canada and the US during the war. When he returned in 1945 he was sent to Eton, where he discovered the delights of gambling and horse racing, two things which were to blight him over the following two decades.

In 1963, he met Veronica Duncan and in November that year they were married. Only two months later, Bingham succeeded to the earldom when his father died. His many money worries also seemed to be over, as he inherited £250,000. Two sons and a daughter followed, and everything seemed right with the world. At least to outsiders, anyhow.

Lucan became a professional gambler, but his losses always outweighed his winnings, and his financial position became increasingly precarious. His home life also deteriorated as his wife suffered long-term mental health problems due to post-natal depression. In early 1973, the couple separated. In a bid to gain custody of the children, Lucan resorted to underhand methods to impugn the character of his wife, but to no effect as the court ruled in her favour.

On the evening of 7 November 1974, Lucan broke into his wife's house. The nanny, Sandra Rivett, was in the basement kitchen. She was bludgeoned to death with a piece of lead piping. Hearing noises from downstairs, the Countess descended the stairs and was also attacked. After a prolonged struggle she managed to escape and raised the alarm in a nearby pub.

Lucan, meanwhile, left the house, visited his sick mother and then drove to Uckfield in East Sussex. His car was found in Newhaven on the south coast two days later.

The murder and disappearance were media sensations. To this day no one has been able to definitively find out where Lord Lucan spent the rest of his days. He was officially declared dead in October 2016.

PRITI PATEL RESIGNS AFTER SECRET MEETINGS WITH ISRAELI OFFICIALS ARE REVEALED

Priti Patel resigned as Secretary of State for International Development, in Theresa May's government, on 8 November 2017. Prior to the resignation, it emerged that she held a number of private meetings with Israeli officials while on holiday in August 2017. All such meetings have to be reported to the government. In an interview, Patel suggested that Boris Johnson, who was the Foreign Secretary at the time, and the Foreign Office were aware of those meetings. This was later denied by Number 10. She was formally reprimanded for failing to report such meetings through official channels and was forced to apologize after they were revealed.

In the following days, it was reported that Patel held two other meetings with Israeli officials in September of the same year, putting further pressure both on her and the government to address it. Patel, who at the time was on a visit to Africa, had to cut short her trip after being ordered to return to the country and summoned to Downing Street. Her flight back was tracked by many on a website used to spot planes online.

After her meeting with the Prime Minister, Theresa May, Patel in her resignation letter admitted that her 'actions also fell below the standards of transparency and openness that I have promoted and advocated'. May, in her response letter, said that 'it is right that you have decided to resign and adhere to the high standards of transparency and openness that you have advocated.' It is believed that May gave Patel the option to resign rather than be sacked to avoid further embarrassment. She was replaced by Penny Mordaunt.

Priti Patel was elected as a Conservative MP in 2010. She served in the Treasury and the Department of Work and Pensions in David Cameron's government, before joining Theresa May's cabinet. Following her resignation, she remained a backbencher until July 2019, when she joined Boris Johnson's cabinet as Home Secretary, the fourth woman to hold that office and the first ethnic minority woman to occupy one of the four Great Offices of State.

RAMSAY MACDONALD DIES

Ramsay MacDonald did have by any standard a distinguished life and career. He had been the first man of undoubtedly working-class background to have achieved the distinction of becoming Prime Minister of the United Kingdom, in 1924. He had also served in that office between 1929 and 1935, securing the biggest landslide win in any general election under universal suffrage, in 1931. He was the first Labour prime minister, and he did much to confirm them as a viable and respectable 'party of government'. Yet instead of being hailed as a hero of his party, he is often castigated as its biggest traitor.

The reason for this is clear. Faced with the challenge of leading the government in the face of the Great Depression and mass unemployment in 1931, MacDonald had formed a multi-party coalition, and then, more culpably still, he had led it later that year into an election, thus splitting the party and condemning it to a wretched defeat in which it won only 52 seats to the coalition's 554. Subsequently, the National Government MacDonald technically led had been vastly dominated numerically by Conservative MPs.

His final years therefore formed a dramatic contrast from his early history. Born of unmarried parents in the north of Scotland in 1866, the self-educated MacDonald had played a key role in organizing, then leading, the early Labour Party. It secured a significant foothold in Parliament through his electoral pact with the Liberals in 1903, before MacDonald bravely entered a period of wilderness through his principled opposition to the Great War.

His first two administrations had performed creditably, given that both were in a minority in the Commons. The 1929–31 Labour government was also unfortunate to have to face the effects of the Wall Street Crash. MacDonald will always be criticized by left-wingers for his response, but at that time even the ideas of Keynes were far from accepted, and King George V himself requested that he lead with broad-based support. Yet his reputation will forever remain clouded, if only by those last few years before his death aboard a liner in the Atlantic, on holiday en route to South America.

MICHAEL FOOT IS ELECTED LABOUR LEADER

Labour's defeat in the 1979 election did not lead to the immediate resignation of the Leader, James Callaghan, but in November 1980, he was replaced by Michael Foot, who had been Deputy Leader of the Labour Party since 1976 and also Leader of the House of Commons.

Foot was born in Plymouth in 1913. He read PPE at Wadham College, Oxford, where he converted from liberalism to socialism. He stood for Parliament unsuccessfully for Monmouth in 1935, aged twenty-two.

Working as a journalist for the *New Statesman* and *Tribune* magazines, he backed a Unity campaign between Labour and other left-wing parties that opposed fascism.

Winning his home seat of Plymouth Devonport in the 1945 Labour landslide, he held the seat until 1955. Twice editing *Tribune* magazine, Foot opposed Britain's engagement in the Suez Crisis and was a founder member of the Campaign for Nuclear Disarmament.

Returning to Parliament in a 1960 Ebbw Vale by-election, caused by the death of Aneurin Bevan, Foot had the whip withdrawn between 1961 and 1963 for rebelling over spending on the Royal Air Force. Turning down a place in Harold Wilson's first government, he became a staunch left-wing critic from the backbenches, where he strongly opposed joining the EEC and reform to trade union law.

Employment Secretary when Harold Wilson returned to Downing Street in 1974, he stood for the leadership against Jim Callaghan in 1976, coming a close second.

Beating Denis Healey in the 1980 Labour leadership election, Foot proved to be a disastrous Leader of the Opposition. He failed to thwart extremists who were determined to take over constituency Labour parties, and although normally a great orator, he rarely landed a blow on Margaret Thatcher. The formation of the SDP–Liberal Alliance didn't help, as it split the opposition vote.

The Falklands War all but guaranteed his defeat at the 1983 election, with only 209 MPs being returned for Labour.

Foot resigned immediately, with Neil Kinnock elected as his successor. Retiring from Parliament in 1992, he remained politically active, writing regularly for *Tribune* and publishing books. He died aged ninety-six in March 2010.

ARMISTICE SIGNED

The war to end all wars. That's how it was described at the time. It took less than three decades to render that quote obsolete. By Armistice Day, the First World War had been fought for four and a quarter years. Nearly ten million military personnel lost their lives, together with another ten million civilians. Another twenty million were wounded. Of those who were killed, 880,000 were British males, 12.8 per cent of those who fought, and 6 per cent of the adult male population.

The turning point in the Allied campaign came in April 1917 when America entered the war. By August 1918, the German military had recognized that things were not going their way. By the end of September, German Supreme Army Command told the Kaiser that the situation was hopeless. General Ludendorff recommended an immediate ceasefire and the acceptance of President Woodrow Wilson's famous 'Fourteen Points'. A few days later, Prince Maximilian of Baden replaced Georg von Hertling as German Chancellor with the specific mandate to negotiate the peace. Fighting continued, however. My great uncle Clifford Nordon was to be killed on 31 October, only ten days before the Armistice was signed.

The delay was caused by the German refusal to countenance the abdication of the Kaiser. Wilson wrote on 23 October: 'If the Government of the United States must deal with the military masters and the monarchical autocrats of Germany now, or if it is likely to have to deal with them later in regard to the international obligations of the German Empire, it must demand not peace negotiations but surrender.'

On 5 November, the Allies agreed to discuss a truce and negotiating teams were despatched to France. The main difficulty was that the Allies weren't united in their aims. France, Britain and Italy rejected several of Wilson's 'Fourteen Points'.

The Armistice was signed at 5.45 a.m. by Marshal Foch for the Allies, and it came into force at 11 a.m. on 11 November 1918. A total of 2,738 men lost their lives on the last day of fighting.

The Treaty of Versailles, which formally ended the war, was signed on 28 June 1919 and took effect on 10 January 1920.

SEX DISCRIMINATION ACT IS PASSED

It is now almost unthinkable that just fifty years ago it was perfectly legal to discriminate against someone because of their sex. Not only was it legal, it was commonplace. However, it was a time when women were finding a collective voice and gradually emerging from centuries of being expected to bow to the wishes of men and live a life dominated by *Kinder, Küche, Kirche* (Children, Kitchen, Church).

In 1931, only 34 per cent of women were in full-time employment, a figure which had barely changed twenty-five years later. However, by 1971, 52 per cent of adult women were working full-time, a figure which is now around 72 per cent.

In 1988, only 10 per cent of women had a degree. That figure has now risen to 42 per cent. Since 1975, the number of households where both parents are in full-time work has increased from 48 per cent to 67 per cent.

In 1970, prior to the passing of the Sex Discrimination Act, women's earnings were 63 per cent of those of men. By 1994, the proportion had risen to 80 per cent. Today it stands at around 93 per cent.

The Sex Discrimination Act protected both men and women from discrimination on the grounds of sex or marital status. The remit of the Act extended to employment, training, education, harassment, the provision of goods and services and the disposal of premises. It was heavily amended over the years and was eventually repealed and replaced by the Equality Act 2010.

The legislation also established the Equal Opportunities Commission, whose remit was to eliminate discrimination, to promote equality between the sexes and monitor the workings of the Equal Pay Act 1970 and the Sex Discrimination Act.

In addition, job advertisements would have to be non-gender-specific and it would no longer be allowed to advertise a position exclusively for males or females.

The academic Ann Morris commented: 'The Sex Discrimination Act 1975 was immensely significant for a whole generation of women who needed no longer to accept that sexism was just the way of the world. They could point to the Act and challenge the discrimination they faced.'

HUGH DALTON RESIGNS

It is rare for a budget to force a Chancellor's resignation. Generally, given their annual occurrence, ministers and civil servants at the Treasury make sure the budget is watertight before its presentation. However, that was not the case for Hugh Dalton, Clement Attlee's first Chancellor of the Exchequer in the post-war Labour government. Leaving office after only two years, what was his resigning offence? Revealing a sentence of the budget to a reporter minutes before the budget speech had been delivered.

It is just one demonstration of the political and media landscape's transformation.

Dalton was born in Neath in Wales in 1887. Educated at Eton and Cambridge, he expressed rare socialist views among the students. Dubbed 'Comrade Hugh', he became President of the Cambridge University Fabian Society, though was unsuccessful three times in a bid to become Secretary of the Cambridge Union.

Serving in France and Italy during the First World War, he became a lecturer at the University of London. Standing four times for Parliament unsuccessfully, he was eventually elected for Peckham at the 1924 election, and then succeeded his wife as MP for Bishop Auckland in 1929.

Dalton became Labour's foreign-policy spokesperson. Sceptical about the left's support for the Spanish Civil War, he reversed his position on appeasement, recognizing the threat from Hitler.

Serving as Minister for Economic Warfare between 1940 and 1942, he became President of the Board of Trade until 1945. Appointed Chancellor of the Exchequer after the war, Dalton managed the nationalization programme in the post-war recovery.

Nonetheless, rationing had to be tightened, with cheap money through interest rates still a problem. Yet the end of his time in the cabinet came not from economic instability but an off-the-cuff remark he made to journalist John Carvel of the *Star* newspaper, telling him about some of the budget tax changes. This was before the speech was delivered and while stock markets remained open.

When the changes appeared in the paper, Dalton faced no alternative but to resign the following day. Replaced by Stafford Cripps, Dalton later returned to the cabinet as Chancellor of the Duchy of Lancaster, but never enjoyed the same influence again.

1935 GENERAL ELECTION

The election of November 1935 saw the second successive land-slide outcome, with a government overall majority of 243. This was somewhat reduced from the massive 494 majority of October 1931, though that did not disturb the strength of the effective control of the Commons. However, there were some significant differences to note.

Technically, it was a 'National' government that won both of these decisive victories: a 'government of national unity'. In 1931, Ramsay MacDonald had effectively ended his second Labour Party administration by inviting the Conservatives and one Liberal faction to coalesce in the face of mass unemployment, and his continued leadership did give the impression of a genuine cross-party coalition. But in June 1935, the Tory Leader, Stanley Baldwin, had taken over as prime minister, and the notion that the government was 'National' had looked increasingly hollow. The election on 14 November further strengthened that impression, or, in fact, that reality.

Although Baldwin essentially campaigned in 1935 for continuity, when the results were announced, his Conservative Party held 387 of the government's 429 seats. The 'National Liberals' under Sir John Simon won thirty-three. National Labour, the remnants of MacDonald's supporters in the great split of the Labour Party in 1931, won only eight. MacDonald lost his own seat at Seaham on the Durham coalfield in probably the bitterest contest of the election against Labour's Manny Shinwell.

Far behind though they were, Labour had more than trebled their own number of MPs to 154, an encouraging sign for their new Leader, Clement Attlee, though few can have foreseen that they (and he) would further multiply their numbers in the next election to be held.

Nor would they have known in 1935 that the next general election would not take place for another ten years. In the second half of the Thirties, the government was in effect dominated by the Conservative Party rather than being a true coalition. The National Liberals gradually became indistinguishable from the Tories, and National Labour did not really outlast MacDonald. But instead of the general election due in 1940, there was a new coalition – brought about by the cataclysmic onset and course of a fresh World War.

ANGLO-IRISH AGREEMENT SIGNED

John Major and Tony Blair are often the prime ministers given credit for bringing peace to the island of Ireland. However, Margaret Thatcher did the groundwork by signing the Anglo-Irish Agreement in November 1985. The treaty confirmed that Northern Ireland would remain part of the union unless a majority of citizens voted to join the Republic.

However, it gave the Irish government an advisory role in shaping Northern Ireland's government. Signing with Irish Taoiseach Garret Fitzgerald, Thatcher had previously failed to persuade Fitzgerald's predecessor, Charles Haughey, to enter serious talks. The IRA hunger strikes in 1981 damaged relations, and Ireland taking the side of Argentina in the 1982 Falklands War didn't exactly help matters.

Thatcher's decision to sign an agreement was undoubtedly shaped by being a target of the Brighton bomb in October 1984, which made her realize never-ending violence was a true possibility.

The Irish-American lobby was huge in the United States and President Reagan encouraged Thatcher to enter talks with the Irish in a spirit of compromise. The Agreement established the Anglo-Irish Intergovernmental Conference, which contained officials from the British and Irish governments. Prioritizing political, legal and security matters in Northern Ireland, it had a consultative role, with no powers to change laws.

This was the precise change designed to encourage unionists to buy into the conference, given they had always opposed any involvement by the Irish government in policymaking. Parliament voted for the Agreement by 472 votes to 47. Only Ulster Unionists vehemently opposed the Agreement, with the DUP and UUP organizing a petition of 400,000 signatures against it. Unionist MPs resigned in protest, holding by-elections.

The Agreement itself failed to end violence in Northern Ireland, with power-sharing only taking effect after the 1998 Good Friday Agreement. Nonetheless, it did dramatically improve British–Irish relations, showing the two countries could work together beneficially. Opposition from some republican quarters argued any agreement permanently partitioned Ireland.

The Anglo–Irish Agreement was a precursor to the peace process and the Good Friday Agreement only thirteen years later.

JOHN BRIGHT IS BORN

John Bright was one of the most influential political figures of the nineteenth century. He was a pioneering Radical and Liberal statesman who strongly supported free trade. He was best known for opposing the Corn Laws, which raised food prices by protecting landowner interests against imported wheat. Sitting in the House of Commons for more than four decades, he championed what were then considered radical causes like electoral reform and religious freedom.

Bright was born in Rochdale to Quakers as the eldest surviving son in a family of eleven children. Educated at boarding schools, he became well known as an effective orator, with the phrases 'flogging a dead horse' and 'mother of all Parliaments' attributed to him.

It was with Richard Cobden that Bright founded the Anti-Corn Law League, a group whose aim was to repeal the protectionist Corn Laws and embrace overseas imports. Seeking to defend free trade, he was elected to represented Durham in an 1843 by-election. Cobden and Bright balanced one another, with the former a serious philosopher and the latter using effective, populist oratory. In his maiden speech, on 7 August 1843, he called for lower import duties, and the movement continued to grow.

It was thanks to a bad harvest in 1845 that the Corn Laws were repealed and free trade triumphed.

Bright later represented Manchester and Birmingham in Parliament, where he opposed reducing the hours in which people could work, as well as clerical control of national education. As a Liberal, he strongly supported enfranchising working-class people and celebrated open protest. He later went on to serve in Gladstone's cabinets as President of the Board of Trade and Chancellor of the Duchy of Lancaster.

Bright had a key interest in Ireland, standing up for the rights of Protestants. Opposing the Home Rule Bill bought forward by Gladstone, this forced the 1886 general election, which led to a landslide for the Conservative Party. Bright was widely believed to have been more responsible for Gladstone's defeat than anyone else.

Illness affected Bright from 1888. He died in March. Prime Minister Lord Salisbury's tribute said he was the 'greatest master of English oratory that this generation has produced'.

BRITAIN ELECTS ITS FIRST COMMUNIST MP

John Turner Walton Newbold, commonly known as Walton Newbold, might sound like the name of someone from the aristocracy, but it actually belonged to Britain's first ever Communist MP. Born in May 1888 in Lancashire, Newbold was educated at Buxton College and the University of Manchester. A Quaker, Newbold came from a wealthy background.

Though initially part of the Fabian Society from 1908, following a period of industrial and economic research, he joined the Independent Labour Party in 1910. A pacifist, Newbold became part of the No Conscription Fellowship, where he was a conscientious objector.

During the First World War, in 1917, Newbold joined the British Socialist Party (BSP), and he regularly wrote for the *Call*, the BSP's paper. Nonetheless, by 1920, Newbold had become a communist, and he joined the Communist Party of Great Britain.

The Communist Party had been founded in 1920 through several smaller Marxist parties merging together. Gaining numerous supporters after the Russian October Revolution, the party was founded around Marxist–Leninist ideology. There existed within the party a debate over whether seeking election to Parliament should be encouraged, as it might prioritize reforming systems over a socialist revolution.

Newbold was successfully elected in 1922 to represent Motherwell. Helped by his wife, Marjory, being well known in socialist groups and adult education campaigns, Newbold also received support from the Labour Party (though he explicitly stood under the Communist label). Though Cecil L'Estrange Malone defected from the Liberals to the Communist Party in 1920, Newbold was the first to be elected.

Though Newbold tried to stand up for the unemployed and promote cheaper housing and rents, he was damaged by a perception of ineffectiveness in Parliament. Newbold lost his seat in the 1923 general election.

Following his short-lived career in Parliament, Newbold rejoined the Labour Party, unsuccessfully standing as its candidate in Epping in 1929. Like many, Newbold drifted to the right with age, supporting Winston Churchill's independent Conservative candidacy in Epping Forest. He passed away in February 1943 aged just fifty-four.

DEVALUATION OF THE POUND

Harold Wilson's first Labour government lasted six years, from 1964 until 1970. One reason for the loss in June 1970 was the state of the economy. Unemployment was rising, inflation was a problem and strikes bedevilled the economy, but it was the devaluation of the pound in November 1967 which stayed long in voters' memories.

Wilson was well aware that devaluing the pound in 1949 had weakened Clement Attlee's Labour government. Having promised that Labour would not devalue, Wilson avoided this prospect in the early years of his government through tariffs and raising $3 billion from foreign central banks. The government were desperate to keep an exchange rate of £1 to $2.80.

In 1966, the pressure on sterling intensified, with Deputy Prime Minister George Brown arguing for devaluation. A trade deficit and low productivity continued making UK goods less competitive. Instead of devaluing, Wilson froze wages and implemented austerity measures.

However, by 1967, a dock strike, the Six-Day Arab–Israeli War, the Suez Canal's closure and the Arab oil embargo made devaluation inevitable. Instead of the government's limiting import spending and boosting exports, the reverse took place. Securing no French or American bailout, Wilson announced on 18 November 1967 that a devaluation of the pound from $2.80 to $2.40 would occur. Cuts to defence and higher interest rates were also announced.

Wilson argued on television that the measure 'does not mean that the pound in your pocket is worth 14 per cent less to us now than it was.' The Prime Minister tried to argue that the internal value of money had not changed, but only when buying goods abroad. The measure was not well received by the electorate. Unemployment had already increased from 1.3 per cent (280,000) to 2.3 per cent (540,000), with a cut in interest rates failing to reflate the economy.

The Chancellor, Jim Callaghan, promised to resign if sterling was devalued, swapping positions with Home Secretary Roy Jenkins. Wilson's further inability to achieve British membership of the EEC further weakened his position. A prospect of another devaluation in March 1968 was avoided thanks to loans.

FIRST DRAW OF NATIONAL LOTTERY

Lotteries of some form have taken place in the UK since 1569, beginning under Queen Elizabeth I. However, the current National Lottery began operations under the Camelot Group in 1994, who still run the competition to this day. Requiring individuals to select numbers that correspondend to those on lottery balls, it has created 6,300 millionaires and given away over £80 billion in prizes.

Of the money spent on National Lottery games, 53 per cent is donated to the prize fund, while 25 per cent goes to good causes set out by Parliament. Indeed, a further 12 per cent reaches the UK government as lottery duty. It may not seem like it, but the Lottery draw – a staple of some people's week – has always been immensely political.

It was Margaret Thatcher's government that investigated whether a private lottery fund could raise money for the NHS. However, her government later cancelled the proposal, realizing such a lottery could be illegal. Instead, John Major, her successor, argued a lottery would not fund government projects but good causes. Indeed, Major said it would be 'the people's lottery'. Camelot beat seven other bidders for running the competition, with their franchise not expiring until 2023.

The first draw took place on 19 November 1994, involving a special TV show hosted by Noel Edmonds and Anthea Turner. Seven million tickets were sold within twelve hours of the launch as seven prize winners shared a total of over £5.8 million. The first show attracted an audience of more than 22 million people.

One area of European relations not affected by Brexit was the Euromillions. Launched in February 2004 by Camelot, it operated across the UK, France and Spain, with other nations including Austria, Ireland and Belgium joining that October. Draws currently take place in Paris every Tuesday and Friday.

Though cynics have argued the Lottery fuelled a culture of greed and materialism, funding has gone to over 560,000 individual projects, with more than £40 billion raised for good causes. Lottery money helped fund the London Olympics and many elite sports, as well as countless cultural and artistic endeavours.

CHRIS SMITH COMES OUT AS BRITAIN'S FIRST OUT GAY MP

Looked at from the perspective of the early 2020s, when the UK Parliament is one of the most diverse in the world, it might seem fairly unremarkable and of little news value that an MP has come out as gay. But back in 1984, it certainly was remarkable and did make the news.

The MP in question was the then Labour MP for Islington South and Finsbury, Chris Smith. There had, of course, been gay MPs before him; but they were all, to a greater or lesser extent, in the closet, and never had a sitting member made a public statement.

That all changed when, at a rally in Rugby in Warwickshire against a town council's potential attempted ban on having gay employees, Mr Smith started his speech with 'Good afternoon. I'm Chris Smith. I'm the Labour MP for Islington South and Finsbury and I'm gay.' He only decided to include the bit about his sexuality just before saying it and reports state he immediately received a standing ovation from those present.

It was only in 1967 that homosexual acts were decriminalized in England and Wales. In addition, Smith's statement happened only two years before 'Section 28' was passed, which stated that councils 'shall not intentionally promote homosexuality or publish material with the intention of promoting homosexuality'.

And it was in her Conservative Party conference speech in 1987 that Prime Minister Margaret Thatcher bemoaned 'hard Left education authorities and extremist teachers', saying that 'children who need to be taught to respect traditional moral values are being taught that they have an inalienable right to be gay.'

Much of the tabloid news media also ran vile campaigns against gay people at the time. Coming out as gay and as a gay MP in the early 1980s was, indeed, remarkable and it was brave.

Chris Smith went on to become Secretary of State for Culture, Media and Sport following the Labour landslide victory of 1997. He made history again when, in 2005, he became the first MP to acknowledge they were HIV positive. Now ennobled as Lord Smith of Finsbury, he continues to champion the rights of LGBT+ people.

BY-ELECTION RECORD BROKEN

Parliamentary by-elections regularly cause upsets, especially if the seat was previously held by the governing party. In 2014, Conservative MP for Rochester and Strood Mark Reckless resigned his seat as he defected to UKIP. Unusually, he decided to submit himself to a by-election. It was a two-horse race between him and Conservative candidate Kelly Tolhurst. He won with a majority of just under three thousand. Labour and the Liberal Democrats failed to make an impression. Indeed, Lib Dem candidate Geoff Juby came fifth, scoring only 349 votes, the lowest ever by a Lib Dem candidate in a by-election. He lost his deposit, winning only 0.87 per cent of the vote.

Lib Dems are an enigma in by-elections. They often score spectacular victories which few had seen coming and on other occasions are nowhere to be seen. In 2021, they took Chesham and Amersham from the Conservatives on a massive 25.2 per cent swing. They followed it up six months after by winning North Shropshire with an even bigger swing of 34 per cent, the seventh-largest swing in by-election history. However, in the next by-election, in Birmingham Erdington in March 2022, the Lib Dems scored a paltry 173 votes. Rumour is, they didn't deliver a single leaflet or knock on a single door.

By-elections offer fringe candidates the chance to share in the political limelight. The most candidates in any by-election ever was twenty-six in Haltemprice and Howden in 2008, when David Davis was the victor.

In the North Shopshire by-election in 2016, caused by the resignation of Conservative MP Owen Paterson, there were fourteen candidates, each paying a deposit of £500. In order to get it back they have to achieve 5 per cent of the vote. In North Shropshire only the three main candidates did so. Independent candidate Yolande Kenward got a grand total of three votes, the lowest ever achieved in a UK by-election since 1918. Of the twelve candidates in the Erdington by-election only those representing Labour and the Conservatives retained their deposits.

The largest ever swing in a by-election came in Bermondsey in 1983, when the Liberal candidate, Simon Hughes, overturned a Labour majority with a swing of 44.2 per cent. Of the ten biggest swings in by-elections, the Liberals or Liberal Democrats achieved half of them.

MARGARET THATCHER RESIGNS

Everyone in the United Kingdom still remembers where they were when they heard the news. Having served as prime minister for eleven and a half years, Margaret Thatcher had resigned. The news broke at 9.30 a.m., minutes before she was due to preside over a cabinet meeting. The previous night, one by one, most of her cabinet had told her she needed to go in order to prevent a humiliating defeat by her charismatic challenger, Michael Heseltine, in the second round of parliamentary voting in the leadership contest. She had learned, while at an international conference with world leaders in Paris the previous evening, that she hadn't gained enough votes to win the leadership contest outright. 'I fight on, I fight to win,' declared the Iron Lady.

Despite late-night and early-morning visits to 10 Downing Street by loyal backbench supporters, urging her to fight on, she decided to quit. An astounded world looked on askance. People scratched their heads in disbelief. Why would her own party ditch a leader who had never lost an election and had restored Britain's reputation around the globe? The truth was, she had come to believe she was invincible. While her economic reforms had borne fruit, her increasingly belligerent and sceptical attitude towards the EEC, and her refusal to U-turn over the hated Community Charge or 'poll tax' led many of her MPs to think she had lost her political touch.

At her cabinet meeting that morning, she broke down in tears as she read out her resignation statement. Several of her ministers followed suit. Later that day, she appeared in the House of Commons to reply to a singularly ill-timed No-Confidence motion tabled by the Labour Leader of the Opposition, Neil Kinnock. It was a tour de force moment as she slayed all her critics and at one stage cried out: 'I'm enjoying this.' Meanwhile, Tory MPs looked on, and if speech bubbles could have appeared over their heads, they would have read: 'What on earth have we done?'

Six days later, having been succeeded by John Major, she left Downing Street for the last time, telling waiting journalists, 'We're very happy that we leave the United Kingdom in a very, very much better state than when we came here eleven and a half years ago.' More than thirty years on, the country is still debating the truth of that statement.

MARY WHITEHOUSE DIES

Make any criticism of our sexualized culture and you'll likely be labelled a 'Mary Whitehouse' figure. The conservative activist, who built her life around opposing social liberalism in the media, died in November 2001 after decades of campaigning against the so-called permissive society.

Whitehouse was born in Nuneaton in 1910 and educated at Chester City and County School for Girls. Joining the Wolverhampton branch of Moral Re-Armament in 1935, she met Ernest Whitehouse, who she married in 1940 and had five children with.

Teaching art and involvement in evangelical Christian groups were two combined interests for Whitehouse, who also formed the Clean-Up TV pressure group in 1964, which gained half a million signatures. That same year, Whitehouse quit teaching to focus on her campaigns.

In 1965, Whitehouse founded the National Viewers' and Listeners' Association (NVLA), which campaigned against the BBC. In particular, she was opposed to rapid social and political changes, demonstrated through excessive swearing and portrayals of sex and violence within the media. Supported by Bill Deedes, who would later edit the *Daily Telegraph*, and Lord Hailsham, the group presented itself as representing the moral majority. She stood accused of homophobia in 1977 when submitting a successful private prosecution case against *Gay News* on the grounds of blasphemous libel, which was the first case of its type for more than fifty years.

Her opposition to media coverage also extended to war programming, where she argued the horror portrayed in wars on TV could deter nations from protecting themselves. At its height, the NVLA had 150,000 members, though this had declined to 30,000 by April 1977. Despite the vocal support of Margaret Thatcher, Whitehouse became a figure of parody, including in shows like *The Mary Whitehouse Experience* and *That Was the Week That Was*. Whitehouse stepped down as President of the NVLA in May 1994.

Critics saw Whitehouse as a figure who defended censorship and bigotry. By contrast, her supporters regarded her as a heroine, trying to stem the tide of moral decline. Her only tangible achievement was to persuade the government to pass the Protection of Children Act 1978.

LORD MELBOURNE DIES

William Lamb, Viscount Melbourne, was probably Queen Victoria's favourite among the ten prime ministers during her long reign. This may well be mainly because he was the first, and thus able to act as a father figure and tutor in politics to the impressionable and needy eighteen-year-old when she first ascended the throne. Victoria desired to escape the baleful influence of her mother, with her oppressive 'Kensington system', and had not yet met the dominant figure in her life, her husband, Albert – dominant both while he was present and in her many years of grief thereafter.

Melbourne's career had been relatively undistinguished before Victoria's accession. A hereditary peer, he was one of no fewer than twenty prime ministers to be educated at a single school, Eton, and the last resident of 10 Downing Street who can unquestionably be labelled as of the Whig Party. Lord John Russell and Viscount Palmerston were Whigs at the start of their careers, but generally regarded as Liberals by the end.

There wasn't much liberal about Melbourne. As Home Secretary he vigorously suppressed the agricultural 'Captain Swing' protests of 1830–31, and played a significant role in the transportation of the Tolpuddle Martyrs to Australia in 1834.

Melbourne was actually prime minister twice, but his first term was brief and rather ignominious. When appointed by William IV to replace Lord Grey in July 1834, he admitted that he did not fancy the extra work it would entail. He needn't have worried, as the King intervened personally to dismiss him in November of the same year. Melbourne was twice involved in sex scandals. Following the notorious affair between his wife and 'Bad Lord Byron' back in 1812, in 1835 Melbourne himself was blackmailed, then sued for adultery, by the husband of society beauty Caroline Norton.

It was the young Victoria who rescued Melbourne's career and reputation. His image is now of the kindly counsellor and friend, retained in office instead of Peel at the Queen's insistence after the so-called Bedchamber Crisis of 1839. However, Victoria married Albert the next year and in 1841 Melbourne really was replaced by Peel. His brief moment had passed.

THE SCARMAN REPORT IS PUBLISHED

The Brixton riots, which broke out in April 1981, were the worst seen in Britain for many years. The policing of the riots provoked outrage in the local community and among opposition politicians.

Only two days after the rioting stopped, on 14 April, Home Secretary William Whitelaw appointed the High Court judge and Law Lord Lord Scarman to conduct an in-depth inquiry into what had happened, why, and to make recommendations. Scarman reported seven months later.

His report did not make easy reading for Margaret Thatcher and her ministers, as Scarman didn't pull any punches. Scarman concluded that the riots were a spontaneous outburst of built-up resentment. He said that 'complex political, social and economic factors' created a 'disposition towards violent protest'.

Scarman examined the issue of inner-city decline, warning that 'urgent action' was required to prevent racial disadvantage becoming an 'endemic, ineradicable disease threatening the very survival of our society'.

He criticized what he called the 'disproportionate' and 'indiscriminate' use of 'stop and search' powers by the police against ethnic minorities. He said that *Operation Swamp 81* was conducted by the police without any consultation with the community or local officers. Police liaison had collapsed prior to the riots and there was an atmosphere of mistrust between the local community and police.

He asked for changes in training and law enforcement, and the recruitment of more ethnic minorities into the police. Unlike the 1999 Macpherson report into the murder of Stephen Lawrence in 1993, Scarman did not accuse the police of being 'institutionally racist', but he did urge the Metropolitan Police force to embrace positive discrimination to tackle racial disadvantage. He said it was a 'price worth paying'.

Indeed, the Macpherson report concluded that many of Scarman's recommendations had been ignored. The 1984 Police and Criminal Evidence Act contained proposals for a new code of police behaviour, and a new independent Police Complaints Authority was created a year later.

Willie Whitelaw described Lord Scarman's recommendations as 'a statement of philosophy and direction for the future'.

344

LILY MAXWELL BECOMES FIRST WOMAN TO VOTE IN BRITAIN

Most of us think the first time women were able to vote was in the December 1918 general election. Not so. Due to a mistake in the compilation of the electoral register in Manchester in 1867, Mrs Lily Maxwell became the first British woman ever to cast a vote. She had to be escorted to the polling station by a bodyguard to protect her from those who were opposed to women's suffrage.

Lily was born in Scotland in 1800 and had spent much of her life as a servant for a Manchester businessman. She eventually owned her own shop. In 1866, she was fined £1 for defrauding her customers with inaccurate weights and measures.

As a shop owner, Lily was obliged to pay rates to her local council, which was also responsible for drawing up the electoral register. Somehow, her name appeared on the list of voters. The local suffragists encouraged her to use her vote, and as a fan of the Liberal MP Jacob Bright, who himself supported women's suffrage, she was resolute in deciding to do so.

When she entered the polling station in Chorlton Town Hall, eyebrows were more than raised. She was accompanied by local suffragist voice Lydia Beckett. At that time, there was no secret ballot and voters had to voice their choice of candidate. She announced in a loud voice her choice of candidate, Jacob Bright, which caused more than a whisper to resonate around the hall. Indeed, the whispers turned into cheers.

Given that she was listed on the electoral register, the voting clerk had little choice but to accept her vote as valid.

A year later, a court closed the loophole.

At the time, the *Englishwoman's Review* paid tribute to Lily, writing: 'It is sometimes said that women, especially those of the working class, have no political opinion at all. Yet this woman, who by chance was furnished with a vote, professed strong opinions and was delighted to have a chance of expressing them.'

Lily Maxwell came to a rather sad end, dying in the Withington Workhouse nine years later. She deserves to be better remembered.

DE GAULLE VETOES BRITAIN JOINING EEC FOR SECOND TIME

Brexit demonstrated the difficulty of removing a nation state from an international body. However, in 1967, Charles de Gaulle, the President of France, highlighted that it was possible to be just as obstructive when a state was trying to join an intergovernmental institution. Vetoing Britain's second application to join the European Economic Community (EEC), the first having been rejected in 1963, he showed that Britain's road to joining Europe's economic institutions was far from smooth.

France was the exception in being so against British membership. The other five members – Belgium, the Netherlands, Luxembourg, Italy and Germany – all stated that they had a far more open mind about the prospect of British entry. Effectively foreshadowing the future, de Gaulle argued Britain had a 'deep-seated hostility' towards European integration and possessed a 'lack of interest' in the Common Market. Though open to commercial exchanges with the UK, he rejected any kind of associate membership.

Entry to the EEC had been attempted under both Conservative and Labour prime ministers. In 1963, the Conservative Harold Macmillan, having already signed Britain up to the European Free Trade Association, applied, believing the EEC was where real economic activity would take place. However, de Gaulle was the barrier to this taking place. EEC entry was therefore a common position shared by the Conservative, Labour and Liberal parties.

De Gaulle openly said his opposition to British membership was purely economic, stating that the UK's economy had a deficiency in its balance of payments, and also went against British practices of obtaining cheap food from around the world. However, de Gaulle's cultural criticisms of Britain at times extended as far as wanting to use the EEC to create a European economic, political and fiscal union separate from the UK.

Nonetheless, the economic picture in Britain was hardly one of strength when trying to apply for membership. In 1967, Harold Wilson was forced to devalue the pound, something which would dramatically affect Britain's ability to export.

Ultimately, Britain would prevail after a third application, under Edward Heath in 1970, the year Charles de Gaulle died.

SINN FÉIN FORMED

Arthur Griffith founded Sinn Féin, translated as 'We Ourselves', in 1905 as a focal point for Irish nationalism. Over its history, frequent splits and disagreements weakened its ability to promote reunification, but it is now in a position in both the Republic and in Northern Ireland where it has reached undreamed-of levels of popular support.

Arthur Griffith, who was the third President of Sinn Féin, had the idea of uniting Irish nationalist parties. As editor of the *United Irishman* newspaper, he used the publication to outline his policies. On 28 November 1905, the first annual convention of the National Council took place.

The party was not initially successful, with funding so poor that it could not pay its headquarters' rent by 1915. Following the 1916 Easter Rising, Count Plunkett, father of the executed leader Joseph Plunkett, was elected to Westminster and represented North Roscommon as an independent. However, Plunkett announced he would not take his seat in the House of Commons, a policy Sinn Féin MPs follow to this day. In December 1918, Sinn Féin won 73 of Ireland's 105 seats in the British House of Commons.

However, the Anglo–Irish Treaty, signed in December 1922, doomed Sinn Féin. Causing divisions among those who supported or opposed the Treaty, it led to new parties. Indeed, the then President, Éamon de Valera, resigned from Sinn Féin over its abstentionism in 1926, forming Fianna Fáil.

Sinn Féin was initially linked to the Irish Republican Army (IRA), but relations soured in the 1930s, and this was followed by many IRA members joining Sinn Féin after the Second World War.

During the Troubles, Sinn Féin gained notoriety for selecting prisoners as parliamentary candidates, with hunger striker Bobby Sands elected MP for Fermanagh and South Tyrone just before his death.

Broadly supportive of the 1998 Good Friday Agreement, Sinn Féin played a pivotal role in creating the Northern Ireland executive. Nonetheless, just as in previous times, some dissident republicans left the party. The party saw increased electoral success in the twenty-first century, overtaking the SDLP as the largest nationalist party in Northern Ireland. In the 2020 Irish general election, Sinn Féin won the largest number of votes, keeping Irish reunification firmly on the agenda.

ENGLAND'S FIRST NEWSPAPER IS PUBLISHED

England was behind the curve when it came to newspapers. In Strasbourg back in 1605, Johann Carolus acquired a printing press and set to work producing the *Relation aller Fürnemmen und gedenckwürdigen Historien*, or 'Account of all Distinguished and Commemorable News' to you and me.

It wasn't until 1641 that the London publisher John Thomas released the first of his small pamphlets entitled *The Heads of Severall Proceedings in This Present Parliament*. It was a folded, printed version of a weekly manuscript which described what had happened in Parliament, so there wasn't much original content.

Brits had previously been getting their news from these manuscripts, from word of mouth and from imports of foreign newspapers. King Charles I had banned the printing of domestic news in order to keep his opponents from getting their word out to his subjects. But the King's relationship with Parliament was breaking down, and as it fell away, so did the prohibition. The advent of John Thomas's publication made English political news far more accessible, and paved the way for the Parliamentary comings and goings to be opened up to the masses. But newspapers, or 'newsbooks' as they were known at the time, were about to achieve a much greater significance, as the need for journalism was about to rocket...

The English Civil War was one of the bloodiest conflicts in British history. King Charles was essentially trying to do away with Parliament, attempting to undo 350 years of Britain's democratic development because he believed he was only answerable to God. This also opened up a deep religious schism in England between the Puritans, who supported Parliament, and the Anglicans who backed the King.

As the war raged, the public on either side were keen to keep abreast of the latest news and, really, to be told what to think. Newspapers chose their faction in the conflict, and tailored their reporting of events to their supportive audiences. With hardly any controls over the press at all, papers like the *London Gazette* boomed and cemented their place in English society, adopting puzzles, advertising, human interest stories and international news.

WINSTON CHURCHILL IS BORN

There was never anything ordinary about Winston Churchill. From the day of his birth at Blenheim Palace, he lived an extraordinary life.

A direct descendent of the Duke of Marlborough, his father was the Conservative MP and future Chancellor of the Exchequer, Lord Randolph Churchill. His mother, Jennie Jerome, was an American socialite. Winston was an unruly child who did not perform well at school. It then took three attempts after Harrow to get into Sandhurst. His father died a month after Winston graduated from Sandhurst in 1895. Some say Winston devoted the rest of his life to trying to please the memory of Lord Randolph.

He joined the 4th Queen's Own Hussars and immediately travelled to Cuba to observe the War of Independence. Observing was never quite enough for Winston and he briefly joined Spanish troops in helping put down the independence fighters. He then went to India for two and a half years, before returning to involve himself in politics. He portrayed himself as a 'Liberal in all but name', but initially allied himself to the Conservatives as he could not bring himself to support Irish Home Rule. He also opposed votes for women.

He then went to the Sudan where he saw action in the Battle of Omdurman in September 1898. In 1899, he left the Army for a career in politics. He lost a by-election in Oldham in June 1899 and then travelled to South Africa to cover the Boer War as a war reporter, where he was captured as a prisoner of war. Being Winston Churchill, he naturally escaped.

In 1900, he fought Oldham again and became a Member of Parliament at the age of twenty-five. His drift towards the Liberals started early in his parliamentary life and he rebelled against the Tory whip on many occasions. In 1904, he defected after an influential wing of the Conservative party adopted protectionism.

He allied himself to the up-and-coming David Lloyd George and after the Liberal victory in 1906 became Under Secretary of State for the Colonies. Two years later, Churchill entered the cabinet as President of the Board of Trade.

DECEMBER

WILLIAM CUFFAY LANDS IN TASMANIA

Like Lily Maxwell, William Cuffay is one of the forgotten names of nineteenth-century British political history. A man of mixed race, he stood only 4 feet 11 inches tall, and was instantly noticeable. He was married three times.

Cuffay was born in 1788. His father was a liberated slave who worked at Chatham docks. In his teenage years, William trained as a tailor, and he moved to London in 1819. In 1834, he took part in the London tailors' strike. As a consequence, he lost his job, and he entered the world of radical politics, becoming involved with the Chartists, a growing movement which supported the so-called People's Charter for democratic reform.

Cuffay was instrumental in forming the Metropolitan Tailors' Chartist Association, and in 1841 he joined the Metropolitan Delegate Council as the Westminster Chartists' representative. He had become one of the most important Chartist organizers in London, and at the 1845 Chartists' National Convention moved 'that the Conference now draw up a plan to enable the people to purchase land and place the surplus labourers who subscribe thereto on such land'.

A year later, he was one of London's three delegates to the Chartist Land Conference. In 1848, Cuffay was also an organizer of the 12 April Chartists National Convention, an open-air event held on London's Kennington Common.

He was appalled by the apparent timidity of the Chartist leaders, and set up a more radical grouping with the Chartists and drew up plans for a display of 'physical force'. However, in August 1848, he was arrested for conspiracy, having been betrayed by a spy, and in October he was convicted at the Old Bailey of 'levying war on the Queen'. He was sentenced to be transported for life to Tasmania.

Designated a political prisoner, he was allowed to work and he went back to his previous trade as a tailor. Eight years later, Cuffay was pardoned, but decided to stay in Tasmania. He became something of a local celebrity as he continued his political activities.

When he died in 1870 at the age of eighty-two, there were numerous obituaries in Australian and British newspapers.

FIRST *KINDERTRANSPORT* ARRIVES IN BRITAIN

Government is often thought of as slow and cumbersome, yet on occasion it can move with incredible speed. So it was with the *Kindertransport*. On 9 November 1938, Jewish homes and businesses were attacked and vandalized by Nazis in Germany. It became known as *Kristallnacht*. Five days later, a delegation of Jewish and Quaker leaders met Prime Minister Neville Chamberlain. They had one demand – to ask him to permit unaccompanied children of Jewish people in Germany to be granted asylum in Britain.

Chamberlain put the proposal to the cabinet the next day and legislation was immediately prepared. In the debate on 21 November, Home Secretary Sir Samuel Hoare said that the Home Office 'shall put no obstacle in the way of children coming here', consequently 'to show that we will be in the forefront among the nations of the world in giving relief to these suffering people'. Hoare told the House of Commons that housing and monetary and other aid required had been promised by the Jewish and other communities.

Four days later, Viscount Samuel made an appeal for foster families to come forward to take a refugee child.

On 2 December, the first *Kindertransport* of 196 children arrived at Parkeston Quay, Harwich. Most were from a Berlin orphanage which had been burned down during *Kristallnacht*. Others came from Hamburg.

More than ten thousand children came to Britain during the ten months that the programme operated, between December 1938 and the outbreak of war in September 1939. They initially came predominantly from Germany, but later also Austria, Czechoslovakia, Poland and Danzig. All the normal visa requirements were waived and the children were placed in foster homes and with British families. Most of them never saw their own families ever again, as their relatives perished in the Nazi death camps. Britain was the only country to organize such a programme, although there were private initiatives in other European countries.

The last *Kindertransport* left Germany on 1 September, the day Germany invaded Poland. Two days later, a group seeking to leave Czechoslovakia was turned back at the border.

EDWINA CURRIE SAYS BRITAIN'S EGG PRODUCTION IS INFECTED WITH SALMONELLA

Since December 1988, the broadcaster, author and former politician Edwina Currie has been unkindly labelled 'Egg-wina'. Why? Because of her dramatic revelation that month that most of Britain's egg production contained salmonella bacteria.

The Conservative MP for South Derbyshire since 1983, the Health minister dropped this bombshell revelation to the anger of farmers, politicians and egg producers. She'd already attracted a reputation for being outspoken and unafraid to speak her mind.

With thirty million eggs consumed every day in 1987, twenty-six outbreaks of salmonella had been reported. However, the controversy grew when Department of Health civil servants seemed unable to provide the evidence for her allegation. It was to be the first nail in her ministerial coffin.

The British Egg Industry Council labelled Currie's remarks 'factually incorrect and highly irresponsible', saying the chances of an egg containing bacteria were less than 200 million to one. Indeed, the Council threatened to sue Currie personally. Initially receiving support from Margaret Thatcher, Currie resigned two weeks later as the controversy continued to rage.

Naturally, Currie's remarks caused egg sales in 1989 to bomb, with the government having to offer a compensation package to pay for companies purchasing surplus eggs and kill millions of hens. Sales of eggs plummeted by 60 per cent, with 400 million unwanted eggs destroyed and four million hens killed.

Currie argued her remarks had been made because salmonella cases had almost tripled in a year. Thanks to vaccinations for hens against salmonella from 1998, British eggs were seen as being as safe as they could be. To this day Currie remains unrepentant.

Currie remained an MP until she lost her seat in Tony Blair's 1997 landslide. She later returned to fame with the publication of her diaries in 2002, which detailed an affair she'd had with John Major. Still residing in Derbyshire, she unsuccessfully sought a return to elected politics on Derbyshire County Council in May 2021.

LORD LIVERPOOL DIES

When Robert Jenkinson, the 2nd Earl of Liverpool, died in 1828, he was only fifty-eight years old. Yet he had been the longest serving prime minister except for Walpole and Pitt the Younger: continuously for nearly fifteen years from 1812 to 1827. No subsequent incumbent of the office has matched this length of tenure, the closest being Lord Salisbury, with over thirteen years in total, and as a single span, Margaret Thatcher's eleven years.

Liverpool's achievement is especially impressive given that his premiership coincided with a dramatic and troubled period in the history of the United Kingdom, and also one when changes of government were more likely to be caused by the interplay of the many factions and the preferences of the monarch than by general election results.

Having succeeded the only prime minister ever to be assassinated, Spencer Perceval, Liverpool had to navigate the stormy waters of the last three years of the war with Napoleonic France, the European settlement afterwards, and a period of social and political unrest within Britain combined with a post-war economic slump. Liverpool managed to complete such a sustained period of office because of his personality.

He was a mediator and conciliator of men and ideas, at least within the accepted political parameters of his day. However, his time in office also coincided with repression of protest, such as by the Six Acts of 1819, though the blame for the worst oppression, such as the Peterloo Massacre, fell more on his Home Secretary, Castlereagh. Liverpool also survived the Cato Street Conspiracy in 1820, a plot to murder the Prime Minister and entire cabinet.

In many ways, Liverpool's term came just before the transformations caused by the onset of democracy. He resisted both Catholic emancipation and parliamentary reform, which were to make advances in 1829 and 1832 respectively. He also cannot be associated with any of the political parties that developed later; he would have considered himself as a Pittite and perhaps as a Tory. His relationship with George IV was very important, both as Regent and King. Liverpool was a manager and survivor, not a modernizer.

CIVIL PARTNERSHIP ACT COMES INTO FORCE

It was a day of mixed emotions for Matthew Roche and Christopher Cramp on 5 December 2005. They were the first couple in England to take advantage of the Civil Partnerships Act 2004, which had come into force at midnight that day. The fifteen-day notice period had been waived as Matthew was suffering from a terminal illness. In fact, he died the next day.

The Act, an initiative of the Blair government, enabled gay and lesbian couples to avail themselves of all the advantages and benefits enjoyed by straight couples. It had met strong resistance from most religious institutions during its passage through Parliament, mostly on the basis that civil partnerships would undermine the institution of marriage. Yes, really. As a compromise the Act forbade civil union ceremonies from taking place in churches or from being conducted by religious celebrants.

The legislation had the support of the opposition Conservatives at the time, with shadow Home Secretary David Davis deputing his gay colleague Alan Duncan to speak for the party. It was a landmark piece of social legislation, which even its opponents would not even think of reversing.

In 2010, Liberal Democrat Home Office minister Lynne Featherstone made it her mission to introduce Equal Marriage and in 2014 the Equal Marriage Act came into force, allowing civil partners to convert their civil partnerships into marriages. In 2018, the Civil Partnership Act was amended to allow straight couples to become civil partners too.

In the first twelve months, more than eighteen thousand civil partnerships were registered. Since then the average number of civil partnerships and/or equal marriages registered have been between seven and nine thousand per annum. Lesbian couples have a greater tendency to divorce than gay male couples.

Denmark was the first country to introduce civil unions, in 1989. It may have taken Britain more than fifteen years to follow suit, but few would deny that this piece of legislation did not deserve the epithet 'landmark'. It has brought undiluted joy to more than 200,000 couples and their families, and there aren't many laws which are able to make that boast.

ANGLO–IRISH TREATY SIGNED CREATING IRISH FREE STATE

The Anglo–Irish Treaty was an agreement which had a profound effect on the course of the United Kingdom. It was ratified by both the UK Parliament, and the Dáil, the Parliament of Southern Ireland.

Like the Good Friday Agreement signed over seventy years later, the Anglo–Irish Treaty was intended to bring a long-running conflict to a close. Concluding the Irish War of Independence, it sought the creation of an Irish Free State, which would have the same status as Canada in being a self-governing Dominion. Northern Ireland was given the chance to opt out of the Free State.

Michael Collins and Arthur Griffith were the main Irish representatives in the negotiations. Griffith had been a major player in the nationalist movement, while Collins had fought in the Easter Rising. Agreements within the Treaty included removing British forces from most of Ireland, while the new Free State's Parliament would require citizens to take an Oath of Allegiance to the Irish Free State. The agreement was officially signed at 2 a.m. on 6 December 1921 in the Cabinet Room of 10 Downing Street.

Conservative MPs, like Colonel John Gretton, were less than pleased with the concessions given to Ireland due to the impact on Protestants and removing the monarch's authority overseas. The decision was to be key in the collapse of the Liberal–Conservative coalition in late 1922.

The Irish Free State officially came into existence exactly a year later on 6 December 1922, when its constitution became law. The Treaty did not receive overwhelming praise within Ireland, partially because of Ireland's status as a Dominion rather than an independent republic. Indeed, the dispute was such that it sparked the outbreak of the Irish Civil War, leading to the assassination of Michael Collins by anti-Treaty republicans in August 1922.

The Civil War lasted only for ten months but remained imprinted in the memories of voters. In 1949, the twenty-six counties of the Irish Free State officially became the Republic of Ireland. Nationalist divisions have subsequently turned to the status of Northern Ireland, the focus of the Troubles between 1968 and 1998.

LLOYD GEORGE BECOMES PM

David Lloyd George, as Chancellor of the Exchequer, had worked closely with Herbert Henry Asquith in the latter's radical 'New Liberal' government from 1908 to 1916. Together they had faced down the House of Lords and the Conservative Party in the great crisis following Lloyd George's People's Budget of 1909. In December 1916, however, the Liberal Party suffered what may have turned out to be a fatal split as these two titans clashed, and the Welsh wizard ousted his long-time colleague.

The causes of the split were twofold: the state of the First World War and the ambition of the younger Liberal. By 1916, the conflict had been going for two years and it was clear that there was to be no quick or easy finish. The slaughter at the Somme confirmed that it had degenerated into a trench-bound war of utter attrition. Asquith no longer seemed like the man to win the war. He appeared old and lethargic, and his known fondness for drink did not help.

Already, in May 1915, Asquith had invited the Conservatives into a coalition cabinet. At this point Lloyd George had switched from Chancellor to be Minister of Munitions, spotting that it would now be a key position. In December 1916, Lloyd George made his bid for the top job.

His strategy was to argue for a restructuring of government. On 1 December, he proposed that the war should henceforth be run by a small committee of three with himself in the chair. Asquith, rightly seeing that he would be sidelined, initially refused. However, the Tory Leader, Bonar Law, then supported Lloyd George's plan. Asquith resigned on 5 December. The King sent for Law, who refused to lead a government and advised that Lloyd George should be invited to do so.

Lloyd George's small war cabinet included the Labour Leader, Arthur Henderson, as well as three Conservatives, with LG as the lone Liberal. However, his party was effectively split, still led by Asquith, who refused to join the government in any capacity. Lloyd George had achieved his ambition of becoming prime minister – but he was to be the last Liberal to do so.

RACE RELATIONS ACT PASSES

Until the Second World War, the United Kingdom was, with some notable exceptions, a very white country. Then, from the late 1940s, people from the far-flung former empire started to migrate in search of economic opportunities and in response to invitations to help with the post-war labour shortage – those on the *Empire Windrush* ship being the most famous, but not the first, example.

Before the 1962 Commonwealth Immigration Act, entry had been freely available. By 1965, at least half a million had immigrated from the 'New Commonwealth': Caribbean-heritage communities had formed in south and west London, and the South Asian subcontinent was well represented in Northern industrial towns and in the West Midlands. Britain was becoming multicultural, but problems were also becoming apparent.

The new arrivals and their families were often greeted with resentment, hostility and racial discrimination, for example in housing. On the other hand, some of the host population felt that resources, services and jobs were being squeezed by those who looked and sounded different. In the 1960s, successive Conservative and Labour governments tried to alleviate the concerns of both communities.

The 1965 Act, introduced by Labour Home Secretary Roy Jenkins, outlawed discrimination on the 'grounds of colour, race, or ethnic or national origins' in public places in Great Britain, and in 1966 led to the creation of the Race Relations Board. Thus, for the first time, there was to be official protection of the rights of ethnic minorities, but the Act also pointed up the continued need for such protection. Within three years Enoch Powell had delivered his famous 'Rivers of Blood' speech at Birmingham, and the influence of his views among many voters became clear in the 1970 election results. Legislation to limit immigration was passed in the Commonwealth Immigrants Act (1968) and the 1971 Immigration Act.

The Race Relations Act of 1965 did not effectively ban racism. Only 10 per cent of all complaints to the Race Relations Board were upheld, and complaints could not be made about the police. Yet it was a milestone in the transformation of Britain, recognizing the need to grapple with the challenges of multiple ethnicities and identities.

DAVID CAMERON VETOES NEW EU TREATY

Battles between British prime ministers and the European Union (EU) were nothing new, so when David Cameron vetoed a new EU Intergovernmental Treaty only eighteen months after coming to power, few should have been surprised. But because he was in coalition with the pro-Europe Liberal Democrats, they were. Cameron told his twenty-three fellow heads of government it was 'not the right thing for Britain'. Hungary, the Czech Republic and Sweden were undecided on whether to join, with Britain's decision meaning it would not be part of any new fiscal rules.

Key proposals within the Treaty mandated states to have balanced budgets, with no structural deficit higher than 0.5 per cent of GDP, meaning automatic sanctions would apply for a country whose deficit exceeded 3 per cent.

Further aspects of the Treaty Cameron criticized included a financial transaction tax, with fears that a eurozone-only tax could still encompass the City of London. Alongside this, the government saw new European-wide regulators as potentially superseding national regulators, resulting in further European protectionism potentially reducing trade with the US or Asian countries.

Nonetheless, Cameron's veto was regarded as unexpected, not least because of the summit's importance in the wake of the financial crash. It meant that, for the first time since Britain joined the European Economic Community in 1973, it would not have a central role at key future fiscal summits.

Labour were scathing about David Cameron's decision, with Ed Miliband arguing that the Prime Minister had severely mishandled negotiations and left Britain with a 'bad deal'. Internationally, the picture was more concerning, with European leaders regarding Britain as an obstacle to improving economic governance. Critics further argued that Cameron was trying to appease his Eurosceptic backbenchers rather than prioritize Britain's domestic interests.

The veto can be seen as a continuation of British prime ministers portraying their relationship with the EU as a duel. Indeed, the French President, Nicolas Sarkozy, argued 'two Europes' were in play, with different attitudes towards integration. Just over a year after his veto, Cameron promised an in-out referendum on European membership if he won the 2015 election.

EDWARD VIII ABDICATES AND IS SUCCEEDED BY GEORGE VI

In December 1936, a constitutional crisis emerged which laid bare the realities of life as a monarch. At its heart was the question of whether love or duty came first. King Edward VIII faced this dilemma as he sought to marry Wallis Simpson, an American socialite already once divorced and seeking to divorce a second time.

The couple met in January 1931 while Edward was the Prince of Wales, and they became lovers in 1934. Followed secretly by members of the Metropolitan Police, investigation of Simpson's private life raised many questions about her suitability. When Edward became king in January 1936, Simpson regularly attended functions as the King's guest.

A potential marriage was fiercely contested in the UK and across the empire. The monarch remains the head of the Church of England, which then did not allow divorced people to remarry if their ex-partners were still alive. Prime Minister Stanley Baldwin considered numerous potential outcomes, including the King's abdication. Backbencher Winston Churchill was the only notable politician who supported the King's decision.

Indeed, there was little sympathy towards Wallis Simpson. Any marriage would lead to her becoming queen, an outcome which was regarded with disdain because of her divorced status. The motivation of Simpson was sharply called into question, with accusations that she sought the marriage not out of love for King Edward VIII but for money-grabbing reasons.

Though duty over personal desire carried far more weight in the 1930s, King Edward VIII was a convention breaker. Edward declared that his love for Simpson would not change and their marriage would happen once her second divorce was finalized. The unwillingness to accept Simpson as the monarch's consort made his abdication inevitable.

On 10 December 1936, at Fort Belvedere in Surrey, King Edward signed his abdication notice. His tenure as monarch lasted 327 days, the shortest since Lady Jane Grey 380 years previously. The couple married in France in June 1937, but Simpson was denied the title Her Royal Highness.

It was left to Edward's brother Albert, who took the title of George VI, to steady the monarchy.

RHODESIA REVERTS TO BRITISH RULE

December 1979 proved to be an important month for Rhodesia, a country which would change its name four months later to Zimbabwe.

In 1978, an 'internal settlement' was signed by the Rhodesian Prime Minister, Ian Smith, and the leader of the United African National Council, Bishop Abel Muzorewa. This was followed in January 1979 by a referendum, in which only white Rhodesians were eligible to vote, to approve a new constitution. Then in April, Muzorewa won elections to the transitional legislature, although these were boycotted by Joshua Nkomo's ZAPU and Robert Mugabe's ZANU PF. Muzorewa became prime minister but because his government of national unity did not have a majority, international sanctions remained in force.

In September, talks began at Lancaster House in London, chaired by British Foreign Secretary Lord Carrington, about the future constitutional settlement for Rhodesia/Zimbabwe. All sides were represented, including Ian Smith, Prime Minister Abel Muzorewa, Robert Mugabe and Joshua Nkomo, along with the UK government. Signed on 21 December, the Lancaster House Agreement effectively ended the civil war, with a ceasefire being signed. All sides agreed to the temporary resumption of British rule, which happened on 11 December when the Rhodesian Parliament voted to approve the Constitution of Zimbabwe–Rhodesia Bill. It revoked the 1965 illegal unilateral declaration of independence. The following day, the country reverted to being the British Dependency of Southern Rhodesia as Lord Soames flew to Salisbury (to be renamed Harare) to become the temporary Governor until elections were held in April 1980.

Robert Mugabe's ZANU won the elections and he took over as prime minister of the new Zimbabwe to coincide with formal granting of independence on 18 April.

Margaret Thatcher herself played little part in the Agreement and left it entirely to Lord Carrington. A skilled diplomat, he brought all the parties together and achieved what may people had believed was impossible.

Initially, Zimbabwe remained a member of the Commonwealth but it was suspended in 2002 for breaching the 1991 Harare Declaration. A year later, when the Commonwealth refused to lift sanctions, Mugabe took Zimbabwe out completely.

BORIS JOHNSON WINS GENERAL ELECTION

There can rarely have been such a contrast between the political balance before and after a general election, even with the same party and Prime Minister, Boris Johnson, in office. The reasons for this are due to the unique circumstances of 2019.

Not for nothing has this been called the 'Brexit election'. British politics since the 2016 referendum had been dominated, and arguably paralysed, by the difficulties caused by its Leave result. Theresa May had not managed to get Parliament to agree to her 'deal' arrangements for actually leaving the EU. Nor had Boris Johnson. The obstruction was caused by a combination of those in all parties who regretted the result of the referendum and were trying to frustrate it, and Europhobes who wanted a 'harder' exit. By autumn 2019, the government had almost completely lost control of the Commons, with no overall majority, open rebellion by Remain Conservative MPs, and even the passing of an act unwanted by the government to stop Brexit without a deal.

Finally, despite the Fixed-term Parliaments Act, the situation was to be resolved by a general election. The rebel Tories were barred from standing, Labour's Jeremy Corbyn appeared too left-wing and unable to give a lead on the key issue, and the official Conservative line was clear – 'Get Brexit Done!'

Johnson was returned with an overall majority of eighty. The most striking thing about the results of the 12 December 2019 election was that class voting, the single most dominant feature of twentieth-century voting behaviour, was statistically insignificant. The Conservatives secured 42 per cent of the middle-class vote – and 42 per cent among the working class. This is what led to their remarkable gains in what had been Labour heartlands, such as Bolsover (the seat of Dennis Skinner) and Sedgefield (which had been Tony Blair's). Instead, the key demographic cleavages now were age and education – these both in fact being surrogates for the Brexit issue.

It remains to be seen whether this dramatic realignment will have permanence (as it has in the USA), but it gave Boris Johnson secure control from 12 December – but three months later, coronavirus invaded Britain...

THREE-DAY WEEK ANNOUNCED FROM 1 JANUARY

In December 1973, Prime Minister Edward Heath announced that 1974 would begin not as a Happy New Year, but one in which power cuts would become the norm, as a three-day week would be introduced.

The aim was to conserve electricity, which had been limited in supply due to widespread strikes by coal miners and others. Business users were therefore limited to three consecutive days of consumption per week, and overtime was banned. Television companies had to end their broadcasts at 10.30 p.m. each day. Subsequently released cabinet papers reveal that the government contemplated permanently taxing electric toothbrushes and hedge trimmers.

The industrial action was linked to desperately high inflation in the UK economy throughout the 1970s. To resolve this, the government sought to cap public sector pay rises, which proved anathema to the trade unions, with workers' pay not keeping up with inflation. The National Union of Mineworkers (NUM) demanded a 35 per cent pay rise.

Though the NUM initially rejected strike action by two to one, a ban on overtime was imposed, which deeply damaged the level of coal supplies. The dependence on coal became even stronger with the onset of the 1973 oil crisis, which was caused by an embargo against countries that supported Israel in the Yom Kippur War. With 81 per cent of NUM members eventually voting to strike on 24 January 1974, it forced Edward Heath to call an election in February 1974 using the slogan 'Who Governs Britain?'.

Despite restrictions being lifted on 7 March, the damage had been done. Heath aimed to present the unions as holding Britain hostage and believed the public would reward him with a mandate for reform. Indeed, most of the media staunchly opposed the strike action (with the exception of the *Daily Mirror*). The election itself resulted in a hung Parliament with the Conservatives enjoying a greater share of the vote while Labour won more seats.

The new Labour government immediately caved to the NUM's demands but it was only delaying the inevitable. Within two years, the economic situation had become so bad that the government had to seek a bailout from the IMF.

1918 GENERAL ELECTION

It is sometimes assumed that there is an absolutely fixed timespan within which general elections must take place, but that is not correct. The life of Parliament may be extended in circumstances considered appropriate, such as world war. There was an eight-year gap between the elections in 1910 and 1918 – and a ten-year gap between those in 1935 and 1945. However, it is expected that an election will be called at the earliest convenient date after the wars come to an end. There was, however, a very significant difference between the elections of 1918 and 1945.

In 1945, Churchill discontinued the Second World War multi-party coalition, and, as is well known, went down to an unexpected defeat by the Labour Party. In December 1918, on the other hand, Prime Minister David Lloyd George decided to try to keep his coalition going into peacetime. The Labour Party would have none of that, but his own Liberal Party was divided, and ended up being hopelessly split – and this permanently damaged its chances of being returned as a party of government in its own right. There had already been a bitter quarrel in December 1916, when Lloyd George ousted his own party leader, Herbert Asquith, as prime minister, but it was the 1918 election that cemented the schism.

In all, 145 candidates 'accepted the coupon', as Lloyd George's letter of support came to be known, and stood as 'National Liberal'. But 277, under Asquith's leadership, did not. The result appeared decisive. Only thirty-six of these were returned. Asquith lost his own seat at East Fife. Meanwhile, the vast majority, 127, of Lloyd George's Liberals won. However, these were massively outnumbered by the 379 Coalition Conservatives, who could have formed an overall majority in their own right.

Therefore, while Lloyd George continued as prime minister, 'the man who won the war', he was utterly dependent on his former Tory adversaries.

This election also saw women voting for the first time, and being able to stand. Countess Markiewicz became the first woman to be elected, but she never took her seat. That honour was left to Nancy Astor the following year when she was elected in a by-election.

BRITAIN ASKS THE IMF FOR A BAILOUT

During the 1979 election campaign, the Conservatives pro-duced a brilliant election poster of an unemployment queue, with 'LABOUR ISN'T WORKING' as the slogan. This theme arguably developed from the moment in December 1976 when the Labour Chancellor, Denis Healey, asked the International Monetary Fund (IMF) for a financial bailout for the UK.

The pound was in crisis, as was the economy in general. The weak state of the public finances and the increases in energy costs following the oil crisis were making an already tense economic situation even worse. Essentially, the UK was experiencing a combination of stag-flation – a recession, increasing unemployment and high inflation.

Healey was asking for a $3.9 billion loan ($17.7 billion at 2020 prices), the largest ever requested from the IMF.

Denis Healey had to resort to setting out his approach towards the IMF from the Labour conference floor, rather than the platform, as he had been voted off Labour's National Executive Committee. Boos from some on the floor did not deter him from making his case that the only alternative was a Conservative government. Jim Callaghan argued that being able to 'spend your way out of a recession' was no longer an option. Inevitably, the conditions set by the IMF were anathema to Labour adherents of a Keynesian economic policy.

Part of the Labour Party, led by Energy Secretary Tony Benn, thought Jim Callaghan's government was being insufficiently radical. Benn's proposals included import restrictions and radically increased industrial investment. However, he enjoyed little support in cabinet. Most ministers backed Denis Healey's policies of reduc-ing government spending and increasing taxation and interest rates, as mandated by the IMF.

The sterling crisis led to the Bank of England temporarily with-drawing from the foreign exchange market, not least because of the pound's record low against the dollar.

The IMF loan was repaid by May 1979, the day Margaret Thatcher became prime minister. It may have performed an eco-nomic task, but politically it was a humiliation for Labour. It, together with the Winter of Discontent and consistent picture of Britain as the 'sick man of Europe', played a large part in Labour's removal from power and Margaret Thatcher's ascent.

MIKHAIL GORBACHEV VISITS CHEQUERS

Any kind of diplomacy requires the courting of potentially unsavoury figures. It was in this vein that Margaret Thatcher welcomed Mikhail Gorbachev to Chequers, the prime minister's country home, in December 1984. While Gorbachev was only Minister for Agriculture, he was increasingly being tipped as the next General Secretary of the Soviet Communist Party.

Initially arriving in London, Gorbachev had a robust meeting with Thatcher, where she accused him of funding the miners' strike, something that was a pressing issue of domestic concern.

Thatcher, as a strong ally and friend of President Ronald Reagan, was fully supportive of US strategy towards the Soviet Union, which was summed up in the NATO slogan 'Peace Through Strength'. NATO was in the course of deploying cruise missiles in Europe in response to the Soviet stationing of SS-20 nuclear weapons in East Germany and elsewhere in Eastern Europe.

Believing Chequers as a country home to be the best place for a second conversation to occur, Thatcher welcomed Gorbachev and his wife, Raisa, for lunch. Topics of discussion included Soviet economic and industrial policy, as well as foreign and defence matters.

A strong ideological debate was far from off the table. Thatcher was unafraid to celebrate Western free enterprise against the Soviet Union's priority of redistributing wealth. In her memoirs, *The Downing Street Years*, Thatcher was laudatory towards Gorbachev, arguing he had a sharp debating style and 'went beyond Marxist rhetoric' in his arguments. At times it became a shouting match, with each giving as good as they got.

Part of Thatcher's strategy aimed to reassure Gorbachev, discussing arms control and arguing Reagan did not want to pursue war. With their conversation overrunning by over an hour, Thatcher expressed her view to the British press that Gorbachev was a man whom she 'could do business' with. She immediately phoned Reagan and urged him to meet him.

The Chequers meeting played a key role in bringing the Cold War to an end.

Gorbachev would become General Secretary of the Communist Party in March 1985, overseeing the decline and fall of the Soviet Union.

HARRODS BOMB KILLS SIX

'The Troubles' is a euphemistic term most associated with the conflict between unionists and nationalists in Northern Ireland. In reality, the whole United Kingdom was dramatically affected. Such pain was especially felt in December 1983, when six people were killed by an IRA bomb outside Harrods in Knightsbridge. Occurring in the run-up to Christmas, ninety-one others were injured. The IRA's Army Council said they had not authorized the volunteers who planted the bomb, yet, despite a forty-minute warning being given, that was not enough to avert tragedy.

Leon Brittan, the Home Secretary, condemned the attack, arguing that any terrorist organization would have members 'not under disciplined control'. He saw little sympathy in the IRA's attempt to distinguish 'legitimate' and 'illegitimate' brutal murder. The bomb, which contained between 25 and 30 lb of explosives, and was operated by a timing device, was left in a 1972 blue Austin.

The warning of the bomb came with details of bombs inside and outside Harrods and in Oxford Street. As a police car, dog handler and foot patrol officer approached the Austin, the device exploded. It was only thanks to the heroism of the police officers inside the police car taking the full force of the explosion that more casualties were avoided.

It was clear why terrorists would target Harrods. It is a large, upmarket department store in affluent Knightsbridge, not far from Buckingham Palace. Previous bombings had occurred in the 1970s within the store, where evacuations were possible. This time, twenty-four cars were damaged, while all five floors on the side of Harrods were affected, sending glass showering on to the street.

Financially, Harrods lost roughly £1 million in turnover from the bombing, though it reopened defiantly three days later.

The legacy of the Harrods bomb persists to this day, not least in relation to the conflation of IRA terrorists with British police officers as part of the Northern Ireland legacy proposal. Susanna Dodd, whose father, police officer Stephen Dodd, was killed in the Harrods attack, has regarded the compensation awarded to victims as totally inadequate.

CAPITAL PUNISHMENT FOR MURDER IS ABOLISHED

There is little doubt that the 1964–70 Labour government did more than any other to reform all sorts of social and moral laws, including the legalization of homosexuality and abortion, divorce reform and the abolition of capital punishment. The then Home Secretary, Roy Jenkins, was accused of creating the 'permissive society', when in reality he saw a need to adjust our laws to meet the prevailing social attitudes of the day. He should go down in history as a great social reformer.

In November 1965, Labour MP Sidney Silverman introduced a private member's bill, supported by the government, to abolish capital punishment for murder. It sought to replace the sentence of death with one of mandatory life imprisonment. It replaced the Homicide Act 1957, which had reduced hangings to only a few per year.

The Act contained a sunset clause, which meant that it would expire on 31 July 1970 unless Parliament voted for it to continue. Parliament did just that and the Act was made permanent on 18 December 1969.

The last hangings for murder took place on 13 August 1964, when Peter Allen and Gwynne Evans were hanged for murdering John West during a theft. The last hanging for treason took place in 1946.

The 1965 Act did not, however, abolish all forms of capital punishment. If you committed high treason, piracy with violence, arson in royal dockyards and espionage, you could still be hanged. In addition, the 1965 Act did not extend to Northern Ireland. It wasn't until 1973 that capital punishment for murder was abolished there. It wasn't until the 1998 Human Rights Act that all forms of capital punishment were abolished.

There were various debates in Parliament on restoring capital publishment in the 1970s and 1990s, but as public support for restoration has dwindled, these debates became rarer and rarer.

In 2004, the UK accepted the 13th protocol to the European Convention on Human Rights (ECHR), which prohibits the restoration of the death penalty for as long as the UK is party to the Convention. Britain's departure from the European Union has no impact on its adherence to the ECHR.

WILLIAM PITT THE YOUNGER BECOMES PM

The circumstances under which the younger Pitt first became prime minister – at the age of twenty-four, the precocious son of a previous PM – reveal much about the nature of British politics in the late eighteenth century, and how different government was from today.

We are accustomed now to changes of office being caused by the democratic vote of the mass electorate, with the occupancy of 10 Downing Street being taken by the leader of the party with the most MPs. The monarch plays a purely ceremonial role in politics. However, when Pitt took office in 1783, none of this applied.

The government had previously consisted of a highly unlikely coalition between two politicians who had traditionally been bitterly divided. Lord North, a Tory, had been prime minister from 1770 to 1782 and was most known for provoking the American Declaration of Independence and subsequent war. His partner was Charles James Fox, a supporter of the Americans and a radical Whig. Yet neither of these was actually prime minister. That position belonged to the rather colourless Duke of Portland.

King George III detested the Fox–North coalition, because Fox was not only a radical but a close friend of the Prince of Wales, and was determined to intervene to destroy it. His opportunity came when the government proposed an East India Bill in November 1783. The King secretly made it clear that any peer who voted in favour would be his enemy. The Lords duly voted the Bill down on 17 December. Thereupon George dismissed Portland, Fox and North and offered Pitt the seals of office.

The young PM had no majority, and his government was initially called the Mince-Pie Administration, as it was not expected to last beyond Christmas. Yet Pitt showed courage and determination, and survived until the inevitable general election, in March 1784. Then over a hundred of Fox's supporters lost their seats, and followers of Pitt (and the King) increased, gaining such key constituencies as Middlesex and Yorkshire. Pitt went on to remain prime minister for all but three of the next twenty-two years, dying in 1806 at the still young age of forty-six.

1910 GENERAL ELECTION RESULTS

Years in which two general elections take place are very rare in the United Kingdom. There have only been two since the 1832 Reform Act, in 1910 and 1974. Such short Parliaments are caused by the lack of a working overall majority, or a political crisis. 1910 had both.

The context of the 1910 elections lay in the unprecedented radical programme of the Liberal government. Lloyd George's so-called 'People's Budget' of 1909 included new and increased taxation of the landed classes. When it was rejected by the Conservative-dominated and entirely hereditary House of Lords, a constitutional crisis ensued. Asquith went to the country to seek a mandate for the budget in January 1910.

The Liberal majority of the 1906 landslide was lost and the Conservatives drew neck-and-neck. The outcome was sufficient for his immediate purpose, because Asquith could rely on the support of both Labour and the Irish Nationalists. However, if the obstruction of the upper House was to be addressed more generally, a lasting structural solution was needed.

Therefore, Asquith called a second election, which ran from 6 to 19 December – the last when voting was not confined to a single day. The results themselves were not spectacular. There was almost no change from January, with the Liberals down two seats to 272 and the Conservatives down one to 271. But there were two very significant consequences.

One was the passage of the 1911 Parliament Act, which for the first time formally limited the Lords, who henceforth could not veto money bills like the budget, and could only delay other legislation by two years (reduced to one year in 1949). This confirmed the supremacy of the elected House, the Commons.

The second consequence was that the Irish Nationalists, seventy-four MPs, again held the balance in a hung Parliament, which pushed Asquith into the Home Rule Bill, passed in the Commons in 1912, with the use of the new Parliament Act overcoming the Lords' opposition in 1914 – only for it to be stymied by the outbreak of World War I. The second 1910 election permanently reduced the power of the unelected Lords, but did not solve the thorny issues of Ireland.

LOCKERBIE

Mention Lockerbie and there is one tragic event that everyone associates with the Scottish town. On 21 December 1988, Pan Am Flight 103 exploded over Lockerbie when a bomb detonated shortly after 7 p.m. The attack killed all 259 people on board and 11 people on the ground. The plane, which was en route to Detroit from Frankfurt, with stopovers in London and New York, was flying at an altitude of 31,000 feet when the time-activated bomb, hidden in a cassette player within a suitcase, exploded.

The plane's wreckage covered 850 square miles and destroyed 21 houses. Though the passengers on board were from 21 countries, 189 were American. Those investigating the blast believed two Libyan intelligence agents carried out the bombing as revenge for a 1986 US bombing campaign against Libya.

Warnings had been given – a man telephoned the US Embassy in Finland on 5 December to say a Pan Am flight would be blown up within the next fortnight. Similarly, the West was on a high alert with threats from the Palestine Liberation Organization.

Colonel Gaddafi, the Libyan dictator, initially refused to hand over the suspects, leading to US and UN sanctions. Eventually, extradition was agreed in 1998.

The largest criminal inquiry was led by the smallest police force in Britain, Dumfries and Galloway Constabulary, collaborating with the FBI. Their investigation involved more than 15,000 interviews and 180,000 pieces of evidence. Abdelbaset Ali Mohmed al-Megrahi was convicted and sentenced to 20 (later 27) years in prison for 270 counts of murder, while Lamin Khalifa Fhimah was acquitted.

Gaddafi finally accepted responsibility for the bombing, paying compensation to families of victims. However, the Libyan leader denied ordering the attack.

In 2009, Megrahi was released from prison in Scotland following a terminal cancer diagnosis, dying in May 2012. The American government was furious, especially when it came to light that BP had lobbied for a prison exchange between the UK and Libya.

The Lockerbie bombing remains the deadliest terrorist attack in the UK's history. On 21 December 2020, exactly thirty-two years after the attack, a Libyan national in custody was charged with crimes related to the Lockerbie bomb's construction.

IRA BOMBS HOME OF EDWARD HEATH

Nineteen-seventy-four did not prove to be a good year for Edward Heath. It started with the three-day week and the miners' strike, which led to him losing office following a general election on 28 February. He lost a second election in October, and the knives were out for him and his leadership. He reluctantly agreed to stand for re-election. Also in October, he was dining at Brooks's Club when an IRA bomb detonated. He was uninjured. In mid December, Heath had also been shopping at Harrods when the IRA bombed the department store, killing six and injuring ninety.

Then, on 22 December, his London home in Wilton Street, Victoria, was also the target of an IRA bomb attack. A man got out of a Ford Cortina and hurled a two-pound bomb on to the first-floor balcony of the house. It detonated and the first-floor window was blown in, and the front door and sitting room were damaged. The only valuable item that was damaged was a painting by Sir Winston Churchill.

The *New York Times* reported: 'The police, fearful that the explosion was a "come-on" tactic – first a small bomb, then a larger one when the first had attracted crowds – sealed off all streets around the house for several hours.'

Although the Cortina was pursued through the streets of Victoria and Chelsea, several men managed to escape after the car crashed.

The former prime minister had been conducting a carol service in his home town of Broadstairs, but arrived home ten minutes after the bomb went off. His housekeeper and her daughter had been in the house at the time of the explosion but were uninjured. Heath was due to visit Northern Ireland the next day and fulfilled the engagement. 'This could happen anywhere, any time,' he said.

Prime Minister Harold Wilson sent Heath a message which he said was 'very much appreciated'. It read: 'Dear Ted, This attack will only strengthen our united resolve to bring these thugs to justice.'

The attack came only hours before a Christmas truce was due to come into force.

PETER MANDELSON RESIGNS

Christmas 1998 is not a period fondly remembered by anyone close to the New Labour project. Why? Not because they received a lump of coal but because Peter Mandelson, MP for Hartlepool, Trade and Industry Secretary, and at the heart of New Labour, resigned from the cabinet.

Mandelson had taken a £373,000 loan from Geoffrey Robinson, the Labour MP for Coventry North West, to fund the purchase of a flat. Robinson was also in government as Paymaster General. There was a clear lack of transparency over the loan, which had not been properly declared. Mandelson had only been Business Secretary since July 1998, but Prime Minister Tony Blair had little choice but to demand his resignation.

Initially, Downing Street had come out in support of Mandelson. It was clear why. The Director of Communications under Neil Kinnock and election manager in 1987, Mandelson had been vital in helping Labour to rebuild and change its image over the previous decade.

However, his position proved unsustainable. The newspapers, far more influential than today, were relentless in portraying New Labour as no less corrupt and full of sleaze than John Major's administration.

Eventually, both Robinson and Mandelson resigned. At the same time as loaning Mandelson money for his apartment, Geoffrey Robinson had himself been under scrutiny by the Trade and Industry department for some of his other business dealings. The conflict of interest was just too much. Indeed, it is unclear, when applying for his £150,000 mortgage, whether Mandelson had declared his loan. Mandelson lacked any personal support within the party to fall back on and was gone in an instant.

Mandelson would later re-enter the cabinet as Northern Ireland Secretary before his resignation in January 2001. This time, it concerned his involvement with the passport application of Indian tycoon Scrichand Hinduja. Though a subsequent investigation exonerated him, rejoining Blair's cabinet for a third time was a stretch.

Resigning as MP for Hartlepool to become a European Commissioner, he was later appointed to the House of Lords under Gordon Brown to become Business Secretary and First Secretary of State.

THE UK AND EU REACH A POST-BREXIT TRADE DEAL

Since becoming prime minister, Boris Johnson had been able to defy the odds. His critics said he couldn't get a new Brexit Withdrawal Agreement. He did. His opponents argued he couldn't get an election and wouldn't win. Thanks to the Liberal Democrats, an election took place which he won with an eighty-seat majority. It completely changed the atmosphere with the European Union (EU) and in Westminster. Having taken Britain officially out of the EU on 31 January 2020, the nation now entered an eleven-month transition period where a future trade relationship would need to be struck.

Even though this was an immense task, it didn't prevent the Prime Minister from abolishing the Department for Exiting the European Union. Lord David Frost became the Chief Negotiator for the UK, facing Michael Barnier for the EU. Ten negotiating rounds took place between March and December 2021.

At many points, it appeared no agreement would be found due to disagreements over core issues like fisheries and Northern Ireland. Lord Frost in particular wanted a looser relationship between the UK and EU. The Office for Budget Responsibility had argued a no-deal withdrawal could reduce Britain's economic output by more than £40 billion, costing 300,000 jobs.

At least five calls between Boris Johnson and the President of the European Commission, Ursula von der Leyen, in the final twenty-four hours eventually ensured the two-thousand-page trade Agreement could be signed off. This included the continuation of the controversial Northern Ireland Protocol, which, though preventing checks between the Republic of Ireland and Northern Ireland, created checks down the Irish Sea. It was to prove a hostage to fortune.

The eventual Trade and Cooperation Agreement between the EU and UK included widespread alignment in digital trade, intellectual property and road transport.

The trade deal also dealt with the thorny issue of fishing rights. Ending freedom of movement, a key aim of Brexiteers, it also required exporters to face a far greater number of border checks. The Agreement provisionally became law on 1 January 2021, before it was endorsed by the European Parliament on 27 April 2021.

KING GEORGE V'S FIRST CHRISTMAS BROADCAST

The Queen's Christmas Message has been a foundational part of Christmas Day for as long as most people can remember. With music, and a short speech from the monarch reflecting on the year, it provides one of the few occasions where the monarch makes an active intervention on the public stage.

The tradition began on 25 December 1932, when King George V broadcast live from Sandringham. The speech itself was written by Rudyard Kipling, as the monarch celebrated the power of the wireless to unite the empire's citizens.

Famously, the speech began: 'Through one of the marvels of modern Science, I am enabled, this Christmas Day, to speak to all my peoples throughout the Empire.'

The time of broadcast was 3 p.m., allowing many countries of the empire across time zones to tune in. Indeed, the idea of radio broadcasting came from the BBC's Director-General, John Reith, who had recognized the important value of radio for transmitting information.

The speech marked the inauguration of the BBC Empire Service, which launched in December 1932 and later became the BBC World Service. The microphones at Sandringham used Post Office land lines to communicate with the control room at Broadcasting House, which reached BBC transmitters across the world.

A monarch's speech continued under King George VI. Despite his stammer – famously portrayed by Colin Firth in the Oscar-winning film *The King's Speech* – George VI's speeches during the Second World War became vital for rallying the troops and maintaining morale.

The Queen's first Christmas message was broadcast in December 1952 following her father's death. Using the same desk and chair as her father and grandfather, she wanted to maintain this tradition. The first televised message eventually arrived in 1957, following the boom in television purchases for the Queen's coronation in 1953.

After 1960, broadcasts were recorded rather than taking place live, which enabled the tapes to be sent around the world to Commonwealth countries.

Until 1996, the speech was produced by the BBC. However, the Queen announced in 1997 that the speech would be produced alternately by the BBC and ITN, with Sky later added.

WINSTON CHURCHILL ADDRESSES CONGRESS

Ever since the day Winston Churchill had become prime minister in May 1940, he had strained every sinew to persuade President Franklin Delano Roosevelt to enter the war. The American public was still in isolationist mood so Roosevelt was only able to give tacit support by supplying military hardware. That all changed on 7 December 1941 when Japan attacked Pearl Harbor. Germany then declared war on the US and Roosevelt's decision was made for him.

Churchill lost no time in hotfooting it across the Atlantic to discuss Allied military strategy for the next stages of the war. On Boxing Day, he was given the honour of addressing a joint session of Congress. Unusually, it took place in the Senate as many Congressmen were at home for Christmas and the House of Representatives would have looked empty.

Churchill started his address by observing: 'If my father had been an American, and my mother British, instead of the other way around, I might have gotten here on my own. In that case, this would not have been the first time you would have heard my voice.' He went on to predict that Allied forces would need at least eighteen months to turn the tide of war and warned that 'many disappointments and unpleasant surprises await us.'

On Japan, he asked, 'What kind of a people do they think we are? Is it possible that they do not realize that we shall never cease to persevere against them until they have been taught a lesson which they and the world will never forget?'

On Germany, he said: 'With proper weapons and proper organization, we can beat the life out of the savage Nazi.' He described the Nazi leadership as 'wicked men' who must 'know they will be called to terrible account if they cannot beat down by force of arms the peoples they have assailed.'

As he finished his half-hour-long oration, he gave a 'V' for victory sign and left to loud applause and a standing ovation. The US Senate website quotes one journalist describing the address as 'full of bubbling humor, biting denunciation of totalitarian enemies, stern courage – and hard facts'.

PRESIDENT WOODROW WILSON BECOMES THE FIRST US PRESIDENT TO VISIT BRITAIN

Woodrow Wilson was the twenty-eighth President of the United States, yet incredibly none of his twenty-seven predecessors had visited Britain while in office. It was the first of twenty-eight visits serving US presidents have made to Britain, at the time of writing. Ten of these were made by President Bill Clinton.

Relations between the United States and Great Britain had never been easy ever since the US War of Independence and the War of 1812, when British troops burned down the White House and razed Washington, D.C. to the ground. Even at the turn of the twentieth century there were strained relations over ownership of Latin American territories. It wasn't until America entered the First World War that the two countries became closer.

The red carpet was rolled out for President and Mrs Wilson as they arrived at Charing Cross Station. They were met by King George V and Queen Mary, along with crowds in The Strand who were standing ten deep on both sides of the road. The dignitaries proceeded via Trafalgar Square to Piccadilly and then down Constitution Hill to Buckingham Palace. As dusk fell, they all made an appearance on the balcony to cheering crowds. Queen Mary passed a Union Flag for the President to wave to the cheering throng.

At a state banquet later that night, the King began his toast by acknowledging the groundbreaking nature of their visit: 'Nearly 150 years have passed since your Republic began its independent life, and now for the first time a President of the United States is our guest in England.'

During his visit he travelled north to Manchester, where he made a speech in the Free Trade Hall, and then visited his mother's home town of Carlisle. He called it a 'Pilgrimage of the Heart'.

In his speech he said that America had never had a vested interest in European politics, and still didn't. 'Interest does not bind men together,' he said. 'Interest separates men... There is only one thing that can bind people together, and that is a common devotion to right.'

PEAK DISTRICT BECOMES FIRST NATIONAL PARK

We all know the words of the hymn 'Jerusalem' and rejoice in singing '... in England's green and pleasant land'. One of the reasons why we still enjoy so much green and pleasant land is the establishment of Britain's national parks. In some ways, we were a bit late to the party given that Yellowstone National Park in the USA was established way back in 1872.

The 1945–51 Labour government led by Clement Attlee is best known for establishing the NHS, giving India its independence and nationalization. But another of its lasting legacies was the National Parks and Access to the Countryside Act 1949. Back in 1884, James Bryce had introduced a 'freedom to roam' bill but it wasn't for nearly another fifty years that the creation of a National Park Authority was recommended by a government committee chaired by the Minister for Agriculture, Christopher Addison. The committee was also tasked with choosing sites for national parks. The 1931 general election then intervened and the whole subject was put on the backburner. It wasn't until 1945 that a white paper on national parks was published.

In 1947, former Liberal MP Sir Arthur Hobhouse was appointed to chair a National Parks Committee and to draft legislation which eventually turned into the 1949 Act. The legislation went through both Houses of Parliament with all-party support.

There are now ten national parks in England, three in Wales and two in Scotland. Unlike in some other countries, the land in areas covered by national parks is not owned by the state. The land is owned primarily by private citizens, but also by public bodies. The Peak District became the first designated national park, followed by the Lake District, Snowdonia and Dartmoor within a year. By the end of the 1950s, the total had risen to ten with the Pembrokeshire Coast, the North Yorkshire Moors, Yorkshire Dales, Exmoor, Northumberland and Brecon Beacons all joining the party.

In 1988, the Norfolk Broads became a quasi national park. In 2002, Loch Lomond and the Trossachs followed, with the Cairngorms being designated a year later. The New Forest followed in 2005 and the South Downs in 2010.

GLADSTONE IS BORN

A politician whose career spanned the nineteenth century, from his initial election as Tory MP for Newark in 1832 at the age of twenty-two, to his final retirement as Liberal prime minister sixty-two years later, W. E. Gladstone is often nominated as one of Britain's greatest ever politicians. He was prime minister four times, compared with his great rival Disraeli's twice. Yet in all the twists and turns of his long political life, it can be hard to discern exactly why he so frequently receives such accolades.

He was the most prominent Victorian-age politician of all, yet was detested by Queen Victoria herself, who found him intolerably pompous. Gladstone was a man of principles, although their application could mutate. He was a Tory who then became a Pittite after the split in the 1840s over free trade and the Corn Laws, then a Liberal. However, he split the Liberal Party due to his conversion to the cause of Irish Home Rule in the 1880s. As a result, the Liberals were in government for only three of the twenty years between 1886 and 1906. Nor did he achieve Home Rule.

Gladstone's liberalism was very much 'classical' rather than 'modern'. He believed that being free meant freedom from external constraints, whether these were caused by economic protectionism or high taxation. Since his time, the Liberal Party itself has been transformed in attitudes and policies, regarding classical liberalism as 'negative', with 'positive' liberalism holding that people cannot be truly free unless they are released from poverty, ignorance and ill health.

Therefore, modern Liberals usually believe that government has a much larger role to play in enabling individuals to fulfil their potential – which in turn will require higher taxation. Scarcely more than ten years after Gladstone's death in 1898, under a Liberal government, Lloyd George introduced his radical People's Budget. Therefore, it could be argued that Gladstone's influence was very much confined to the nineteenth century.

So much did twentieth-century Liberalism move away from Gladstone's philosophy that it has been argued that his true heir was Margaret Thatcher – in which case, however, his impact would indeed look far less confined to his own epoch.

COVID VACCINE APPROVED BY UK REGULATOR

It had been a miserable Christmas for many, as last-minute lockdown regulations meant that families and friends were prevented from mixing on Christmas Day. The country had been in and out of Covid lockdowns since late March, and people were becoming increasingly weary and frustrated with government announcements which appeared to make little sense to them. However, there appeared to be light at the end of the tunnel when, in early December, it was announced that Oxford University and Astra Zeneca had developed a vaccine which was said to be highly effective in preventing transmission of Covid-19 and mitigating its worst effects. Health Secretary Matt Hancock became quite emotional when he announced that it would soon be made available to the entire adult population. First, however, it had to be approved by the UK medical regulator.

On 30 December, it received approval and became the first Covid vaccine in the entire world to be licensed for public use. The government prioritized the elderly and the clinically vulnerable. The NHS organized a superbly efficient vaccination programme, staffed by doctors, nurses and volunteers. But it wasn't all plain sailing. Other EU countries, led by France, rubbished the effectiveness of the vaccine, causing mistrust in their own populations, and preferred to wait for the Pfizer vaccine, which was a few weeks behind the Oxford/AZ vaccine in its rollout. That delay undoubtedly caused thousands of extra deaths across the EU.

The vaccine had been developed after funding by UK taxpayers, and Astra Zeneca announced it would be made available throughout the world without them making any profit. However, because of the misinformation propagated by those who should have known better, the uptake wasn't as high as it should have been, with various EU countries having stockpiles of the vaccine lying unused. At the same time they threatened to take the UK to court over alleged non-supply of the vaccine.

In the end, the UK was around three months ahead of most other countries in its vaccine rollout, although by the end of 2021, they had caught up. It was the one thing the UK government got right during the pandemic.

NATIONAL SERVICE ENDS

Despite the Second World War ending in 1945, National Service remained until the end of 1960. The National Service Act 1948 extended conscription to all healthy young men not registered as conscientious objectors. Though the war had been won, the British government realized the armed forces needed to be larger than a voluntary service would allow.

The process of demobilization of those who served in the forces during the Second World War had already begun in 1944 through the Reinstatement in Civil Employment Act, which allowed individuals to reclaim their old jobs. Given Britain's strong ongoing commitments in Germany, Palestine and India especially, large manpower was necessary. Indeed, given the commencement of the Cold War, geopolitical tensions were far from eased.

Previously, the age range for National Service during the war was eighteen to forty-one, which was altered to seventeen to twenty-one. Requiring men (not women) to serve for eighteen months, they remained on the reserve list for four years. The duration was increased to two years following the Korean War in 1950. Men working in the merchant navy, farming and coal mining were exempt for eight years.

Conscripts received six weeks of basic training, before being issued equipment, uniform and boots (regardless of whether they fitted). Paid roughly twenty-eight shillings (£1.40) and residing in wooden barrack huts, their living conditions were far from luxurious. Yet the process created a bond among the men that most never forgot.

There were also exemptions on the grounds of ethnicity, with black and British Asian men not conscripted. Similarly, to avoid civil unrest in Northern Ireland, men there were also exempt. Ironically, the large number of men conscripted into the forces eventually became a burden to the Army, as regular soldiers spent large amounts of time training new recruits.

From 1957, National Service was gradually ended. Those born on or after 1 October 1939 were not required to take part, and call-up formally ended on 31 December 1960. The last servicemen left National Service in May 1963. In total, more than two million men were conscripted into the British Army, Royal Navy or Royal Air Force.

Acknowledgements

I would like to acknowledge the following sources, which have been used by me and my team in the research for this book.

Al Jazeera, AlistairLexden.org, AP, *The Argus*, Bank of England, BBC website, Beautiful Britain, *Belfast Telegraph*, *Birmingham Mail*, Bodleian Library, British Library, Brookings Institute, Channel 4, CNN, Conservative Party, ConservativeHome, Constitution Unit, The Conversation, *Daily Mirror*, *Daily Telegraph*, EdinburghLive, EDP24.co.uk, *Encyclopaedia Britannica*, *Express & Star*, *Financial Times*, France24, Gov.uk, *The Guardian*, Guido Fawkes, *The Herald*, History Extra, History Hit, History of Parliament Trust, *History Today*, House of Commons Library, House of Lords Library, Huffington Post, *The Independent*, iNews, Insider, Institute for Government, *Irish Examiner*, *Irish Times*, Labour Party, LabourList, Liberal History Group, *London Evening Standard*, Mailonline, MargaretThatcher.org, *Morning Star*, *The National*, National Archives, *New European*, *New Statesman*, *New York Times*, *The News Letter*, OnThisDay.com, Open Democracy, Parliamentary Archives, Politics.co.uk, Politicshome, *Reading Chronicle*, Reuters, RTE, *The Scotsman*, *Shropshire Star*, Sky News, Spartacus Educational, *The Spectator*, *The Sun*, Tides of History, *Time*, *The Times*, *Tribune*, TUC, Unherd, US Senate, Walesonline, *Washington Post*, *The Week*, Wikipedia and last but not least, the *Yellow Advertiser*.

Index

Abbott, Diane 80, 156
Abse, Leo 218
Adams, Gerry 219,
 250, 294
Adams, John 195
Addington, Henry 77
Addison, Christopher
 379
Addison, Paul 226
Aethelstan, King 21
Ahern, Bertie 105, 242
Aislabie, John 72
Aislabie, William 72
Aitken, Jonathan 179
Al Assad, Basher 253
Al-Megrahi Abdelbaset
 372
Ali, Ali Harbi 302
Allen, Peter 369
Amery, Leo 137
Amess, Sir David 175,
 302
Amin, Idi 230
Ancram, Michael 268
Anne, Queen 224
Applegarth, Adam 55
Armstrong, Sir Robert
 278
Ashdown, Paddy 60,
 66
Asquith, H H 13, 34,
 43, 102, 227, 233,
 241, 306, 358, 365,
 371
Assange, Julian 178
Astor, Nancy 365
Attlee, Clement 5, 6,
 13, 25, 36, 53, 57, 59,
 96, 99, 181, 206, 217,
 238, 252, 290, 295,
 308, 312, 332, 333,
 337, 379

Aung San 5
Aveling, Edward 14

Bader, Douglas 201
Bailey, David 67
Bailey, Michael 106
Baker, Steve 279
Baldwin, Stanley 6, 23,
 45, 96, 130, 145, 155,
 156, 244, 248, 275,
 306, 316, 333, 360
Balfour, Arthur 13, 28,
 115, 141, 203
Barrington, Jonah 4
Barrow, Tim 92
Barry, Charles 158, 303
Beackon, Derek 272
Beckett, Dame Margaret
 267
Beeching, Dr Richard
 90
Bell, Richard 48
Bellotti, David 221
Bellingham, John 291
Ben-Gurion, David 141
Benes, Edvard 285
Benn, Stephen 121
Benn, Tony 121, 144,
 164, 210, 234, 278,
 317, 366
Bercow, John 20, 146
Berkeley Humphrey
 218
Berlin, Isiah 304
Berry, Sir Anthony 175,
 299
Bevan, Aneurin 47, 78,
 196, 211, 290
Beveridge, William 196
Bevin, Ernest 59, 99,
 135, 290, 312
Biden, Joe 251

Bin Laden, Osama 266
Birkenhead, Lord 8
Black, Mhairi 117
Blackford, Ian 280
Blair, Tony 6, 12, 20,
 31, 38, 51, 60, 66, 76,
 80, 83, 105, 128, 134,
 139, 156, 186, 192,
 198, 242, 253, 261,
 265, 266, 273, 294,
 313, 325, 354, 374
Blunt, Anthony 24
Boaeteng, Paul 156
Bonaparte, Napoleon
 235, 247, 291
Bonar Law, Andrew
 155, 306, 358
Bond, Edward 281
Bondfield, Margaret
 166
Bonzo, Hector 129
Boothby, Lord 67
Boothroyd, Betty 122
Brabourne, Lady 250
Brewer, Eleanor 24
Bright, John 335
Brittan, Leon 7, 204,
 368
Brocklebank-Fowler,
 Christopher 89
Brook, Sir Norman 252
Brown, George 47, 78,
 110, 176, 337
Brown, Gordon 55, 60,
 114, 123, 133, 138,
 146, 184, 186, 262,
 273, 314, 374
Brown, Louise 216
Bruce, Fiona 280
Bryce, James 379
Buckley, Sheila 229
Budgen, Nicholas 133

Bukharin, Nikolai 140
Bulganin, Nikolai 78
Bunting, Ronald 88
Burgess, Guy 24, 312
Burnham, Andy 267
Burns, John 227
Burns, Lord 51
Bush, George H W 225
Bush, George W 83, 266
Bute, Earl of 71
Butler, Sir David 304
Butler, R A 11, 144, 226, 307
Byrn, Lord 343

Cairncross, John 24
Callaghan, James 6, 18, 47, 52, 91, 93, 130, 131, 212, 262, 293, 298, 329, 337, 366
Cambon, Paul 103
Cameron, David 17, 31, 38, 66, 110, 138, 153, 182, 183, 189, 198, 205, 248, 253, 268, 273, 300, 327, 360
Campbell, Alastair 128
Campbell-Bannerman, Henry 13, 34, 102
Campbell, Menzies 280
Canning, George 65, 84, 231, 269, 291
Carolus, Johann 348
Carrington, Lord 97, 99, 100, 362
Castle, Barbara 208, 293
Carswell, Douglas 146, 300
Carvel, John 332
Casement, Sir Roger 119
Castle, Barbara 18
Castlereagh, Viscount 65, 84, 231, 235, 291, 355
Catesby, Robert 324
Caunt, Benjamin 158
Cavendish, Lord 118
Chadwick, James 59

Chamberlain, Austen 53, 155, 306
Chamberlain, Joseph 28, 155, 203
Chamberlain, Neville 53, 73, 137, 155, 258, 285, 307, 353
Charles I, King 46, 49, 51, 55, 82, 153, 174, 245, 313, 348
Charles II, King 46
Charles, Prince 250, 261
Charmley, John 312
Chatfield, Lord 96
Chesterfield, Earl of 257
Chichester-Clark, James 117
Churchill, Lord Randolph 25, 349
Churchill, Winston 6, 11, 25, 34, 37, 45, 54, 57, 59, 68, 96, 100, 135, 137, 142, 155, 158, 165, 185, 201, 211, 217, 237, 238, 243, 244, 248, 263, 275, 295, 311, 312, 336, 349, 361, 365, 373, 377
Clark, Alan 179, 249
Clarke, Kenneth 11, 80, 268, 280
Cleese, John 144
Clegg, Nick 60, 74, 110, 123, 138, 153, 248, 273, 313
Clemenceau, Georges 187
Clinton, Bill 378
Cobbett, William 239
Cobden, Richard 335
Cockerell, Michael 249
Cole, John 299
Collins, Michael 8, 357
Colquhoun, Maureen 282
Colston, Edward 321
Cook, Robin 80, 242
Cooke, Judith 212
Cooper, Yvette 267

Corby, Jeremy 16, 80, 89, 161, 267, 289, 363
Cornell, George 67
Cosgrave, Liam 212
Cousins, Frank 42
Cox, Brendan 175
Cox, Jo 175, 302
Cramp, Christopher 356
Creasy, Stella 309
Cripps, Sir Stafford 312, 332
Crookshank, Harry 54
Cromwell, Oliver 82, 154, 245, 292
Cromwell, Richard 154
Cromwell, Thomas 322
Crosland, Anthony 52
Cross, Richard 114
Cross, John 303
Cubbon, Brian 212
Cudlipp, Hugh 144
Cuffay, William 352
Cullen, Lord 76, 276
Cummings, Dominic 182
Currie, Edwina 171, 353
Curzon, Lord 115, 306
Cutler, Carmen 259

Dalton, Hugh 52, 332
Darling, Alistair 278
Davies, Gavyn 305
Davis, David 199, 268, 340, 356
Davison, Emily Wilding 163
Day, Sir Robin 249, 280, 311
De Gaulle, Charles 2, 15, 37, 50, 200, 296, 315, 346
De Montfort, Simon 21
De Valera, Eamon 8, 347
Deedes, Bill 342
Dempster, Nigel 282
Derby, (16th) Earl of 28, 62, 114, 202
Derby, (17th) Earl of 43

Devlin, Bernadette 31, 117
Dewar, Donald 134
Diana, Princess Diana 261
DiCaprio, Leonardo 109
Dilke, Charles 6
Dimbleby, David 152, 182, 280, 304
Dimbleby, Jonathan 152
Dimbleby, Richard 26, 152, 304
Disraeli, Benjamin 27, 62, 77, 114, 117, 118, 138, 202, 226, 380
Dobson, Frank 176
Dodd, Stephen 368
Dodd, Susanna 368
Donoughue, Lord 51
Douglas-Home, Alec 44, 47, 100, 177, 183, 211, 307, 317
Dowding, Sir Hugh 201
Downing, Sir George 277
Driberg, Tom 67
Duffy, Gillian 123
Duncan, Alan 356
Duncan Smith, Iain 268, 325
Dundas, Henry 3, 220
Dyke, Greg 305

Eddington, Paul 323
Eden, Anthony 11, 25, 53, 100, 142, 144, 296, 317
Edmonds, Noel 338
Edward I, King 21
Edward III, King 82
Edward VII, King 13
Edward VIII, King 361
Edwards, Robert 216
Eisenhower, Dwight D 144, 165, 296, 318
Elizabeth I, Queen 322, 324, 338
Elizabeth II, Queen 25, 131, 150, 152, 208, 213, 214, 263, 279, 296, 317, 376
Elliot, Sir Charles 27

Engels, Friedrich 132
Evans, Gwynne 369
Everett, Kenny 228
Ewart-Biggs, Christopher 212
Ewing, Margaret 274

Farage, Nigel 153, 182, 300
Falmouth, Viscount 84
Farthing, Pen 251
Faulkner, Brian 31, 232
Fawcett, Millicent 193
Fawkes, Guy 324
Fayed, Dodi 261
Fearnley-Whittingstall, Hugh 183
Featherstone, Lynne 38, 356
Ferguson, Richard 169
Fhimah, Lamin Khalifa 372
Fitzgerald, Dr Garret 212, 334
Fletcher, Yvonne 112
Foch, Marshall 330
Foot, Michael 58, 91, 168, 280, 329
Foote, Geoffrey ix
Forster, E M 265
Foster, Arlene 150
Foster, Michael 51
Fowler, Norman 101
Fox, Charles James 65, 370
Frampton, James 81
Fraser, Sir Hugh 44
Friedman, Milton 297
Frost, Lord 375
Frost, Sir David 254, 281
Furlong, Patrick 303

Gaddafi, Muammar 112, 372
Gaitskell, Hugh 47, 52, 78, 318
Galtieri, Leopoldo 173
Gandhi, Mahatma 238
Garland, Judy 67
Gaunt, John of 172
George I, King 72

George II, King 277, 310
George III, King 29, 77, 174, 195, 224, 263, 291, 370
George IV, King 355
George V, King 23, 163, 241, 248, 328, 358, 376, 378
George VI, King 155, 312, 361, 376
Gilmour, Sir Ian 297
Giuliani, Rudi 136
Gladstone, Herbert 13, 48, 255
Gladstone, William 6, 28, 102, 114, 118, 180, 202, 206, 209, 233, 255, 335, 380
Goderich, Viscount 269
Goering, Hermann 201
Goldsmith, James 182
Golitsyn, Anatoliy 24
Gorbachev, Mikhail 259, 292, 367
Gordon, General 118
Gordon, Lucky 260
Gott, Richard 208
Gould, Bryan 108
Gove, Michael 110, 189, 215
Gow, Ian 175, 210, 221
Grafton, Duke of 29
Grande, Ariana 162
Grant, Bernie 156
Grantham, Joseph 284
Greenspan, Alan 275
Greer, Bonnie 213
Grenville, George 71
Grenville, Lord 3, 65, 291
Gretton, Colonel John 357
Grey, Earl 85, 291, 343
Grey, Sir Edward 13, 227
Grey, Lady Jane 361
Griffin, Nick 213, 272
Griffith, Arthur 8, 347, 357
Grimond, Jo 18
Gummer, John 143

Hague, William 268, 301, 325
Hain, Peter 261
Hale, Lady 279
Halifax, Lord 25, 137
Hall, Benjamin 158
Hallett, Lady Justice 198
Hamilton, Thomas 76
Hancock, Matthew 86, 381
Hannan, Daniel 300
Hands, Greg 184
Harcourt, Sir William 180, 256
Hardie, Keir 14, 48, 289
Hardinge, Sir Henry 84
Harry, Prince 261
Hartington, Marquess of 28, 118
Hatton, Derek 171
Haughey, Charles 334
Hawkesbury, Lord 65
Hawthorne, Nigel 323
Hawtrey, William 292
Hay Hill, Alsager 34
Healey, Denis 52, 329, 366
Heath, Edward 2, 18, 35, 41, 44, 50, 61, 69, 100, 130, 148, 164 176, 200, 211, 230, 232, 249, 283, 297, 298, 307, 315, 346, 364, 373
Henderson, Arthur 358
Henry III, King 21, 322
Henry VI, King 149, 183
Henry VII King 82
Henry VIII, King 224
Heseltine, Michael 7, 38, 320, 341
Hiddleston, Tom 183
Hill. Christopher 245
Hitler, Adolf 68, 135, 136, 155, 186, 201, 258, 285, 332
Hoare, Sir Samuel 53, 353
Hobhouse, Sir Arthur 379

Hogg, Quintin (Lord Hailsham) 200, 342
Hoon, Geoff 266
Hooson, Emlyn 19
Hore-Belisha, Leslie 75
Howard, Michael 215, 249, 325
Howe, Sir Geoffrey 44, 320
Hoyle, Lindsay 146
Hughes, Cledwyn 308
Hughes, Simon 340333
Huhne, Chris 74
Hume, John 105
Hunt, Sir Rex 97
Hurd, Douglas 40, 183, 246
Hussein, Saddam 83, 225, 246

Ingham, Bernard 323
Ingrams, Richard 281
Ismay, General 'Pug' 99, 243
Ivanov, Yevgeny 260

James I, King 124
James II, King 46, 111, 174
Jefferson, Thomas 195
Jellicoe, Earl 148
Jenkins, Roy 6, 26, 50, 52, 66, 89, 164, 204, 218, 249, 263, 281, 310, 315, 337, 359, 369
Jerome, Jenny 349
Jiang, Zemin 192
Jinnah, Muhammed Ali 197
John, Elton 261
John, King 21, 174
Johnson Boris ix, 16, 20, 79, 86, 136, 176, 183, 184, 189, 199, 215, 249, 263, 279, 327, 363, 375
Johnson, Robert Underwood 115
Jones, Nigel 175
Joseph, Sir Keith 44
Joyce, William 4

Juby, Geoff 340

Keays, Flora 301
Keays, Sara 301
Keeler, Christine 148, 260
Keith, Penelope 323
Kelly, John 225
Kendall, Liz 267
Kennedy, Charles 66
Kennedy, John F 110, 122, 296
Kent, Bruce 58
Kenward, Yolande 340
Keyes, Sir Roger 137
Keynes, John Maynard 116, 183, 186, 275, 297
Khan, Sadiq 136
Khomeini, Ayatollah 70
Khruschev, Nikita 78, 140, 292
King, Anthony 304
King, Tom 40
Kinnock, Neil 7, 80, 94, 104, 108, 139, 156, 170, 171, 329, 341
Kipling, Rudyard 376
Kitchener, Lord 43
Knight, Dame Jill 151
Kray, Ronnie & Reggie 67

Lambton, Lord 148
Lammy, David 267
Lamont, Norman 40, 271
Lansbury, George 206
Laud, William 245
Lavasani, Abbas 125
Lawrence, D H 263, 281
Lawrence, Stephen 344
Lawson, Nigel 101
Leach, Sir Henry 97
Leadsom, Andrea 189
Lee, Arthur 292
Lee, Jennie 177
Leicester, Earl of 21
Lenthall, William 49
Levy, Nora 148

Lewis, Brandon 309
Lewis, Damian 183
Liddle, Rod 171
Lilley, Peter 40
Liverpool, Earl of 31,
170, 187, 223, 235,
239, 355
Livingstone, Ken 136,
156, 176, 272, 294
Lloyd George, David 8,
13, 19, 23, 34, 45, 96,
102, 115, 116, 137,
155, 156, 163, 187,
206, 227, 241, 248,
292, 306, 349, 358,
365, 371, 380
Lockwood, Stuart 246
Lubbock, Eric 19
Lucan, Earl of 229, 326
Ludendorff, General
330
Luther, Martin 322

Macclesfield, Earl of
257
MacDonald, Ramsay
13, 23, 48, 73, 91,
157, 248, 288, 316,
328, 333
Maclean, Donald 24
Maclennan, Robert 66
Macleod, Iain 144, 177,
211, 301, 307
Macmillan, Dorothy 67
Macmillan, Harold ix,
11, 15, 19, 24, 25, 36,
44, 47, 100, 144, 199,
263, 292, 296, 307,
311, 317, 346
Macpherson, Lord 344
Maddicott, John 21
Madison, James 247
Magee, Patrick 169,
299
Maguire, Frank 91
Mair, Thomas 175
Major, John 40, 76, 94,
104, 105, 128, 139,
144, 147, 179, 183,
225, 271, 312, 320,
325, 334, 338, 341,
354, 374

Malone, Cecil
L'Estrange 336
Mandelson, Peter 144,
374
Marples, Ernest 90
Markham, Joseph 229
Markiewicz, Countess
365
Marlborough, Duke of
349
Marlow, Anthony 282
Marr, Andrew 186
Martin, Michael 20,
145
Marx, Karl 14, 132
Mary, Queen 378
Mary I, Queen 322
Massey-Mainwaring,
William 197
Maudling, Reginald 31,
117, 177 207
Maxwell, Paul 249
Maximilian of Baden,
Prince 330
Maxwell, Lily 345
Maxwell-Fyfe, Sir David
145
May, James 234
May, Theresa 16, 30,
38, 92, 161, 183, 184,
189, 199, 215, 267,
327, 363
Mayhew, Sir Patrick 40
McAlpine, Lord 108
McDonnell, John 80,
186
McGinn, Conor 309
McGuinness, Martin
88, 150
McIntosh, Andrew 176,
294
McMahon, Thomas
250
McVitie, Jack 67
Melbourne, Viscount
81, 180, 343
Mellor, David 40
Menendez, Mario 173
Meyer, Sir Anthony 221
Miah, Raja 272
Miliband, Ed 253, 267,
273, 360

Mill, John Stuart 193,
233
Millar, Ronald 7
Miller, Gina 92, 279
Millerand, Alexandre
115
Mitford, Diana 288
Mitterand, Francois
214
Mohammed, Oan Ali
125
Monckton, Sir Walter
144
Moore, General Jeremy
173
Mordaunt, Penny 327
More, Sir Thomas 322
Moreno, Lenin 178
Morley, John 227
Morris Ann 330
Morrison, Herbert 290
Mosley, Oswald 4, 73,
222, 288, 305
Mountbatten, Earl 25,
238, 250
Mousavi, Mir-Hossein
70
Mowlam, Mo 105, 242
Mugabe, Robert 362
Mussolini, Benito 53
Muzorewa, Bishop Abel
362

Naoroji, Dadabhair
197
Nasser, Gamal Abdel
17, 311, 318
Neave, Airey 44, 93,
131
Newbold, Walton 336
Newcastle, Duke of 29
Nicholson, Samuel 161
Nitti, Francesco 115
Nixon, Richard 110,
254
Nkomo, Joshua 362
Norden, Clifford 330
North, Lord 29, 195,
247, 370
Northcote, Sir Stafford
28
Norton, Caroline 343

Nott, Sir John 97, 100, 120
Nye, Sue 123

O'Brien, Edna 280
O'Driscoll, Brian 212
O'Flynn, Patrick 89
Oakeshott, Isabel 74
Obama, Barack 253
Obote, Milton 230
Orwell, George 22, 167, 183, 240
Osborne, Bernal 62
Osborne, George 123
Ostarius, Elias 292
Owen, David 26, 66, 89, 164

Paisley, Revd Ian 88, 105, 150
Palmerston, Viscount 343
Pankhurst, Emmeline 163
Paterson, Owen 340
Pankhurst, Sylvia 140
Park, Keith 201
Parkinson, Cecil 301, 314
Patel, Priti 327
Patten, Chris 27, 30, 192
Paul, Henri 261
Paxman, Jeremy 325
Pearse, Patrick 119
Pearson, Lord 207
Peck, John 35
Peel, Sir John 205
Peel, Sir Robert 31, 61, 187, 235, 269, 284
Pelham, Henry 257
Pennington, Andrew 175
Pepys, Samuel 55
Perceval, Spencer ix, 65, 231, 291, 355
Pettitt, Ann 259
Peyton, John 44
Philby, Kim 24, 312
Philip, Prince 261
Pitt the Elder, William 29

Pitt the Younger, William 3, 10, 65, 77, 220, 235, 291, 355, 370
Plunkett, Count 347
Plunkett, Joseph 347
Pollard, Albert 304
Pollitt, Harry 140, 305
Pompidou, Georges 50
Portillo, Michael 268
Portland, Duke of 65, 231, 291, 370
Pottinger, Sir Henry 27
Powell, Enoch 41, 50, 61, 177, 307, 359
Powell, Jonathan 105
Prior, James 44, 297
Profumo, John 148, 260, 296
Pryce, Vicky 74
Purdy, Jean 216
Pym, Francis 297, 315
Pym, John 245

Raab, Dominic 251
Reagan, Ronald 58, 259, 367
Reckless, Mark 300, 240
Rees, Merlyn 64
Reith, Lord 305, 376
Richard II, King 171
Ridley, Matt 55
Robbins, Olly 199
Robens, Lord 308
Robertson, Lord 99
Robinson, Geoffrey 374
Roche, Matthew 356
Rockingham, Marquess of 65, 71
Rodgers, William 26, 89
Roosevelt, Franklin D. 37, 59, 116, 165, 235, 377
Rose, Richard 304
Rosebery, Earl of 6, 47, 102, 180, 202
Ross, Maj Gen Robert 247
Rothermeere, Lord 288
Ruddock, Joan 58

Rushdie, Salman 70
Rushton, Willie 281
Russell, John 292
Russell, Lord John 31, 62, 81, 209, 343

Said, Wafic 30 (put two dots above the I in Said)
Salisbury, Marquess of 11, 28, 62, 103, 180, 202, 203, 256, 335
Salmond, Alex 110, 131, 273, 274
Samuel, Herbert 248, 353
Sands, Bobby 64, 347
Sankey, Lord 248
Sarkozy, Nicolas 360
Saville, Lord 31
Scargill, Arthur 12, 69
Scarman, Lord , 106, 344
Scott, Norman 19
Seward, Liney 252
Shackleton, David 48
Shaw, George Bernard 14
Shelburne, Earl of 65
Sheridan, Jim 146
Shinwell, Emmanuel 333
Short, Clare 80
Sidmouth, Lord 235
Silverman, Sidney 369
Simon, Sir John 333
Simpson, Wallis 360
Sinatra, Frank 67
Sissons, Peter 280
Skinner, Dennis 363
Smith, Adam 10
Smith, Chris 339
Smith, Ian 362
Smith, John 108, 128, 139, 241
Smith, Owen 267
Snow, Dan ix
Snow, Peter 244, 304
Snowden, Philip 23, 248, 275
Soames, Christopher 25
Solomos, Harry 208

Sombre, David Dyce 197

Somerset, Duke of 149

Spencer, Charles 261

St Clair, Malcolm 121

Stagg, James 165

Stalin, Josef 37, 68, 140, 165

Stanley, Lord 32

Starmer, Sir Keir 289

Steel, David 66, 91, 205

Steptoe, Patrick 216

Stevenson, Melford 67

Stewart, Alastair 110

Stewart, John 9

Stoltenberg, Jens 99

Stonehouse, John 229

Strathclyde, Lord 313

Straw, Jack 169, 265

Stuart, Charles Edward 111

Sunderland, Earl of 72

Sturgeon, Nicola 274

Taylor, A J P 58

Taylor, Teddy 280

Tebbit, Margaret 280

Tebbit, Norman 299

Thatcher, Carol 179

Thatcher, Denis 131, 299

Thatcher, Margaret x, 7, 13, 18, 30, 40, 44, 52, 54, 61, 64, 69, 70, 79, 89, 91, 93, 94, 97, 100, 101, 104, 105, 106, 107, 112, 120, 122, 125, 129, 131, 147, 151, 161, 168, 169, 170, 171, 173, 175, 176, 179, 192, 200, 204, 214, 221, 225, 234, 244, 249, 250, 262, 265, 266, 268, 271, 277, 292, 294, 297, 298, 299, 308, 311, 320, 323, 325, 330, 338, 339, 341, 342, 344, 353, 355, 362, 366, 367, 380

Thomas, J H 248

Thomas, Johann 348

Thorpe, Jeremy 19, 50, 61, 177

Tillett, Ben 14

Todd, Barbara 282

Timms, Stephen 175

Tolhurst, Kelly 340

Trimble, David 105

Trimingham, Carina 74

Truman, Harry 59, 68

Trump, Donald 20, 251

Truss, Liz 246

Turnbull, Malcolm 278

Turner, Anthea 338

Tusk, Donald 92

U Saw 5

Vansittart, Robert 115

Varadkar Leo 113

Vaz, Keith 156

Victoria, Queen 17, 28, 62, 81, 114, 118, 158, 180, 263, 317, 343, 380

Vine, Jeremy 123, 304

Von Hertling, Georg 330

Wakeham John 40

Walker, Johnny 228

Walker, Peter 297

Walpole, Robert 72, 98, 263, 277, 281, 355

Ward, Stephen 260

Warwick, Countess of 53

Watson, Tom 186

Watson-Watt, Robert 201

Weatherill, Bernard 122

Webb, Sidney 48, 248

Wellington, Duke of 84, 183, 187, 231, 269

Whibley, Richard 303

Whitehouse, Mary 281, 342

Whitelaw, William 44, 150, 244, 344

Whittemore, Lynne 259

Widdecombe, Ann 221

Widgery, Lord 31

Wilberforce, William 3, 220

William IV, King 85, 343

William of Orange 46, 56, 111

William, Prince 261

Williams, Shirley 26, 66, 89, 164, 280

Willink, Henry 196

Wilson, Harold 2, 6, 17, 18, 25, 47, 52, 61, 78, 79, 87, 90, 96, 121, 130, 164, 177, 200, 207, 208, 234, 263, 278, 293, 298, 307, 308, 315, 329, 337, 346, 373

Wilson, Richard 266

Wilson, Woodrow 187, 330, 378

Winchilsea, Earol of 84, 269

Winner, Michael 112

Winslett, Kate 109

Wolfenden, Lord 218

Woolton, Lord 194, 312

Worlock, Archbishop David 280

Wright, Peter 278

Wyn Jones, Ieuan 110

York, Richard, Duke of 149

Young, Brian 120

Young, Edward 114

Zaghari-Ratcliffe, Nazanin 70